MW00719231

Josef Fuchs

on

Natural Law

Moral Traditions Series

A series edited by James F. Keenan, S.J.

Aquinas and Empowerment: Classical Ethics for Ordinary Lives
G. Simon Harak, S.J., Editor

The Banality of Good and Evil: Moral Lessons from the Shoah and Jewish Tradition
David R. Blumenthal

Bridging the Sacred and the Secular: Selected Writings of John Courtney Murray
John Courtney Murray, S.J.
J. Leon Hooper, S.J., Editor

The Catholic Moral Tradition Today: A Synthesis
Charles E. Curran

The Christian Case for Virtue Ethics
Joseph J. Kotva, Jr.

The Context of Casuistry
James F. Keenan, S.J., and Thomas A. Shannon, Editors

Democracy on Purpose: Justice and the Reality of God
Franklin I. Gamwell

Ethics and Economics of Assisted Reproduction
Maura A. Ryan

The Ethics of Aquinas
Stephen J. Pope, Editor

The Evolution of Altruism and the Ordering of Love
Stephen J. Pope

The Fellowship of Life: Virtue Ethics and Orthodox Christianity
Joseph Woodill

Feminist Ethics and Natural Law: The End of the Anathemas
Cristina L. H. Traina

Jewish and Catholic Bioethics: An Ecumenical Dialogue
Edmund D. Pellegrino and Alan I. Faden, Editors

John Paul II and the Legacy of *Dignitatis Humanae*
Hermínio Rico, S.J.

Love, Human and Divine: The Heart of Christian Ethics
Edward Collins Vacek, S.J.

Medicine and the Ethics of Care
Diana Fritz Cates and Paul Lauritzen, Editors

The Origins of Moral Theology in the United States: Three Different Approaches
Charles E. Curran

Shaping the Moral Life: An Approach to Moral Theology
Klaus Demmer, M.S.C.
Translated by Roberto Dell'Oro
James F. Keenan, S.J., Editor

Who Count as Persons? Human Identity and the Ethics of Killing
John F. Kavanaugh, S.J.

Josef Fuchs

on

Natural Law

Mark E. Graham

Georgetown University Press
Washington, D.C.

Georgetown University Press, Washington, D.C.
© 2002 by Georgetown University Press. All rights reserved.
Printed in the United States of America

10 9 8 7 6 5 4 3 2 1   2002

This volume is printed on acid-free offset book paper.

Library of Congress Cataloging-in-Publication Data

Graham, Mark E.
    Josef Fuchs on natural law / Mark E. Graham.
        p. cm.—(Moral traditions series)
    Includes bibliographical references and index.
    ISBN 0-87840-382-5 (cl. : acid-free paper)
        1. Fuchs, Josef, 1912—Contributions in law. 2. Natural law—
    Philosophy. 3. Christian ethics. I. Title. II. Series.
    K468. G73   2002
    340'.112—dc21

                                              2002023641

To Laura and Peter

Contents

Foreword

In 1981, my Jesuit superior decided that I was to do doctoral studies. Inasmuch as I had been preparing myself for work in the social/pastoral apostolate, his news was unsettling. Still, he allowed me to determine the area of study as well as the doctoral program itself. After consulting a number of colleagues, I decided on moral theology, but then needed to deliberate whether I would study in Münster with Bruno Schüller or in Rome with Josef Fuchs and Klaus Demmer. (Demmer and Schüller were Fuchs's most celebrated students, but each was so remarkably different from the other—Demmer is always interested in hermeneutics; Schüller, with linguistic analysis—that it is hard to imagine that they shared the same mentor.) In order to discern where to go, the historian John O'Malley nudged me in the direction of Rome by arranging for me to spend that summer in Florence with a private tutor learning Italian.

During these Italian studies, I went to Rome to meet Josef Fuchs. He met me on the steps of the Gregorian University. At the time he would have been about 65 years old. As he approached, I thought he looked like a German twin of Cary Grant. He invited me to his office and then to supper, and by the time I returned to Florence, I decided that I would return in the fall of 1982 to do a licentiate and a doctorate at the Gregorian.

I had learned about Josef Fuchs while doing my Master of Divinity (1979–1982) at Weston Jesuit School of Theology. There, a rather extraordinary person, the late Sr. Mary Emil Penet, I.H.M., taught us fundamental moral theology. She had studied with him only a few years earlier when, after years of being an administrator, she decided to become a moral theologian. She visited him in Rome and proposed to him that she would organize his notes and papers and basically serve as his secretary, if he would in turn be her mentor. In her lectures whenever she wanted to underline the seriousness and profundity of a fundamental point, she would preface it by saying, "I tried to understand what this author meant and as hard as I tried, I couldn't and so

I went to Fuchs. . . . " The name of Fuchs entered into the folklore of first year studies at Weston. (Years later Fuchs would tell me what an extraordinary first meeting he had had with Penet. He had never met her; she wrote asking for a meeting, he agreed, she arrived, looked around his office and made her proposal. Fuchs agreed immediately. They remained close friends until her death this past year.)

I arrived in September 1982 and was not in my new residence more than an hour when he phoned. "Keenan, this is Fuchs. Come to supper here tonight and then we will go beer drinking." I remember after the second beer telling him that I had jet lag and needed to retire. "Very well," he said, "but come back to my office in a few days. I have a project for you."

The project was to proof the galleys of a collection of his essays that had been translated into English. I accepted his offer. Having been a high school English teacher, I found the task an easy one and discovered quite a number of errors. The German Fuchs was delighted to report all these grammatical discrepancies to the Americans, and in that delight he developed a positive estimation of my own abilities. (The collection, *Personal Responsibility and Christian Morality*, would be the first of four published by Georgetown University Press and it was through Fuchs that I first came into contact with the Press.)

That first semester I took a seminar with him in bioethics and he so liked my paper that he sent it to *Stimmen der Zeit*, where it was translated into German and published. Ironically, not yet knowing German, I was unable to read my first published essay. The next semester, I took another course with him, the last he taught at the Gregorian. Because of Fuchs's retirement, I did my major seminar with Fr. Klaus Demmer, M.S.C., and wrote my licentiate under his guidance. Still, Fuchs loved having his students with him and so occasionally he would invite us to supper at the Gregorian and to return to his room to drink and discuss ethics. Here I got to know many of my contemporaries. Similarly, whenever a licentiate or doctoral student wanted to invite Fuchs to his residence for dinner, I would be invited, usually by the student, as Fuchs's protégé.

At the end of my first two years of studies, I began a series of three successive summers during which I spent two months learning German and then let an aging pastor have his month's vacation (every September) from a tiny German village in the Würzburg diocese. Almost every year, Fuchs would go to Germany or Austria in the summer to work in a parish or a convent, read a bit, and provide a variety of ordinary priestly services. He was especially disposed to hearing confessions, telling me that a moralist should know how to respond to those who suffered over their sinfulness. Because it did not matter where I studied

German, for those three years I went to whatever city he chose. Inevitably, I lived in a nearby Jesuit community. We would meet often for suppers, and weekly he would take me by train to tour some Germanic city or town like Melk, Krems, Salzburg, Munich, Augsburg, Vienna, Ulm, or Cologne.

I did my doctoral dissertation with him. It was a study of Thomas Aquinas through the contemporary distinction between goodness and rightness. The more I considered the distinction, the more I moved from my earlier understanding of it as it appeared with all its clarity in Schüller's writings to the more nuanced and complicated insights of Demmer. I was afraid that Fuchs would side with Schüller's interpretation, and so I made a long, extended (about seventy pages) argument in my first chapter. Fuchs was not pleased with the chapter and wanted it to be dramatically reduced. For several weeks we disagreed and things became unpleasant. He would express his annoyance at the different dinner gatherings that we would attend. On top of this, he was often in the United States lecturing at Georgetown, Weston, Notre Dame, and the seminary in Boynton Beach, so my access to him was limited. In due time we came to a compromise: He let me stay with Demmer's interpretation and I cut the chapter to twenty pages.

I learned much from him during these years. A few vignettes might serve to highlight who the man is.

One weekend, he invited about twenty of us to a villa outside of Rome at Lake Nemi. It was again a colloquy. He slept in the room next to me. I remember that I could not sleep the entire night because he coughed loudly and interminably, sounding as if he had the worst case of bronchitis imaginable. In the morning he appeared perfectly dressed telling us what a wonderful sleep he had had in the clear, clean air of Nemi.

On another occasion, a few of us sat in his room discussing a contemporary essay by a moral theologian who blamed Fuchs for the Vatican's diminished moral authority. We thought the essay was idiotic and so I did a dramatic reading of the accusations against Fuchs. As I was concluding, I realized my colleagues had become quiet: Fuchs was tearful. He hated being attacked.

Fuchs was, like the meaning of his name, clever. He remarked often that though he never said something he didn't believe, he didn't always say everything that he did believe. He told me that whenever I wrote, I should learn to let readers come to the evident conclusions. Learn to use a question mark at the end of your work and be less emphatic with the period, he would advise me, so as to avoid investigations by Rome.

About these investigations, he told me how he was censored for his position on situation ethics. He was forbidden to teach the first-cycle students who were studying for the Roman equivalent of the Masters of Divinity. But he was allowed to teach licentiate and doctoral students. He found the punishment ironic: The Vatican didn't allow him to teach future priests, but he was allowed to teach future moral theologians!

He demanded that I take a course with an incredibly aged and infamous moral theologian who was known for attacking in class any number of his opponents. After four classes I finally withdrew; Fuchs was pleased and added, "You have now seen what he is like: you have had the experience!"

Likewise, when I first arrived in Rome, the pope declared that all clergy wear their Roman collars at all times. At all the residences there was considerable pressure and within a month, the Gregorian student population went from 30 percent being "collared" to 98 percent "collared." He asked me about my residence where seventy Jesuit priests who were doing licenses and doctorates lived. I told him that nine of us refused, and of those, eight were moralists. The defender of the conscience chuckled at the news.

He considered that one of his greatest achievements occurred in 1968 when he was asked by the dean to broker the complaints of some seminarians protesting at the Gregorian (assuredly, the demonstrations were modest). The account of the students' satisfaction with his arbitration was something that he often told with great pride. His delight over these negotiations is ironic, because at the same time he was having extraordinary influence on the members of the birth control commission whose work would be rejected by Pope Paul VI in the encyclical *Humanae Vitae.*

When Mark Graham invited me to do the foreword to this extraordinary book, I was honored. It seemed, inasmuch as I—like so many others—learned so much from Fuchs about mentoring, about being a theologian, and about loving the church, that perhaps I could somehow convey here how those lessons were communicated. I hope these vignettes have helped to do that.

Essentially, each of those lessons by Fuchs were about the virtue of openness: openness to the conservative moralist, openness to the conscience, openness to new students, and openness to experience. Fuchs often remarked on the essential importance of openness, for instance, in grasping the concept of moral goodness.

Graham beautifully captures that openness throughout his work. You will find, I think, two ways that Fuchs was particularly open. First, he was, above all, open to moral truth. As a young moralist he was open to the innovative claims of the situational ethicists, but he was convinced that the traditional teachings of the natural law more closely approximated moral truth than that of any of the innovators. Later, when he was a member of the papal commission examining birth control, his openness to the testimonies of the married witnesses and commission members prompted him not only to rethink his position on birth control, but more importantly to rethink his entire understanding of how one ascertained moral truth. It was at this point that Fuchs, having been so open to the claims of the magisterium, became open to the competency of the moral agent.

This openness to moral truth was also an openness to the Spirit. Throughout Graham's work there emerges the profile of a very flexible man. By the Spirit, Fuchs literally abandoned not only his earlier premises, but also his earlier writings. This Spirit was not, therefore, some private source of inspiration. Rather, the Spirit that animated Fuchs's persistent search to develop anew the foundations for moral theology was the same Spirit that inaugurated and guided Vatican II. In turn, Fuchs's openness to the Spirit gave him the confidence and the vision to remain continuously committed to his pursuit of moral truth, and this openness is thoroughly in evidence throughout Fuchs's writings.

One final word. In *Feminist Ethics and Natural Law: The End of the Anathemas* (Georgetown University Press, 1999), Cristina Traina explored, among other contributions, Fuchs's theology of the natural law. Traina significantly affected the agenda of Christian ethics by validating as a feminist enterprise the revisiting of the natural law in general and Fuchs's writings in particular. Now with Mark Graham's work we have a definitive presentation and critique of Fuchs's theology and therefore a new but constitutive element for that program. I am sure that this contribution, like Traina's very successful work, will lead us all to better grasp the reality of moral truth as well as that Spirit who leads us to it.

James F. Keenan, S.J.

Acknowledgments

To those who have contributed in various ways to this book, I offer my sincere thanks. The Theology and Religious Studies Department at Villanova University provided me with a graduate assistant every semester since my arrival at Villanova. In particular, my thanks to those responsible for assigning graduate assistants Thomas Martin, O.S.A., and Paul Danove, whose spirit of generosity to junior faculty members is appreciated. My former graduate assistants, Joshua Snyder and Assely Etienne, spent many hours in the library locating articles and books. Mark Medwig, my current graduate assistant, provided valuable and timely assistance, especially at the end of my project.

David Hollenbach, S.J. and Stephen Pope read an earlier version of my manuscript and offered numerous constructive comments that helped clarify issues and prompted me to think and write better. For their time, energy, and thoughtfulness, I am grateful.

James Keenan, S.J., my former professor, influenced this book in so many ways. Jim initially sparked my interest in Josef Fuchs in his course on 20th Century Roman Catholic moral theologians, and later suggested a long-term project on Fuchs that eventually culminated in this book. It was a labor of love from which I have benefited enormously.

Jim's generosity throughout the course of this project was breathtaking. He labored many hours over various drafts of my manuscript, offering constructive criticisms, posing pertinent questions, and suggesting helpful changes, all of which greatly improved my book in substance and style. I would be remiss, however, not to mention one of Jim's qualities that indirectly shaped my book by shaping me. Jim can nurture people and tease out their full potential unlike anyone I've ever known. To a great extent, the ideals to which I aspire as a professor and scholar have been forged by my contact with Jim, during which I observed the many ways he continually enriches the lives of his students, colleagues, and friends. For everything you have given me, thanks, Jim.

Finally, this book is dedicated to my wife, Laura, and our baby, Peter. Peter greets me every morning with a hearty smile and is a constant source of joy in our lives. Words of thanks seem starkly inadequate when I consider Laura's daily support, encouragement, patience, and enthusiasm for my work—and also the gentle and much needed prodding to finish the book! Laura assumed more than her fair share of childcare responsibilities to allow me time to write and edit, and without her help this book would have taken much longer to write. For being a wonderful spouse, a treasured friend, and for contributing to my professional life so substantially, my deepest thanks, Laura.

Introduction

The need for a credible, persuasive natural law theory is perhaps no more pressing than today. Since Pope Leo XIII's Thomistic revival in the late 1800s, natural law has attained notable, maybe even unprecedented, prominence in Roman Catholic moral theology, principally through numerous papal documents that have employed natural law analysis to assess a host of diverse moral issues in the social, political, economic, and personal spheres. From Leo XIII's critique of labor and the miserable working conditions prevalent in the late nineteenth century in *Rerum Novarum*, to John XXIII's defense of a broad spectrum of human rights in *Pacem in Terris*, to John Paul II's attack on the unequal distribution of the world's wealth and the rapidly increasing incidence of dire poverty in the Southern hemisphere in *Sollicitudo Rei Socialis*, natural law has been the conceptual tool for analyzing a multitude of ethical questions and for making normative moral statements about structures, institutions, and human conduct both to the Catholic faithful and to the world at large.

For better or worse, natural law analysis has become an integral part of Roman Catholic moral theology and will not be jettisoned in the foreseeable future. The last four decades, however, have been a turbulent, unsettling time for Roman Catholic natural law theory. The collapse of the neo-Thomist manuals of moral theology in the 1960s, which dominated Roman Catholic moral theology during the first half of this century and provided an extraordinarily influential synthesis of natural law widely accepted within Roman Catholic circles, as well as the maelstrom of controversy surrounding the contraception issue and the publication of Pope Paul VI's encyclical *Humanae Vitae*, have engendered an ongoing debate that has raised a series of foundational questions: What is natural law? How is it known? Who can know it? What is the role of human nature in natural law deliberation? Can natural law be codified in propositional moral norms, particularly exceptionless moral norms? What is moral objectivity? What are the necessary ingredients for making objectively right choices conforming to natural law?

1

The general consensus among contemporary Roman Catholic moral theologians is that the reexamination of the basic tenets of Roman Catholic natural law theory prompted by the controversy ignited in the 1960s was fundamentally on target. The palpable cracks identified by moral theologians were real, systemic, and foundational and could not be rectified by minor adjustments or tinkering on the periphery of Roman Catholic natural law theory. To become an intellectually credible tool of moral analysis, natural law would have to undergo a significant, substantive refurbishment.

Josef Fuchs, S.J., (b. 1912) has been perhaps the most productive thinker in Roman Catholic natural law theory both before and after the 1960s. His *magnum opus* on natural law, *Lex Naturae. Zur Theologie des Naturrechts,* originally published in German in 1955 and later translated into English, French, and Italian, immediately distinguished Fuchs as one of the premier figures in Roman Catholic natural law theory and was hailed as a "radical," landmark work.[1] As one commentator wrote, "One hardly could do better than to begin by studying Fr. Fuchs'[s] masterful theological approach to the subject."[2]

Fuchs's enthusiasm for the presentation of natural law in *Lex Naturae,* however, proved to be short lived. A mere eight years after its publication, Fuchs was appointed by Pope John XXIII to the Pontifical Commission on Population, Family, and Birth, and during his three years of service on the pontifical commission Fuchs underwent a profound intellectual conversion that dramatically altered his notion of natural law and culminated in an explicit repudiation of most of his earlier positions.

After his intellectual conversion, Fuchs began reconstructing his understanding of natural law, beginning with theological anthropology. Appropriating insights from Karl Rahner's conception of transcendental Thomism, Fuchs explored the implications of human subjectivity, personhood, transcendence, fundamental option, and historicity, and produced a conception of the human being substantially different from that presented during his preconversion period.

For the next thirty-odd years, Fuchs turned his attention to other foundational questions, addressing and revisiting a broad array of issues pivotal to his project of reconstructing Roman Catholic natural law theory: the roles of human nature, reason, and experience; moral epistemology; moral competency and the magisterium's ability to perceive natural law; the function and validity of moral norms in natural law deliberation; the soteriological import of natural law; the role of concrete knowledge of circumstances in ascertaining natural law; and the individual moral agent's function in uncovering natural law.

Fuchs's insights not only have altered the landscape of Roman Catholic natural law theory, but have provided a constructive foundation that might successfully indicate solutions to the divisive impasse plaguing Roman Catholic natural law theory since the 1960s. In my opinion, the time is ripe to begin a critical, systematic, and comprehensive assessment of Fuchs's notion of natural law that identifies both the dead-ends and areas of incompleteness characteristic of any relatively new, ambitious intellectual endeavor as well as the solid ideas that form a reliable foundational platform and will continue to bear fruit for subsequent commentators attempting to construct a natural law theory serviceable for use within Roman Catholic moral theology.

Despite Fuchs's stature as a first-rate thinker on natural law, to date there has been no attempt to present a sustained, critical analysis and assessment of his natural law theory. Although several important chapter-length discussions of Fuchs's notion of natural law have been published, their brevity precludes the scope and detail necessary to explore the full import of Fuchs's presentation of natural law.[3]

This study is an attempt to remedy that lacuna. The first part, consisting of the first three chapters, examines Fuchs's preconversion natural law theory. Chapter 1 focuses on the situation ethics controversy in the 1950s and Fuchs's defense of natural law against the challenges posed by situationism. In chapter 2 a more comprehensive account of Fuchs's natural law theory is presented, including natural law's relation to personal salvation, the status of "nature" and "human nature" in natural deliberation, the validity of moral norms, and the role of the individual moral agent. Chapter 3 treats Fuchs's intellectual conversion during the pontifical birth control commission and the key insights and experiences leading to his unexpected shift.

The second part of this study develops and critiques Fuchs's postconversion natural law theory. Fuchs's Rahnerian turn to the subject and other anthropological issues form the basis of chapter 4. Chapter 5 treats Fuchs's notion of *recta ratio* as the proximate norm of morality and the port of entry to natural law, along with its implications for our understanding of moral epistemology, moral competency, and a method for determining right and wrong behavior. In chapter 6, two issues are explored: the role of Christian faith in natural law deliberation and the ability to reduce natural law to propositional moral norms, especially exceptionless moral norms. Finally, the conclusion of this study addresses what I believe to be the most significant strengths and weaknesses of Fuchs's natural law theory and suggests possible avenues of development that would contribute positively to the ongoing quest to rehabilitate Roman Catholic natural law theory.

Notes

1. Michael Bertram Crowe, review of *Natural Law,* by Josef Fuchs, *Irish Theological Quarterly* 33 (1966): 276.

2. Germain Grisez, review of *Natural Law* by Josef Fuchs, *Month* 34 (1965): 331.

3. Timothy O'Connell, "Changing Roman Catholic Moral Theology: A Study in Josef Fuchs (Ph.D. diss., Fordham University 1974): 20–86; Ronald Amos Mercier, "What Is Nature? The Development of Josef Fuchs' Thought on Moral Normativity" (Ph.D. diss., Regis College, 1993): 57–110; Cristina L. H. Traina, *Feminist Ethics and Natural Law* (Washington, D.C.: Georgetown University Press, 1999): 169–202; and Vincent MacNamara, *Faith and Ethics: Recent Roman Catholicism* (Washington, D.C.: Georgetown University Press, 1985): 9–66.

PART I

THE PRECONVERSION PERIOD (1941–66)

Natural Law and the Confrontation with Situation Ethics

Introduction

Traditional Roman Catholic natural law theory has faced formidable challenges in the twentieth century, but perhaps none as unnerving as the so-called "situation ethics"[1] that created a firestorm of controversy in Europe in the 1940s and 1950s. Decried as a rebellion against the moral law, a chaotic system of ethical thought, a rejection of objective moral norms, and a denial of natural law's validity, situation ethics evoked visceral reactions, pointed commentary, and dark references to moral relativism.[2]

During the situation ethics controversy Josef Fuchs emerged not only as an authoritative commentator on issues pertaining specifically to situation ethics, but also as an astute expositor and defender of the Roman Catholic natural law tradition. From 1952 to 1956 Fuchs focused, almost exclusively, on systematizing his understanding of natural law and defended it against the "inadmissible relativism"[3] of Protestant situation ethics. During this period he published several influential articles[4] and a book[5] on situation ethics. These works demonstrated considerable familiarity with the works of noted Protestant situationists and were widely cited among Fuchs's Roman Catholic counterparts. In 1955 he published his *magnum opus* on natural law, *Lex Naturae. Zur Theologie des Naturrechts*,[6] a significant portion of which Fuchs described as "a dialogue in progress with Protestant theology."[7] Fuchs clearly regarded many aspects of situationism as incompatible with natural law properly understood. But Fuchs's antipathy toward situationism was not total. Years after he had stopped writing on situation ethics Fuchs wrote, "What went by the name of a *nouvelle Morale* or a certain *Situationsethik* in post-war middle Europe, and what is now appearing in Anglo-Saxon countries as a 'new morality,' is not totally in error. It contains some valuable insights too."[8] Indeed, the Vatican regarded Fuchs's writings on situation ethics as so tolerant and congenial that it imposed punitive measures on him: Fuchs was forbidden to teach fundamental moral theology to priesthood candidates in the Gregorian University for one year, although he retained the privilege of instructing licentiate and doctoral candidates during this time.

Situation Ethics and Roman Catholic Moral Theology

The attribution of a label usually requires an identifiable convergence of thought, shared concepts and themes, and comparable methods of analysis. However, the label "situationism," as it was employed by Roman Catholic moralists during most of the European situation ethics controversy, functioned as an umbrella term including nearly anyone who, for whatever reason, questioned the validity of universal moral norms. "Existentialism" was generally considered the seedbed of situationism, with such diverse thinkers as Søren Kierkegaard, Jean-Paul Sartre, Simone de Beauvoir, Karl Jaspers, and Martin Heidegger numbered among the proponents of situationism. On the theological side, a personalistic and voluntaristic conception of ethics was favored by Protestants such as Karl Barth, Emil Brunner, and Helmut Thielicke, which led not to a wholesale rejection of all moral norms, but only those claiming universal validity.[9]

Although these various strands of situationism were not unknown to Roman Catholic moralists in the first half of the twentieth century, their proponents were either ignored or chastised for their alleged moral relativism. It was only amidst the ruins of post–World War II Germany that situation ethics began to receive a favorable hearing among Catholic theologians.[10] The turbulence and extreme conditions facing postwar Germany raised a host of unusual moral problems that never would have arisen under normal circumstances.

> The problems of cooperating with the invading conquerors, of joining resistance movements, of the black market, of retaliation, of avoiding torture, of professing the faith in the face of diabolical persecution, of observing rigid laws of conjugal morality in the midst of the most dire poverty, of having children who would be just so much 'gun fodder,' of preserving premarital chastity when almost every form of innocent entertainment seemed beyond the reach of youth—these and countless other difficult problems be-

came a part of the very atmosphere created by the War and its aftermath.[11]

German theologians began to recognize that moral norms formulated in a more stable environment could not encompass the adverse and bewildering conditions created by the collapse of the political, economic, and social order. But who or what could answer the moral questions pressing upon postwar Germans?

Several influential theologians suggested that situation ethics, or at least some qualified version of situation ethics, could. The Jesuit Hans Wulf maintained that the Catholic Church's authoritative posture toward the faithful in moral matters was partially responsible for the moral confusion of many Germans. Instead of fostering the skills and insights necessary to solve new and complex moral issues, the Catholic Church's practice of handing down moral laws to the faithful had dulled their moral decision-making skills and left them unable to deal effectively with the emerging moral issues.[12]

Another Jesuit, Hans Hirschmann, praised situationism's emphasis on attending to concrete circumstances and questioned the assumption prevalent in Roman Catholic moral theology that universal norms can adequately capture all the morally relevant factors in concrete situations. For Hirschmann, moral awareness requires not only attending to moral norms, but a keen understanding of local conditions, the network of social relations affected by moral decisions, and changing historical situations.[13]

During the late 1940s the eminent theologian Karl Rahner also exhibited some sympathy toward situationism. Although Rahner upheld the validity of universal moral norms, he identified a "sphere of individual morality" pertaining to each person in her or his uniqueness and individuality that "is not subject to universal norms, laws and rules."[14] In this sphere each person is addressed by God "in a free, unrepeatable and incalculable way" and each person must respond not simply as one human being among many, but as a distinctive, original, unduplicated person.[15] According to Rahner, this sphere is, in principle, beyond the church's moral jurisdiction and must be left to each individual's discretion: "Now we must expressly add that *this individual morality cannot be directly governed by the Church.*"[16]

Perhaps the most unabashed supporter of situation ethics was Walter Dirks, the coeditor of the popular *Frankfurter Hefte*, a magazine published by lay German Catholics. Dirks argued that situation ethics arose in response to a growing awareness of historical consciousness, a consciousness that recognized the contingency of social institutions, patterns of self-understanding, and established rules and customs. In this new atmosphere Germans were forced to acknowledge that history unfolded not according to a predetermined plan, but according to their free decisions. "If today we seek the will of God in terms of the situation, this does not indicate a collapse of basic norms, but rather a response to a collapse which is independent of us and which we cannot remedy, a collapse of the objective social framework, the result of which is that the individual is forced to take a position which is more free, more conscious, and more fully responsible."[17] Dirks also criticized the tendency to absolutize moral norms in traditional Roman Catholic moral theology. Moral norms, for Dirks, are instruments constructed to protect the "corporeal, psychical, and intellectual" well-being of persons, and if the application of a norm to a concrete situation does not serve these purposes, the norm must be regarded as deficient and inapplicable.[18]

Alarmed at the sympathetic hearing some of the tenets of situationism were receiving in Germany, Pope Pius XII (1939–58) launched an aggressive attack on situation ethics in two addresses in 1952.[19] In the first address he attempted to counteract the subjectivism of situation ethics by outlining the proper function of conscience in moral decision making. According to Pius, situationists treat the conscience as a self-sufficient originator of moral laws capable of generating moral criteria in isolation from any external referents (divine law, natural law). Pius argued, on the contrary, that conscience is correctly understood not as a generative, but an interpretive, faculty that discerns moral obligations already given through divine and natural laws.[20] But Pius was not content merely to identify the function of conscience in subservience to higher laws; for this does not settle the issue of whether a person's conscience could be understood as a legitimate interpreter of higher laws, thus leading to precisely the type of subjectivism Pius wished to avoid.[21] Pius then argued that morality properly belongs to revelation, which has been given to the church alone and not to individuals:

> Our Divine Redeemer entrusted His revelation, of which moral obligations are an essential part, not to individual men, but to His Church, to which He gave the mission to bring men to accept faithfully this sacred deposit.
>
> Similarly, the divine aid, which is meant to preserve revelation from error and deformation, was promised to the Church, and not to individuals.[22]

By linking morality with revelation,[23] and by locating the capacity to interpret revelation exclusively in the magisterium (i.e., the "Church"), Pius effectively severed the conscience's—and by extension the individ-

ual's—ability to formulate or construct moral norms. The proper function of the conscience, according to Pius, is limited to applying received
moral teaching, which is defined by the magisterium alone.

In his second address Pius shifted his focus from conscience and
moral decision making to the status of moral norms. Situationists,
according to Pius, refuse to acknowledge the obligatory nature of moral
norms and consider them simply as indicators that may be dismissed
if an individual judges them inappropriate in a concrete situation.
As a consequence, situationism relegates moral norms to the periphery
of moral deliberation and undercuts their rightful status as binding directives.[24]

The primary reason why situationists regard the obligatoriness of
moral norms as limited, Pius stated, arises from the uniqueness and
originality of each concrete situation that cannot be captured fully by
moral norms.

> The distinctive mark of [situationism] is that it is not based in effect
> on universal moral laws, such as, for example, the Ten Command-
> ments, but on the real and concrete conditions or circumstances in
> which men must act, and according to which the conscience of the
> individual must judge and choose. Such a state of things is unique,
> and is applicable only once for every human action. That is why
> the decision of conscience, as the advocates of this ethic assert,
> cannot be commanded by ideas, principles, and universal laws.[25]

Pius responded that situationism had conflated the sphere of moral
norms with that of their prudent application. Because moral norms
arise from human nature, which is present wherever humans are found
and independent of changing circumstances, they can be applied across
a diverse range of concrete situations. Prudence, on the other hand,
refers to the correct application of moral norms to concrete situations
and demands attention to the specific factors that make every situation
unique and unrepeatable.[26] In short, Pius accepted situationism's claim
that every concrete situation is new and original, but he considered
this irrelevant to the issue of the status of moral norms.

Any lingering doubts about reconciling situation ethics with Roman Catholic moral theology was settled decisively four years later by
the Sacred Congregation of the Holy Office, which prohibited situation
ethics from being "taught or approved in Universities, Academies,
Seminaries and houses of formation for religious, or [from being] propa-
gated and defended in books, dissertations, assemblies . . . or in any
other manner whatsoever."[27]

The Holy Office's condemnation focused on two distinct themes: the objectivity of human nature and moral decision making.[28] Concerning human nature, the Holy Office chastised those rejecting an "absolute and unchangeable" human nature in favor of an "existent human nature" that is relative and changeable and "can always be adapted to every situation."[29] The import of these divergent notions of human nature is enormous for understanding moral objectivity. If moral objectivity is directly linked to the moral order arising from human nature, and if human nature is to a certain degree malleable, then moral objectivity also must be regarded as a fluid and changeable phenomenon that is as adaptable as human nature.[30] And this conclusion, according to the Holy Office, must be rejected.

On the second theme, moral decision making, the Holy Office complained that situationists advocate an erroneous subjectivism that regards an individual's judgment as the "ultimate norm of conduct," a self-sufficient standard of morality that need not conform to the dictates of reason:

> The authors who follow [situationism] hold that the decisive and ultimate norm of conduct is not objective right order, determined by the law of nature, and known with certainty from that law, but a certain intimate judgment and light of the mind of each individual, by means of which, in the concrete situation in which he is placed, he learns what he ought to do. And so, according to them, this ultimate decision a man makes is not, as the objective ethics handed down by authors of great weight teaches, the application of the objective law to a particular case, taking into account at the same time and weighing according to the rules of prudence the particular circumstances of the "situation," but that immediate, internal light and judgment. This judgment, at least in many matters, is not measured ultimately, is not to be measured, and is not measurable with regard to its objective correctness and truth, by any objective norm outside man, and independent of his subjective persuasion, but is entirely sufficient unto itself.[31]

Although most of Fuchs's writings on situation ethics were published before the Holy Office's condemnation, Fuchs was well aware from Pius XII's stern admonitions that certain boundaries could not be crossed and that any attempt to appropriate the valid insights of situation ethics into his natural law theory would be an extremely delicate task. Interestingly, although the validity of universal moral norms was indisputably the principal bone of contention during the situation ethics controversy, Fuchs's diagnosis of situationism's ailments noticeably departs from Pius's and the Holy Offices'. Although Pius XII and the Holy Office tended to focus on issues closely related to practical moral decision making and exhibited great care in specifying and delineating loci of authority in the moral life, Fuchs thought that situationism's errors in the sphere of practical morality were a foreseeable extension of prior theological positions. Thus, in Fuchs's mind, the most pressing issues raised by situationism were not the staple topics treated by many participants in the situation ethics debate, such as the functions of conscience and prudence, the uniqueness and originality of the individual, or the self-sufficient "internal light and judgment" condemned by the Holy Office. Instead, Fuchs proposed, situationism fails on a practical level because it first misconstrues God, how God grounds morality, and the theological significance of creation, which in turn lead to errors in the realm of practical moral decision making.

Fuchs's Natural Law Theory and the Conflict with Situationism

In the preface of his *Natural Law* Fuchs mentions that for centuries natural law was typically treated philosophically while its theological presuppositions were largely neglected. In Fuchs's estimation this was a mistake because natural law is an abstraction from the total reality of human life, which includes the supernatural dimension, and can be understood properly only within a larger theological context. One of the primary goals of Fuchs's project to systematize his understanding of natural law, therefore, is to raise natural law's neglected theological presuppositions to explicit consciousness and to address them adequately.[32]

Fuchs's attempt to give a "more decidedly theological cast"[33] to natural law explains why his critique of situationism focuses almost exclusively on Protestant theologians, specifically Emil Brunner, Helmut Thielicke, and Karl Barth. Although significant differences exist between each of these theologians, the common factor unifying them is their rejection of traditional Roman Catholic natural law for specifically theological reasons. From their theological understanding of the "situation" to their notions of original sin, their conception of the moral significance of "nature," and their personalistic conception of the God-human relationship, each of these Protestant theologians adhered to fundamental theological positions that placed them sharply at odds with traditional natural law theory.

What Sort of God?

How does God ground and communicate moral obligations to humans? How are God's attributes to be understood? Is God principally conceived as creator? commander? eternal mind? absolute mystery? Is God jealous? loving? forgiving? demanding? Behind every theological ethic lies a particular conception of God that influences and sometimes determines how morality is understood.[34] Throughout his writings on situation ethics Fuchs was highly critical of the dangers the situationist conception of God posed to absolutely binding moral norms, while simultaneously being sympathetic to the personalistic understanding of the God-human relationship prevalent in the writings of the situationists.

A passage in *Natural Law* isolates the basic problem between Fuchs's understanding of natural law and the situationist conception of God. Fuchs writes,

> As men we are not merely obliged to behave according to certain objective moral *norms*. God personally commands everyone in every immediate situation. What is being asked (and doubted) is whether a natural law that is not only a general directive but is an absolute demand, is extensive enough for the God of Revelation and his ever actual freedom. The question is whether absolute and objective moral norms do not deprive him of the possibility of laying free and unlimited claim to the individual at every moment.[35]

This statement is clearly aimed at Karl Barth's understanding of God's freedom. Barth adamantly refused to accept any limitations on God's freedom to act in any way God chooses. God is preeminently a free being, subject to no extrinsic conditioning or compulsion: "God is . . . unlimited, unrestricted and unconditioned from without. He is the free Creator, the free Reconciler, the free Redeemer . . . His divinity is not exhausted in the fact that in His revelation it consists throughout in this freedom from external compulsion: in free utterance and action, free beginning and ending, free judgment and blessing, free power and spirit."[36] In Fuchs's mind, this notion of God's freedom posed grave difficulties in the moral sphere. Because God is ultimately free, according to Barth, God can issue whatever command God wishes in the moment. Not only can God's command to a person in a concrete situation never be predicted beforehand with certainty, but even an obvious pattern among God's commands in similar situations does not guarantee that God will give the same command in another comparable situation. Barth admits that analogies may be drawn from God's prior commands contained in Scripture to predict, in a general way, what God will probably command in the future, but God is not bound by Scripture and is always free to issue new and different commands. The absolute freedom of God, according to Barth, must be preserved even if it results in the demise of theological ethics in any traditional sense. This is a fundamental limit in Barth's theology that he will not abandon under any circumstances.[37]

Fuchs was also concerned with the situationists' "divine voluntarism," which located the source of moral obligation in God's will. Throughout the history of Christian ethics divine voluntarism has found favor among various influential theologians as disparate as Augustine, Peter Abelard, the Franciscans Duns Scotus and William of Occam, the Spanish Jesuit Francisco Suarez,[38] and twentieth-century Protestant theologians including Karl Barth and Emil Brunner. The recurrent problem divine voluntarism poses for ethical deliberation is its tendency toward irrationality, insofar as God's will need not conform to, and sometimes contradicts, the dictates of human reason.[39] According to one commentator, Barth's divine command ethic poses precisely this problem. By locating the source of moral obligation in God's will and insisting on God's absolute freedom, Barth not only places an individual's actions beyond rational assessment or criticism, but he undermines any "publicly intelligible justification of moral decision": "The good [for Barth] is literally arbitrary, purely the product of the absolute power and freedom of the divine will. It is absolutely heteronomous, and therefore irrational. It stands beyond the range of any human measure of what is rational and moral."[40] Brunner, in contrast, presents a more modified version of divine voluntarism. Although he holds that the "good" is always defined in relation to God's will, he maintains that the divine will is conveyed, at least partially, through the "orders of creation."[41] Although this acceptance of the ethical significance of orders of creation seems to establish some common ground between Brunner and traditional Roman Catholic natural law theory, Brunner is unwilling to concede that these orders convey absolutely binding moral obligations. In his mind the orders of creation are capable of transmitting the divine will only "in a fragmentary and indirect way"[42] because they act as mediators between God and humans, and cannot attain the clarity, forcefulness, and unambiguousness characteristic of God's direct commands.

If protecting the freedom of God represented a fundamental concern in Barth's theology, Fuchs was equally insistent in specifying certain limitations to God's freedom. The gravamen of Fuchs's objection to the situationists's conception of God is its faulty metaphysics, or more precisely, its failure to distinguish between the divine nature and the divine will. The divine nature, for Fuchs, is a stable principle of action preceding and limiting the divine will. As Fuchs writes, "God's personality and freedom do not exclude but presuppose that his own essence is 'given before' all personal and free volition. It therefore constitutes the measure of everything."[43] This is a crucial statement with important consequences in the sphere of moral obligation. The priority of the divine nature necessitates that everything God wills corresponds to the divine nature and that no opposition can ever arise between God's nature and will. Thus it cannot be asserted, as the situationists do, that God possesses the absolute freedom to issue whatever command God chooses; for the "good" arises from God's nature and restricts God from willing anything contrary to the divine nature:

> [I]n all genuine theonomy there is room for the good "in itself." It is recognized by God because he has no choice but to recognize it as good. This is not to be understood as if God were merely the guardian of the good "in itself," a good facing God in its absoluteness. It has been said that God is not the guardian but the Creator of the good. Yet even this can be denied: God cannot be said to decide arbitrarily what he wants to describe and present to man as good. This would be nominalism. . . . What is good cannot be defined according to something which is not in God—an idea for example; neither can it be declared alien to God by God's own arbitrary will. God *is* good. What is good, is, to speak in human terms, already good antecedently to God's will and *a fortiori* previous to all ideas and all creatures.[44]

The conception of God permeating Fuchs's writings on natural law is God the creator. God, for Fuchs, is preeminently the creator of an ordered, stable, and harmonious universe, a God grounding creation and giving it moral significance while remaining distinct from it. This is not to imply that Fuchs understands creation as independent from God and capable of bearing moral meaning in itself.[45] On the contrary, Fuchs holds that moral significance is attributed to creation only because it participates in God's goodness[46] and makes the divine nature manifest in varying degrees.[47] In this way creation is correctly understood as God's self-revelation, conveying to humankind the moral demands consonant with the divine nature.[48] Fuchs is so intent on forging an intimate link between God and creation that some of his statements seem to flirt with pantheism, equating God with creation.[49]

Although God the creator underlies Fuchs's entire natural law project, he was also highly sympathetic to the situationists' personalistic

understanding of the God-human relationship: the moral life as a continual dialogue between God and the individual, with God addressing
each person and offering concrete directives.[50] Fuchs agreed that conceiving the moral life as obedience to laws arising from the created
order fosters a desiccated and unpalatable understanding of morality
that fails to grasp the moral life ultimately as an expression of the
intimate, personal, and loving relationship between God and each individual person.[51] Although Fuchs never considers, in any critical manner,
the theoretical difficulties involved in reconciling his notion of God as
creator with a personalistic understanding of the God-human relationship, he frequently employs situationist language and themes to describe God's relationship to humankind via creation. He writes that
creation represents a "word and demand of the living and personal
God"[52] through which God "address[es] us as part of an uninterrupted
and highly personal call."[53] By attending to the obligations arising from
created reality, humans are drawn into perpetual and intimate dialogue
with God:

> This is the main point, always to understand one's own reality as
> word and demand of God, reverently to know and see the reality
> of beings more and more and thus to understand the contents of
> the divine words and demands deeper and more thoroughly. Then
> our lives can be consciously fulfilled as a dialogue between the
> continually addressing and demanding God and the continually
> answering person through his actions.[54]

Although Fuchs resolutely maintains that God's self-communication
occurs through creation, he does admit that in extremely rare cases it
is possible that God addresses an individual directly through private
revelation: "The possibility cannot be excluded—it must in fact be
considered as *fundamentally* possible—that God gives us his moral
directives through the Holy Ghost in a completely personal way."[55] But
Fuchs qualifies this apparent concession to Barth with such stringent
restrictions that, in the end, it does not even remotely resemble Barth's
conception of the divine command. First, any private inspiration given
to an individual can never contradict the moral demands arising from
natural law. It might clarify and illuminate natural law's demands
and their application to the concrete situation at hand, and it might
recommend a course of action surpassing the requirements of natural
law, but conflict can never exist between natural law and a genuine
private revelation.[56] Such conflict "would be totally impossible because
it would imply a contradiction of his own essence by God himself."[57]
Furthermore, evidence substantiating the claim of a divine inspiration

must be more compelling than mere personal testimony. In order for a divine inspiration to be considered authentic it must be confirmed by miracles.[58]

In the final analysis, Fuchs's presentation of God is not unproblematic. Although he is especially concerned to present God as immanent, as intimately present to every person through created reality, Fuchs's version of personalism still places humans in direct relationship with creation, not with God. Despite Fuchs's comments to the contrary, his creator God appears more as an eternal and immutable mind who has created an ordered universe of objects bearing moral meaning, a God grounding creation yet remaining notably distant from it,[59] a God whose love and affection never seem to grasp the person directly and personally, but only mediately through a structured and stable world.

"Human Nature" as the Source of Moral Obligation

One of the tenets of traditional Roman Catholic natural law theory from the Thomistic revival of Pope Leo XIII in the late 1800s to Pope Pius XII in the mid-twentieth century was that the order observable in "nature" reflects the eternal order intended by God and that it can be known by reason apart from revelation. The general idea is that "creatures have 'impressed' in their very being inherent tendencies which reflect the ordering and orientation which God their creator wishes for them."[60] Humans, as rational beings, are capable of understanding their God-given nature and thus can intentionally cooperate in God's providential activity by acting in accordance with the moral demands arising from their nature. "This knowing and free acceptance of his nature as created and destined by God is man's observance of the law of his nature, or of the 'natural law.' "[61] By the mid-twentieth century this notion of nature as the basis for discerning God's intentions for humankind was widespread in official church teaching[62] and received considerable support from the neo-Thomist manualists that dominated Roman Catholic moral theology in the first half of the twentieth century.[63]

The idea of human nature as a conduit for God's intentions proved to be a major point of contention between Fuchs and the situationists. Barth, one of the most outspoken critics of natural theology in recent times, rejected the analogical reasoning predominant in Roman Catholic theology that placed confidence in the ability to draw inferences about the eternal order intended by God from the order observable in creation.[64] God, for Barth, is not an object that can either be observed directly or known analogically through other objects, but a subject known only through action, through God's self-revelation.[65] But Barth grants that even if God's intentions could be known through created reality, the notion of God derived from such an understanding could only be a partial glimpse of the total reality of God. God has been revealed in Scripture not only as creator, but as lord, redeemer, and reconciler who has entered human history through Jesus Christ and redeemed humankind. To the extent that metaphysical speculation fails to capture the whole being of God, its conception of God cannot claim adequately to represent the God of Christianity, but only an idolatrous construct of the human mind.[66]

Brunner and Thielicke also rejected human nature as a reflection of the divine order based on their understanding of original sin's effects. Brunner, for instance, agrees that in its uncorrupted state in paradise human nature served as a unifying force between God and humans. But human nature has been so perverted by original sin that it is now a source of hostility and enmity toward God:

> As a sinner, man is a being whose nature has been perverted, one who has been severed from God, one who is remote from God. He is—whether he knows it or not—in conflict with the nature in which he was created; he is "sick" with that "sickness unto death" which, when it breaks out, manifests itself in the form of despair. . . . Not merely the individual personal acts are hostile to God, but hostility to God now forms part of the very nature of man; the "nature," the character of the existence of man as a whole is now dominated by the contradiction.[67]

Postlapsarian human nature, in Brunner's view, is precisely what must be resisted in order to act morally; it not only impels the human person toward an enveloping and self-destructive narcissism, but it vents its malice on God and neighbor alike, thereby intensifying the human person's isolation and alienation.[68]

Thielicke, an astute commentator on natural law theory, finds original sin as the "basic difference between Roman Catholic and Reformation theology."[69] The orders of creation in the original state did reflect God's eternal wisdom and purpose, but after the Fall they are better characterized as "orders of divine patience"[70] that have deviated from God's original plan and have become objectifications of humankind's sinful condition.[71] The basic mistake of traditional Roman Catholic natural law theory is trying to establish an analogy or corridor between the original state and the fallen world that provides a sufficient basis for comparison through an abstract metaphysical concept of human nature impervious to change and unaffected by original sin.[72] In

Thielicke's view this attempt must fail; original sin has effected a qualitative change in the human person extending to the entire being.[73]

Fuchs was convinced that a correct understanding of human nature could avoid the theological pitfalls posed by the situationists and remain a valid basis for natural law. If, as the situationists maintained, human nature was equated with the original condition of humans, a natural law based on existing, fallen human nature—the only human nature currently available for inspection—is correctly regarded as a degradation of God's original intention for humankind, a collection of "urgency measures" designed to avoid complete chaos.[74] As Fuchs says, "If the original state of man is *not* merely a particular realization of man's essence (certainly, willed and created by God) and *is* purely and simply the nature of man in all the ramifications of his being and if the effects of original sin destructively touch this integral totality, it follows that natural law cannot be affirmed of his present condition nor can it be God's will for him."[75]

Against Brunner and Thielicke, Fuchs maintains that they have confused human nature with a particular realization of human nature. Human nature, according to Fuchs, must be understood metaphysically as "abstracted from any determinate mode of being, real or possible";[76] it is the reality underlying all types of human existence and discoverable in every human being.[77] In this sense, human nature was and is present in both *pre-* and *postlapsarian* humans, although the manner in which it was realized before the Fall was conditioned by the presence of supernatural and preternatural gifts. Given this metaphysical understanding of human nature, the problem of original sin corrupting human nature is seen to be misplaced; the effects of the Fall pertain to the supernatural level while the sphere of nature remains intact. As Fuchs says,

> The Catholic conception [of human nature] presupposes this very distinction between nature and the supernatural. It understands nature only and precisely in as far as it is distinct from the supernatural. This is the only sense in which it is *nature* and of which the Church can say that it was not destroyed but remains as the foundation of a valid natural law. The original *state* of man in its integrity was destroyed and does not survive into our present condition.[78]

Against Barth, Fuchs steadfastly maintained the ontological link between God and human nature through the *analogia entis*.[79] Fuchs was especially concerned that absent this ontological grounding the God-human relationship could be construed in a "*purely* actual, personal and dynamic" way, thus opening the door to moral relativism.[80] According to Fuchs, Barth's conception of the God-human relationship fundamentally misunderstands the theological significance of creation. All of nature, because it is created by God, ontologically participates in the being and goodness of God and thus remains a visible image of the original image, God. Fuchs says,

> Behind all of creation stands the "yes" of the creator God, and indeed not only as God putting creation into effect, but—basically, so to speak—as image. When he creates, he lends his unending being as an "image," as a "vestige," one in an ultimate reality. Since outside of God nothing "exists," there is a "creation-becoming" only as part of the being of God and thus as his image. . . . Man and everything which belongs to him, his qualities, his inner life, his environment, all bear the mark of God in themselves and are the images of God.[81]

Because of this ontological relationship between God and creation, the entire natural world—including human nature—is rightly regarded as God's self-revelation[82] through which God makes manifest the divine being and will for humankind. Fuchs is particularly emphatic on this point: "the reality which we call 'nature' . . . comes directly from the hands of God. God speaks through it and reveals himself in it. It bears his features and it is his image. How could it be otherwise since nature is the creature of God?"[83] Therefore, the moral task of humans is to seek to understand human nature more thoroughly, to uncover the finalities and orders in human nature more precisely in order to comprehend as well as possible the moral demands conveyed by God through human nature.[84]

This relationship being noted, it is clear in Fuchs's preconversion writings that he makes no substantive distinction between "nature" and "human nature." For Fuchs, nature represents all created realities, a collection of objects whose structure and finalities could be understood with precision by the power of human reason. In consequence, Fuchs treats human nature like all other objects in nature, as a reality mediating God's will, placing demands and limitations on the moral agent, and capable of being known objectively without any reference to the knower. Nowhere in Fuchs's early work does he acknowledge human nature as a reality more complex than other natural objects that can be known with "scientific" exactness.[85]

Although Fuchs maintains throughout his early writings that natural law is related primarily to metaphysical human nature, or human nature "in general" as he calls it, Fuchs was also aware that this metaphysical definition of human nature fails to capture the full reality of concrete human beings existing in time and history. Human nature "in general" is an abstraction—albeit a valid abstraction—that is always actualized in a determinate mode of existence conditioned by variable historical circumstances, and if natural law is to regulate the behavior of concrete human beings in the here and now it must descend, as it were, into history. Although Fuchs's concern with the issue of historicity and natural law would become more pronounced and sophisticated in his postconversion writings, at this point he equated historicity with particularity, which is quite different from contemporary understandings of "historical consciousness" and the extensive anthropological, epistemological, and hermeneutical questions it raises.[86] For now Fuchs's objective remains to construct a natural law theory grounded in metaphysical human nature, and therefore universally applicable, while rendering it capable of attending to the manifold ways human nature is realized in diverse historical situations, particularly different epochs in salvation history. But Fuchs claims that even within the same state of salvation history natural law must be historical[87] in the sense that it considers the unique conditions of groups in society as well as of individuals: "The absolute natural law demands a consideration of the historical peculiarities of society, that is of certain peoples and groups in human community. It must take cognizance, for example, of the special social and human situation of the working class today as well as the peculiarities of the individual and his respective singular situations."[88]

Fuchs reconciles this potential disparity between metaphysics and history by distinguishing two types of natural law. "Absolute natural law" is the moral order arising from human nature comprising a series of immutable moral principles that are valid in every historical period. "Relative natural law," which is contained in the absolute natural law in a " 'hypothetical,' 'latent,' and 'potential' way,"[89] refers to the applications of the absolute natural law's principles in diverse historical situations. As Fuchs explains,

> The order given us with nature *as such* can be called "absolute" natural law. . . . The "concrete" forms of this principle in the different situations of our history—for example for man in the original state or in the state of sin—could accordingly be called "relative" natural law. It is relative in the sense of being an *application* of the absolute natural law to a certain situation in salvation-history. It is relative but not in the sense of being a modification of an absolute order of the original state which would adapt that state *in the very*

mode of its being. Yet the formal force of this relative natural law stems from the absolute law whose intrinsic openness to determination is actualized in a purely material way. Considered in this way the relative natural law which takes into account the particular situation of fallen man is, therefore, not a *transformation* of the absolute natural law but rather its genuine application to concrete circumstances. It is purely a material determination of formal moral enunciations. The principles of the absolute natural law do not change formally in man's changing states of salvation-history. They are changed materially according to the accidental changes of the various modes of being in human nature. *The absolute natural law is realized in the relative law. Seen from a different point of view, it contains the relative natural law in a hypothetical yet truly original and essential way.*[90]

It is vital to note that Fuchs sees no discontinuity between absolute and relative natural law. Because the entirety of relative natural law is contained hypothetically in absolute natural law, it forms an extension of, and participates in the absoluteness of, the latter. In this way relative natural law remains as binding as absolute natural law and its principles admit of no exception in the particular historical situation for which they were intended: "The absolute natural law is always valid; the relative natural law proper to our state in the history of salvation knows of no exception for the duration of this state. *Any principle of the natural law remains efficacious in every situation that realizes the facts involved by this principle.*"[91]

To illustrate the transition from absolute to relative natural law, consider the state's right to exercise coercion. Because humans are by nature social beings there must exist in any historical situation an authoritative body—the state—to care for the common good. Therefore it is a principle of the absolute natural law that the state must exist and must be allowed to make decisions regulating communal life. By itself, this principle does not specify what type of government is permissible or the means the government may use to seek the common good. The application of this principle of absolute natural law in different states of salvation history, however, yields divergent principles on the level of relative natural law. In the state of paradise humans would have voluntarily submitted to the state's legitimate decisions, rendering coercion superfluous. But after the Fall, when humans are much less inclined to cooperate with the state, coercion would sometimes be necessary for the state to achieve its proper goals.[92] In each case "[t]he same immutable and eternal truth [of absolute natural law] is being conditioned by *nature* to act in one way in this situation and in another way in that situation. It requires different measures in different situations: *diversa diversis mensuris mensurantur.*"[93]

The preceding example should not give the impression that a principle of absolute natural law always yields diverse principles on the level of relative natural law when applied to concrete historical situations. In addition to the positive principle discussed above, which identified a good to be pursued (the common good), absolute natural law also grounds negative principles or prohibitions that sharply circumscribe the number of potential applications in the sphere of relative natural law. Direct abortion,[94] lying, and sterilization for contraceptive purposes are some of the examples Fuchs mentions that are forbidden by absolute natural law and are never permitted in any historical period.

Fuchs's attempt to wed a universal human nature as the source of natural law to a sustained concern for diverse historical circumstances conditioning human life is perhaps his most significant contribution to Roman Catholic natural law theory in his preconversion period. Yet there is a certain innocence pervading this synthesis that raises several important issues. First, Fuchs never articulates the contents of metaphysical human nature in any systematic manner. Despite Fuchs's confident assertion that metaphysical human nature can be known[95] and the surety with which he derives universal and immutable principles from human nature and applies them on the concrete level,[96] he never offers a clear explanation of the contents of human nature or how principles are derived from it. Not only does this create an aura of arbitrariness surrounding his derivation and application of moral principles, but it makes it difficult, if not impossible, to construct a comprehensive understanding of human flourishing and the concrete goods that must be pursued in order to achieve this objective.

Second, Fuchs's restricted notion of historicity as particularity or situatedness allows him to forge a deceptively unproblematic wedding between metaphysics and historicity, between universal human nature and the human person conditioned by historical circumstances, and between absolute natural law and relative natural law. In Fuchs's mind, the historical is always an extension of the metaphysical, a particular embodiment and manifestation of an eternal and unvarying form, an ontological "accident" that can be subsumed under the "substantial."[97] Nowhere in Fuchs's early work do we witness any perceived discontinuity between metaphysics and history or the possibility that metaphysics itself might be historically conditioned.

Third, although Fuchs spends a considerable amount of energy establishing the structural unity of absolute and relative natural law, he offers little guidance on how to determine a proper "application" of absolute natural law's principles to the sphere of relative natural law, particularly when dealing with positive principles.[98] Take, for example, the principle of absolute natural law discussed above, "the state must be allowed to act for the common good." When this principle is applied to the sphere of relative natural law, it both permits and prohibits capital punishment depending on the particular historical circumstances. But what criteria determine that allowing capital punishment is a legitimate application in one historical period but not in another? Fuchs certainly does not regard all applications as equally correct, nor does he regard the indeterminacy and elasticity of the absolute natural law's positive principles as allowing any concrete application whatsoever, yet he fails to specify in any substantial manner how to determine legitimate from illegitimate applications.

The "Situation" and the Validity of Universal Moral Norms[99]

The issue that greatly troubled the Roman Catholic magisterium—and drew sharp criticism from natural law theorists, including Fuchs—was the validity of universal moral norms in concrete situations.[100] Situationists did not deny that moral norms are a relevant component of moral deliberation and that they offer a general indication of God's will in a concrete situation. Even Karl Barth, who vociferously rejected the metaphysical grounding of traditional Roman Catholic natural law theory, gave credence to moral norms patterned on God's prior commands recorded in Scripture. But situationists agreed that whereas moral norms possess an indicative or directive character, they can never claim universal validity in concrete situations.

It is revealing to note the significant differences Fuchs displays in his pre- and postconversion writings when assessing the validity of moral norms in terms of his breadth of interest, the ability to question critically, and the components of his Roman Catholic natural law tradition that he simply presumes as true and indisputable. In his postconversion work Fuchs offers a panoramic, far-ranging, comprehensive, and thorough treatment of moral norms. Most of his attention focuses on epistemological issues, in other words, the role of reason in the formulation of moral norms and the inability of human reason to foresee all the possible circumstances in which moral norms are applied. But Fuchs also considers the implications of historicity (at this point Fuchs had embraced a more sophisticated understanding of "historical consciousness"), diverse cultural backgrounds, and newly emergent conceptions of theological anthropology on the validity of moral norms,[101] as well as the competency of the magisterium in formulating moral norms.[102] In addition, Fuchs also investigates the relationship between moral norms and concrete circumstances and challenges the dominant paradigm in Roman Catholic moral theology that moral objectivity consists in simply applying a norm to a concrete situation. In Fuchs's postconversion period we see a theologian assessing the validity of moral norms from a variety of angles, probing, raising further relevant questions, challenging the received tradition, and taking little for granted.

Standing in stark contrast to this is Fuchs's limited scope and the dearth of direct analysis he offers on the issue of universal moral norms in his preconversion period. At this time the paramount issue for Fuchs was the metaphysical grounding of moral norms. Situationists were able to reject the validity of universal moral norms because of their nominalistic understanding of God's will that denied any stable, enduring, and consistent foundation for moral norms. As we have seen, Fuchs's strategy in combating this nominalism was to establish a metaphysical basis for natural law that is located remotely in the divine nature and proximately in human nature, thus attaining the constancy Fuchs so craved. It is fair to say that the validity of universal moral norms remained the central point of contention in the situation ethics controversy, whereas for Fuchs it was subservient to prior metaphysical issues, and once these were resolved adequately, so too was the question of universal moral norms. Indeed, at the beginning of one of Fuchs's earliest articles on situation ethics, he states that the problem of universal moral norms simply dissolves if a proper metaphysical basis for natural law is established.[103]

Another reason for the paucity of direct analysis Fuchs gives to universal moral norms stems from his acceptance of the Roman Catholic natural law tradition's understanding of the relation between universal moral norms and concrete situations. From the situationist's perspective, a concrete situation represents a moment of suspense and uncertainty, a moment of decision regulated ultimately not by prefabricated universal moral norms but by an absolutely free and sovereign God whose commands can be entirely unpredictable.[104] As Brunner says, "[W]e can never know beforehand what God will require. God's command can only be perceived at the actual moment of hearing it. It would denote a breaking away from obedience if we were to think of the Divine Command as one which had been enacted once for all, to be interpreted by us in particular instances."[105] On the other hand, in traditional Roman Catholic natural law theory concrete situations are not pregnant with pendency and unsurety; they are either instances in which universal moral norms are applied or concrete realizations of a universal. Although the uniqueness and complexity of concrete situations might cast confusion on which universal moral norm should be applied, the question is never raised whether a concrete situation can elude the grasp of norms entirely or whether certain circumstantial data might render a norm inapplicable in a concrete situation. The preconversion Fuchs, who at this point considered himself an ex-pounder and guardian of received teaching, fully accepted the traditional Roman Catholic paradigm of applying universal moral norms to concrete situations and perceived no contradiction between them. Years after he had ceased writing on situation ethics he lauded situationism's insistence on attending to concrete circumstances, which for-bade "a simple, matter-of-fact, cold 'imposition' of prefabricated principles on living reality."[106] But this statement was untenable for the preconversion Fuchs.

Fuchs wished to rectify one lingering doubt concerning the potential discrepancy between universal moral norms and individual human persons. Situationists claimed that God's command is addressed to individuals, not simply as one person among many, but as an unrepeat-able, unique, and singular being whose subjective qualities and attri-butes are relevant not simply to the determination of moral culpability but to the specific command God decides to give. Fuchs, too, was concerned that the originality and uniqueness of each person be given due respect: "The uniqueness of the human person is absolute. Nobody can represent me; perhaps it can be said of another that he is of my age, my size, or my beliefs; and in many more ways commonalities can exist between me and another person; even if another person has no ascertainable differences from me, he always remains the other, he is never me."[107] Fuchs's incipient personalism also depicted God calling each person individually, in the fullness of their concrete existence, through the created structures of reality.[108] But Fuchs was unwilling to concede any conflict between universal moral norms and either the absolute uniqueness of each individual or the personal call of God in the situation. Fuchs continually beckons his readers back to the proximate source of natural law, human nature:

> But with all the emphasis on the absolute uniqueness of humans and human situations and of particular qualitative features it may not be overlooked that every person is a human, although in a singular and particular way; and all persons express what human-ness is in itself. What we understand concerning "human" is totally

and wholly realized in each person, and indeed at all times, although entirely uniquely and always in its own way. The significance of this statement for morality is no less important than the observation of the absolute uniqueness and distinctiveness of persons.[109]

Fuchs's solution to this potential conflict was to distinguish two planes of morality. On the first, the plane of "universal essences," human nature grounds universal moral norms that bind the moral agent regardless of her or his unique characteristics and must be applied in her or his particular historical circumstances. The second supernatural plane, on which the "the absolute originality of each individual" comes to expression, is the forum for the moral agent's personal response to the call of God that determines her or his existence.[110] But, as Fuchs explains, this response never stands in contradiction to the demands of universal moral norms; indeed, God's purposes in the supernatural sphere are to strengthen the moral agent's resolve, to offer added insight, and to help the agent overcome her or his subjective weaknesses so the agent can act in accordance with universal moral norms: "Through this [supernatural] inspiration God leads the person, not so that he imposes obligations where the moral order grants freedom, or that he acknowledges freedom where the moral order places demands, but rather that through an inner effect he guides the person to an appropriate insight and act of the will."[111]

A similar pattern of reverting to human nature as the proximate source of natural law is found in Fuchs's discussion of the "situation." Note the priority given to human nature in every concrete situation:

> Elements of the situation: (1) *The fundamental element: human nature.* (2) *Individual qualities of the subject* . . . (3) *Relations to external circumstances* . . . (4) *The divine disposition in regard to the individual person as such* . . . (5) Nor should the *extraordinary intervention of God* be absolutely excluded.[112]

Time after time, Fuchs poses the question, Are universal moral norms valid without exception in concrete situations? and his immediate response is always to identify human nature as the source of moral norms.[113] Although this might seem to evade the question, in Fuchs's mind it was a sufficient response; metaphysical human nature is present wherever humans are found, grounding universal moral norms that regulate the entirety of human behavior.

Notes

1. The label "situation ethics" and cognates are not intended as terms of abuse. There was a tendency in this particular controversy to discredit authors by labeling them without adequately assessing the quality of their ideas. Although labels will be employed in the following essay, they are not meant to convey disparagement.

2. John Mahoney, *The Making of Moral Theology: A Study of the Roman Catholic Tradition* (Oxford: Clarendon Press, 1989), 205. See also Paul Hilsdale, "The Real Threat of Situation Ethics," *Homiletic and Pastoral Review* 58 (1957): 173; Kenneth Moore "Situational Ethics," *American Ecclesiastical Review* 135 (1956): 33; and Paul H. Besanceney, " 'Situation Ethics' or the 'New Morality,' " *American Ecclesiastical Review* 137 (1957): 101, for ominous warnings about situationism's dangers.

3. Josef Fuchs, *Natural Law: A Theological Investigation,* trans. Helmut Recker and John Dowling (New York: Sheed and Ward, 1965), xi.

4. Josef Fuchs, "Situationsethik," *Seelsorgehilfe* 4 (1952): 245–55, 273–78; Josef Fuchs, "Situationsethik in theologischer Sicht," *Scholastik* 27 (1952): 161–82; Josef Fuchs, "Morale théologique et morale de situation," *Nouvelle Revue Théologique* 76 (1954): 1073–85; Josef Fuchs, "Ethique objective et éthique de situation," *Nouvelle Revue Théologique* 78 (1956): 798–818; and Josef Fuchs, "Positivistisches Naturrecht?" *Orientierung* 20 (1956): 113–15, 127–29.

5. Josef Fuchs, *Situation und Entscheidung: Grundfragen christlicher Situationsethik* (Frankfurt: Knecht, 1952).

6. Josef Fuchs, *Lex Naturae: Zur Theologie des Naturrechts* (Düsseldorf, Germany: Patmos, 1955).

7. Fuchs, *Natural Law*, xi.

8. Josef Fuchs, *Human Values and Christian Morality,* trans. M. H. Heelan et al. (Dublin: Gill and Macmillan, 1970), 72.

9. For discussions of the philosophical aspects of situationism, see Anthony Manser and Albert Kolnai, "Symposium on Existentialism," *Aristotelian Society Supplementary Volume* 37 (1963); Mary Warnock, *The Philosophy of Sartre* (London: Hutchinson, 1965); Anthony Manser, *Sartre: A Philosophic Study* (London: Althone Press, 1966); Robert L. Cunningham, introduction to *Situationism and the New Morality*, ed. Robert L. Cunningham (New York: Appleton-Century-Crofts, 1970); Dietrich von Hildebrand, *True Morality and Its Counterfeits* (New York: McKay, 1955); J. Newman, "The Ethics of Existentialism," *Irish Ecclesiastical Record* 71 (1952); and W. A. Wallace, "Existential Ethics in a Thomistic Appraisal," *Thomist* 27 (1963). For discussions of theological issues raised by situationism, see Ernst Michel, *Der Partner Gottes: Weisungen zum christlichen Selbtverstandnis* (Heidelberg: Lambert Schneider, 1946); Francis Hürth, "Instructio Supremae Sacrae Congregationis S. Officii: De Ethica Situationis," *Periodica de Re Morali, Canonica, Liturgica* 45 (1956); Richard Egenter, *Von der Freiheit der Kinder Gottes* (Freiburg: Herder, 1949); Richard Egenter, "Kasuistik als christliche Situationsethik," *Münchener Theologische Zeitschrift* 1 (1950): 54–

65; and G. Sohngen, "Die biblische Lehre von der Gottebenbildlichkeit des Menschen," *Münchener Theologische Zeitschrift* 2 (1951): 52–76.

10. John A. Gallagher, *Time Past, Time Future: An Historical Study of Catholic Moral Theology* (Mahwah, N.J.: Paulist Press, 1990), 226–35.

11. John C. Ford and Gerald Kelly, *Contemporary Moral Theology*, 2 vols. (Cork, Ireland: Mercier Press, 1958–64), 1: 125. See also Walter Dirks, "How Can I Know What God Wants of Me?" *Cross Currents* 5 (1955): 81.

12. Hans Wulf, "Gesetz und Liebe in der Ordnung des Heils," *Geist und Leben* 22 (1949): 356.

13. Hans Hirschmann, "Im Spiegel der Zeit," *Geist und Leben* 25 (1951): 301–03.

14. Karl Rahner, *Nature and Grace*, trans. Dinah Wharton (New York: Sheed and Ward, 1964), 19.

15. Ibid., 18–19.

16. Ibid., 28. For a later article addressing the potential tension between the individual and universal moral obligations, see Karl Rahner, "On the Question of a Formal Existential Ethics," in *Theological Investigations*, vol. II, trans. Karl-H. Kruger (Baltimore, Md.: Helicon Press, 1963), 217–34.

17. Dirks, "How Can I Know What God Wants of Me?," 81.

18. Ibid., 84–85.

19. Pope Pius XII, "Address to the World Federation of Catholic Young Women," *Catholic Documents* 8 (1952): 15–20; Pope Pius XII, "The Christian Conscience as an Object of Education," *Catholic Documents* 8 (1952): 1–7.

20. Pope Pius XII, "The Christian Conscience," 2.

21. For treatments of conscience in the neo-Thomist manuals of moral theology, see Henry Davis, *Moral and Pastoral Theology*, 7th ed., 4 vols. (London: Sheed and Ward, 1958), 1: 64ff; Antony Koch and Arthur Preuss, *A Handbook of Moral Theology*, 3d ed., 5 vols. (St. Louis, Mo.: B. Herder, 1925), 1: 182ff; Thomas Slater, *A Manual of Moral Theology*, 3d ed., 2 vols. (New York: Benzinger Brothers, 1908), 1: 57ff; John A. McHugh and Charles J. Callan, *Moral Theology: A Complete Course Based on St. Thomas and the Best Modern Authorities*, 2 vols. (New York: Joseph F. Wagner, 1929), 1: 23ff; Dominic Prümmer, *Handbook of Moral Theology*, trans. Gerald W. Shelton, ed. John Gavin Nolan (New York: P. J. Kennedy and Sons, 1957), 58ff; Francis Hürth and P. M. Abellan, *De Principiis, De Virtutibus et Praeceptis* (Rome: Pontificia Universitatis Gregoriana, 1948), 120ff; H. Noldin and A. Schmitt, *Summa Theologiae Moralis*, 3 vols. (Innsbruck, Austria: Sumptis and Typic Feliciani Rauch, 1940), 1: 193ff; Marcellinus Zalba, *Theologiae Moralis Compendium: Juxta Constitutionem Deus Scientiarum*, 2 vols. (Madrid: Editorial Catolica, 1958), 1: 381ff; Aloysius Sabetti and Timothy Barrett, *Compendium Theologiae Moralis* (Rome: Frederick Pustet, 1931), 35ff; and Arthur Vermeersch, *Theologiae Moralis*, 3d ed., 3 vols. (Rome: Pontificia Universitatis Gregoriana, 1933), 1: 293ff.

22. Pope Pius XII, "The Christian Conscience," 3.

23. Pius's link between morality and revelation, which in the preceding quotation seems to imply that no sphere of morality lies outside of revelation,

needs to be understood properly. Following the First Vatican Council, Pius is asserting that moral truths, to be known with certainty and without error, must be revealed. Although Pius agrees that some moral truths are knowable absent revelation, the persistent negative effects of original sin, which weaken the mind considerably, render most moral truths—especially practical moral truths—unknowable. Thus without revelation, the range of moral knowledge available to *postlapsum* humans is confined to general moral truths, whereas knowledge of concrete right and wrong remains intractably elusive. See Pope Pius XII, "Humani Generis," in *The Papal Encyclicals 1939–1958*, ed. Claudia Carlen (1950; reprint, Raleigh, N.C.: McGrath Publishing, 1981), #2–3.

24. Pius XII, "Catholic Young Women," 16.

25. Ibid., 16.

26. Ibid., 18–19.

27. Quoted in Ford and Kelly, *Contemporary Moral Theology*, 1: 123.

28. Mahoney, *Making of Moral Theology*, 206.

29. Ford and Kelly, *Contemporary Moral Theology*, 1: 122.

30. Mahoney, *Making of Moral Theology*, 206.

31. Ford and Kelly, *Contemporary Moral Theology*, 1: 121–22.

32. Fuchs, *Natural Law*, xi.

33. Ibid.

34. After his conversion Fuchs returned to this issue, but the God he portrays is markedly different from that in his preconversion writings. See Josef Fuchs, *Christian Morality: The Word Becomes Flesh*, trans. Brian McNeil (Washington, D.C.: Georgetown University Press, 1987), 28–49.

35. Fuchs, *Natural Law*, 128.

36. Karl Barth, *The Doctrine of God*, vol. 2, bk. 1 of *Church Dogmatics*, trans. T. H. L. Parker et al., ed. G. W. Bromiley and T. F. Torrance (Edinburgh: T. and T. Clark, 1957), 301. For commentary on Barth's notion of God's freedom, see Robin W. Lovin, *Christian Faith and Public Choices: The Social Ethics of Barth, Brunner, and Bonhoeffer* (Philadelphia: Fortress Press, 1984), 28–30; and Nigel Biggar, *The Hastening that Awaits: Karl Barth's Ethics* (Oxford: Clarendon Press, 1993), 9.

37. Lovin, *Christian Faith and Public Choices*, 29–30. See also, Biggar, *Hastening that Awaits*, 9.

38. For a discussion of some of the significant proponents of divine voluntarism, see Mahoney, *Making of Moral Theology*, 225–29.

39. For critical discussions of this problem, see the essays in Paul Helm, ed., *Divine Commands and Morality* (New York: Oxford University Press, 1981).

40. Biggar, *Hastening that Awaits*, 24. See also James Gustafson, *Protestant and Roman Catholic Ethics* (Chicago: University of Chicago Press, 1978), 44–46.

41. Emil Brunner, *The Divine Imperative*, trans. Olive Wyon (Philadelphia: Westminster Press, 1947), 330–39. For a discussion of Brunner's understanding of the "orders of creation," see Reinhold Niebuhr, "The Concept of 'Order of Creation' in Emil Brunner's Social Ethic," in *The Theology of Emil Brunner*, ed.

Charles W. Kegley and Robert W. Brethall (New York: Macmillan, 1962), 265–71.

42. Brunner, *The Divine Imperative*, 291.

43. Fuchs, *Natural Law*, 129.

44. Ibid., 70.

45. Ibid., 67, no. 7.

46. The fundamental goodness of creation pervades Fuchs's writings. See Josef Fuchs, *Die Sexualethik des Heiligen Thomas von Aquin* (Cologne: J. P. Bachem, 1949), 21–30.

47. Fuchs, "Situationsethik," 164; Fuchs, *Situation und Entscheidung*, 35; and Fuchs, "Morale théologique et morale de situation," 1077–78.

48. Fuchs, *Natural Law*, 67–68.

49. For example, Fuchs writes, "It is therefore God who is before my eyes in creation and, through it, he addresses the world of his creation in me, and in this very moment" (ibid., 132).

50. For the situationist, the moral law, codified in propositional moral norms, represents an unnecessary, unpalatable, and sometimes deceptive medium that can never compare to God's direct command to an individual, indicating precisely and unambiguously what must be done. Commenting on how notions such as "the good" and "the law" place a barrier between God and the individual, Brunner writes, "This personal estrangement from God transforms personal union with Him into an impersonal abstract idea; thus 'the Good,' the 'Idea of the Good,' 'the Law,' becomes the principle of life, an abstract idea, which has no vital connexion with life and therefore does violence to life. For the *Idea* of the Good did not create life, it has no interest in life. It is an alien force which has invaded life" (Brunner, *The Divine Imperative*, 114). See also Thomas C. Oden, *The Promise of Barth* (Philadelphia: J. B. Lippincott, 1969), 58–62; Aidan M. Carr, "The Morality of Situation Ethics," *Catholic Lawyer* 5 (1959): 81–82; and Louis Dupré, "Situation Ethics and Objective Morality," in *Situationism and the New Morality*, ed. Robert L. Cunningham (New York: Appleton-Century-Crofts, 1970), 98–99.

51. Josef Fuchs, *General Moral Theology*, pt. 1 (Rome: Pontificia Universitatis Gregoriana, 1963), 22.

52. Fuchs, *Situation und Entscheidung*, 24.

53. Fuchs, "Morale théologique," 1078.

54. Fuchs, *Situation und Entscheidung*, 24.

55. Fuchs, *Natural Law*, 134. See also Fuchs, *Situation und Entscheidung*, 77–92.

56. Fuchs, "Situationsethik," 171–73.

57. Fuchs, *Natural Law*, 134.

58. Fuchs, "Situationsethik,"172.

59. Ronald Amos Mercier, "What Is Nature? The Development of Josef Fuchs' Thought on Moral Normativity" (Ph.D. diss., Regis College, 1993), 68–72.

60. Mahoney, *Making of Moral Theology*, 78.

61. Ibid.

62. For a review of papal statements on nature and natural law, see Fuchs, *Natural Law*, 6–9.

63. Henry Davis, writing on the theological significance of the natural realm, represents the neo-Thomist position well: "The proof that there is an intelligent purpose behind nature is that physical activities are regular, uniform and mutually useful, or in other words, that they are productive of order. Furthermore, the existence of the Natural Law is a necessary result of creation, for given the natural order, the Wisdom of the Creator must be interested in His work, especially as the work continues so long as Providence maintains nature in existence. Consequently, Divine Wisdom must wish reasonable creatures to be directed towards their ultimate end conformably to the nature proper to them, and must, therefore, wish man to choose what is in accordance with his nature and to reject what is not" (Davis, *Moral and Pastoral Theology*, 1: 125). For other neo-Thomist manualists on the theological status of nature, see Slater, *Manual of Moral Theology*, 1: 92; Koch and Preuss, *A Handbook of Moral Theology*, 1: 122; Prümmer, *Handbook of Moral Theology*, 29; McHugh and Callan, *Moral Theology*, 1: 96; and Zalba, *Theologiae Moralis Compendium*, 1: 182.

64. Barth, *Doctrine of God*, vol. 2, bk. 1, 76–78. Recent commentators claim that the later Barth was more sympathetic to certain aspects of natural theology. See Stanley Hauerwas, *With the Grain of the Universe: The Church's Witness and Natural Theology* (Grand Rapids, Mich.: Brazos Press, 2001), 141–204; and Alister E. McGrath, *Nature*, vol. 1 of *A Scientific Theology* (Grand Rapids, Mich.: William B. Eerdmans, 2001), 267–72.

65. Lovin, *Christian Faith and Public Choices*, 34.

66. Barth, *Doctrine of God*, vol. 2, bk. 1, 79–84.

67. Brunner, *The Divine Imperative*, 154–55.

68. Ibid.

69. Helmut Thielicke, *Foundations*, vol. 1 of *Theological Ethics* (Philadelphia: Fortress Press, 1966), 398.

70. Ibid.

71. Ibid., 419, 439.

72. Ibid., 398, 405.

73. Ibid., 394.

74. Fuchs, "Morale théologique," 1082.

75. Fuchs, *Natural Law*, 46–47.

76. Ibid., 50

77. Ibid., 90.

78. Ibid., 47.

79. See Mercier, "What Is Nature?," 66–67.

80. Fuchs, *Natural Law*, 62.

81. Fuchs, *Situation und Entscheidung*, 22.

82. Fuchs, *Natural Law*, 67. See also Fuchs, "Morale théologique," 1077–78; Fuchs, "Situationsethik," 164.

83. Fuchs, *Natural Law*, 60.

84. Fuchs, *Situation und Entscheidung*, 24; Fuchs, "Morale théologique," 1077–78; and Fuchs, *Natural Law*, 71.

85. For constructive proposals on the use of human nature in ethical theory, see Larry Arnhart, *Darwinian Natural Right: The Biological Ethics of Human Nature* (Albany: State University of New York Press, 1998); Robert J. McShea, *Morality and Human Nature: A New Route to Ethical Theory* (Philadelphia: Temple University Press, 1990); Mary Midgley, *Beast and Man: The Roots of Human Nature* (Ithaca, N.Y.: Cornell University Press, 1978); Stephen Pope, *The Evolution of Altruism and the Ordering of Love* (Washington, D.C.: Georgetown University Press, 1994); and John Kekes, "Human Nature and Moral Theories," *Inquiry* 28 (1985): 231–45.

86. For criticism of Fuchs's preconversion notion of historicity, see Norbert J. Rigali, "The Uniqueness and Distinctiveness of Christian Morality and Ethics," in *Moral Theology: Challenges for the Future*, ed. Charles E. Curran (Mahwah, N.J.: Paulist Press, 1990), 74–93.

87. Fuchs, *Natural Law*, 100.

88. Ibid., 111.

89. Ibid., 94.

90. Ibid., 91–92.

91. Ibid., 123.

92. Ibid., 96.

93. Ibid., 95, citing Thomas Aquinas, *Summa Theologiae* I–II.104.3 ad 1.

94. Fuchs, *General Moral Theology*, pt. 1, 28.

95. Fuchs, *Natural Law*, 54.

96. Ibid., 56.

97. Josef Fuchs, "De Valore Legis Naturalis in Ordine Redemptionis," *Periodica de Re Morali, Canonica, et Liturgica* 44 (1955): 51–55; Fuchs, "Ethique objective et éthique de situation," 810–11; and Fuchs, *Natural Law*, 111.

98. This was Brunner's principal objection to the notion of relative natural law, because according to him the supposed variable application of absolute natural law's moral principles in different historical contexts is nothing more than a fanciful theoretical construct designed to justify a predetermined moral agenda. See Brunner, *The Divine Imperative*, 630.

99. Fuchs employs the adjective "universal" to denote any moral norm admitting of no exception in which the facts envisioned in the norm are realized in the concrete situation. As we have already discussed in the section on natural law's historicity, some moral norms are universally valid in a particular state of salvation, but not in another. Thus according to Fuchs moral norms can possess universal validity either in any state of salvation history, or in a particular state of salvation history, or within a particular state of salvation history in which certain cultural or social conditions are realized.

100. See, for example, J. Kunicic, "Ethicae situationis' multiplex error," *Divus Thomas* 60 (1957): 305–13; Moore, "Situational Ethics;" Thomas A. Wassamer, "A Re-examination of Situation Ethics," *Catholic Educational Review* 57

(1959): 20–37; and Robert W. Gleason, "Situational Morality," *Thought* 32 (1957–58): 533–58.

101. See Josef Fuchs, *Personal Responsibility and Christian Morality*, trans. William Cleves et al. (Washington, D.C.: Georgetown University Press, 1983), 115–52.

102. See Josef Fuchs, *Christian Ethics in a Secular Arena*, trans. Bernard Hoose and Brian McNeil (Washington, D.C.: Georgetown University Press, 1984), 131–53.

103. Fuchs, "Situationsethik," 162.

104. Karl Barth, *The Doctrine of God*, vol. 2, bk. 2 of *Church Dogmatics*, trans. T. H. L. Parker et al., ed. G. W. Bromiley and T. F. Torrance (Edinburgh: T. and T. Clark, 1957), 522.

105. Brunner, *The Divine Imperative*, 117.

106. Fuchs, *Human Values and Christian Morality*, 72.

107. Fuchs, *Situation und Entscheidung*, 14.

108. Fuchs, "Morale théologique," 1077–78; and Fuchs, *Situation und Entscheidung*, 26.

109. Fuchs, *Situation und Entscheidung*, 17.

110. Fuchs, "Morale théologique," 1079–81.

111. Fuchs, "Situationsethik," 173.

112. Fuchs, *General Moral Theology*, pt. 1, 26.

113. Fuchs, "Ethique objective," 803; Fuchs, "Morale théologique," 1075; Fuchs, *Situation und Entscheidung*, 31–32; and Fuchs, *Natural Law*, 123–24.

2

A Fuller Account of Natural Law

Our point of departure, in chapter 1, for reconstructing and analyzing portions of Fuchs's natural law theory was his confrontation with situation ethics and the various divisive issues that occurred during this controversy: theological conceptions of God and the manner in which God grounds natural law; the status of "nature" in natural law deliberation; and the validity of universal moral norms. In this chapter I develop a more comprehensive account of Fuchs's understanding of natural law from foundational concepts to practical moral issues, focusing on four topics: (a) the structure, derivation, and justification of moral norms; (b) moral epistemology and the magisterium's competency to interpret natural law; (c) the individual moral agent's role in Fuchs's natural law theory; and (d) the relation between natural law and the supernatural moral order.

Natural Law and the Structure of Moral Norms

Interpreting and analyzing Fuchs's preconversion understanding of natural law's relation to moral norms poses formidable difficulties. His discussions of moral norms are piecemeal and cryptic, and the examples he offers to demonstrate how moral norms are derived, specified, and justified are often generic and do not lend easily to a nuanced or precise understanding. The problem is compounded by Fuchs's ambiguous notion of human nature, which he repeatedly mentions as the proximate foundation of natural law. Fuchs explicitly endorses an abstract definition of human nature based on attributes common to all persons in all times. But Fuchs's metaphysical definition fails to specify what constitutes metaphysical human nature: natural inclinations, the finalities inherent in the human body, reason, or something else. For instance, after discussing the types of natural inclinations grounding absolute natural law in his manual of moral theology, Fuchs offers the following definition of human nature: "[Human] nature is understood as the essence of man, both according to his metaphysical being ('rational animal,' with all the consequences necessarily flowing from this) and according to his physical being, by which his metaphysical being by the will of the Creator is in fact real, together with all its attendant relations."[1] I surmise that Fuchs employs metaphysical human nature univocally, which partially explains his vacillation in justifying the validity of certain moral norms.

Despite these obstacles, a major lacuna would exist in Fuchs's natural law theory if the relation between natural law and moral norms remained unexplored. Given Fuchs's (and his neo-Thomist contemporaries') preoccupation with articulating natural law's contents precisely and concretely in the form of propositional moral norms, it would be remiss not to offer some explanation, however tentative, of Fuchs's process of reducing natural law to a series of ordered moral norms.

Fuchs understands natural law in two senses: first, as an unwritten, internal law corresponding to the demands arising from human nature;[2] second, as a series of ordered moral norms cast in propositional form that specify, in varying degrees of concreteness, how these demands are to be fulfilled. The transparency of human nature is, of course, one of the pivotal issues concerning the transition from an unwritten law to a codified set of moral norms. If human nature remains impenetrable and inscrutable to human reason, the ability to construct accurate moral norms regulating purposive action is virtually nonexistent; without knowledge of human nature, human reason would have no basis to determine how or what actions impede, contradict, or support natural law's demands.

In Fuchs's opinion, human nature can be understood with sufficient precision for two reasons. First, revelation testifies to at least some of human nature's components. Although revelation does not offer an exhaustive presentation of human nature, its partial account can be regarded as correct.[3] Second, what revelation has omitted human reason can know through ordinary human experience: "[W]e can come to a specific representation of man 'in general,' with his concomitant moral and juridical order, by means of concrete human experience. We can achieve a knowledge of man's metaphysical essence in the strict sense of *definition metaphysica*. From this point of departure . . . the natural law as pertaining to man with metaphysical necessity will be open to us."[4]

The capacity of the human mind to comprehend the contents of metaphysical human nature opens up the vast sphere of absolute natural law, which remains the supreme regulative measure of all human action, even though it does not, and sometimes cannot, specify exactly what should be done in certain concrete, historical situations. As I discussed in chapter 1, Fuchs distinguishes between two types of natural law: *absolute natural law*, which arises from human nature in general and comprises a series of universal and immutable moral norms valid in every historical period; and *relative natural law*, which corresponds to the various states of nature, in other words, the diverse soteriological, historical, social, and cultural circumstances in which human nature in general is realized, and that grounds mutable moral norms that accommodate the unique conditions of specific times or locales.[5] Fuchs maintains that eternal law, or God's mind ordering the universe and drawing all things to their due ends, is the supreme regulative measure of human conduct. Because it is impossible for humans to grasp the mind of God directly, however, absolute natural law—which is grounded in metaphysical human nature and thus can be known—is the highest regulative principle for us.[6]

The scope of absolute natural law is unlimited; because it is grounded in universal and immutable human nature it is present wherever and whenever humans are found and either permits or forbids every human action. But the universality of human nature also functions as a limiting principle. Absolute natural law can be only as specific as its ground, human nature, allows, and because human nature prescinds from individuality, particularity, and historicity—literally all the ontological "accidents" that differentiate one person from another—the contents of absolute natural law must remain indeterminate if knowledge of particulars or contexts is morally relevant in assessing an action's rightness or wrongness.

In perhaps his clearest presentation of the structure of moral norms derived both from absolute natural law, which is the universal and immutable moral order arising from human nature in general, and from relative natural law, which is the moral order arising from human nature as it is actualized in a determinate mode of existence and conditioned by variable historical circumstances,[7] Fuchs writes,

> The examples which follow can be considered as natural law in particular. Take first the most general principles, for example, to do good, to give every man his due; secondly the primary 'consequences'—that is the primary applications to objective individual spheres of nature 'in general': not to kill, to steal, or lie etc. just as one likes; thirdly, the application to more concrete facts which, however, presuppose to a great extent a certain state in the history of salvation: for example, the question of the interruption of preg-

nancy in extremely difficult circumstances. Finally we must consider the application to particular concrete situations.[8]

This passage is significant for two reasons. First, even before assessing the potential implications of historicity, Fuchs considers it possible to derive immutable and universal moral norms from absolute natural law. In Fuchs's mind, the movement is always from the universal to the particular, from metaphysical human nature to the historically embedded individual person, with relative natural law and its norms becoming a relevant factor in moral deliberation only if a particular issue or action cannot be settled on the level of absolute natural law.

Second, in both language and structure Fuchs's account of moral norms derived from natural law is remarkably similar to Thomas Aquinas's.[9] Both identify three grades of moral norms, beginning with the most general norms known easily by everyone that identify "goods" to be pursued and the acceptable ways of pursuing these "goods."[10] From these first principles certain "consequences"[11] (Fuchs) or "conclusions" (Thomas)[12] follow that comprise the second grade of moral norms. The third, and final, grade consists of norms derived from the second set of principles that can be grasped only through "much consideration of different circumstances"[13] (Thomas) or through "a consideration of the historical peculiarities of society, . . . of certain peoples and groups in human community" (Fuchs).[14] These structural and conceptual similarities do not, of course, imply an identical method of deriving norms from natural law; only that Fuchs's obvious reliance on Thomas might help illuminate certain elements of Fuchs's presentation.

Fuchs's derivation of universal and immutable moral norms occurs in various ways. First, Fuchs seems to rely on a phenomenology of natural inclinations from which he proceeds to construct moral norms ensuring the existence of various goods constitutive of human flourishing in any historical context. In this instance, the moral norms Fuchs derives are intended to legitimate the institutional structures necessary for at least a minimal degree of human flourishing. Although Fuchs does not link any of these institutions with specific natural inclinations, one can infer the connections: the natural inclination to live in community requires the existence of human society; the desires to mate and procreate require the institutions of marriage and the family; and the need for peace, security, and order necessitate the state in some form.[15] On this basic level, moral norms may be either positive ("the state has a right to exist") or negative ("anything threatening the state's existence is impermissible"), but they are always formal and give no material indication how these goods are to be realized (e.g., what type of state or the extent of its powers).

Another class of universal and immutable moral norms concerns the manner in which the goods indicated by the natural inclinations are and are not to be pursued. These norms, too, are formal ("*suum cuique*,"[16] "be merciful"[17]) and susceptible to different material realizations. For Fuchs, these norms are self-evident, or at least readily perceivable to nearly all rational persons.

Fuchs, however, does not consider absolute natural law reducible only to formal moral norms. Although limited in number, Fuchs maintains that certain concrete, negative moral norms derived from absolute natural law are universal and immutable. It is interesting to note that Fuchs's method of justifying this class of norms shifts noticeably; no longer does he appeal to the "goods" to which humans are naturally inclined and which must be protected in order for humans to flourish or to moral norms patently true with only a modicum of consideration, but to the criterion that certain actions are against nature (*contra natura*).[18] Sexual intercourse within the context of marriage is an example of this. As noted above, Fuchs maintains that absolute natural law requires the existence of the institution of marriage based upon the natural inclination to mate. But when Fuchs considers sexual acts between spouses, the focus shifts to an analysis of the sexual organs' natural finality, namely, procreation.[19] Fuchs concludes that every act of intercourse must remain open to conception and any attempt to alter or impede one's natural fecundity through artificial means is always morally wrong.[20]

Perhaps the most intriguing aspect of Fuchs's natural law theory is his method of deriving moral norms from relative natural law. Relative natural law, in Fuchs's writings, serves as an extension of absolute natural law, regulating human behavior that requires a consideration of concrete persons in various "states of nature."[21] In other words, relative natural law corresponds to the moral demands arising from persons embedded in particular historical contexts and conditioned both by internal and external factors, from original sin's effects to such differences among persons as cultural and social influences, political and economic arrangements, and various regional and local considerations. Literally all the factors arising from occupying a determinate place in space and time are in principle potentially relevant to determining relative natural law's requirements.

The key to grasping relative natural law's function in Fuchs's overall conception of natural law is the indeterminacy of absolute natural law. To be sure, Fuchs does not consider absolute natural law to be so indeterminate that no universally valid and immutable concrete moral norms can be derived from it. But in most instances, Fuchs regards absolute natural law, grounded in metaphysical human nature, as capable of supporting only formal moral norms that must be further specified in reference to various specific circumstances in order to indicate what is permitted or forbidden in a concrete situation.

Although Fuchs's catalogue of the "historical peculiarities"[22]—conditions potentially germane to a determination of relative natural law—is extensive, there is little doubt he is primarily concerned with the pervasive and deleterious effects of original sin. Indeed, in *Natural Law* Fuchs begins his discussion of relative natural law by identifying original sin as the fundamental problem in assessing natural law's historicity:

> Human nature and its likeness to God are immutable in their essentials. In this sense the natural law too must be regarded as immutable and independent of time and history. On the other hand man endures through time and lives in history. The history of salvation, especially, knows nothing of an unchangeable historical concept but is instinct with the effects of the cataclysm that was decisive for man's history: original sin. How is the immutability of the natural law to be reconciled with this enormous tension between the original state of grace and the present state of original sin? The problem of the historicity of the natural law is primarily a question for us of its function in this violent change in the history of salvation.[23]

The particular difficulty with original sin occurs during the process of "applying" absolute natural law's formal moral norms to concrete, historical situations before and after the Fall. Consider, for instance, the absolute natural law norm, "The state must be allowed to care for the common good." When this norm is applied to a concrete situation before the Fall, the sinless condition of *prelapsum* humans renders coercion superfluous. In this particular state of nature, in which humans are graced with preternatural gifts, malice, selfishness, ill will, avarice, illicit motivations, opportunism, and other negative qualities are virtually absent; communal life reflects this state of sinlessness, being characterized by harmony, cooperation, and respect. Coercion, in these concrete circumstances would be gratuitous and illicit brutality; for *prelapsum* humans willingly accept and embrace the state's rightful decisions in regulating the common good.[24]

One of the hallmarks of *postlapsum* humans, in contrast, is resistance to the state's efforts to care for the common good. This might range from surreptitious attempts to avoid one's individual contribution to the common good, overt violations of public safety, to violent acts intended to overthrow a legitimate government. In these cases, in order for the state to achieve its legitimate goal, when the absolute natural law norm "The state must be allowed to care for the common good" is applied to the situation of *postlapsum* humans, it yields the principle, "The state may exercise coercion." As Fuchs explains, these divergent applications of the same formal moral norm should not be understood as contradictions or inconsistencies within relative natural law, but simply the recognition that differing human conditions—before and after the Fall—warrant variable applications if the common good is to be maintained:

> If the gift of grace given to the original man made possible a State *without coercion* and required its actual existence as a State-without-coercion, then this fact constituted relative natural law for this particular State. Nonetheless it resulted from the absolute necessity in natural law to have a State—but for men for whom coercion was superfluous. As soon as sin disturbed the harmony of man, the State *with the right of coercion* became relative natural law in this condition of man. The absolute natural law demands, on the one hand, the existence of the State for any human condition including the present. The natural destination of the state, on the other hand, cannot be achieved without the use of coercion; thus the absolute natural law itself is the foundation for the realization of the State as exercising the function of coercion in man's actual condition.[25]

Finally, Fuchs maintains that even within a particular period of salvation history the application of particular moral norms will exhibit a certain degree of variability due to differing and continually changing local circumstances. In Fuchs's mind, even if the Fall had never occurred, historicity would still be a constitutive aspect of human existence, affecting and shaping the conditions in which humans act and live and thus necessitating flexibility in the application of norms.[26] The norm "A worker must be paid a just wage," for instance, permits a number of legitimate applications in our period of salvation history depending on a wide variety of circumstances, including the cost of living in a particular region; the revenue generated by a respective business; the skill level of individual workers and their importance to the company; financial burdens imposed by state or local regulations and/or taxes; and the amount of overhead costs necessary to operate a business.[27]

This cursory presentation of the structure of moral norms in Fuchs's natural law theory is not intended to settle the numerous theoretical and substantive issues raised by Fuchs's synthesis. To a great extent, Fuchs's presentation is a reiteration of the traditional neo-Thomist understanding of moral norms, which has been severely criticized by many natural law thinkers over the past thirty years. Instead of delving into these technical and detailed objections (many of which Fuchs addresses directly in his postconversion writings) and revisiting territory already well-trod by others, let me offer a few general comments on the suitability of Fuchs's understanding of moral norms.

First, let us ask the question, "What has Fuchs's catalogue of moral norms offered in the way of positive guidance in constructing a substantive, coherent life-plan and in identifying goods that lead to human flourishing?" Fuchs mentions society, marriage, family, and the state as goods worthy of pursuit, and other goods can be inferred from his writings. But this brief list hardly begins to exhaust the multifarious goods comprising even a general anthropology. Like his neo-Thomist counterparts, Fuchs's moral norms are primarily prohibitions intended to help the moral agent avoid acting wrongly. Although this is undoubtedly a vital component of any natural law theory, a series of prohibitions, even if true, cannot offer the positive content needed to direct human development and allow human beings to flourish.[28]

Another problematic aspect of Fuchs's presentation is his undifferentiated conception of the moral agent. The driving force behind Fuchs's construction of moral norms is a quest for universality in which the human person is considered primarily as one human being among others,[29] dominated by "metaphysical principles" applicable to all.[30] It is true that Fuchs accords some moral significance to ontological "accidents" that create the need for diverse applications of universal moral norms on the level of relative natural law, but this consideration of particularity still fails to grasp the moral agent as a developing and maturing being who faces unique moral challenges and opportunities in different stages of her life.[31] The moral concerns paramount in adolescence should not coincide with those of young adulthood, mid-life, or old age, and any adequate catalogue of moral norms, if it is to help individuals clarify and successfully meet the demands specific to any respective period of life, must be formulated with these particular conditions in mind.

Finally, Fuchs often presents moral norms, especially moral norms derived from absolute natural law, as self-validating, self-evident, and unvarying conclusions following necessarily from human nature.[32] Such bold claims were made possible by Fuchs's moral epistemology,[33] which attributed such penetrating and superior, almost invincible, moral insight to the magisterium. But such an understanding betrays not only an erroneous ahistorical conception of the genesis of moral norms, but also a faulty notion of their function in moral deliberation.

Historical studies[34] have shown that moral norms originate in a specific location and at a specific time in response to a wide variety of circumstances and needs. They are "extracted from conventional conduct prevailing in [a] society" and reflect its considered judgments about right and wrong behavior.[35] Over time these norms are accepted, rejected, or refined as society continually reassesses their validity and applicability. Contrary to Fuchs's suggestion, the process of formulating moral norms is not governed by necessity, nor are norms self-evident or self-validating. Moral norms are subservient to, and legitimated by, moral judgments of historical communities; they mirror a community's obtuseness and biases as well as its insightfulness and self-awareness; they are the result of reflection occurring over longer or shorter durations during which knowledge of goods integral to human fulfillment and the appropriate means to realize these goods are gradually appropriated and tested.[36]

Moral Epistemology and the Magisterium's Competency to Interpret Natural Law

Even a cursory examination of Fuchs's writings on natural law cannot fail to detect an uncharacteristic hesitancy in his discussion of moral epistemology. Although Fuchs remained ever-cognizant of the magisterium's teaching on any given moral issue and respected the boundaries and limitations imposed by his ecclesial tradition, his deference did not prevent him from creatively probing, expounding, and refining traditional teachings. On the issue of natural law's perceptibility, however, Fuchs's intellectual vigor seems unduly restrained and his presentation atypically cautious, sometimes resembling more a plodding exegesis of defined doctrine than a critical and lively examination of the issues at hand.

Fuchs's tentativeness stemmed from Pius XI's and Pius XII's doctrinal statements that erected clear and definite boundaries around human reason's ability to grasp natural law.[37] During their pontificates, these two popes attempted to solidify the magisterium's teaching authority in moral matters by constructing a highly skeptical moral epistemology that denied individual moral agents any consistent, practical knowledge of natural law. In Pius XI's and Pius XII's views, the moral knowledge attainable by individuals is vague, partial, indeterminate, and limited to the most general moral principles that provide scant guidance in concrete situations. The only possibly remedy for overcoming this inability to grasp natural law concretely is to turn to the magisterium, the authentic interpreter of natural law.[38]

Given the direct link forged by the popes between moral epistemology and the magisterium's teaching authority, the tone of restraint and submission permeating Fuchs's presentation of natural law's perceptibility is understandable. Moral epistemology represented a minefield for a careless, imprecise, or overly adventurous theologian who dared to stray into forbidden territory.

Fuchs's discussion of moral epistemology begins with an analysis of the First Vatican Council's statements on the power of human reason. Fuchs readily grants that natural knowledge of God, not moral knowledge, was the primary concern of the council fathers. Indeed, morality is mentioned explicitly only once in the council's documents, but Fuchs, as well as other interpreters—including Popes Pius XI and Pius XII—draw important inferences from this single reference. It reads, "If anyone says that divine faith is not to be distinguished from natural knowledge about God and moral matters, and consequently that for divine faith it is not required that revealed truth should be believed because of the authority of God who reveals it: let him be anathema."[39] Fuchs believed the council fathers intended to affirm in this canon that knowledge of natural law is coextensive with natural knowledge of God, and thus whatever can be affirmed of human reason's ability to know God must also be affirmed of its capacity to grasp natural law. As Fuchs says frequently, "knowledge of God includes knowledge of morality."[40]

Fuchs focuses on two paragraphs in the second chapter of *Dei Filius* to demonstrate natural law's perceptibility. In the first paragraph, the council fathers maintained that "God, the source and end of all things, can be known with certainty from the consideration of created things, by the natural power of human reason."[41] In Fuchs's estimation, this is a very restricted endorsement of natural knowledge of God, being limited to the most fundamental truths about God. Fuchs accordingly maintains that human reason is naturally able to perceive "the principal foundations of the natural law."[42] But in the second paragraph the council fathers affirmed more extensive natural knowledge of God, stating that "matters concerning God which are not of themselves beyond the scope of human reason, can, even in the present state of the human race, be known by everyone without difficulty, with firm certitude and with no intermingling of error."[43] Fuchs comments,

> In this [paragraph] the Council defined the object of our knowledge in a way that is quite different from the previous paragraph. In

place of a knowledge of God 'as origin and end' it said here: knowledge of 'things divine which are *per se* not inaccessible to human reason.' This expression is more general and does not restrict the assertion to fundamental truth, as does the previous paragraph and its definition. If we are to understand 'things divine' not in the sense of theoretical but practical knowledge of God, this paragraph speaks of the entire sphere of the natural law and its knowledge. This is stated to be *per se* accessible to human reason, even in the present state. ... The Council taught, therefore, *the natural ability to know the natural law in its complete extension.*[44]

Although Fuchs is convinced that human reason, considered in itself, is capable of grasping the entirety of natural law, from general principles to the most proximate, detailed conclusions, he is equally convinced that original sin distorts the operations of reason and renders the attainment of knowledge of natural law a highly dubious process. Fuchs is not asserting that original sin has diminished or stifled human reason's powers. The capacity of human reason to know moral truth remains the same before and after the Fall. Similar to his argument against the situationists that human nature remains intact whereas the subjective realization of the same human nature manifests varying degrees of distortion due to original sin,[45] Fuchs argues that human reason's powers and potentialities remain the same, but original sin produces various subjective impediments in each person that stifle the actualization of knowledge of natural law.[46] Original sin's effects, according to Fuchs, act like blinders: they obscure the field of vision without injuring or destroying the ability to see.[47]

Although Fuchs speaks ominously about original sin's effects on human reason, maintaining that "the power of moral understanding is ... massively endangered by forces outside [human reason's] powers," he does not consider *postlapsum* humans incapable of grasping the basic rudiments of natural law. Citing the First Vatican Council and Popes Pius XI and Pius XII, Fuchs agrees that natural law's "first moral principles" are easily accessible to all rational persons.[48] But as human reason attempts to specify and concretize the first principles it becomes difficult, if not impossible, for it to overcome the subjective obstacles posed by original sin's effects and to grasp concretely natural law's demands.[49] Fuchs writes, "first moral principles are easily known by all; the others, on the contrary, not without difficulties. To the first principles belong, for example: it is not lawful to kill *anyone at all*; there is *some* order in the sexual life. To the other (secondary) principles belong: it is not lawful for any man, on his own private authority directly to kill; masturbation and fornication are unlawful."[50]

Fuchs holds out the possibility that someone with formal "training in sound philosophy"[51] who also has attained a notable degree of mastery over the "mighty power of the senses, of imagination, concupiscence and the prejudices formed through education and habit"[52] might be able to grasp natural law's more proximate and detailed principles. But even for an intelligent, self-controlled, and well-informed person uninstructed in the systematic and "scientific" study of morality, concrete knowledge of natural law remains elusive: "One who thinks little in moral categories must not assume that he will be able to find the proper solution to difficult moral questions with any real facility."[53]

If Fuchs is correct, the subjective epistemological barriers induced by original sin prevent the vast majority of humankind from consistently—or, perhaps, even infrequently—attaining detailed knowledge of natural law. Like captives in Plato's cave, they possess only nondescript and obscure images of natural law's full reality, and this level of understanding of natural law's first principles can offer only general and indeterminate advice when an individual is faced with the practical question confronting every concrete moral decision, "What should I do?"

Most importantly, as will be discussed more thoroughly below, these epistemological limitations bear directly and deleteriously on one's capacity to gain eternal life. Given Fuchs's link between right actions and merit, the inability to acquire concrete knowledge of natural law dramatically increases the probability—unless one is extremely lucky—that actions will not conform to natural law's demands, thereby imperiling one's soteriological standing.

Yet the epistemological morass engendered by original sin does not inevitably foreclose the possibility of concrete knowledge of natural law. God, omniscient and loving, not only perceives natural law down to its most minute details, but reveals this knowledge to humankind clearly and unambiguously, rendering natural law's opacity transparent. In Fuchs's opinion, only God's revelation of natural law guarantees that humans can consistently grasp natural law to any morally relevant degree:

> Yet the [First Vatican] Council holds the *Revelation of the natural law to be of such importance that it calls it morally necessary in the state after original sin*. It is not necessary in the sense that man's reason may, in general, be able to come to knowledge. It *is* necessary in the sense that all men, intellectually mature and "open," may be able to come to a knowledge of the natural law easily, securely and free of error. God himself must therefore provide a practical

knowledge of the natural order for man. Otherwise many will never come *de facto* to a sufficiently comprehensive knowledge of the natural law, and certain spheres of this law will in fact never be known at all.[54]

Official Roman Catholic moral teaching from Vatican I to the mid-twentieth century claimed that the exclusive ability to interpret revelation, whether scripture or tradition, belongs to the magisterium. From Vatican I's *Dei Filius* to Pius XI's *Casti Connubii* to Pius XII's allocutions on situation ethics and his *Humani Generis*, interpreting revelation has been decisively defined as the prerogative of the magisterium alone. Pius XII, for instance, reiterating the positions of Vatican I and Pius XI, forcefully admonishes anyone challenging the magisterium's teaching authority in moral matters: the "sacred Office of Teacher in matters of faith and morals must be the proximate and universal criterion of truth for all . . . since to it has been entrusted by Christ Our Lord the whole deposit of faith—Sacred Scripture and divine Tradition—to be preserved, guarded and interpreted."[55]

An ardent supporter and defender of the tradition, Fuchs acknowledges the magisterium's indispensable and unique role as the authoritative conveyor of God's revelation of natural law: "It is from [the magisterium] *as the authentic interpreter* that we must receive the divine Revelation and the natural law."[56] But the magisterium's teaching authority is not limited to interpreting only natural law contained explicitly in revelation. Fuchs makes a more extensive claim: "[I]t belongs to the Church not only authentically to propose propositions of the law of nature that are *explicitly contained in revelation,* but *all* propositions of the natural law."[57] Fuchs, again citing the First Vatican Council, claims that the entire sphere of natural law is the proper object of the magisterium's teaching authority: "[The] Vatican holds matters of faith and *morals* without distinction as the object of the magisterium of the Church."[58]

Fuchs's conclusion is clear: the magisterium alone can authentically propose and interpret natural law, from its most general principles to its most proximate principles, thereby guaranteeing that natural law is understood easily and securely: "The Church, as our guide on this way, has the obligation of proclaiming and protecting the entire moral law, including the natural law, even in as far as it has not been formally revealed and even down to its concrete applications."[59]

Despite Fuchs's enthusiastic confidence in the magisterium's ability to grasp natural law correctly, he does not imply that every doctrinal proposition of the magisterium is infallible or that the magisterium is incapable of future error in moral matters. He states that many of the magisterium's statements "do not have that character of infallibility that gives ultimate security."[60] But he firmly believes that the assistance of the Holy Spirit promised to the church creates so strong a presumption in favor of the magisterium that no personal conviction, however sincere, is capable of overriding it.[61] Although this presumption does not warrant "ultimate security" in the magisterium's ordinary teaching, there is little doubt that Fuchs considers the magisterium a font of moral truth, a safe haven in a world beset by confusion and unknowing.[62]

It is important to note that Fuchs's confidence in the magisterium's ability to teach natural law authoritatively is not determined by prior ecclesiological concerns to centralize power in the magisterium by portraying it as the ultimate arbiter of moral truth. Ann Patrick, in her insightful recent work,[63] argues persuasively that such an ecclesiological vision was in fact the impetus behind the classical paradigm of Roman Catholic moral theology which remained highly skeptical of the individual moral agent's ability to know natural law, accorded negligible importance to circumstances and particularity, and tended to equate moral objectivity with universality.[64] The intent of the classical paradigm, according to Patrick, was to convince the faithful that their moral insights were irremediably vulnerable, thereby creating the need for the magisterium to articulate objective moral truth.

It is not unreasonable to suspect, particularly given Fuchs's background in ecclesiology, that on some level Fuchs's moral epistemology might have been unduly influenced by the ecclesiological concerns of preserving and protecting the magisterium's teaching authority in the sphere of natural law. Fuchs was originally trained in ecclesiology, not moral theology. His 1940 dissertation, *Magisterium, Ministerium, Regimen: Vom Ursprung einer ecclesiologische Trilogie,* investigated the church's roles as teacher, minister, and ruler.

There are two compelling reasons to reject this suspicion in Fuchs's case. First, both before and after his conversion Fuchs was singularly interested in moral objectivity, that is, objective rightness and wrongness, not ecclesiological matters. He explicitly rejects the possibility that the magisterium's teachings on natural law are objectively correct simply because they are proposed by the magisterium. Fuchs asks the question directly: In what does moral objectivity consist? He responds, "[Not] in the fact that these laws are externally *proposed* to us, for example, by theologians or by the Church. . . . [Moral] *objectivity is in this, that this order is grounded in (human) being and consequently can be known from (human) being.*"[65] Throughout his writings, Fuchs makes it abundantly clear that moral objectivity consists in correspondence to the moral demands arising from human nature regardless of whether or not they are proposed by the magisterium.[66]

What, then, is the basis for Fuchs's confidence in the magisterium's ability to grasp and articulate natural law correctly? Has Fuchs simply accepted the magisterium's claims of interpreting revelation and teaching natural law authoritatively without offering credible reasons why these functions, which imply superior competency in moral matters, rightly belong to the magisterium? In the final analysis, Fuchs's confidence in the magisterium is grounded in the belief that God's grace allows the magisterium greater and more penetrating insight into natural law; thus, the magisterium should be obeyed not because of some functionalism or because of its own claims to competency in moral matters, but solely for the reason that its teachings on natural law are substantially correct.

In one of his earliest articles, which investigates the relation between episcopal ordination and the magisterium's teaching authority, Fuchs asserts that the increase of sanctifying grace attendant to episcopal ordination produces a pervasive modification of the ordained that increases his ability to comprehend natural law.[67] One effect of the sanctifying grace is an increase of the acquired and infused virtues that effectively stifles the negative subjective impediments caused by original sin, thereby creating a rightly ordered person possessing the necessary detachment to understand natural law's demands clearly and consistently.

Furthermore, Fuchs maintains that sanctifying grace not only instills in the ordained a persistent desire to grasp natural law more and more completely, but also makes it easier to comprehend natural law, both revealed and unrevealed.[68] As a consequence, a bishop, in Fuchs's estimation, represents a "teacher of truth," an "instrument of God" whose superior insight into natural law legitimizes the deference given to him by the faithful.[69] In Fuchs's later preconversion writings the sacramental basis for the magisterium's competency in moral matters is de-emphasized in favor of the classic *assistentia Spiritus*,[70] but in both instances God's grace produces the same effect: superior insight virtually guaranteeing that the magisterium understands and proposes natural law correctly.

Another reason to reject ecclesiological concerns as a formative influence on Fuchs's moral epistemology arose during his service on the Papal Commission on Population, Family, and Birth (1963–66). As will be explained in greater detail in the next chapter, during the commission's deliberations proponents of the church's ban on artificial methods of contraception were petrified that changing the church's official teaching would seriously undermine the magisterium's credibility to teach natural law authoritatively. In their minds, such a change is tantamount to admitting error, an error that not only calls into question the validity of other past teachings, but future teachings as well. The American Jesuit John Ford, perhaps the most outspoken supporter of the tradition, sounds an ominous warning about the disastrous ecclesiological implications that would surely follow such a change:

> If the Church should now admit that the teaching passed on is no longer of value, teaching which has been preached and stated with ever more insistent solemnity until very recent years, it must be feared greatly that its authority in almost all moral and dogmatic matters will be seriously harmed. For there are few moral truths so constantly, solemnly and, as it has appeared, definitively stated as this one for which it is now so quickly proposed that it be changed to the contrary. . . . For the Church to have erred so gravely in its grave responsibility of leading souls would be tantamount to seriously suggesting that the assistance of the Holy Spirit was lacking to her.[71]

Ford openly admitted that he could not provide "clear and cogent" arguments supporting the traditional teaching "based on reason alone";[72] his primary, perhaps even sole, motivation for upholding the ban of artificial methods of contraception was to prevent the magisterium's teaching authority from being eroded. Ford epitomizes a theologian whose moral theology is dictated by ecclesiological concerns. The fundamental question for Ford is not, Is artificial contraception objectively moral or immoral? but, How will the magisterium be affected if the traditional teaching is changed?

Fuchs, in contrast, never appealed to the magisterium's credibility as a reason for reaffirming past teaching. Indeed, when ecclesiological concerns began to overshadow other considerations and threatened to dominate the commission's proceedings, Fuchs reminded the members of their duty to determine the requirements of objective morality, not to protect or bolster the magisterium's teaching authority in moral matters: "Many confuse objective morality with the prescriptions of the church. . . . We have to realize that reality is what is."[73]

Throughout the commission's proceedings, and despite pointed and dire predictions from influential bishops and theologians of the potential loss of the magisterium's credibility to teach on moral issues, Fuchs consistently refused to allow ecclesiological concerns to direct or impede his quest to determine natural law's requirements. As Fuchs writes, the paramount issue is not "fidelity or infidelity to prior teachings," loss of teaching authority, constancy in moral doctrine, or admission of past error;[74] the sole issue is moral objectivity, in other words, whether natural law prohibits or allows artificial methods of contraception.

The absence of ecclesiological concerns motivating Fuchs's moral epistemology, however, does not imply that his moral epistemology is entirely satisfactory. One internal problem Fuchs fails to acknowledge is the magisterium's potential limits in grasping relative natural law, especially when specific, local, factual knowledge is required in order to determine natural law's demands.

Fuchs's analysis of relative natural law focuses on salvation history and how the differences in which human nature is realized in both *pre-* and *postlapsum* humans condition the movement from absolute to relative natural law.[75] Because Fuchs regards many of the Fall's effects as relatively uniform throughout humankind, he maintains that certain moral norms are universally applicable to all humans after the Fall. But certain issues cannot be settled by knowledge of what is common to all *postlapsum* humans; these issues require more detailed knowledge of regional, local, and sometimes individual circumstances.[76]

Take, for example, the problem of acquiring goods on the black market in Germany during World War II. Under ordinary conditions Fuchs maintains that natural law forbids any cooperation with the black market.[77] But "under certain circumstances," Fuchs writes, natural law permits one to purchase goods on the black market. It is significant that Fuchs, who in his preconversion period was interested in articulating precisely and concretely what natural law allows and prohibits, fails to settle the issue of purchasing goods on the black market with any degree of specificity. The reason is that the presence or absence of certain concrete circumstantial data determines whether or not purchasing goods on the black market is deemed permissible or impermissible. Although Fuchs does not mention the morally relevant circumstances, it is not difficult to imagine what he had in mind: the cost of the goods and whether paying an exorbitant price would impose hardship on oneself or one's family; the ability to acquire the goods in another manner; whether dealing with the black market might expose one's friends or family to potential violence; the likelihood that supply lines will be reopened in the near future; the ability to flee the country in order to procure the needed goods; whether the black market is illegally siphoning goods from the armed forces and thus weakening the war effort; and the probability that the war will end soon, among others. The point is that Fuchs considers the morality of purchasing goods on the black market irresolvable without knowledge of concrete circumstances.

Fuchs's insistence on knowledge of specific circumstantial data in order to determine some of natural law's requirements undermines his assertion that the magisterium possesses the competency to proclaim and protect natural law even in its most specific details.[78] If concrete knowledge is necessary to determine what is consonant with natural law, how can the magisterium, which might possess no knowledge of a particular situation's unique circumstances, be considered competent to determine what should be done?

Like all human beings, the members of the magisterium face obstacles that limit their acquisition of knowledge: time constraints, both professional and personal; lack of interest in a specific issue; potential insufficient factual information on a particular event, situation, or topic; difficulties in isolating and interpreting morally relevant factors; biases, prejudices, and indifference; and possible lack of moral imagination. But even for the exceptional person who has overcome these impediments, practical and detailed knowledge of concrete circumstances, which might be changing rapidly, are needed to determine what natural law requires in the situation, and often these circumstances are known only by persons in the situation or by specialists following the latest developments.

These considerations do not imply a blanket denial of the magisterium's competency to interpret natural law; but they do suggest that if superior insight into natural law is the foundation for Fuchs's notion of moral competency, Fuchs must add nuances to his understanding of moral competency and acknowledge that the epistemic limitations generally present among all humans, as well as the impediments to gathering and interpreting knowledge on any given particular situation, do not permit the facile assumption that when concrete, local circumstances must be known to determine natural law's requirements the locus of moral competency should rest with the magisterium.

Another problematic aspect of Fuchs's moral epistemology is the disputable evidence he offers in support of the magisterium's superior insight into natural law. As we mentioned earlier, Fuchs maintains that both episcopal ordination and the assistance of the Holy Spirit allow the magisterium to grasp natural law more clearly and comprehensively than the faithful or unbelievers. In each instance, Fuchs ultimately appeals to God's grace either as modifying the knowing subject (the individual bishops)[79] or guiding the magisterium to moral truth to the extent that its teachings are substantially free from error.[80]

As John Boyle indicates, however, God's grace must still contend with the manifold human limitations, both intrinsic and subjective, conditioning the acquisition of knowledge.[81] Unless Fuchs conceives God's grace as a direct and unimpeded infusion of knowledge of natural law, which I cannot detect in any of his writings, the assistance offered would still require that knowledge of natural law be obtained through the normal and fallible processes of human knowing, the accuracy of which is intimately dependent on the authenticity of the knower and therefore is susceptible to error.

One unfortunate consequence of Fuchs's belief that the magisterium is the focus of God's grace leading the church to correct knowledge of natural law is the negligible contribution he accords to the nonordained faithful, both as individuals and as a collective body, and unbelievers, in uncovering natural law. Never in Fuchs's preconversion writings is the discovery of natural law envisioned as a mutual and collective undertaking in which the timely, fruitful, and perceptive insights of all persons are given due consideration; nor does Fuchs entertain the idea that the Holy Spirit's assistance might be directed toward persons outside the episcopacy; nor does he envision the faithful or any other group as a potentially corrective influence to the magisterium's teaching. Fuchs's moral epistemology, which accords such superiority to the magisterium in interpreting natural law, effectively relegates nonmembers of the magisterium to the periphery of the church's moral discourse and regards them solely as receivers of the tradition whose limited functions are to listen attentively to defined teaching and to apply the teaching in concrete situations.

Finally, Fuchs's moral epistemology is plagued by an insufficiently developed conception of historicity and its effects on human knowing. To be sure, Fuchs does not consider historicity irrelevant in constructing a persuasive natural law theory, remarking in *Natural Law* that the connection between natural law and historicity is "the main subject of this study."[82] The problem is that Fuchs fails to attribute to historicity any modifying influence on human knowing.

Historicity, in Fuchs's writings, is a phenomenon external to human reason, affecting society, culture, politics, economics, and other orders affecting human life, without concomitantly altering human reason's perception or ability to grasp natural law. Yet as proponents of a more sufficient conception of historical consciousness have insisted, there is no impregnable shield behind which human reason can be sheltered from historicity's effects. Bernard Lonergan, for example, has persuasively demonstrated that the formal processes of human knowing are invariant, whereas the contents of our knowledge are radically conditioned by historicity,[83] in other words, by the beliefs dominant in one's particular period; by the language, concepts, symbols, and images available; by notable systems of thought and their capacity either to distort or clarify; by a particular society's or culture's values, the quality of its prior insights, its tolerance for novel and imaginative ideas, and its promotion of learning; and by the enormous array of self-understandings that have emerged, developed, and either flourished or decayed in the course of history.[84] All these factors, more of which could be listed, condition human reason by affecting what is considered worthy of attention; what information is actively sought or ignored; whether, to what degree, and how data are understood; the conceptual tools and categories used to interpret reality; the degree of thoroughness considered acceptable in formulating, explaining, and verifying insights; and the ability to integrate ideas into a larger, more comprehensive viewpoint.

At the very least, the contingent and provisional character of human knowledge suggests that Fuchs's bold assertions about natural law's perceptibility need to be tempered by a dose of realism. Yet historical consciousness pertains to more than simply the tone of Fuchs's presentation. The historicity of human reason necessitates a more critical examination of the knowing subject, an explanation of how and to what degree historical embeddedness conditions consciousness, perception, understanding, judgment, and imagination, any of which might indicate needed revisions in Fuchs's conceptions of moral epistemology and moral competency.

Natural Law and the Role of the Individual Moral Agent

Fuchs's preconversion natural law theory is replete with clear and distinct boundaries:[85] between the metaphysical and historical; between the objective and subjective; between absolute and relative natural law; between human nature in general and the concrete person living in unique circumstances; and between the supernatural and natural orders. The individual moral agent's relation to natural law is similarly circumscribed by a definite boundary: between formulating and proposing moral norms and applying them in concrete situations.

As we have seen, the magisterium remains the crucial link between the objective moral order established by God and the possibility of grasping this moral order and articulating its contents in propositional form that offer specific directives for action. This extensive process of reducing natural law to a series of ordered moral norms is exclusively the province of the magisterium by virtue of its superior insight into moral matters. The individual moral agent's role emerges only subsequent to the establishment of normative morality and is confined to determining what and how norms should be applied.

According to Fuchs, once the morally relevant aspects of a situation have been isolated and identified, they are subsumed under a moral norm intended to regulate such situations, which gives a specific directive to the individual moral agent:

Ordinarily some already known universal laws are applied to the situation to be judged. (1) *Under laws that are sufficiently determined as to their matter* are simply *subsumed* those elements of the situation about which the general law determinately speaks: "direct killing of a fetus is never licit," and therefore not now. (2) *Under laws that are less determinate as to their matter, or more formal,* are likewise subsumed the corresponding elements of the situation; but as, for example, the less material principle "be merciful" is grounded in the being of man and thus known, so also *such* mercy to be exercised is grounded in *such* a being of man, determined by his situation, and thence known.[86]

In the case of material norms, whether of absolute or relative natural law, the individual moral agent's task is simple: to recognize one's situation or case as a particular instance envisioned by a norm and to act in accordance with it. These norms are almost always negative and prohibit certain actions.

Formal norms present a different scenario for the individual. Lacking specific material content, the process of subsumption in this instance does not necessarily culminate in a particular proscription or prescription. The moral agent in this case is faced with more flexibility and latitude in determining what concrete behavior corresponds with the moral norm in her given circumstances. It should be noted that formal moral norms in Fuchs's writings are predominantly positive. Whenever Fuchs discusses prohibitions he sometimes begins by articulating formal moral norms that apparently allow diverse applications, but he usually specifies them sufficiently so that definite and precise material content is eventually yielded.

Regardless of the type of moral norm, Fuchs regards the individual moral agent's role as obediently applying received teachings in concrete situations.[87] As we saw earlier, Fuchs is not advocating obedience to the magisterium simply because a teaching is defined and proposed. Moral norms cannot be arbitrary or unintelligible edicts disconnected from reality; they must be rational insights into the objective moral order based on natural law. To this extent, it is the moral agent's duty not simply to obey received teaching, but to reflect on its "inner content and causes"[88] and to try to understand its meaning and significance.

The "catch," of course, is that the more an individual penetrates the intelligible bases of received teachings, the more she recognizes the unreasonableness of her personal doubts and the magisterium's superior wisdom because, according to Fuchs, it is substantially correct on moral issues: "[T]he teaching authority of the Church constituting a higher authority than personal consideration, if accepted in the true attitude of the Christian, will silence these contradictions and exclude the general suspicion of considerations purely personal. Thus a life based upon the truth of the natural law will become easier, happier and more intense."[89]

Let us assume for a moment that an individual has made reasonable attempts to understand a particular moral norm's meaning and significance. If, after this reflection, conflict still exists between her judgment in conscience and the particular application indicated by the norm, may she follow her conscience in opposition to the objective moral order (i.e., the magisterium's teaching)?

This is an extremely delicate question for Fuchs. Like Thomas Aquinas, Fuchs considers the dictate of conscience inviolable: one must never intentionally act contrary to one's conscience. Yet Fuchs is also concerned that appeals to conscience in the past have been employed to undermine the magisterium's ability to bind individuals through its official teaching.[90] Fuchs avoids any antinomy between conscience and the magisterium by assigning a very specific and limited function to the conscience: to apply moral norms in concrete situations.[91] Conscience does not determine whether particular moral norms are correct or incorrect, but only which moral norm should be applied in the here and now. Therefore anyone claiming her conscience dictates that a moral norm proposed by the magisterium not be followed because of its falsity has not, by definition, made a judgment in conscience. Instead, she is conflating conscience with mere "subjective opinion":

> It is not so infrequent that men appeal to their own conscience against the teaching of the Church or of learned men [i.e., moral theologians]. This is true, for example, in the case of so many doctors with regard to medical ethics. The truth of the matter is that they appeal not really to *conscience*, but to a *subjective opinion*, to which however, the authority of the Church or that of men learned in morals is superior. ... Since, however, it is the function of conscience to dictate according to the truth, and not according to subjective opinions, *the judgment of conscience* on the act to be placed must be formed ... according to *that* teaching which carries either certainty or a greater presumption of the truth. This obligation many men apparently do not perceive, either because they do not clearly see the function of conscience, or because they are mistaken on the decree of respective authority.[92]

Fuchs diffuses this potentially divisive conflict between an individual's conscience and official church teaching by ruling conscience "out of court" in the domain of determining normative morality, but there still exists the possibility that a person's judgment in conscience might contradict natural law by failing to grasp "the existence, meaning, nature, object [or] extension of a norm."[93] According to Fuchs, this is an entirely different issue; for the validity of a moral norm, assuming it is known, is at least implicitly acknowledged and accepted. In this instance, Fuchs regards an individual's judgment as actually a judgment in conscience, which must be followed even in opposition to received teaching.

Assuming Fuchs's conception of the individual moral agent as an applicator of moral norms, What characteristics are essential to applying norms well? In other words, What is Fuchs's vision of the ideal moral agent? First, knowledge of natural law is the indispensable prerequisite for right action. To this end, the moral agent must not only be well-versed in received teaching, but she must also possess intricate and detailed knowledge of the hierarchy of moral norms.[94] Stated differently, the ideal moral agent's conscience must be formed by the objective moral order so that in concrete situations she is able to grasp the meaning of norms and the circumstances for which they were intended. Fuchs acknowledges that in concrete situations not only is it sometimes difficult to select one moral norm over others that seem to be applicable, but norms also appear to conflict in their requirements, indicating irreconcilable courses of action.[95] This conflict, according to Fuchs, is apparent, not real; moral norms correspond to a hierarchy of goods, and this lexical ordering of norms precludes any conflict even though a norm's position in the overall hierarchy is not always immediately evident to certain individuals.[96]

Second, the ideal moral agent possesses the virtue of prudence, the habit of judging the contingent and particular well.[97] Like the conscience, prudence does not pertain to determining normative morality, in other words, formulating and proposing moral norms, but to selecting the appropriate means to an end that requires skill in evaluating the various "accidental" features of a situation. As Fuchs explains, a moral norm can be applied in manifold ways, and the prudent person is noted for her keen grasp of particular conditions as well as her ability to select the best means available for applying a norm.[98] Fraternal correction, for instance, can be done sternly and openly or gently and unobtrusively depending on whether the corrected person is shy, mild-mannered, assertive, or recalcitrant. The prudent person assesses these individual qualities as well as the social context in which the correction occurs and determines which manner of correction is best in these particular circumstances.

Third, the ideal moral agent would have attained a notable degree of self-control. Fuchs warns that the "mighty power of the senses, of

imagination, concupiscence and the prejudices formed through education and habit, together with the corresponding negative dispositions
of will and intellect, are all realities [that] prevent only too easily a
correct activation of our real native ability to come to a true moral
knowledge."[99] The word resurfacing continually in Fuchs's discussion
of subjective impediments to moral knowledge is "detachment." *Postlapsum* humans will never be entirely free of original sin's negative
effects; the goal is to master oneself, to restrain and subdue the emotions
and affectivity, to manage and control the numerous subjective im-
pulses perpetually threatening to swamp rationality, in order to attain
the requisite detachment necessary to grasp the objective moral order
calmly and deliberately. Even moral theologians, according to Fuchs,
must be vigilant not to allow emotional concerns to jeopardize their
moral reasoning: "[H]ow difficult it is even for the specialist versed in
ethical thinking to understand correctly the moral structure of certain
actions, in themselves immoral, but employed to kill unborn life in
situations which bear so agonizingly upon the mother! This is difficult
even for the trained moralist, not only because it is difficult to come
into possession of the correct knowledge but because the feelings of
mercy and compassion prevent the mind from maintaining its calm
and necessary detachment."[100]

Finally, the ideal moral agent would possess "training in sound
philosophy."[101] Although Fuchs maintains that being raised in a stable
and nurturing family, being well educated, and having the benefit of
moral exemplars as friends and acquaintances certainly is advantageous to moral development and most likely culminate in a moral
agent more capable of acting rightly than most, the above-average
moral sensibilities of this moral agent, although laudable, still fall short
of the "scientific" moral knowledge possessed by one formally trained
in ethics. In Fuchs's mind, there is a substantial gulf separating someone
gifted by heredity and environment and someone similarly gifted but
also having undertaken a more critical and sophisticated examination
of morality; the former might possess the resources to deal effectively
with all normal situations arising in daily life, but the latter is able to
bring to explicit consciousness the concepts, categories, and methods of
analysis that enable a more precise understanding of human behavior.[102]

Fuchs's conception of the ideal individual moral agent succeeds
in capturing one essential component of moral agency: the willingness
to follow moral norms. Moral norms serve indispensable functions in
human life, from protecting physical safety, to ensuring the integrity
and limitations of political, economic, and social institutions erected
to enhance human life, to indicating standards of fairness and equity
in our daily relations with other persons, to identifying appropriate

types of behavior in marriage, in raising and educating children, and in the workplace, to instructing those whose occupations or roles are governed by an internal code of conduct that poses unique obligations and restrictions. Standards of behavior, enshrined in moral norms, exist in virtually every aspect of human life, ordering our commitments and priorities, safeguarding our values, and attempting to protect the goods necessary for individual and communal flourishing.

Although an unpalatable paternalism underlies Fuchs's conception of the individual moral agent's role in concretizing natural law, he cannot be accused of denigrating the importance of adhering to and obeying moral norms. Fuchs, I think, would readily agree with Jean Porter, who writes, "it is apparent that an ability and willingness to follow rules is one of the most fundamental capacities that a (potentially) rational creature can possess. Without this capacity, persons can neither emerge as fully rational social beings, nor can they act or sustain a course of activity."[103] At the very least, Fuchs's paradigm of the moral agent as an obedient listener to received tradition and applicator of moral norms helps to counteract the ever-present and destructive tendencies of rationalization, self-deception, and hard-heartedness that often obscure moral reasoning and impede the performance of right actions.

Yet Fuchs's account of moral agency is incomplete in several crucial respects. The most obvious problem is that a willingness to follow norms has contributed greatly to horrific and appalling acts committed throughout human history. The twentieth century alone has witnessed atrocities defying the imagination that were perpetrated by persons willing to obey the dictates of their governments, their organizations, and their leaders.[104] On a more mundane level, the willingness to follow moral norms often results in the all too familiar "principled person" whose obedience to norms arises more from a concern to acquiesce to authority figures than a reflective grasp of the goods norms are designed to protect and a sincere desire to promote human well-being.[105] But let us focus for a moment on what I believe to be a broader and more pervasive negative consequence of Fuchs's account of moral agency, which perhaps underlies the first two criticisms: insufficient moral development.[106]

Under normal conditions, a child is indoctrinated in the rudiments of moral behavior by the examples and instruction of parents, teachers, caretakers, family friends, relatives, peers, and various social institutions. Much of this initial moral education is conveyed through statements intended to reinforce or eradicate certain kinds of actions: "Do not hit your brother!" "You must learn to share your toys!" "Do not interrupt your mother while she is talking on the telephone!" "That was very kind of you to help her." In addition to these verbal commands and affirmations, a child is also formed by symbols, metaphors, and images, by characters and familiar themes in storybooks, by observing the behavior of people around her and their reactions to various events and persons, and by the roles assumed by significant adults in her life. As she becomes more proficient at deciphering and interpreting the moral messages conveyed to her, she internalizes the dominant paradigms of her society and begins to identify with various social roles presented to her by imitating and play-acting, by learning how persons in these roles think, feel, and assess others, and which patterns of behavior are expected in certain familiar situations. Throughout this socialization process, the child gradually appropriates the ideals offered by her community, discovers the claims and expectations placed on her, establishes an identity conveying meaning and purpose, and learns with increasing precision what types of behavior are deemed acceptable both as a member of the human community and as a determinate individual occupying a particular social role.

If a child's socialization proceeds well, at some point her moral development undergoes a critical turn. Now she begins to perceive and understand the reasons that undergird the moral norms imposed, sometimes coercively, by her parents and caretakers. She develops a "feel" for appropriate behavior, is able to understand on her own what types of actions either correspond to or contradict the moral ideals promoted in her society, and begins extending her repository of moral knowledge through analogical reasoning that offers her an intelligible framework for solving unprecedented, and potentially more complex, situations independently of external advice or instruction.

Her nascent critical awareness also allows her to transcend her relative passivity as an untutored child to a more active assessment of the moral truth either embodied in, or absent from, certain norms and ideals. This does not obviate her perpetual need to refer to norms and ideals for moral guidance; it acknowledges only that the transition to full moral maturity includes the capacity to form one's own conception of the good and an unwillingness to accept the moral claims of others at face value without testing the truthfulness of their contents as thoroughly as she can.

Thus, my ideal moral agent differs significantly from Fuchs's. Yes, one's conscience must be formed by the standards of objective morality; it is necessary to be able to judge the contingent and particular well; it is beneficial to have overcome one's subjective impediments that obfuscate moral reasoning and perception; and formal training in ethics is sometimes very helpful in rendering concepts, categories, and methods of analysis clearer, more penetrating, and more accurate. But I disagree with Fuchs's paramount conception of the moral agent as an applicator of moral norms.

As I indicated in my brief sketch of moral development, childhood is characterized by submitting to a superior's will and wisdom, by doing what one is told to do, by obeying various authority figures and applying the norms they impose in a wide variety of situations. For a child, this initial moral training is invaluable and imparts to her a sense of identity and expectations that are integral to her moral development. Moral agency in adulthood, however, requires a more refined set of skills that are not gained simply by applying moral norms in concrete situations.

Mature moral agency requires a sufficient level of moral reasoning that can begin to render intelligible the many nonprototypical situations or cases that occasionally arise and that cannot be solved on the basis of past experience or conditioning.[107] It also requires that moral imagination be cultivated, which not only allows the mature moral agent to envision appropriate ways of acting in new, unique, and sometimes highly complex, circumstances, but also better ways of structuring existing institutions, relationships, social roles, and recurrent patterns of behavior. As Mark Johnson writes:

> We really must be innovators, if we hope to meet in an intelligent way the demands of these various sorts of change that confront us daily in all aspects of our lives. We must decide which attitudes, traits of character, human goods, and actions serve our purposes and aims within communities that represent continuing and developing moral traditions. This will involve critically scrutinizing our own purposes and values, as well as imaginatively envisioning alternative perspectives and possibilities for human flourishing.[108]

Mature moral agency depends on the ability to form images, symbols, metaphors, prototypes, and ideals that provide an imaginative basis for understanding, developing, revising, improving, and critiquing our commitments and actions; it depends on the capacity for "resourceful problem solving" that meets complex situations not by reverting to clichés or familiar patterns of thinking or behavior or by discounting complexity as irrelevant, illusory, or inconsequential, but by forging new concepts and categories that allow us better to comprehend the goods at stake and the proper manners of realizing these goods; it depends on the ability to empathize and identify with others, to imagine how it feels to be harmed or benefited, to be despised, ridiculed, and ignored, or loved, affirmed, and noticed; and it depends on the capacity for mental exploration of particular possibilities and the consequences, sometimes remote, of certain types of behavior.[109]

Fuchs's conception of moral agency, I fear, fails to cultivate any of these qualities to any significant degree. His emphasis on applying received teaching might create individuals adept at grasping morally relevant aspects of a situation and the appropriate norm to be applied under given conditions, but it also leaves adult moral agents with inadequate resources and skills to deepen and extend their understanding of human behavior and to assess critically the many obligations, commitments, sacrifices, goods, and conflicts that are part of our daily lives.

Finally, let me pose one last criticism of Fuchs's conception of the moral agent's relation to natural law. If, as Fuchs claims, natural law regulates the entirety of human life, from the most momentous and formative decisions to our more mundane and commonplace actions,[110] it would be either arrogant or foolhardy to believe that the magisterium either has proposed, or can propose, a series of moral norms comprehensive enough to indicate what should or should not be done in every concrete situation. In other words, there is an irreducibly individual element in grasping and specifying natural law's demands, not in the sense that there exists some private sphere remaining immune from external criticism, but in the sense that the individual moral agent often encounters situations in which received teaching is so formal that it offers no substantive, determinate advice, or there is simply no official teaching on a respective topic.

I have in mind certain issues that, during Fuchs's preconversion writings, were relegated to the periphery of moral deliberation, or were not considered as "moral issues" at all, even though, in my opinion, they are pregnant with moral meaning and bear directly on human flourishing: whether to get married, to take religious vows, or to remain single; when to have children and how many children to have; where and how children are to be educated; the type of job one takes or the selection of a particular career path or occupation; how disposable income is spent; the amount of time and resources designated for leisure activities; whether and in what ways one contributes to the life of the community; which companies, corporations, or local businesses one supports; whether one participates in charitable or political organizations; whether living accommodations are ornate and lavishly furnished or spartan and frugal; how many natural resources one is willing to deplete or pollute in order to increase mobility, living space, or the ability to acquire nonessential goods; what types of food are consumed regularly and the ecological and cultural costs incurred in producing and transporting these foods; whether one embraces modern conveniences or technology—television, automobiles, computers, kitchen appliances, tractors, heavy construction equipment, airplanes, power tools—or forsakes these in favor of a simpler life.

The point of this illustrative, and very incomplete, list is not to suggest that once the moral horizon is expanded beyond the standard topics treated in traditional Roman Catholic moral theology the complexity of these issues is so formidable and bedeviling that moral norms, however precise and well-formulated, cannot begin to render them intelligible. Not at all. I am suggesting that these issues depend on specific knowledge of the individual moral agent's commitments, resources, talents, limitations, personality traits, and external circumstances, without which a truly well-informed and reasonable judgment cannot be made.[111]

The issue of having one's child educated in a public or parochial school, for example, depends on a host of considerations that require concrete, detailed, and local knowledge of a variety of factors: the importance to the parents and/or to the child of daily religious instruction; the quality of the teachers; the school's academic reputation; the educational theory and pedagogy dominant at each school; course diversity and class size; parent involvement and support, either formally or informally, in each respective school; the characteristics of a particular class or the entire student body, in other words, whether the students tend to be diligent, attentive, supportive, enthusiastic, or well-disciplined, or ill-mannered, disruptive, lazy, belligerent, or lacking in self-control; the parents' financial condition and their ability to pay the increased cost of tuition at a parochial school, and the potential sacrifices that either the parents or the family as a whole would have to make in order to send a child to a parochial school; the need for individual attention and the school's ability and willingness to provide it; and opportunities for extracurricular activities, among others.

This example illustrates vividly the inherent limitation in Fuchs's conception of the moral agent as an applicator of moral norms. What is the correct norm to be applied when a parent is trying to decide where to have her child educated? The question strikes me as odd and misplaced. Situations like this cannot be resolved adequately by hauling out prefabricated norms, even though general statements such as "Choose in your child's best interests, not yours," "Parochial school education should be a high priority," and "Be willing to make sacrifices to ensure the best education for your child" might offer some guidance and direction, however vague. The concrete, objectively right course of action in this instance emerges through an examination of relevant particulars, by understanding the child's unique needs, the family's resources and commitments, and the strengths and weaknesses of each school. Of course, not all moral issues require such extensive consideration of concrete particulars in order to determine their rightness or wrongness; sometimes knowledge of a few salient elements suffices. But if I am correct, many of the issues confronting us in our daily lives are not immediately resolvable without detailed knowledge of concrete particulars possessed by individuals in the situation.

This suggests an important modification of Fuchs's conception of moral agency and the church's role in enhancing it. Moral agency is not necessarily perfected by mastering the entire corpus of received teaching; for this still would not provide sufficient determinate advice to settle all, or perhaps even most, of the moral issues an individual is likely to encounter regularly. In order for natural law to be grasped and specified in a wide variety of concrete situations, the magisterium's traditional role of defining, proposing, and defending moral norms must be supplemented by the equally vital function of creating capable and competent individual moral agents whose skills allow them to negotiate uncharted territory, to comprehend and assess the validity of moral norms, social ideals and roles, and the various self-understandings prevalent in a particular age, and to identify and cultivate the personal qualities that will serve them well in all stages of life.[112] This is an admittedly broad agenda, but I think its objective is on target. If there are limitations in the magisterium's moral competency, particularly when knowledge of concrete circumstances is necessary to discern natural law's requirements, the best possibility of realizing natural law concretely lies with competent individual moral agents.

Natural Law and the Supernatural Destiny of the Human Person

Natural law, according to Fuchs, does not exhaust the totality of the moral order. It remains a valid, necessary, yet ultimately incomplete expression of the Christian moral life because it prescinds from the supernatural reality of the human person. As Fuchs writes, "It is the *total reality of man that regulates his behavior. The Christian moral order is neither that of nature nor that of the supernatural but an order constituted by nature* AND *the supernatural together*. Both 'nature' and 'the supernatural' taken separately are mere abstractions."[113] Thus far our discussion of Fuchs's conception of natural law has participated in the abstraction, focusing on "nature" and the moral order derived from it. Our objective now is to explain natural law's function in a wider, and much more religiously significant context: the reality of the supernatural.

Following the Thomistic tradition closely, Fuchs understands human nature to direct the human person to two distinct ends. One, natural happiness, consists in a rightly ordered person whose powers have been perfected, thus enabling her to act rightly consistently.[114] The other, supernatural happiness, consists ultimately in union with God[115] in the beatific vision.[116] The "basic conundrum"[117] characterizing Fuchs's Thomistic anthropology is that human nature impels the human person toward both ends, while supplying the requisite resources or powers to realize only one of these ends. The ability to attain natural happiness, on the one hand, lies entirely within the capacities given through human nature. Various subjective impediments might prevent certain individuals from attaining natural happiness, but it remains in principle capable of being realized through one's native powers. In contrast, the human person remains impotent when faced with the task of attaining her ultimate end, supernatural happiness, which inexorably transcends human nature's potentialities and can be bestowed only through God's free gift of grace.[118]

The absolutely gratuitous character of supernatural happiness means that natural law, considered strictly in itself, can neither direct nor enable the human person to attain union with God.[119] Actions in accordance with natural law perfect the human person's powers, order her appetites correctly, and actualize certain external goods, but they remain bereft of any supernatural significance: "In itself the natural law can never be a power by which we are able to gain the supernatural."[120] Thus even a life lived entirely in accordance with natural law's demands, a life involving perhaps extraordinary sacrifices, a life recognized as exemplary and morally laudable, in itself remains ineffective in the supernatural sphere.[121]

Even though natural law possesses no intrinsic significance in the supernatural realm, Fuchs perceives no antinomy or exclusivity between the natural and supernatural orders; indeed, Fuchs considers them in continuity, with natural law serving as a receptacle for the supernatural order, always remaining open to supernatural fulfillment and completion:[122] "God, who ordains his creation to the beatific vision positively 'fulfills' the natural law accordingly. This 'fulfillment' consists in the fact that man must accept and strive for his supernatural *destiny* and must therefore likewise attend to the co-natural beginnings of eternal life by living a life of grace and supernatural love (*caritas*) in this world."[123]

Charity, according to Fuchs, is the sine qua non of natural law's potential supernatural significance. As a theological virtue, charity has God as its object. But unlike faith and hope, which by definition imply distance between the human person and God as unseen and unpossessed, charity is actual and immediate union with God, through which the human person loves God *propter seipsum* and all things in relation to God.[124] When animated by charity, actions in accordance with natural law arise out of love of God and are referred to God as our final end, thus transcending their natural meaning and value and becoming supernaturally meritorious.[125] Fuchs writes of those in a state of charity, "The accomplishment of the demands of the natural law [has] truly the power to *merit* an increase of God-given sanctity, achieve the beatific union with God in heaven and an increase of our eternal participation in God's glory."[126]

Fuchs's wedding of the natural and supernatural orders through charity (love), however, involves no denigration or lessening of natural law's requirements. One of Fuchs's criticisms of the situationists was their tendency to relativize the demands arising from the natural order, based on an erroneous conception of love:[127] "A one-sided understanding of the 'Christian' virtue of love often involves the danger of considering all norms (including those of the natural law) as general yet . . . *in the end* not absolutely binding directives. . . . It may be asked: is not every natural law being rendered relative, indifferent, ultimately unimportant and therefore without any absolute and demanding character?"[128]

The situationists's principal mistake, Fuchs contends, is to assign material content to the virtue of charity, which either creates conflict between the natural and supernatural orders, or regards natural law's norms as provisional, nonobligatory directives that may be supplanted by the requirements of the higher supernatural order. In either case, the validity and bindingness of natural law is directly undermined. Fuchs avoids this false antinomy by assigning charity a formal function in moral deliberation. Beyond the general commands principally to love God above all things and secondarily to love oneself and one's neighbor as partakers in the divine image,[129] charity has no specific norms. In Fuchs's writings, charity functions within the motivational sphere;[130] out of love for God it prompts one to perform right actions, but it does not specify concretely what love for God requires.[131] Many actions can express love for God (such as almsgiving, telling the truth, not harming others, and contributing to the common good), but charity cannot be reduced to, or identified exclusively with, any particular act or class of acts.

Every act, therefore, is subject to two distinct measures. Natural law measures the rightness of proximate objects and their conformity to the demands arising from human nature. Charity, in contrast, measures one's motivation for acting and is concerned with attaining greater union with one's ultimate end, God. According to Fuchs, both components—an act conforming to natural law, and the presence of charity—are necessary for a particular act to be meritorious. Absent charity, an act in accordance with natural law realizes certain natural goods, but it does not arise principally from love for God, who as the most perfect being must be loved above all other things, and it fails to seek the proper remote object, greater union with God. As such, the act is not morally blameworthy, but it possesses no supernatural significance: "A fulfillment of the natural law that is not to some extent animated by *caritas* does not lead to God and remains, as such, sterile for life everlasting."[132]

Without a right action, a loving motivation alone is insufficient to render an act meritorious. Intentions and motivations might be laudable, as might feelings of goodwill toward friends, family, the entire human race, and perhaps even one's enemies, but for Fuchs the necessary precondition for human perfection, both natural and supernatural, is right action.[133] Through right acts not only are the powers supplied by human nature ordered properly, but the human person, through the gift of charity, moves toward her ultimate destiny, God, and participates in God's life more intimately.

Fuchs notes that charity need not exclude self-interested acts. Contrary to many Protestant moralists, who regard love as self-sacrificing, self-abnegating, giving higher priority to others' needs, or strict impartiality, Fuchs holds that the order of charity, in which self-love is prior to love of neighbor, sometimes requires that one's own well-being be sought before that of others:

> A genuine love for oneself is indeed reconcilable with the essence of man's likeness to God, that is, in the man who recognizes the image of his God in himself and acknowledges this image. The true and highest love of God is conformable to man's created nature and is therefore always the highest form of self-love, precisely because God and man who is his image are not contradictory concepts. It is therefore necessary that man's love for himself as the image of God does accompany, somehow, every moral decision and act of man.[134]

Fuchs is not implying that self-interest can or should be the predominant motive in a life animated by charity. The general principle underlying the order of charity is this: the closer someone is united to oneself, the more one is able to influence her union with God. Because outside of God nobody can affect one's union with God to the extent that one's self can, self-love must precede love of neighbor. Neighbor-love is ordered similarly: family and friends should be loved more than casual acquaintances or strangers, because one is usually able to affect the former's union with God more than the latter's.[135]

One of the most interesting—and intractably problematic—issues in Fuchs's natural law theory is the relationship between natural law and supernatural merit; more precisely, the ability of actions conforming to natural law to be meritorious and thus to contribute to one's soteriological standing. The neo-Thomist manualists unanimously concurred that in addition to being animated by charity, an act must be right, that is, its object, intention, and circumstances must each be right for the act to be meritorious. If any component is judged to be morally wrong, the entire act is vitiated and cannot be meritorious.[136] Henry Davis summarizes the neo-Thomists's reasoning well: "[I]t would be absurd to think that any morally evil act could possibly lead to God, Who necessarily abhors evil."[137]

Fuchs agrees that moral wrongness is contrary to God and can never contribute to one's salvation, but his judgment on whether rightness or wrongness should be attributed to the act as a whole or to certain parts of an act shifts noticeably during his preconversion period. In *Lex Naturae: Zur Theologie des Naturrechts*, originally published in German in 1955, Fuchs offers no challenge to the traditional teaching. By 1963, however, in *General Moral Theology* Fuchs's incipient discontent with the neo-Thomistic understanding is apparent. The problem for Fuchs is the status of a "mixed act," or an act attendant by both right and wrong ends. Can such an act be meritorious? Fuchs responds by differentiating each end and assessing its moral quality separately:

> But often the evil end is *not* the *only* end or motive of an act good in its object. Then the act is rendered *virtually twofold* from a moral standpoint . . . for in these cases not only the evil end but also the good end informs the act which is good in its object—then there is brought to realization in the same physical act moral good and moral evil at once. And if the evil end is not grave, a man who is living in grace merits from such an act insofar as it is good.[138]

Fuchs is a divided man in this passage. The basic idea impelling his reexamination of the tradition, as he mentions in the final sentence, is that an act should be meritorious insofar as it is right. But Fuchs also is reluctant to overturn the longstanding precedent that each component of an act must be morally right for the act as a whole to be meritorious. Fuchs adopts a compromise solution that revises the traditional understanding slightly: If and only if an act, morally right in its object and performed under fitting circumstances, possesses two contrary ends, one right and the other wrong, merit is awarded to that part of the act intended for a right purpose, but not for that part intended for a wrong purpose. Fuchs rejects the possibility that merit might be awarded to the components of an act individually, so that a right object, for example, in itself and despite the moral wrongness of the other two aspects of the act, would be meritorious.

Although the nuance and precision of Fuchs's discussion of the multiple ends present in mixed actions is a welcome refinement of the tradition, his critique functions entirely within the confines of the neo-Thomist understanding of the relationship between actions and supernatural merit, directly linking the former as the necessary prerequisite for the latter. Nevertheless, despite his adherence to the fundamental presuppositions of traditional teaching, Fuchs was simultaneously laying the conceptual groundwork in his preconversion writings that, years later and after significant development, would culminate in a direct and explicit repudiation of the traditional wedding of actions and merit. To be sure, these incipient beginnings of Fuchs's substantive critique represent only partial, fragmentary, and undeveloped ideas, the implications of which remained largely unexplored. Nonetheless, they signal the birth of intellectual doubt, nagging questions, and a growing sense of internal discontent that Fuchs was unwilling to brush aside.

The genesis of Fuchs's postconversion critique lay in his understanding of conscience. Based on a twofold function of conscience detectable in Thomas Aquinas's writings, Fuchs began distinguishing between conscience's *operatum* and *operationem*.[139] In every freely chosen human act, Fuchs maintained, conscience performs two operations. First, in the *operatum* conscience judges whether the act conforms to natural law. The *operationem*, in contrast, refers to the judgment of conscience concerning the moral quality of what the person intended to do, which prescinds entirely from the issue of whether the act actually conformed to natural law. Based on conscience's two functions, Fuchs distinguishes two types of "goodnesses":

> The distinction set forth in the title is between the good 'performed' (*operatum*) and the good 'performance' (*operationem*), or between the 'good act placed' and the 'good placing of the act.' *Objective-material moral goodness*, therefore, consists in that quality of the act itself on account of which this act is according to right reason ordainable to the last end. But *personal-formal moral goodness* consists in the *intention of the good* which man sees in the act he performs (whether rightly or wrongly). *Per se* these goodness[es] coincide in personal action; *per accidens*—because of an error in the knowledge of the objective-material good—they do not coincide.[140]

Two distinct moral evaluations are emerging here, one for the external act's conformity to natural law, and another for the inner act of the will, or what the person actually intended to do. The problem for Fuchs, as his final sentence indicates, is that inadequate or incorrect knowledge or factual information occasionally causes an agent to act contrary to what she intended to do. Consider, for example, a parent who mistakenly punishes the wrong child for a broken window. The parent's external act—punishing an innocent child—clearly violates objective-material moral "goodness." Yet the parent did not wish to reprove the wrong child; she was either mistaken, mislead, or deceived into thinking that her identification of the culprit was correct. Had she known differently, she would have punished the actual perpetrator.

The pivotal question for Fuchs is, What contributes more decisively to the parent's moral standing, the external act of punishing the wrong child or her actual intention to punish the right child? Fuchs responds: the inner act of the will, not the external act: "What makes man, above all, either moral or immoral, is not the act in itself, but the inner personal decision."[141] In Fuchs's estimation, whether a person "owns" an action and should be assigned responsibility for it, or whether an action reflects or conditions a person's moral standing is determined by her inner consent to the action.

Yet despite Fuchs's distinction between "objective-material moral goodness" and "personal-formal moral goodness" to account for the potential disparity between external acts and internal acts of the will, and despite his explicit admission that the latter—not the former—shape and mold the person's moral standing, he nonetheless fails to reconsider his traditional understanding of merit and salvation in light of the distinction. For Fuchs, merit is awarded only for the performance or attainment of right action (assuming the act is animated by charity). The decisive issue is not striving or intending to do what is right, but actually doing what is right. As Fuchs writes, "*A man who lives in grace and charity, in choosing and **performing** a good act as good implicitly realizes and actuates himself, that is to say as tending by charity toward God.*"[142]

The incongruity of Fuchs's position becomes manifest when the soteriological import of the parent's action is assessed. By Fuchs's standards, the mother's act of punishing the wrong child clearly violates "objective-material moral goodness" and thus cannot be meritorious. On the other hand, because she intended to punish the guilty perpetrator, her action increased her "personal-formal moral goodness." One would assume that this increase of "personal-formal moral goodness" possesses some soteriological significance, but this is precisely the conclusion Fuchs fails to draw; within Fuchs's framework, the necessary prerequisite for the bestowal of merit is actual performance of a right action. The implications of "personal-formal moral goodness," then, at this point do not extend to the soteriological sphere. But as Fuchs continues to refine his understanding of the distinction between "objective-material moral goodness" and "personal-formal moral goodness" in his postconversion writings, he eventually arrives at a more satisfactory notion of the relation between actions conforming to natural law and the supernatural sphere.

This example of the parent punishing the wrong child highlights another problem with Fuchs's link between merit and the performance of right actions: merit is dependent upon correct knowledge, both factual and moral. This presupposition unwittingly engenders a "disturbing intellectual moral elitism"[143] that is inherently biased against the unintelligent. Consider two persons equally well-ordered and well-intentioned, equally loving and concerned for the well-being of themselves and others, but obviously unequally intelligent. Who is more likely to perform meritorious acts? The one most adept at gathering and interpreting factual information, knowing which moral principle to apply, assessing the moral relevance of various circumstances, and judging the likely consequences of the act; in short, the one possessing the most intellectual acumen.

Regardless of whether intelligence is understood as innate or cultivated by environmental factors, insurmountable difficulties arise. If the first, one has simply hit the jackpot in the natural lottery. Intelligence, in this instance, is a stroke of undeserved luck, and the capacity to improve one's soteriological standing must rest on a more plausible foundation than the vicissitudes of heredity. If intelligence is shaped by environmental factors, the capacity to earn merit becomes contingent upon the presence or absence of a vast array of conditions that are largely, if not entirely, beyond an individual's control: the willingness and ability of one's parents, relatives, friends, and church to convey moral insights; society's interest in promoting and supporting education; the means sufficient to ensure a quality education; the vitality or decadence of one's culture; a lack of political conflict disruptive of the educational process; and research indicating how intelligence is nurtured or hindered, among others. If intelligence is conditioned by these environmental factors, merit should be measured not by a uniform standard—performing right actions—but by a graduated scale that recognizes both the limitations and strengths of one's background and the degree to which it has fostered moral ineptitude, moral competency, or perhaps even moral heroism.

Fuchs's lack of any antecedent evaluation of the person, independent of her actions, also is a glaring deficiency that strains the credibility of his link between right actions and merit. The emergence of the "personal-formal moral goodness" category indicates an inchoate desire to supplement his traditional act analysis with a moral assessment of the person, but he fails to distinguish the person from her actions adequately, considering the person's moral status solely in relation to the good intended through her actions.[144]

The fundamental problem with Fuchs's act analysis is that acts, in some instances, are imperfect, and sometimes incongruent and deceptive, expressions of a person's character. Consider the anti-Semite portrayed by Jean-Paul Sartre, who surreptitiously conceals his hatred for Jews and leads, by all external accounts, a noble and praiseworthy life: "A man may be a good father and a good husband, a conscientious citizen, highly cultivated, philosophic *and* in addition an anti-Semite. He may like fishing and the pleasures of love, may be tolerant in matters of religion, full of generous notions on the condition of the natives of Central Africa *and* in addition detest the Jews."[145] In this instance, the anti-Semite's poisonous attitude is never manifested by his external actions. Perhaps he lacks opportunity or reason to display his anti-Semitism, perhaps he fears social ostracism or moral reprobation, perhaps he is concerned for his and his family's physical safety if his anti-Semitism were uncovered, or perhaps he is simply lazy and does not want to expend the energy to promote his views publicly. Whatever the case, it would be impossible to call the anti-Semite, as a person, morally good even though his external actions are right. Fuchs's moral analysis, on the contrary, because it has only one source for evaluation—the act—would fail even to consider the anti-Semitism as a relevant factor in the person's moral status and remains blind to other equally formative character traits that constitute a person's moral makeup.

Fuchs's preconversion understanding of natural law's relation to salvation needs a substantial overhaul that reevaluates the import of actions on a person's soteriological standing. As contemporary proponents of the goodness/rightness distinction recognize, right actions do not necessarily indicate a good person, nor do wrong actions indicate a bad person. Good persons sometimes act wrongly and bad persons sometimes act rightly. Personal goodness unquestionably requires that one strive consistently and sometimes mightily to fulfill natural law's demands, but failure to accomplish natural law's requirements need not imply personal badness. Lack of self-control, underdeveloped moral imagination,[146] mental handicaps, deleterious environmental influences, addictions and compulsions, fear, and many other factors render us passive subjects whose ability to act according to natural law is restricted in varying degrees and in some cases perhaps even obliterated, and even the brightest and purest moral virtuosos are not exempt from making mistakes.

Within Fuchs's conceptual framework, all the factors limiting or precluding one's ability to act in conformity with natural law negatively affect one's soteriological standing to the extent that they diminish the probability of acting rightly. By adopting the distinction between goodness and rightness, Fuchs would avoid the unwitting link he has forged between salvation and the innumerable accidental and random circumstances affecting every person's life. No longer would it matter soteriologically whether one is blessed or cursed by nature, whether one is talented or inept, or whether one is stifled or nurtured by friends, family, society, or culture. The sole criterion for assessing one's soteriological standing would be the effort a person makes to act rightly, given her internal and external circumstances, which would make the possibility of accepting God's offer of salvation in principle equally accessible to everyone.

Notes

1. Josef Fuchs, *General Moral Theology*, pt. 1 (Rome: Pontificia Universitatis Gregoriana, 1963), 42–43.

2. Ibid., 43, 49–50.

3. Josef Fuchs, *Natural Law: A Theological Investigation*, trans. Helmut Recker and John Dowling (New York: Sheed and Ward, 1965), 57. For discussions of natural and supernatural elements in human beings and the relevance of revelation in identifying them, see C. Boyer, "Morale et surnaturel," *Gregorianum* 29 (1948): 527–43; T. Deman, "Sur l'organisation du savior morale," *Recherches des Sciences Philosophiques et Théologiques* 23 (1934): 258–80; G. de Broglie, "De gratuitate ordinis supernaturalis ad quem homo elevantus est," *Gregorianum* 29 (1948); Gérard Gilleman, *The Primacy of Charity in Moral Theology*, rev. ed., revised by Rene Carpentier, trans. William F. Ryan and André Vachon (London: Burns and Oates, 1959), 218–24; J. P. Kenny, "Reflections on Human Nature and the Supernatural," *Theological Studies* 14 (1953): 280–87; L. Malevez, "L'espirit et désir de Dieu," *Nouvelle Revue Théologique* 69 (1947): 1–31; and Philip J. Donnelly, "Discussions on the Supernatural Order," *Theological Studies* 9 (1948): 213–49.

4. Fuchs, *Natural Law*, 54.

5. Ibid., 88–93; Fuchs, *General Moral Theology*, 49–54; Josef Fuchs, "Naturrecht und positives Recht," *Stimmen der Zeit* 163 (1958–59): 133; Fuchs, "Ethique objective et éthique de situation," *Nouvelle Revue Théologique* 78 (1956): 801–02; Fuchs, "Morale théologique et morale de situation," *Nouvelle Revue Théologique* 76 (1954): 1075; and Fuchs, *Situation und Entscheidung: Grundfragen christlicher Situationsethik* (Frankfurt: Knecht, 1952), 38–39.

6. Fuchs, *General Moral Theology*, 66.

7. For a more detailed discussion of Fuchs's distinction between absolute and relative natural law, see chapter 1.

8. Fuchs, *Natural Law*, 117.

9. This tripartite division of moral norms, beginning with the most general and terminating with specific norms that indicate concrete moral rightness or wrongness, was common among the neo-Thomist manualists. Francis Connell, for example, writes, "We distinguish three classes of commandments of natural law: (1) *Most universal principles,* such as 'Good must be done, evil avoided.' (2) *Immediate deductions from the former,* such as 'It is wrong to steal, to murder, to commit adultery.' (3) *More remote conclusions,* such as 'Things that are found must be restored to their owner, fornication is always wrong, direct suicide is always forbidden' " (Francis Connell, *Outlines of Moral Theology,* [Milwaukee, Wisc.: Bruce Publishing, 1953], 30). See also Antony Koch and Arthur Preuss, *A Handbook of Moral Theology,* 3d ed., 5 vols. (St. Louis, Mo.: B. Herder, 1925), 1: 129–30; and H. Noldin and A. Schmitt, *Summa Theologiae Moralis,* 3 vols. (Innsbruck, Austria: Sumptis and Typic Feliciani Rauch, 1940), 1: 111.

10. Thomas Aquinas, *Summa Theologica,* 5 vols., trans. Fathers of the English Dominican Province (1911; reprint, Westminster, Md.: Christian Classics, 1981) I–II.94.5, 6; 100.1, 3; and Fuchs, *General Moral Theology,* 55.

11. Fuchs *Natural Law,* 117.

12. Aquinas, *Summa Theologica,* I–II.94.4, 5.

13. Ibid., I–II.100.1.

14. Fuchs, *Natural Law,* 111.

15. Ibid., 96.

16. Ibid., 106.

17. Fuchs, "Morale théologique et morale de situation," 1083; and Fuchs, "Ethique objective et éthique de situation," 805.

18. For practical examples of the *contra natura* argument, see Thomas Slater, *A Manual of Moral Theology,* 3d ed., 2 vols. (New York: Benzinger Brothers, 1908), 1: 330–38; Henry Davis, *Moral and Pastoral Theology,* 7th ed., 3 vols. (London: Sheed and Ward, 1958), 2: 211–18, 381; and Aloysius Sabetti and Timothy Barrett, *Compendium Theologiae Moralis* (Rome: Frederick Pustet, 1916), 275–79.

19. Josef Fuchs, *De Castitate et Ordine Sexuali* (Rome: Pontificia Universitatis Gregoriana, 1959), 31.

20. Fuchs, *De Castitate et Ordine Sexuali,* 32. For an explanation of the difference between an action being contrary to nature or contrary to reason, see ibid., 41–42.

21. Fuchs *Natural Law,* 110. For extended discussions on the relationship between absolute and relative natural law, see ibid., 88–95, 99–100, 110–19; Fuchs, *General Moral Theology,* 49–54; Fuchs, *Situation und Entscheidung,* 31–42; Fuchs, "Ethique objective et éthique de situation," 810–18; Fuchs, "Situationsethik in theologischer Sicht," *Scholastik* 27 (1952): 166–68; Josef Fuchs, "De Valore Legis Naturalis in Ordine Redemptionis," *Periodica de Re Morali, Canonica, et Liturgica* 44 (1955): 48–55.

22. Fuchs, *Natural Law*, 111.

23. Ibid., 85.

24. Ibid., 96.

25. Ibid.

26. Ibid., 100.

27. Fuchs, "Naturrecht und positives Recht," 133; and Fuchs, *Natural Law*, 111.

28. This is a criticism directed at "scholastic natural law theory" by Germain Grisez (German Grisez, *Christian Moral Principles*, vol. 1 of *The Way of the Lord Jesus* [Chicago: Franciscan Herald Press, 1983], 105–6).

29. For a perceptive analysis of the ethical implications of the process of homogenization, which discounts uniqueness, difference, and individually and considers commonality as the morally relevant basis for determining right and wrong, see Val Plumwood, *Feminism and the Mastery of Nature* (New York: Routledge, 1997), 41–68.

30. Fuchs, *Natural Law*, 115.

31. James F. Keenan, "Virtue Ethics: Making a Case as It Comes of Age," *Thought* 67 (1992): 116.

32. Recall Fuchs's definition of human nature: "[Human] nature is understood as the essence of man . . . according to his metaphysical being ('rational animal,' with all the consequences [i.e. moral norms] **necessarily** flowing from this)" (Fuchs, *General Moral Theology*, 43; emphasis added).

33. Fuchs's moral epistemology is treated in greater detail in the following section.

34. John R. Connery, *Abortion: The Development of the Roman Catholic Perspective* (Chicago: Loyola University Press, 1977); John T. Noonan, *Contraception: A History of Its Treatment by the Catholic Theologians* (Cambridge, Mass.: Harvard University Press, 1965); and Albert R. Jonsen and Stephen Toulmin, *The Abuse of Casuistry* (Berkeley: University of California Press, 1988), 181–227.

35. John Kekes, *The Examined Life* (University Park: Pennsylvania State University Press, 1988), 50. See also John Kekes, *Moral Tradition and Individuality* (Princeton, N.J.: Princeton University Press, 1989), 128–29; and Martha C. Nussbaum, *The Fragility of Goodness: Luck and Ethics in Greek Tragedy and Philosophy* (Cambridge: Cambridge University Press, 1986), 299.

36. Pamela M. Hall, *Narrative and Natural Law: An Interpretation of Thomistic Ethics* (Notre Dame, Ind.: University of Notre Dame Press, 1994), 99.

37. Pius XI, for example, addressing the possibility of individuals using their unaided reason to arrive at moral truth, writes, "But everyone can see to how many fallacies an avenue would be opened up and how many errors would become mixed with the truth, if it were left solely to the light of reason of each to find it out, or if it were to be discovered by the private interpretation of the truth which is revealed" (Pope Pius XI, *Casti Connubii*, in *The Papal Encyclicals 1930–39*, ed. Claudia Carlen [1930; reprint, Raleigh, N.C.: McGrath Publishing, 1981], #102). Pius XII offers a similar assessment based on the pervasive, distorting influence of original sin on human reason: "Now the

human intellect, in gaining the knowledge of [moral] truths is hampered both by the activity of the senses and the imagination, and by evil passions arising from original sin. Hence men easily persuade themselves in such matters that what they do not wish to believe is false or at least doubtful. It is for this reason that divine revelation must be considered morally necessary so that those religious and moral truths which are not of their nature beyond the reach of reason in the present condition of the human race, may be known by all men readily with a firm certainty and with freedom from all error" (Pope Pius XII, *Humani Generis*, in *The Papal Encyclicals 1939–1958*, ed. Claudia Carlen [1950; reprint, Raleigh, N.C.: McGrath Publishing, 1981], #2).

38. The neo-Thomist manualists agreed with Popes Pius XI and XII that knowledge of natural law is limited, although they offer additional factors for the limitations. For Henry Davis, knowledge of natural law's most general principles is available to everyone, whereas natural law's more proximate conclusions concerning practical action are likely to be misunderstood, especially by the young, uncultured, or uneducated (Davis, *Moral and Pastoral Theology*, 1: 127–28). Likewise, in the realm of practical knowledge of natural law, Arthur Vermeersch lists disordered appetites, ignorance, subjective character flaws, and negative environmental influences as frequently preventing one from attaining moral knowledge (Arthur Vermeersch, *Theologiae Moralis*, 3d ed., 3 vols. [Rome: Pontificia Universitatis Gregoriana, 1933], 1: 69–87).

39. Norman Tanner, ed., *Decrees of the Ecumenical Councils*, 2 vols. (Washington, D.C.: Georgetown University Press, 1990), 2: 810.

40. Fuchs, *Natural Law* 147; and Fuchs, *General Moral Theology*, 54.

41. Tanner, *Decrees of the Ecumenical Councils*, 2: 806.

42. Fuchs, *General Moral Theology*, 54.

43. Tanner, *Decrees of the Ecumenical Councils*, 2: 806.

44. Fuchs, *Natural Law*, 148–49.

45. Fuchs, "Ethique objective et éthique de situation," 811–12; Fuchs, "Naturrecht und positives Recht," 135; and Fuchs, *Natural Law*, 50–51.

46. Fuchs, *General Moral Theology*, 53; and Fuchs, *Natural Law*, 152.

47. Fuchs, *Natural Law*, 147.

48. Fuchs, *General Moral Theology*, 55.

49. There was almost unanimous agreement among Roman Catholic moralists at this time that natural law's most general principles were known easily by every normal, rational person, but the more details and circumstances involved in applying a specific principle to a situation, the more subjective impediments due to original sin, lack of education, improper upbringing, or bad character traits interfered with the ability to discern correctly a proper application. In consequence, most people, if left to their own devices, will have little awareness of natural law's specific principles. See, for example, Koch and Preuss, *A Handbook of Moral Theology* 1: 128–30; Noldin and Schmitt, *Summa Theologiae Moralis*, 1: 112; Davis, *Moral and Pastoral Theology*, 1: 127–28; Connell, *Outlines of Moral Theology*, 30; Slater, *Manual of Moral Theology*, 1: 117–18; and Bernard Häring, *The Law of Christ*, 3 vols., trans. Edwin G. Kasper (Westminster, Md.: Newman Press, 1961–66), 1: 245.

50. Fuchs, *General Moral Theology*, 55.

51. Fuchs *Natural Law*, 155.

52. Ibid., 152.

53. Ibid., 155.

54. Ibid., 157. See also Pius XII, *Humani Generis*, #3.

55. Pius XII, *Humani Generis*, #18.

56. Fuchs, *Natural Law*, 158. See also Fuchs, *General Moral Theology*, 55.

57. Fuchs, *General Moral Theology*, 55.

58. Ibid.

59. Fuchs, *Natural Law*, 158.

60. Ibid.

61. The sole exception, discussed in the first chapter, is a communication given by God to an individual that is confirmed by a miracle. See Fuchs, "Situationsethik in theologischer Sicht," 172.

62. Ronald Amos Mercier, "What Is Nature? The Development of Josef Fuchs' Thought on Moral Normativity," (Ph.D. diss., Regis College, 1993), 117–18.

63. Anne E. Patrick, *Liberating Conscience* (New York: Continuum, 1996).

64. James F. Keenan, "Josef Fuchs and the Question of Moral Objectivity in Roman Catholic Moral Reasoning," *Religious Studies Review* 24 (1998): 253.

65. Fuchs, *General Moral Theology*, 32.

66. Fuchs, "Ethique objective et éthique de situation," 801–3; Fuchs, "Morale théologique et morale de situation," 1075; Fuchs, *Situation und Entscheidung*, 32, 43–44; Fuchs, "Naturrecht und positives Recht," 133; Fuchs, "Situationsethik in theologischer Sicht," 166–68; Fuchs, *General Moral Theology*, 43; and Fuchs, *Natural Law*, 42–58, esp. 49–51.

67. Josef Fuchs, "Weihsakramentale Grundlegung kirchlicher Rechtsgewalt," *Scholastik* 16 (1941): 496–520.

68. Ibid., 515.

69. Ibid., 516.

70. Fuchs, *Natural Law*, 158–59.

71. John C. Ford et al., "The Birth Control Report II: The Conservative Case," *Tablet* 29 April 1967, 485. In a similar vein, Ford argued that changing the church's official teaching would imply that the Holy Spirit had actually been assisting Protestant churches, which had approved artificial contraception: "If contraception were declared not intrinsically evil, in honesty it would have to be acknowledged that the Holy Spirit in 1930, and 1951 and 1958, assisted Protestant Churches, and that for half a century Pius XI, Pius XII and a great part of the Catholic hierarchy did not protest against a very serious error, one most pernicious to souls. . . . Therefore one must very cautiously inquire whether the change which is proposed would not bring along with it a definitive depreciation of the teaching of the moral direction of the hierarchy of the Church and whether several very grave doubts would not be opened up about the very history of Christianity" (ibid., 483–84).

72. Ibid., 480.

73. Josef Fuchs, quoted in Robert Blair Kaiser, *The Encyclical That Never Was: The Story of the Pontifical Commission on Population, Family, and Birth, 1964–66* (London: Sheed and Ward, 1987), 198.

74. Robert McClory, *Turning Point* (New York: Crossroad, 1995), 99.

75. See, for example, his discussions of the state's right to exercise coercion, capital punishment, self-defense, fighting a just war, and the right to resist a despotic government (Fuchs, *Natural Law*, 95–100).

76. Ibid., 111.

77. Ibid., 107.

78. Ibid., 158.

79. Fuchs, "Weihsakramentale Grundlegung kirchlicher Rechtsgewalt," 515.

80. Fuchs, *Natural Law*, 158–59.

81. John P. Boyle, "The Natural Law and the Magisterium," in *The Magisterium and Morality*, Readings in Moral Theology, no. 3, ed. Charles E. Curran and Richard A. McCormick (Ramsey, N.J.: Paulist Press, 1982), 443.

82. Fuchs, *Natural Law*, 111.

83. Bernard J. F. Lonergan, *Insight: A Study of Human Understanding* (New York: Longmans, Green, 1958); Bernard J. F. Lonergan, *Method in Theology* (New York: Herder and Herder, 1972); Bernard J. F. Lonergan, *A Third Collection*, ed. Frederick E. Crowe (Mahwah, N.J.: Paulist Press, 1985), 169–83; and Bernard J. F. Lonergan, *A Second Collection*, ed. William F. J. Ryan and Bernard J. Tyrell (London: Darton, Longman, and Todd, 1974), 1–9.

84. See, for example, Charles Taylor, *Sources of the Self: The Making of the Modern Identity* (Cambridge, Mass.: Harvard University Press, 1989); and Charles Taylor, *The Ethics of Authenticity* (Cambridge, Mass.: Harvard University Press, 1991).

85. Mercier, "What Is Nature?," 101.

86. Fuchs, *General Moral Theology*, 28.

87. This understanding of the moral agent as an applicator of received teaching was widespread among Roman Catholic moralists during this time. In their view, once the morally relevant aspects of a situation are identified, the moral norm intended to regulate such situation is "applied," meaning that the moral agent concretely performs the action specified by the norm. See Koch and Preuss, *Handbook of Moral Theology* 1: 188–90; W. Rauch, *Abhandlungen aus Ethik und Moraltheologie* (Freiburg, Germany: Herder, 1956), 47–48; and Heinrich A. Rommen, *The Natural Law: A Study in Legal and Social History and Philosophy*, (1947; reprint, Indianapolis, Ind.: Liberty Fund, 1998), 195–204.

88. Fuchs, *Natural Law*, 159.

89. Ibid., 160.

90. Fuchs, *General Moral Theology*, 135.

91. Ibid., 122.

92. Ibid., 136.

93. Ibid., 142.

94. See Davis, *Moral and Pastoral Theology*, 1: 68; Heribert Jone and Urban Adelman, *Moral Theology*, 2nd ed. (Westminster, Md.: Newman Press, 1946), 46–49; and Häring, *Law of Christ*, 1: 151–53 for statements on the necessity of forming one's conscience properly.

95. Fuchs, *General Moral Theology*, 141.

96. Fuchs, *Natural Law*, 131.

97. Fuchs, *General Moral Theology*, 120–3; Fuchs, *Situation und Entscheidung*, 129–42; Fuchs, "Ethique objective et éthique de situation," 803. See also Mercier, "What Is Nature?," 88–93.

98. Fuchs, "Ethique objective et éthique de situation," 803.

99. Fuchs, *Natural Law*, 152.

100. Ibid., 160.

101. Ibid., 155.

102. Ibid. Although Fuchs considers moral agency to be enhanced by formal training in ethics, he refuses to establish a similar connection between formal training in ethics and the magisterium's teaching authority. This line of thought, however, would become pivotal in Fuchs's postconversion critique of the magisterium's competency to interpret natural law. See Josef Fuchs, *Christian Ethics in a Secular Arena*, trans. Bernard Hoose and Brian McNeil (Washington, D.C.: Georgetown University Press, 1984), 131—53.

103. Jean Porter, *Moral Action and Christian Ethics* (Cambridge: Cambridge University Press, 1995), 190.

104. See Gerald Reitlinger, *The Final Solution: The Attempt to Exterminate the Jews of Europe, 1939–1945* (New York: A. S. Barnes, 1961); Lucy S. Dawidowicz, *A Holocaust Reader* (West Orange, N.J.: Behrman House, 1976); and Hannah Arendt, *The Origins of Totalitarianism* (New York: Harcourt Brace, 1975).

105. Porter, *Moral Action and Christian Ethics*, 80.

106. My account of moral development is heavily dependent on Porter's *Moral Action and Christian Ethics*, 167–79.

107. J. M. Brennan, *The Open-Texture of Moral Concepts* (New York: Harper and Row, 1977), 116–24.

108. Mark Johnson, *Moral Imagination* (Chicago: University of Chicago Press, 1993), 109. See also Philip Keane, *Christian Ethics and Imagination* (New York: Paulist Press, 1984).

109. John Kekes, *Moral Wisdom and Good Lives* (Ithaca, N.Y.: Cornell University Press, 1995), 101.

110. Fuchs, *Natural Law*, 123.

111. For discussions of individuality and particularity and their implications for moral normativity, see Owen Flanagan, *Varieties of Moral Personality* (Cambridge, Mass.: Harvard University Press, 1991), 65–78; and Lawrence Blum, *Moral Perception and Particularity* (New York: Cambridge University Press, 1994), 65–97.

112. See, for example, John Kekes's accounts of self-control, self-knowledge, and moral imagination in Kekes, *Moral Wisdom and Good Lives*.

113. Fuchs, *Natural Law*, 120.

114. Fuchs, *General Moral Theology*, 15; and Fuchs, *Natural Law*, 178.

115. As I discuss below, for Fuchs perfect union with God occurs only after death in the beatific vision, whereas imperfect union with God can occur during our terrestrial life through charity.

116. For discussions of the twofold ends of the human person, see Connell, *Outlines of Moral Theology*, 7–12; Davis, *Moral and Pastoral Theology*, 1: 6–10; and Noldin and Schmitt, *Summa Theologiae Moralis*, 1: 15–19. With the publication of Henri de Lubac's *Surnatural* (Paris: Aubier, 1946), in which de Lubac rejected the Thomistic notion of "natural happiness," a lively debate ensued on the meaningfulness of partitioning happiness into two spheres, one natural and the other supernatural. See Joseph Buckley, *Man's Last End* (St. Louis, Mo.: B. Herder, 1949); Donnelly, "Discussions on the Supernatural Order;" and Gerard Smith, "The Natural End of Man," *Proceedings of the American Catholic Philosophical Association* 23 (1949): 47–61 for discussions of the natural/supernatural distinction.

117. John A. Gallagher, *Time Past, Time Future: An Historical Study of Catholic Moral Theology* (Mahwah, N.J.: Paulist Press, 1990), 55.

118. Fuchs, *General Moral Theology*, 14.

119. Fuchs, *Situation und Entscheidung*, 36; Fuchs, "Situationsethik in theologischer Sicht," 165–66; and Fuchs, "De Valore Legis Naturalis in Ordine Redemptionis," 62.

120. Fuchs, *Natural Law*, 178.

121. Fuchs, *General Moral Theology*, 15, 57.

122. Fuchs, *Natural Law*, 171.

123. Ibid., 172.

124. Fuchs, *General Moral Theology*, 187.

125. Ibid., 71.

126. Fuchs, *Natural Law*, 179.

127. Fuchs was also critical of Roman Catholic attempts to construct an ethic based on love, insofar as the presence or absence of love as a motivation becomes the sole criterion for determining an action's rightness or wrongness. See Josef Fuchs, "Der Liebe als Aufbauprinzip der Moraltheologie," *Scholastik* 29 (1954): 79–87, esp. 86–87.

128. Fuchs, *Natural Law*, 138.

129. Ibid., 140.

130. Ibid., 141.

131. See Gilleman, *Primacy of Charity*, 29–48 for an explanation of charity's formal function.

132. Fuchs, *Natural Law*, 139.

133. Ibid., 141.

134. Ibid., 140.

135. Ibid.

136. Slater, *Manual of Moral Theology*, 1: 52–55; Davis, *Moral and Pastoral Theology*, 1: 46; John A. McHugh and Charles J. Callan, *Moral Theology: A*

Complete Course Based on St. Thomas and the Best Modern Authorities, 2 vols. (New York: Joseph F. Wagner, 1929), 1: 38; Noldin and Schmitt, *Summa Theologiae Moralis*, 1: 99–101; Marcellinus Zalba, *Theologiae Moralis Compendium: Juxta Constitutionem Deus Scientiarum*, 2 vols. (Madrid, Spain: Editorial Catolica, 1958), 1: 28; Vermeersch, *Theologiae Moralis*, 1: 131; and Connell, *Outlines of Moral Theology*, 25.

137. Davis, *Moral and Pastoral Theology*, 1: 46.

138. Fuchs, *General Moral Theology*, 200.

139. Fuchs, *Situation und Entscheidung*, 107–28, esp. 118–28; and Fuchs, "Morale théologique et morale de situation," 1085.

140. Fuchs, *General Moral Theology*, 107–8.

141. Fuchs, *Situation und Entscheidung*, 116, emphasis added.

142. Fuchs, *General Moral Theology*, 188.

143. James F. Keenan makes this same criticism against Thomas Aquinas in "The Problem with Thomas Aquinas's Concept of Sin," *Heythrop Journal* 35 (1994): 402–3.

144. Fuchs, *General Moral Theology*, 107–8.

145. Jean-Paul Sartre, quoted in Flanagan, *Varieties of Moral Personality*, 288.

146. Kekes, *Moral Wisdom and Good Lives*, 73–113.

3

The Intellectual Conversion: The Pontifical Commission on Population, Family, and Birth, 1963–66

Commentators have noted a substantial conceptual shift in Fuchs's natural law theory in the mid-1960s:[1] traditional concepts were retained after 1966, but redefined and given new meaning; an anthropology dependent on the neo-Thomist manualists was jettisoned in favor of Karl Rahner's transcendental Thomism; the locus of moral competency shifted from the magisterium to the individual moral agent in the concrete situation; Fuchs's preoccupation with discrete, isolated acts gave way to a concern for the individual's athematic relationship with God; the link between actions in accordance with natural law and personal salvation was weakened; moral norms derived from natural law were no longer considered exceptionless embodiments of moral objectivity in concrete situations, but rules of thumb offering general guidance; and natural law shifted from the demands arising from human nature to *recta ratio,* or right reason. Although vestiges of Fuchs's early natural law theory perdured unscathed through this transitional period, most of its conceptual superstructure was either substantially revised or explicitly repudiated.

As I shall argue, the paramount factor precipitating Fuchs's intellectual conversion was his experience on the Pontifical Commission on Population, Family, and Birth. There Fuchs not only openly admitted for the first time the inability of the traditional understanding of natural law to deal adequately with the issue of artificial contraception,[2] but he also began to question whether this deficiency might indicate more systemic flaws that could not be corrected by peripheral adjustments.[3]

The most important factor, however, was that Fuchs's service on the pontifical commission exposed him to faithful and committed Catholic spouses who had either tried, or were trying, to adhere to received teaching on birth control. These couples presented a practical portrait of the multiple, interconnected, and often conflicting, goods at stake in the decision to employ the rhythm method. Instead of limiting their discussion to the traditional twofold ends of marital intercourse, they talked about the rhythm method's effects on marital intimacy and the overall health and strength of their marriages; the financial and social hardships frequently caused by untimely pregnancies or too many children; the couples' lifeplans and their ability to contribute to the life of their communities in ways other than raising good children; how prolonged periods of abstinence, particularly for women with irregular menstrual cycles, engendered resentment, frustration, and emotional distance between spouses; and women suffering from medical conditions for whom pregnancy represented a potentially life-threatening situation.

While listening to the testimony of these couples, Fuchs gradually became convinced that married couples—not the magisterium or moral theologians—were in the best position to judge the liceity of artificial contraception in their concrete circumstances. Fuchs's key insight—which would affect his understanding of natural law immeasurably in subsequent years—was that individual moral agents possess knowledge about themselves, their responsibilities and commitments, the practical effects of their actions, and their particular circumstances that enable them to judge objectively what should be done in their respective situations. This pivotal insight would become the primary force impelling Fuchs to reexamine and reconstruct significant portions of his natural law theory, including his understandings of moral competency, moral objectivity, moral epistemology, and the adequacy of moral norms in concrete situations.

The components of Fuchs's postconversion natural law theory are examined in detail in the final three chapters. In this chapter I will outline the genesis of Fuchs's intellectual conversion. What happened during the commission's proceedings? Why did Fuchs find traditional natural law theory inadequate when faced with the contraception issue? What factors precipitated an abrupt and unexpected about-face?

Birth Control: The State of the Question

John Noonan, author of the erudite *Contraception: A History of its Treatment by Catholic Theologians and Canonists*, notes that in the late 1800s the contraception issue assumed a new degree of urgency. For the first time in history there emerged an organized birth control movement, lead primarily by the Malthusian League, which was dedicated to disseminating contraceptive information, to ensuring access to various types of contraceptives, to mobilizing public opinion, and to establishing "birth control as a social objective in the Western world."[4] By the beginning of the twentieth century, the birth control movement had attained a notable degree of respectability among physicians, government officials, population experts, and social scientists; it had also evolved from a loosely-knit conglomeration of local, grassroots organizations to a consciously international, well-coordinated, and politically influential, movement. By the early 1900s the Malthusian League had established active satellite branches throughout Europe, and also in South America and Cuba.[5] Beginning in 1900, international congresses on birth control were held regularly in Europe and the United States, which were considered "milestones" in the attempt to influence public perception on the legitimacy of contraception.[6] Statistical evidence also indicated uniform declines in birth rates throughout the industrialized nations of Western Europe in the early 1900s, and precipitous declines in Belgium and France, all of which strongly suggested that birth control was being widely practiced.[7] The birth control movement's agenda, it seems, was being realized rapidly. Not only had it succeeded in garnering influential allies in government, medicine, the academy, and the media, but it also witnessed a growing tacit acceptance of its goals and objectives through the birth control practices of a substantial portion of people throughout Europe and North America.

Although these developments prompted predictable reactions from various national hierarchies ranging from calm but stern admonitions to avoid contraceptive practices to near hysterical warnings of the disastrous social and political consequences if declining birth rates were not reversed,[8] the Lambeth Conference of Anglican bishops in 1930 seemed to be the decisive event that roused Pope Pius XI to action. Having condemned contraception in 1908 and 1920, by 1930 a majority of Anglican bishops had changed their minds, adopting a resolution that permitted a qualified use of contraceptives:

Where there is a clearly felt moral obligation to limit or avoid parenthood, the method must be decided on Christian principles. The primary and obvious method is complete abstinence from intercourse (as far as may be necessary) in a life of discipline and self-control lived in the power of the Holy Spirit. Nevertheless in those cases where there is such a clearly-felt moral obligation to limit or avoid parenthood, and where there is a morally sound reason for avoiding complete abstinence, the conference agrees that other methods may be used, provided that this is done in the light of the same Christian principles. The Conference records its strong condemnation of the use of any methods of conception control from motives of selfishness, luxury, or mere convenience.[9]

That a mainline Christian denomination endorsed the use of contraceptives was significant; of even more import, however, was the fact that of all Protestant denominations, the Anglican Church was most similar doctrinally to the Roman Catholic Church. As Noonan notes, "The bishops of the church whose theology was closest to that of the Roman Catholic Church no longer adhered to an absolute prohibition on contraception."[10]

A mere four months after the Lambeth Conference, Pope Pius XI issued an encyclical on Christian marriage, *Casti Connubii*, which was intended to counteract "the false principles of a new and utterly perverse morality"[11] that had begun to sway even the faithful. In an obvious reference to the Anglican bishops, Pius noted that certain persons have openly departed "from the uninterrupted Christian tradition [and] have judged it possible to declare another doctrine regarding this question [of contraception]."[12] In consequence

the Catholic Church, to whom God has entrusted the defence of the integrity and purity of morals, standing erect in the midst of the moral ruin which surrounds her, in order that she may preserve the chastity of the nuptial union from being defiled by this foul stain, raises her voice in token of her divine ambassadorship and through Our mouth proclaims anew: any use whatsoever of matrimony exercised in such a way that the act is deliberately frustrated in its natural power to generate life is an offence against the law of God and of nature, and those who indulge in such are branded with the guilt of a grave sin.[13]

Pius went even further: contraception was not only gravely sinful, but "intrinsically vicious" because nature demanded that each and every act of sexual intercourse be open to procreation and no act *contra natura* can become morally right:

But no reason, however grave, may be put forward by which anything intrinsically against nature may become conformable to nature and morally good. Since, therefore, the conjugal act is destined primarily by nature for the begetting of children, those who in exercising it deliberately frustrate its natural power and purpose sin against nature and commit a deed which is shameful and intrinsically vicious.[14]

The immense doctrinal authority of Pius's solemn declaration effectively ended speculation among Roman Catholic theologians about the liceity of contraception for approximately thirty years. The scope of *Casti Connubii* was debated, theologians discussed whether the principle of double effect might justify the use of contraceptives when certain medical conditions were present, and in the early 1950s Pope Pius XII declared what he and many theologians believed to be implicit in, and consistent with, *Casti Connubii*, namely, that natural law permitted the use of the rhythm method to regulate births. Thus when the papal birth control commission was convened, *Casti Connubii's* fundamental principle—the act of sexual intercourse is naturally ordained to procreation and any direct attempt to stifle or impede one's procreative capacity artificially was immoral—remained publicly unopposed by any reputable authority in the Roman Catholic Church.

The Pontifical Birth Control Commission

The Pontifical Commission on Population, Family, and Birth was created by Pope John XXIII in March 1963 with a limited objective in mind: to construct a strategy for an upcoming international conference on world population problems sponsored jointly by the United Nations and the World Health Organization. The composition of the committee—two medical doctors, a demographer, an economist, a sociologist, and a career diplomat[15]—as well as its recommendations at the conclusion of the first session, which described papal statements on the immorality of contraception as "luminous teachings," indicated that its purpose was not to revisit, and possibly reconsider, the teaching of *Casti Connubii* or to venture into the questions of fundamental moral theology.[16] As John Marshall, a member of the original committee, said, "I don't think any of us felt at that point that the old doctrine could or should be changed. We didn't see ourselves as the sort of group that would move in that direction."[17]

After Pope John's death in June 1963 and the election of Pope Paul VI, the trajectory of the commission changed. Because the original purpose of the commission had been fulfilled—it had issued a twenty-two page report outlining the strategy for dealing with the international conference on population problems—Pope Paul could have simply dissolved it. But he did quite the opposite. In a surprising move, Pope Paul appointed seven new members to the commission, including two sociologists and five moral theologians,[18] including Fuchs. By all accounts, Fuchs was appointed to the commission not only because of his expertise in sexual morality, but because of his agreement with received teaching on birth control.[19] In his popular manual on sexuality, *De Castitate et Ordine Sexuali* (1959), and a number of articles on marriage and sexuality published between 1948 and 1952,[20] *Castii Connubii* and Pope Pius XII's allocutions were cited approvingly and there was never a hint of deviation from papal teaching.

Pope Paul's expansion of the commission did not immediately suggest a desire to reconsider the traditional ban on contraceptives. Most of the appointees publicly adhered to received teaching on birth control, and the committee's agenda, suggested by Pope Paul, remained similar to that of the first meeting.[21] According to papal advisors, the pope was a thorough and deliberate man who preferred to consider all sides of a question or issue before rendering a judgment. In their view, even given the limited objectives of the birth control commission, the pope felt uncomfortable with a lack of theological expertise on the commission and simply desired more input.[22]

The commission's deliberations during the second meeting in 1964, however, soon began to expand beyond the narrow confines of offering advice on the upcoming international conference on population problems. Bernard Häring[23] and Pierre de Locht argued that the commission could not come to any practical conclusions until larger issues had been discussed and settled. Häring objected strongly to the traditional teaching that assigned procreation as the primary end of marital intercourse, claiming that the locus of theological reflection should not be individual acts of intercourse, but the quality of the marital relationship as a whole. In his perspective, whether each act of marital intercourse was open to procreation was unimportant; the crucial issue was fostering mutual love between spouses that not only solidifies their marital relationships but creates a supportive and caring atmosphere in which children are raised.

Concurring with Häring, de Locht suggested that the commission begin "raising fundamental questions" about marriage and the use of contraceptives within marriage.[24] Fuchs, however, staunchly opposed Häring's and de Locht's proposals, claiming that received teaching on contraception still remained valid:

> Since an "ordination to procreation" is inherent in each sexual union . . . "the integrity of the act itself" is destroyed when contraceptive measures are taken. Furthermore, said Fuchs, this new emphasis on love, however well intentioned, seems to distort the time-honored Christian doctrine. After all, he noted, the essence of marital consent is the mutual "exchange by man and woman of their rights to sexual activities apt for procreation."[25]

Although Häring and de Locht failed to convince any other moral theologians at this time, their appeals influenced Pope Paul, whose proposed agenda for the third meeting, also held in 1964, included questions of fundamental moral theology. In particular, he asked for responses to three questions: "What is the relationship of the primary and secondary ends of marriage? What are the major responsibilities of married couples? How do rhythm and the [birth control] pill relate to responsible parenthood?"[26]

At the close of the third session the commission was no closer to answering Pope Paul's questions.[27] A growing number of theologians agreed that the primary end of conjugal intercourse should be the enhancement of marital love, but this position was far from unanimous. The commission's deliberations, according to commentators, tended to deal with peripheral matters such as the conditions required for a valid marriage, continuity of doctrine, and the authority of official church teaching.[28] Fearing that the commission's inability to reach any substantive agreement might prompt Pope Paul simply to reaffirm past teaching, de Locht and Häring informed the pope that answers to such far-reaching questions required insights from a broader spectrum of theologians and from those affected most directly by the church's teaching on birth control: married couples themselves. Pope Paul agreed and proceeded to expand the commission from thirteen to fifty-eight members, including three married couples named specifically as couples, rather than for competency in a particular academic field.[29]

At the beginning of the fourth meeting it was decided to focus on the question of reformability, in other words, whether the received teaching on contraception could be altered, or perhaps even changed entirely. Given the scattered and unproductive discussion of the last meeting, the commission members felt that the scope of their deliberation must be established clearly in order to determine which potential answers to the pope's three questions were permissible. If the received teaching remained irreformable, the parameters of the commission's deliberations would be restricted and certain answers would immediately be eliminated from consideration.

The ensuing debate on reformability produced an avalanche of reports from the moral theologians. Marcellinus Zalba, a Spanish Jesuit, argued that "the centuries-old condemnation of coitus interruptus, the teaching of procreation as marriage's primary end, and the prohibition of direct sterilization" constituted "a universal pattern" in the church's teaching that indicated not only irreformability, but infallibility.[30] John Ford, an American Jesuit, concurred with Zalba's judgment: "We stand before a practically uninterrupted tradition. . . . This prescription [against contraception] is in full force now as it was before, and so it will be tomorrow and forever, because it is not a mere human enactment but the expression of a natural and divine law."[31]

Several theologians, however, disagreed with Zalba's and Ford's conclusions. Philippe Delhaye, a moral theologian at the University of Lisle, maintained that moral issues are not the subject matter of unchangeable judgments; they presuppose malleable cultural and social contexts, which, if changed, might alter the liceity of particular actions. Taking interest on a loan, Delhaye pointed out, was condemned by three ecumenical councils and several popes. Today, on the contrary, it is accepted by the church without reservation as a normal and legitimate business practice.[32] Michel Labourdette, a French Dominican, argued similarly: "A document concerning very precise moral conduct loses its force because it presupposes situations in which many of the elements have changed. . . . Did not Pius XII already start an evolution? His acceptance of regulating births and his approval of periodic continence already strike a new note."[33] Häring pressed Zalba and Ford on different grounds, arguing that irreformability and infallibility pertain only to matters contained in divine revelation, not to interpretations of natural law.[34]

Fuchs surprised many by stating the doctrine is reformable. But he immediately added a caveat: "Declaring these statements 'reformable' does not make them uncertain. . . . Theologians cannot simply abandon them until they have good reason to do so."[35] At this point, Fuchs did not believe that persuasive evidence had been offered to justify changing the church's teaching on contraception, nor did he think that sufficient reasons had been raised to place received teaching under the probabilistic adage "a doubtful law does not oblige."[36] In Fuchs's mind, the church's position on contraception was still valid and obligatory; but unbeknownst to the other commission members, Fuchs was privately struggling with the contraception issue. As he would reveal later, he had already begun to question the church's teaching on contraception, and his growing doubt would not only cause him to stop teaching at the Gregorian University during the 1965–66 academic year because he refused to teach a doctrine about which he was ambivalent, but it would prompt him in 1965 to request that his manual on sexuality, which upheld received teaching on contraception, not be reprinted.[37] By 1965, then, Fuchs's position on contraception was in flux; his doubts were of sufficient magnitude to affect his professional undertakings, but they were not sufficient enough to warrant a public acknowledgement that received teaching on contraception should be revised. A year later, however, his nascent doubts would lead to a thorough intellectual conversion, prompted greatly by the testimony he was about to hear from Catholic married couples who had struggled with the rhythm method and found it wanting.

During the latter part of the fourth meeting, Patrick and Patricia Crowley, founders of the Christian Family Movement (CFM), an international organization created to foster lay participation in the church, presented correspondence they had received from members throughout North America in response to queries on the rhythm method, copies of which were distributed to commission members. Although the survey did not purport to be "scientific," its affect on commission members was substantial.[38] CFM members were not run-of-the-mill Catholics; all attended small-group meetings every other week, and their goal of implementing Catholic social teaching in their respective communities led many to active participation in politics, grassroots organizing, local parishes, and direct aid to the poor. The respondents, in short, were committed Catholics and respected leaders in their communities whose faith was an impelling force in their lives. Their responses to the Crowleys' questionnaire were, for the most part, highly negative. Summarizing the results to the entire commission, Patrick Crowley stated that he and Patricia "have been shocked into a realization that even the most dedicated, committed Catholics are deeply troubled by this problem [of the rhythm method]. We have gathered hundreds of statements from many parts of the Unites States and Canada and have been overwhelmed by the strong consensus in favor of change."[39] One couple, for example, married thirteen years with six children, pointedly relayed their struggles with the rhythm method. The husband wrote,

> Rhythm destroys the meaning of the sex act: it turns it from a spontaneous expression of spiritual and physical love into a mere bodily sexual relief; it makes me obsessed with sex throughout the month; it seriously endangers my chastity; it has a noticeable effect upon my disposition toward my wife and children; it makes necessary my complete avoidance of all affection toward my wife for three weeks at a time. I have watched a magnificent spiritual and physical union dissipate and, due to rhythm, turn into a tense and mutually damaging relationship. Rhythm seems to be immoral and deeply unnatural.[40]

His wife offered a similar assessment:

> My doctor advised me, recommended the basal temperature combined with the calendar method, and was constantly consulted. The psychological problems worsened, however, as we had baby

after baby. We eventually had to resort to a three-week abstinence and since then (three years) we have had no pregnancy. I find myself sullen and resentful of my husband when the time for sexual relations finally arrives. I resent his necessarily guarded affection during the month and I find I cannot respond suddenly. I find, also, that my subconscious dreams and unguarded thoughts are inevitably sexual and time consuming. All this in spite of a great intellectual and emotional companionship and a generally beautiful marriage and home life.[41]

Of course, not all respondents evaluated the rhythm method so negatively. Some stated that periodic abstinence increased self-control and helped them discover other ways to express intimacy. Some expressed stoic resignation: the rhythm method might involve struggles, but acting rightly sometimes requires sacrifices. Others, preferring a chemical- and hormonal-free method of birth control, found the rhythm method the best available option overall. But these positive replies were in the minority. The pattern emerging from the Crowley survey was that the rhythm method, although relatively successful if practiced carefully, had many undesirable side effects that deleteriously affected numerous aspects of their marital and family lives.

In addition to the Crowley survey, Fuchs was also exposed to the practical effects of the rhythm method by John Marshall, a British neurologist, original commission member, and recognized expert on the rhythm method. Fuchs and Marshall became close friends during the commission, taking walks together during breaks and frequently socializing after-hours at a local pub. For years, while working for the London-based Catholic Marriage Advisory Council, Marshall conducted studies attempting scientifically to validate the rhythm method's effectiveness. After the discovery of the new basal temperature method,[42] Marshall conducted a pioneering study of the improved method on the predominantly Catholic population on the Isle of Maritius. Overall, the results were fairly encouraging. As Marshall described the new method, "It certainly was not the Vatican roulette its critics claimed, nor was it as good as its enthusiasts would have wanted it to be."[43] But Marshall was unconvinced that the rhythm method should be the sole morally permissible option available to married couples to regulate births.[44] During their walks and nocturnal visits to the pub, Marshall explained to Fuchs that the rhythm method proved to be unsatisfactory for some married couples either because of medical conditions that might be physically debilitating or perhaps even life-threatening if pregnancy occurred, or because abstinence during the fertile period was difficult and caused tension between spouses.

The fifth and final session of the commission was markedly different from the previous meetings. The first four sessions were brief three or four day events; nearly two months were allotted for the final session. Pope Paul also appointed sixteen new bishops, including seven cardinals, and instituted an important procedural change: the bishops alone would now speak for the commission and report directly to the pope; all other participants formally lost their membership and were designated as *periti* to the committee of bishops. Pope Paul, it seems, was concerned with the commission's trajectory and desired an intermediate buffer zone—the bishops' committee—to temper its recommendations.[45]

The final session has been described as "the rise of the laity." With the exception of the Crowleys' presentation, the lay members were a relatively silent group, offering comments and suggestions only infrequently. In an attempt to gather the laity's insights on marriage and contraception, the chair of the commission, Henri de Riedmatten, a Vatican observer at the United Nations, scheduled a pastoral week intended to spotlight the laity, especially the women. Anticipating such an opportunity, the Crowleys undertook a more extensive survey of CFM members and with the help of the University of Notre Dame sociology department prepared a more scholarly examination of the rhythm method's effects. Their twenty-three page report, summarizing the replies of approximately 3,000 CFM couples in eighteen countries, was circulated to all commission members. The results were similar to those of the last survey: if practiced judiciously, the rhythm method worked reasonably well at regulating births; but for the vast majority of couples, the costs incurred by using the rhythm method were considerably high. On the positive side, 64 percent found the rhythm method helpful to their marriage in some way, 43 percent said it was helpful in spacing children, and 21 percent found it partly helpful. However, a large group, 78 percent, claimed that the rhythm method harmed their marital relationship because of sexual strain and tension, irritability, loss of spontaneity, fear of pregnancy, arguments, or insecurity, and 28 percent found it absolutely unhelpful.[46] After presenting these statistical findings, Patricia Crowley implored the commission to recommend that contraception be deemed a morally permissible method of birth control:

> We think it is time that this Commission recommend that the sacredness of conjugal love not be violated by thermometers and calendars. Marital union does lead to fruitfulness, psychologically as well as physically. Couples want children and will have them generously and love them and cherish them. We do not need the

impetus of legislation to procreate. It is the very instinct of life, love and sexuality. . . .

We sincerely hope and do respectfully recommend that this commission redefine the moral imperatives of fertility regulation with a view toward bringing them into conformity with our new and improved understanding of men and women in today's world.[47]

Colette Potvin, who operated a rhythm method clinic in Ottawa, Canada with her husband, argued that the commission should reject the traditional focus on the act of marital intercourse and begin concentrating on creating healthy marriages and families: "The physiological integrity of the conjugal act is less important than the repercussions of that love on the couple and on their family." Periodic abstinence, she continued,

> can have a positive value if it is agreed on by both husband and wife for the good of one or the other and if it doesn't upset the tranquility of the family. But if it impedes the couple from living a serene, intimate conjugal life, one has to question its value and its effects. Must we sacrifice the psychological benefits of marital relations in order to preserve the biological integrity of an act? Is that a human way to act? Is it Christian? . . . [The church's teaching on contraception] should be adjusted to take into account the good of marriage, the good of the couple, the good of the children and of the whole family community.[48]

Most of the theologians found the married couples' arguments persuasive and were convinced that received teaching on contraception needed to be changed. But the theologians were far from unanimous in their recommendations. A small, but vocal, minority upheld *Casti Connubii* and regarded any use of contraceptives as morally illicit. After several weeks of debate—and a vote among the theologians which affirmed by a 15–4 margin that *Casti Connubii* was reformable and that artificial contraception was not an intrinsically evil violation of natural law[49]—the time arrived to draft a final document representing the commission's definitive recommendation to Pope Paul.

The process of drafting a final document produced three papers, two of which are discussed below. The first, commonly called the "Minority Report," was written by John Ford and Germain Grisez, a young professor of philosophy at Georgetown University. By all accounts, Ford was extremely agitated by the commission's growing consensus to reverse the church's ban on contraception. In a final effort to sway the commission to uphold received teaching, Ford had Grisez flown to Rome where the two labored day and night for more than a week on a passionate and aggressive document defending *Casti Connubii*. Their 9,000-word treatise,[50] which was unsolicited by the commission, was submitted to de Riedmatten on May 23.

Three days later the so-called "Majority Report,"[51] authored primarily by Fuchs with the help of five other moral theologians[52] and representing the position of the commission's majority, was submitted to de Riedmatten. After minor adjustments and eventual approval by the bishops' committee, the "Majority Report" was submitted to Pope Paul as the commission's definitive recommendation on birth control.

After reading Ford's paper, de Riedmatten asked Fuchs, Raymond Sigmond, and Philippe Delhaye to prepare a response to the particular issues raised by Ford. By May 28 their rebuttal was completed and was approved by a majority of moral theologians.[53]

The Beginnings of Change: Natural Law in the Commission Documents

The "Majority Rebuttal" and "Majority Report" reveal clear and definite breaks not only from Fuchs's earlier understanding of natural law in the spheres of sexuality and contraception, but from his overall conception of natural law as well. Perhaps the most apparent and far-reaching change pertained to the meaning and function of "nature." For the first time Fuchs began to distinguish between "nature" (which Fuchs also calls "material nature" or "physical nature" in the two commission documents) and "human nature" (also called "rational nature" and "personal nature"). In his preconversion writings, he used these terms interchangeably, sometimes several times in the same paragraph.[54] The ramifications of this newly articulated distinction, however, were not simply terminological. Fuchs's underlying intention in differentiating nature from human nature was to undermine the functional equivalence they assumed in his earlier works—more precisely—to reevaluate the status of nature in natural law deliberation. Prior to his conversion, nature and human nature occupied identical roles in his natural law theory: both were considered proximate sources of natural law, conduits untarnished by original sin through which the divine essence and will were known, and the standards by which the liceity of all actions were judged. On the specific issue of nature's role in determining the rightness of sexual acts, for example, Fuchs writes, "Nature, according to which the rectitude of an act is judged, is itself the essence of the faculty and act of sexuality, rationally conceived."[55] A more general statement in *Natural Law* attributes the same normative force to nature: "the reality which we call 'nature' . . . comes directly from the hands of God. God speaks through it and reveals himself in it. It bears his features and it is his image. How could it be otherwise since nature is the creature of God?"[56] In both the "Majority Rebuttal" and "Majority Report," however, the status attributed to nature in his earlier writings was directly repudiated. No longer was moral normativity established by perceiving the finalities inherent in nature, nor was nature regarded as the proximate manifestation of God's will. Fuchs now presented nature as raw material that must be shaped and perfected by humankind's intentional activity and intervention.[57]

> [T]he concept of natural law, as it is found in [the] traditional discussion of this question, is insufficient; for the gifts of nature are considered to be immediately the expression of the will of God, preventing man, also a creature of God, from being understood as called to receive material nature and to perfect its potentiality. Churchmen have been slower than the rest of the world in clearly seeing this as man's vocation. . . .
>
> But an unconditional respect for nature as it is in itself (as if nature in its physical existence were the expression of the will of God) pertains to a vision of man which sees something mysterious and sacred in nature, and because of this fears that any human intervention tends to destroy rather than perfect this very nature. . . .
>
> In the matter at hand, then, there is a certain change in the mind of contemporary man. He feels that he is more conformed to his rational nature, created by God with liberty and responsibility, when he uses his skill to intervene in the biological processes of nature so that he can achieve the ends of the institution of matrimony in the conditions of actual life, than if he would abandon himself to chance.[58]

A related and equally significant shift, especially evident in the "Majority Rebuttal," can be detected in Fuchs's identification of the proximate source of natural law. Although Fuchs severely undercut the moral import of nature, he did not directly undermine the normativity of human nature.[59] In the two commission documents, however, Fuchs displayed a growing ambivalence about human nature's status in natural law deliberation, and his identification of natural law's proximate ground often vacillates between human nature and right reason.[60] This incipient movement toward *recta ratio*, or right reason, as the foundation of natural law became much more pronounced in his early postconversion writings, particularly as Fuchs recast his theological anthropology to incorporate the insights of Karl Rahner's transcendental Thomism. Once this process was completed and Fuchs accepted Rahner's premises and theoretical framework, references to human nature in Fuchs's natural law theory become sparse and infrequent, whereas voluminous references can be found equating natural law with right reason. At this point, however, Fuchs's transition was incomplete; his discomfort with the traditional notion of human nature was apparent, yet his willingness to endorse right reason as natural law's proximate source was only partial.

Another notable departure from his preconversion natural law theory concerns epistemology; more precisely, the magisterium's epistemologically privileged position in grasping natural law. As we saw earlier, Fuchs accorded the magisterium superior insight in perceiving natural law for two reasons: the grace bestowed during episcopal ordination that allowed a bishop to penetrate the truths of natural law more easily than the nonordained; and the classic assistance of the Holy Spirit that created an almost insurmountable presumption "in favour of the word of the Church and against a personal conviction standing in opposition to this word."[61] In the "Majority Rebuttal," however, Fuchs disputed his earlier contention about the Holy Spirit's assistance and remained doubtful about the ability to predict beforehand with sufficient accuracy whom or how the Holy Spirit will guide: "[T]he criteria for discerning what the Spirit could or could not permit in the Church can scarcely be determined a priori. In point of fact we know that there have been errors in the teaching of the magisterium and of tradition."[62] Fuchs continued with an astonishing admonition: instead of submitting to the practical tendency of regarding the ordinary teachings of the magisterium as correct, we must begin to expect "that the non-infallible magisterium is sometimes mistaken."[63] More than thirty years after the pontifical commission an admission that the ordinary magisterium is "sometimes mistaken" might seem quite unremarkable. But for Fuchs, who just one year earlier presented the magisterium as a font of moral truth whose teachings on natural law must be accepted obediently, this statement was bold and provocative.

Fuchs's analysis of the specific issue of natural law and birth control also exhibited notable structural and conceptual shifts. Fuchs began with a rejoinder to John Ford, whose principal argument throughout the commission had been the constancy of received teaching which "from the beginning [of Christianity] up to the present decade" had condemned contraception.[64] Fuchs conceded the church's consistent condemnation of contraception, but he challenged Ford's conclusion that the church has no authority to alter prior ordinary teaching. As the church refined its understanding of natural law and applied it to the spheres of sexuality and birth control it has exhibited a willingness to develop its teaching, often in unprecedented ways. In the twentieth century alone the church's teaching on sexuality and birth has undergone two major revisions. First, the primary end of marital intercourse—procreation—championed by St. Augustine and dominant for nearly two millennia was supplemented by Pope Pius XI in *Casti Connubii* through the addition of a secondary end, the enhancement of conjugal love, which was affirmed by Pope Pius XII. Second, in his "Address to Italian Midwives," Pius XII, for the first time in the history of the Roman Catholic Church, explicitly accepted the rhythm method as a morally permissible means to regulate births.[65] These two developments in the church's teaching on sexuality and birth control in this century alone make manifest that the precedents established by prior teachings are not inviolable and do not preclude subsequent alterations. Indeed, as Fuchs wrote, the lesson learned from recent history is that the church's moral doctrine on sexual matters was evolving substantially: "With all this in mind, it becomes evident that the official teaching . . . has been evolving in recent decades, and that the position stated in the text of the encyclical *Casti Connubii* has not yet been found to be definitive."[66]

Another reason Fuchs mentioned to reject Ford's argument was the emergence of new data which renders obsolete the reasons on which prior teachings were based. Fuchs writes,

> The reasons in favour of this affirmation [of the use of contraception within marriage] are of several kinds: social changes in matrimony and the family, especially in the role of the woman; lowering of the infant mortality rate; new bodies of knowledge in biology, psychology, sexuality and demography; a changed estimation of the value and meaning of sexuality and of conjugal relations; most of all, a better grasp of the duty of man to humanize and to bring to greater perfection for the life of man what is given in nature. Then must be considered the sense of the faithful: according to it, condemnation of a couple to a long and often heroic abstinence as the means to regulate conception, cannot be founded on the truth.[67]

These new data, Fuchs asserts, raised pressing questions which received teaching has not addressed adequately, if at all. But more importantly, the mere fact that Fuchs appealed to such data as morally significant signaled yet another shift in his understanding of natural law and birth control. In his preconversion manual on sexuality, *De Castitate et Ordine Sexuali*, the norms Fuchs derived from his analysis of the natural order and applied to the issue of contraception pertained to absolute natural law, or the sphere of natural law comprised of metaphysical principles that were timeless and unvarying in content.[68] In many instances, these norms or principles were formal and did not specify materially what was permitted or forbidden. But this was not the case in the area of sexuality, which Fuchs claimed was replete with highly concrete, material moral norms which suffered no exception in any historical situation. As Fuchs wrote, because the biological reality of the human body and the finality of the sexual organs remained constant, "[t]he sexual order . . . is valid whether it is applied to man before or after original sin, with or without Christ. It is valid because the underlying reality is the same in every historical situation of man."[69] In the passage quoted from the "Majority Report," however, Fuchs made no appeal to unvarying metaphysical principles, nor did he exhibit concern for the finality of the sexual organs; instead, Fuchs was more preoccupied with empirical data arising from the physical and social sciences.

In addition, the "Majority Report" passage cited above illustrates an incipient shift in Fuchs's understanding of moral competency, which will be given much greater attention in his postconversion writings. Before his conversion, Fuchs displayed an outspoken skepticism toward the individual moral agent's ability to grasp natural law's demands concretely. Because of the epistemological privilege accorded to the magisterium, the principal, even exclusive, role of the individual moral agent was to apply received teaching in concrete situations. In the "Majority Report," however, Fuchs's reference to "the consensus of the faithful" explicitly acknowledged that the magisterium was not the exclusive source of moral knowledge and challenged his prior conception of the faithful as passive "listeners"[70] to received teaching who played a negligible role in discerning and articulating natural law's requirements.

At this point, Fuchs offers no substantive reasons for this apparent change of mind (Have the subjective impediments preventing individual moral agents from grasping natural law clearly and consistently been lessened or extinguished? Has the object of the Holy Spirit's assistance been transferred from the magisterium to the faithful? Has Fuchs detected a disjunction between moral norms proposed by the magisterium and concrete situations? Was every concrete situation, as the situationists asserted, unique, unrepeatable, and therefore incapable of being captured adequately by prefabricated moral norms?), but it was clear that for Fuchs moral competency was no longer the exclusive province of the magisterium and that the considered moral judgments of the faithful as a collective body must be accorded greater significance in natural law deliberation than they were previously.

Having overcome Ford's objection that the church does not possess the authority to alter its teaching on contraception, Fuchs outlined the reasons why natural law permits the use of contraceptives within marriage. Since the dawn of Christianity, Fuchs wrote, the church's teaching on sexuality has protected two fundamental values: the good of procreation, and the rectitude of marital intercourse. Throughout the centuries, however, many diverse expressions of these same fundamental values have emerged: some have insisted that marital intercourse is justified only by an intention to procreate; others have denied the use of the infertile period to regulate births; still others have linked the liceity of marital intercourse with a resolve to care for and educate all children conceived, and with the well-being of children already born. These manifold and qualitatively different concrete realizations of the same fundamental values, according to Fuchs, should not be understood as incompatible or contradictory positions. As the church has reflected on natural law and the meanings of marriage and sexuality in different theological and social contexts, it has interpreted and articulated natural law's contents "in expressions and formulas proper to the times,"[71] always seeking a more precise and accurate manner of incarnating the two fundamental values in particular contexts.

In twentieth-century Roman Catholic sexual morality, the magisterium's particular expression of the fundamental values of procreation and conjugal intercourse erected a conceptual boundary between the natural destination of the marital act and artificial methods of birth control designed to prevent conception, based on the belief that God's will was manifested through the natural finalities of the human body, in other words, the finality of the sexual organs. In Fuchs's mind, this distinction between the "natural" and "artificial" was outdated and erroneous and detracted from the more important issue of creating and nurturing "fruitful" marriages:

> The true opposition is not sought between some material conformity to the physiological processes of nature and some artificial intervention. For it is natural to man to put under human control what is given by physical nature. The opposition is really to be sought between one way of acting which is contraceptive and opposed to a generous fruitfulness, and another way which is an ordered relationship to responsible fruitfulness and which has a concern for education and all the essential, human and Christian values.[72]

Fuchs has essentially shifted the terms of the debate. Because "nature" was no longer a locus of moral normativity for Fuchs, contraceptive intervention, or the suspension of one's natural fecundity, was morally neutral. The principal question for Fuchs was, Does contraception promote a stable family life and a healthy marriage?[73]

Nevertheless, Fuchs also realized that the interests of one's own family cannot be the sole criterion by which the liceity of contraception was judged because individuals and families were also part of the larger human community and must contribute to its well-being, albeit in ways relative to particular talents and gifts. Fuchs, accordingly, presented a broad catalog of factors, resembling general points of consideration rather than precise criteria, which must be considered to determine the liceity of contraception. Quoting the Second Vatican Council's *Gaudium et Spes*, Fuchs wrote that couples should " 'thoughtfully take into account both their own welfare and that of their children. . . . For this accounting they will reckon with both the material and spiritual conditions of the times as well as of their state in life. Finally they will consult the interests of the family community, of temporal society, and of the Church herself' " in deciding which manner of birth control is most appropriate.[74]

These "objective criteria" represented a significant departure from Fuchs's preconversion natural law analysis of the liceity of contraception, which was preoccupied with the moral limits inherent in "nature." In contrast, the range of human goods that Fuchs now acknowledges explicitly or implicitly as relevant to the contraception issue have expanded to include the physical and psychological health of each spouse, the overall health of the marriage, the family's economic situation, the welfare of children already born, various communal responsibilities and commitments, professional aspirations, a couple's maturity and ability to raise children well, and tension and stress caused by fear of pregnancy.[75]

An even more important aspect of Fuchs's list of human goods relevant to the decision whether or not to use contraception was its concreteness. The liceity of contraception no longer depends on an abstract metaphysical analysis of natural finalities, which can be applied universally regardless of individual or social considerations, but on the manifold concrete circumstances of each couple. This raised a formidable epistemological problem for Fuchs's preconversion natural law theory: How can the magisterium teach authoritatively on the morality of contraception when it possesses limited or no knowledge of each couple's particular situation? Anticipating this question, Fuchs responded that "It is impossible to determine exhaustively by a general judgment and ahead of time for each individual case what these objective criteria will demand in the concrete situation of a couple."[76]

With this sentence, Fuchs offered a glimpse of the direction his natural law theory would take in his postconversion period as his notions of moral epistemology and moral competency undergo a thorough renovation. By insisting on the necessity of concrete knowledge in order to determine the liceity of a particular act or class of acts, not only has Fuchs placed the individual moral agent in an epistemologically privileged position, because the individual in the concrete situation occupies the best position to assess her responsibilities and commitments, the practical effects of her action, and the precise circumstances in which she must act, but he has also begun to shift the locus of moral competency from the magisterium to the individual moral agent. From this point forward, Fuchs's skepticism about the individual moral agent's ability to grasp natural law diminishes markedly, as does the unflinching confidence characterizing his portrayal of the magisterium's ability to interpret natural law correctly.

Thus, Fuchs's admonition that predetermined moral judgments about contraception's liceity have limited applicability in concrete situations was a strong assertion that sharply curtailed the magisterium's ability to propose concrete moral norms on the subject of contraception, and by implication on other subjects requiring knowledge of concrete circumstances; the competency to determine whether natural law permitted or forbade contraception now rested with the couples themselves, independently of any mediators. As Fuchs wrote, "since moral obligations can never be detailed in all their concrete particularities, the personal responsibility of each individual must always be called into play. This is even clearer today because of the complexity of modern life: the concrete moral norms to be followed must not be pushed to an extreme."[77]

Fuchs's expansive list of goods relevant to the issue of birth control, however, raises several practical questions: Which good (or goods) should be given priority? Is there a hierarchy among these goods? What are one's responsibilities to the local community, to state, country, and the worldwide human community, and to the church? How are conflicts among these goods to be adjudicated? Although Fuchs did not answer all these questions directly, he proposed a criterion to determine which type of birth control, whether total abstinence, the rhythm method, or some form of contraception, should be used. Fuchs wrote,

> every method of preventing conception—not excluding either periodic or absolute abstinence—carries with it some negative element of physical evil which the couple more or less seriously feels. This negative element of physical evil can arise under different aspects: account must be taken of the biological, hygienic and psychological aspects, and personal dignity of the spouses, and the possibility

of expressing sufficiently and aptly the interpersonal relation or conjugal love. The means to be chosen, where several are possible, is that which carries with it the least possible negative element, according to the concrete situation of the couple.[78]

In many ways, this criterion of choosing the method of birth control that minimizes the amount of physical evil raised more questions than it answers. What is the meaning of "physical evil"? Do physical evils comprise any lack of perfection which impedes human fulfillment? Does the notion of physical evil distinguish between those imperfections or limitations which rightly-ordered parents consider relevant to the birth control decision and those which immature, narcissistic, or greedy parents erroneously consider burdensome and intolerable? Is there a standard or measure by which physical evils can be assessed? How are the qualitatively different physical evils of each birth control option compared?

Because the object of the two commission documents was to determine permissible methods of birth control, not to develop a precise method of natural law reasoning, it would be unfair to expect Fuchs to address all these questions directly and in detail (which he does in several postconversion articles). Two insights are necessary for understanding Fuchs's incipient method of moral reasoning. First, once again the locus of moral deliberation was the respective couple's concrete circumstances. In my opinion, Fuchs's "turn to the concrete," which was prompted by his encounter with faithful and dedicated married couples during the commission who relayed in vivid detail the many struggles and setbacks they experienced in attempting to follow received teaching on birth control, was the impelling force behind the numerous shifts we have seen in Fuchs's natural law theory. From his epistemology, to the magisterium's role in interpreting natural law concretely, to his understanding of the locus of moral competency, to the function of the individual moral agent and her ability to grasp natural law, to the adequacy of prefabricated moral norms in concrete situations—all these substantive shifts in the conceptual foundation of Fuchs's natural law theory can be linked directly or indirectly to the pivotal insight that individual moral agents are best able to determine natural law's requirements in the concrete situation.

Second, Fuchs's "turn to the concrete" also signaled a revision of the moral theologian's role in natural law deliberation. Before his conversion, Fuchs presented the moral theologian as an intermediary between the magisterium and the individual moral agent whose functions were hermeneutic, adjudicatory, and constructive: hermeneutic, by interpreting the meaning and content of received teaching;

adjudicatory, by determining whether certain ambiguous situations or actions should be regulated by preestablished moral norms, and by rendering concrete moral judgments about particular individual cases; and constructive, by probing, testing, scrutinizing, revising, and expanding moral concepts and norms in order more accurately and cogently to render natural law's contents intelligible to the faithful.

In the two commission documents, however, the adjudicatory role was transferred from the moral theologian to the married couple in the concrete situation (at least on the issue of contraception); the spouses themselves considered the "objective criteria" in their circumstances and determined what natural law forbade or permitted in their particular case. As Fuchs said bluntly, the "objective criteria are to be applied by the couples."[79] Consistent with this reassignment of the adjudicatory role, Fuchs, as a moral theologian, refused to render a concrete moral judgment on the liceity of contraception and preferred instead to indicate the various goods and disvalues that were typically at stake in the birth control decision.

Indeed, throughout his postconversion writings Fuchs never offers any concrete directives on any practical moral issue; he lays the groundwork for dealing with practical matters by posing questions, ruminating on potentially relevant values, discussing cultural, social, and theological meanings and implications, exploring motivations and intentions, and erecting minimal (and usually formal) criteria which provide general guidance.[80] But Fuchs never encroaches into the domain of practical decision making, which he has placed firmly at the feet of the individual moral agent who possesses concrete, local knowledge unavailable to the moral theologian.

In Christian circles the term "conversion" connotes a sudden, dramatic, and often unanticipated about-face precipitated by an event so existentially compelling that the trajectory of one's life is forever altered. Conversion conjures up images of St. Paul being struck by lightning while riding his horse, hearing God's reproving voice, and being transformed from an ardent persecutor of Christians to a zealous promoter of Christianity, walking several thousand miles on his missionary journeys through forbidding and dangerous territory to spread the Gospel; of an anguished and divided St. Augustine sitting under a fig tree, reading a scripture passage condemning his former lifestyle, and feeling "a peaceful light streaming into [his] heart" which eradicated "all the dark shadows of doubt";[81] of St. Ignatius, a self-admitted gambler, dueler, and womanizer, reading *The Life of Christ* and collections of the lives of the saints during his lengthy convalescence in his family's castle, which prompted him to repudiate his misbegotten ways and to write his famous *Spiritual Exercises*; and of St. Francis of Assisi, the privileged son of wealthy merchants whose vision of Christ crucified impelled him to renounce his inheritance and his adherence to the ideals of medieval chivalry, which he did dramatically by stripping naked publicly and announcing his dedication to a life of extreme poverty and service to others.

Although Fuchs's intellectual conversion involved no divine allocutions, dramatic public gestures, or decisive moments of emotional relief and consolation, it shared with the aforementioned conversions a common trait: a radical, substantive, enduring, and patently detectable reorientation. In *Natural Law* (1965), Fuchs typified traditional Roman Catholic natural law theory dominated by the neo-Thomist manualists: nature and human nature, being created directly by God and remaining immune from the pernicious effects of original sin, revealed God's nature and will to humankind and constituted the proximate source of natural law; universal moral norms were derived from the natural order specifying concretely, and often in great detail, what natural law permitted and forbade; the magisterium, as the focus of the Holy Spirit's assistance, had privileged insight into natural law's contents and must be acknowledged as the authentic interpreter of natural law by the faithful; the moral theologian served as an intermediary between the magisterium and the faithful, interpreting papal teaching and deciding individual cases; and the individual moral agent's role was limited to shaping one's conscience according to the magisterium's teaching and applying it in concrete situations.

One year later all these positions had changed: the moral normativity of nature was explicitly and forcefully denied, and the status of human nature remained unclear; the preoccupation with the universal had given way to a concern for particular persons and their manifold concrete circumstances; the magisterium's epistemologically privileged position had been transferred to the individual moral agent; the moral theologian's role as practical decision maker for the faithful was undercut; and the individual moral agent now assumed the greatly expanded role of determining natural law's contents in particular situations.

Such pervasive and substantive changes throughout the foundation of Fuchs's natural law theory cannot be captured adequately by the popular term "development" with its implication of continuity through change. Fuchs, of course, never denied the existence or validity of natural law; to this extent his natural law theory exhibits continuity. Nevertheless, the defining characteristic of Fuchs's natural law theory during the papal birth control commission is discontinuity; from theological foundations to substantive content to practical conclusions, few aspects of Fuchs's natural law theory remained unchanged.

This chapter has outlined the numerous shifts occurring in Fuchs's natural law theory during the papal birth control commission, but has not critically assessed their merits or validity. Fuchs expanded and refined the insights acquired during the papal birth control commission and began to formulate a more comprehensive account of his postconversion understanding of natural law. Thus, our analysis will now move beyond simple reconstruction to a more detailed critique of his mature natural law theory in order to determine whether Fuchs has produced a natural law theory serviceable for use within Roman Catholic moral theology. We begin by isolating and developing Fuchs's reformulated theological anthropology, which he began constructing immediately after his conversion.

Notes

1. James F. Keenan, "Josef Fuchs and the Question of Moral Objectivity in Roman Catholic Reasoning," *Religious Studies Review* 24 (1998), 254; Timothy E. O'Connell, "Changing Roman Catholic Moral Theology: A Study in Josef Fuchs," (Ph.D. diss., Fordham University, 1974), 81–86; Ronald Amos Mercier, "What Is Nature? The Development of Josef Fuchs' Thought on Moral Normativity," (Ph.D. diss., Regis College, 1993), 120–22; Russell Hittinger, *A Critique of the New Natural Law Theory* (Notre Dame, Ind.: University of Notre Dame Press, 1997), 18; and Cristina L. H. Traina, *Feminist Ethics and Natural Law* (Washington, D.C.: Georgetown University Press, 1999), 169–95, esp. 178–83.

2. Robert Blair Kaiser, *The Encyclical That Never Was: The Story of the Pontifical Commission on Population, Family, and Birth, 1964–66* (London: Sheed and Ward. 1987), 206.

3. Ibid., 206–7.

4. John T. Noonan, *Contraception: A History of Its Treatment by the Catholic Theologians and Canonists* (Cambridge, Mass.: Harvard University Press, 1965), 407.

5. Ibid., 406–7.

6. Ibid., 407.

7. Ibid., 409.

8. For example, in the aftermath of the Franco-Prussian war, the Swiss cardinal, Gaspar Mermillod, chastised the French people during an address on Bastille Day: "You have rejected God, and God has struck you. You have, by hideous calculation, made tombs instead of filling cradles with children; therefore you have wanted for soldiers" (quoted in ibid., 414).

9. *The Lambeth Conference*, 1930, resolution 15, quoted in ibid., 409.

10. Ibid.

11. Pope Pius XI, *Casti Connubii*, in *The Papal Encyclicals 1903–39*, (1930; reprint, Raleigh, N.C.: McGrath Publishing, 1981), #3.

12. Ibid., #56.

13. Ibid.

14. Ibid., #54.

15. The original members of the papal birth control commission were Stanislas de Lestapis, Henri de Reidmatten, Clement Mertens, John Marshall, Pierre van Rossum, and Jacques Mertens de Wilmars. See Kaiser, *Encyclical That Never Was*, 72; Robert McClory, *Turning Point* (New York: Crossroad, 1995), 41; Philip S. Kaufman, *Why You Can Disagree and Remain a Faithful Catholic* (New York: Crossroad, 1995), 53; and Pierre de Locht, *Les Couples et l'Eglise* (Paris: Centurion, 1975), 123.

16. McClory, *Turning Point*, 41–43.

17. Quoted in ibid., 43. For Marshall's account of the commission's proceedings, see John Marshall, "Inside the Commission," *Tablet* (24 July 1993): 938–39; John Marshall, "The Door that Closed," *Tablet* (23 July 1988): 835–37; and John Marshall, "The Council and the Commission," *Tablet* (21 September 1968): 933–34.

18. The sociologists were Thomas Burch and Bernard Colombo, and the moral theologians were Josef Fuchs, Bernard Häring, Jan Visser, Marcellinus Zalba, and Pierre de Locht. See Kaiser, *Encyclical That Never Was*, 72; McClory, *Turning Point*, 47; and de Locht, *Les Couples et l'Eglise*, 125.

19. Kaiser, *Encyclical That Never Was*, 122; and McClory, *Turning Point*, 49.

20. Josef Fuchs, "Die Ehezwecklehre des h. Thomas von Aquin," *Theologische Quartalschrift* 128 (1948): 398–426; Josef Fuchs, "Vom Sinn der Ehe," *Trierer Theologische Zeitschrift* 58 (1949): 65–75; Josef Fuchs, "Elterliche Verantwortung für das kommende Geschlecht," *Scholastik* 26 (1951): 222–43; and Josef Fuchs, "Ehelehre der Kirche und Eheleben der Christen," *Die neue Ordnung* 5 (1952): 413–17.

21. Kaiser, *Encyclical That Never Was*, 73.

22. Ibid.

23 For Häring's account of the commission's proceedings, see Bernard Häring, *My Witness for the Church,* trans. Leonard Swidler (Mahwah, N.J.: Paulist Press, 1992), 70–80.

24. Kaiser, *Encyclical That Never Was,* 73. The particular contraceptive causing considerable controversy at that time was the birth control pill, which was first marketed commercially in the early 1950s. For moral analyses of the birth control pill, see John C. Ford and Gerald Kelly, *Contemporary Moral Theology,* 2 vols. (Cork, Ireland: Mercier Press, 1958–64), 2: 338–77; M. Thiéffry, "Stérilization hormonale et morale chrétienne," *Nouvelle Revue Théologique* 83 (1961): 135–58; Klaus Demmer, "Die Moraltheologische Diskussion um die Anwendung Sterilisierender Medikamente: Versuch einer Übersicht," *Theologie und Glaube* 53 (1963): 415–35; and Marcellinus Zalba, "Casus de usu artificii contraceptivi," *Periodica de Re Canonica, Morali, et Liturgica* 51 (1962): 167–92.

25. McClory, *Turning Point*, 49.

26. Ibid., 53. See also de Locht, *Les Couples et l'Eglise*, 130.

27. Norman St. John-Stevas, *The Agonizing Choice* (London: Eyre and Spottiswoode, 1971), 116–17.

28. Kaiser, *Encyclical That Never Was,* 86; and McClory, *Turning Point,* 54.

29. McClory, *Turning Point,* 62.

30. Marcellinus Zalba, quoted in ibid., 70.

31. John Ford, quoted in ibid., 70.

32. Kaiser, *Encyclical That Never Was,* 126.

33. Michel Labourdette, quoted in McClory, *Turning Point,* 70.

34. Ibid.

35. Josef Fuchs, quoted in Kaiser, *Encyclical That Never Was,* 126.

36. Ibid.

37. Ibid., 206.

38. McClory, *Turning Point,* 72, 74.

39. Patrick and Patricia Crowley, quoted in ibid., 72.

40. Anonymous, quoted in Kaiser, *Encyclical That Never Was,* 129–30.

41. Ibid., 130.

42. The meaning of the phrase "rhythm method" has undergone significant evolution in the past forty years. Technically speaking, the "calendar method" would have been a more accurate phrase to describe the original rhythm method, which proved to be highly unreliable because it was premised on a regular twenty-eight–day menstrual cycle, which many women, in fact, did not experience. The "temperature method," which involves taking a woman's basal temperature upon awakening, is a much more precise indicator of a woman's fertile period, particularly for women with irregular menstrual cycles. Over the years, the rhythm method's effectiveness has been improved through the discovery of other factors indicating potential fertility: the texture and color of cervical mucus, bloody discharge between menstrual periods, and cervical position.

43. John Marshall, quoted in McClory, *Turning Point,* 39.

44. Kaiser, *Encyclical That Never Was,* 129.

45. Jan Grootaers, "The Papal Commission," in *On Human Life,* ed. Peter Harris (London: Burns and Oates, 1968), 162–63.

46. McClory, *Turning Point,* 89.

47. Patricia Crowley, quoted in ibid., 105.

48. Colette Potvin, quoted in ibid., 106.

49. Ibid., 99.

50. John C. Ford et al., "The Birth Control Report II: The Conservative Case," *Tablet* (29 April 1967): 478–85.

51. All citations referring to the Majority Report are taken from Kaiser, *Encyclical That Never Was,* 3–18.

52. The other coauthors of the Majority Report were Pierre de Locht, Michel Labourdette, Raymond Sigmond, Alfons Auer, and Paul Anciaux.

53. Josef Fuchs, Philippe Delhaye, and Raymond Sigmond, "The Argument for Reform," *Tablet* (6 May 1967): 510–13.

54. See, for example, Josef Fuchs, *Natural Law: A Theological Investigation,* trans. Helmut Recker and John Dowling (New York: Sheed and Ward, 1965), 59–60.

55. Josef Fuchs, *De Castitate et Ordine Sexuali* (Rome: Pontificia Universitatis Gregoriana, 1959), 31.

56. Fuchs, *Natural Law*, 60.

57. Beginning in the early 1960s, other reputable moral theologians began to question the meaning and normativity of "nature" as it functioned in official condemnations of artificial contraception. See Louis Janssens, "Morale conjugale et progestogènes," *Ephemerides Theologicae Lovanienses* 34 (1963): 787–826; and Josef M. Reuss, "Eheliche Hingabe und Zeugung: Ein Diskussionsbeitrag zu Einem differenzierten Problem," *Theologische Quartalschrift* 143 (1963): 454–67, for important discussions of this issue.

58. Fuchs, Delhaye, and Sigmond, "Argument for Reform," 511. Similarly, in the commission's final report, Fuchs writes, "It is proper to man, created in the image of God, to use what is given in physical nature in a way that he may develop it to its full significance with a view to the good of the whole person. This is the cultural mission which the Creator has commissioned to men, whom he had made his co-operators" (Josef Fuchs et al., "Final Report of the Pontifical Commission on Population, Family, and Birth," in *The Encyclical That Never Was* by Robert Blair Kaiser, [1967; London: Sheed and Ward, 1987], 8).

59. Shortly after the papal birth control commission, several moral theologians, especially German moral theologians, followed Fuchs's lead in distinguishing the general concept of nature from human nature. See the essays in Franz Böckle, ed., *Das Naturrecht im Disput* (Düsseldorf, Germany: Patmos, 1966); and Franz Böckle and Ernst Wolfgang Böckenforde, eds., *Naturrecht in der Kritik* (Mainz, Germany: Matthias-Grunewald, 1973).

60. See, for example, the "Argument for Reform," where Fuchs writes, "[T]he dominion of God is exercised through man, who can use nature for his own perfection according to the dictates of *right reason*. . . . The decision about the manner of intervention [in nature] therefore must be formulated according to the finalities which can be discovered from *human nature*" (Fuchs, Delhaye, and Sigmond, "Argument for Reform," 512; emphasis added).

61. Fuchs, *Natural Law*, 159.

62. Fuchs, Delhaye, and Sigmond, "Argument for Reform," 511.

63. Ibid.

64. See Ford et al., "Birth Control Report II," 479.

65. Fuchs, Delhaye, and Sigmond, "Argument for Reform," 511.

66. Ibid.

67. Fuchs et al., "Final Report of the Pontifical Commission," 10. See also Fuchs, Delhaye, and Sigmond, "Argument for Reform," 511.

68. Josef Fuchs, *De Castitate et Ordine Sexuali*, 40–42.

69. Fuchs, *Natural Law*, 91.

70. Ibid., 3, 150–62.

71. Fuchs et al., "Final Report of the Pontifical Commission," 9.

72. Ibid., 11.

73. Fuchs, Delhaye, and Sigmond, "Argument for Reform," 513; and Fuchs et al., "Final Report of the Pontifical Commission," 8.

74. Fuchs et al., "Final Report of the Pontifical Commission," 12. It should be noted that the Second Vatican Council took no formal position on the liceity of contraception, in deference to Pope Paul's request that he and his birth control commission settle this issue. The council fathers simply asserted that the faithful "are forbidden to use methods disapproved of by the teaching authority of the Church in its interpretation of the divine law" (*Gaudium et Spes* #51 in Austin Flannery, ed., *The Conciliar and Post Conciliar Documents: Vatican Council II*, vol. 1, rev. ed. [Northport, N.Y.: Costello, 1988]).

75. Fuchs et al., "Final Report of the Pontifical Commission," 12; and Fuchs, Delhaye, and Sigmond, "Argument for Reform," 513.

76. Fuchs et al., "Final Report of the Pontifical Commission," 12. See also Fuchs, Delhaye, and Sigmond, "Argument for Reform," 512 where Fuchs writes, "But it is up to them [spouses] to determine, in view of their personal and social situation, how to achieve this purpose of marriage, and how to bring about a perfect balance between conjugal love and harmonious fecundity."

77. Fuchs et al., "Final Report of the Pontifical Commission," 4.

78. Ibid., 13.

79. Ibid., 12.

80. See, for example, Josef Fuchs, *Christian Morality: The Word Becomes Flesh*, trans. Brian McNeil (Washington, D.C.: Georgetown University Press, 1987), 62–82 and 189–201.

81. St. Augustine, *The Confessions of St. Augustine*, trans. John K. Ryan (New York: Doubleday, 1960), 202.

PART II

THE POSTCONVERSION PERIOD
(1966 – Present)

The preconversion Fuchs's task as a moral theologian was well-defined and abundantly clear in his writings: to articulate, clarify, refine, extend, and defend received teaching on natural law. By the time Fuchs began writing on natural law in the late 1940s, the Thomistic revival begun by Pope Leo XIII in the late 1800s had succeeded in placing natural law deliberation at the forefront of Roman Catholic moral theology.[1] In the hands of Pope Leo and his early to mid–twentieth-century successors, natural law became the principal conceptual tool to address a host of practical political, economic, social, and sexual issues through an increasingly voluminous body of encyclicals and addresses.[2] The neo-Thomist manualists further solidified the emerging natural law discourse by incorporating it extensively into their popular manuals of moral theology.[3] Thus by the mid-twentieth century, a relatively settled body of natural law doctrine had developed, which had received official ecclesiastical approval from the highest offices and had garnered widespread allegiance among the majority of the most respected Roman Catholic moralists.

Until his service on the papal birth control commission, Fuchs regarded the main tenets of this received tradition on natural law as embodiments of moral truth. Although Fuchs was certainly willing to voice disagreement on more peripheral matters, his assent to the core claims of the tradition on issues of metaphysics, the role and function of "nature," the validity of universal moral norms, the magisterium's competency in interpreting natural law, and the moral agent's role in applying received teaching was unflagging. Given Fuchs's intellectual concurrence with the received natural law tradition, his writings exhibited strong constructive and defensive tendencies. On the constructive side, Fuchs did what any theologian attempting to build a positive, thorough, and credible case for an idea would do: attend to foundational philosophical and theological matters, demonstrate the internal coherence and compatibility of concepts, show how the idea offers an adequate explanatory account of important phenomena, and outline the practical implications of the theory. Thus, in his constructive mode, Fuchs focused on solidifying and making intellectually credible the substantive edifice of received teaching on natural law, while also showing how such teaching could legitimately be applied and extended to a host of moral issues.

Fuchs's defensive tendency, shown most clearly during the situation ethics controversy in Europe, also functioned as a constructive moment in his writings. Although one of Fuchs's objectives was to demonstrate the errors of various Protestant moralists, Fuchs did not simply attempt to undermine their positions but indicated how his understanding of natural law offered a better account of certain disputed points. Thus amidst the polemical atmosphere of the situation ethics debate, Fuchs was simultaneously erecting further elements of his natural law theory by addressing specific concerns of situationists and showing how natural law, correctly understood, offered a comparative advantage on certain critical points.

Although the postconversion Fuchs exhibits the same constructive tendency to put forth a positive, substantive case for natural law and to defend his version of natural law against its detractors, there emerges in his writings a vibrant and sharply focussed deconstructionism. In Fuchs's writings during the papal birth control commission, this incipient deconstructionism first became evident when he reconsidered and effectively denied what were then regarded in the Roman Catholic academic community as indisputable truths concerning "nature," the magisterium's competency to interpret natural law (at least on certain issues), the ability to apply moral principles in concrete situations to attain moral objectivity, and the moral agent's role in natural law deliberation. Of course, an isolated pattern of denial does not constitute a deconstructionist inclination; for this a more sustained and systematic effort is needed.

Although Fuchs's deconstructionism is certainly not as unrelenting as Jacques Derrida's or any of his followers, it is important enough to warrant notice. As one of Fuchs's former students said, on certain issues the postconversion Fuchs is comparable to a bulldozer, methodically dismantling a structure and leveling the ground to make way for something else.[4] This is an apt metaphor for the postconversion Fuchs, whose particular stripe of deconstructionism is not intended to breed widespread, pervasive doubt, but only to undercut forcefully a few isolated, yet highly entrenched, ideas in Roman Catholic natural law theory.

I mention these tendencies in the postconversion Fuchs partly for interpretative clarity, but mostly to note the persistent tension engendered by these apparently opposite trajectories, sometimes even in the same article. In his deconstructionist mode, Fuchs's agenda is essentially negative: to discredit certain positions or ideas by exposing erroneous presuppositions, theological inadequacies, internal inconsistencies, or doubtful practical conclusions about right and wrong behavior.

Fuchs's constructive moments, on the other hand, differ in substance from similar moments in his preconversion writings. Probably the most marked shift in Fuchs's constructive endeavors is the appearance of a strong hermeneutical urge to attend closely to the meaning attached to pivotal moral terms and concepts, and to provide a more nuanced and subtle contextualism that acknowledges the importance of concrete embeddedness and relationship to other persons, religion, family, culture, economic arrangements, political scenarios, and other realities influencing human self-understanding and the circumstances in which we live and act. Similar to Klaus Demmer, whose writings typify the hermeneutical approach in contemporary moral theology,[5] Fuchs's constructive, hermeneutical thrust offers a careful, detailed account of the often multiple layers of meaning, commitments, and values relevant to the moral endeavor.

The remainder of this study will show a decided preference for Fuchs's constructive, hermeneutical aspects. Brief attention will be given to Fuchs's deconstructionist accomplishments, because some represent seminal contributions to Roman Catholic natural law theory by indicating positions that should be rejected. But because the principal objective of this study is to contribute positively to the ongoing attempt to formulate a natural law theory serviceable for use within Roman Catholic moral theology, the preponderance of energy will be devoted to outlining Fuchs's constructive contributions and offering an assessment of their validity and merit. I will begin with Fuchs's first constructive attempt to rehabilitate Roman Catholic natural law theory after his intellectual conversion by examining the subject to which he first turned: theological anthropology.

Notes

1. John A. Gallagher, *Time Past, Time Future: An Historical Study of Catholic Moral Theology* (Mahwah, N.J.: Paulist Press, 1990), 37–41

2. See, for instance, Pope Leo XIII, *Rerum Novarum*, in *The Papal Encyclicals, 1878–1903* (1891; reprint, Raleigh, N.C.: McGrath, 1981), #7–8; Pope Pius XI, *Quadragesimo Anno*, in *The Papal Encyclicals, 1903–39* (1931; reprint, Raleigh, N.C.: McGrath, 1981), #41–43; Pope Pius XI, *Casti Connubii*, in *The Papal Encyclicals, 1903–39* (1930; reprint, Raleigh, N.C.: McGrath, 1981), #54–56; and Pope Pius XII, *Humani Generis*, in *The Papal Encyclicals 1903–39* (1950; reprint, Raleigh, N.C.: McGrath, 1981), #2.

3. Francis Connell, *Outlines of Moral Theology* (Milwaukee, Wisc,: Bruce, 1953), 29–31; Antony Koch and Arthur Preuss, *A Handbook of Moral Theology*, 3d ed., 5 vols. (St. Louis, Mo.: B. Herder, 1925), 1: 122–26; Arthur Vermeersch, *Theologiae Moralis*, 3d ed., 3 vols. (Rome: Pontificia Universitatis Gregoriana, 1933), 1: 149–55; Henry Davis, *Moral and Pastoral Theology*, 7th ed., 4 vols. (London: Sheed and Ward, 1958), 1: 124–32; Aloysius Sabetti and Timothy Barrett, *Compendium Theologiae Moralis* (Rome: Frederick Pustet, 1916), 96–97; Thomas Slater, *A Manual of Moral Theology*, 3d ed., 2 vols. (New York: Benzinger Brothers, 1908), 1: 116–18; and H. Noldin and A. Schmitt, *Summa Theologiae Moralis*, 3 vols. (Innsbruck, Austria: Sumptis and Typic Feliciani Rauch, 1940), 1: 9–14.

4. James F. Keenan, personal communication with author, May 1994.

5. Klaus Demmer, *Sittlich handeln aus Verstehen: Strukturen hermeneutisch orientierter Fundamentalmoral* (Düsseldorf, Germany: Patmos, 1980); and Klaus Demmer, "Hermeneutische Probleme der Fundamentalmoral," in *Ethik im Kontext des Glaubens: Probleme—Grundsätz—Methoden,* ed. Francesco Campagnoni and Dietmar Mieth (Freiburg, Germany: Universitätsverlag,1978), 101–19.

4

Theological Anthropology and Natural Law

Although Fuchs had rejected much of the theoretical foundation of his preconversion natural law theory by the close of the papal birth control commission in 1966, one methodological presupposition remained constant: *agere sequitur esse* (action follows being).[1] From Thomas Aquinas to modern papal teaching to the twentieth-century neo-Thomist manualists, Roman Catholic natural law deliberation was inseparable from, and subsequent to, a theological anthropology that situated the human person cosmically in relation to God and other creatures, provided a meaningful theological context for understanding the natural inclinations and intrinsic powers present in the human person, and supplied a vision of goods constitutive of human perfection. Within this framework, natural law deliberation is a second-level order of inquiry the accuracy of which depends on the ability to understand the human person and to identify the moral demands consonant with her *esse*.

Given the methodological priority of theological anthropology in Roman Catholic natural law theory, it is not surprising that immediately after his conversion Fuchs focused his energy on reconstructing his theological anthropology. In a series of articles written between 1966 and 1968 Fuchs began appropriating Karl Rahner's conception of transcendental Thomism, particularly his notion of fundamental option, which allowed Fuchs to recast his understanding of natural law's soteriological import dramatically.[2] Following Fuchs's initial Rahnerian turn to the subject, and throughout the rest of his writing career, he continued to revise his theological anthropology by reconsidering the status of human nature in natural law deliberation, the historicity of human existence, emergent meanings of the "person" in contemporary moral theology, and the criterion of integral human flourishing and its significance for Roman Catholic natural law theory, all of which substantially departed from his preconversion theological anthropology.

The theological anthropology that emerges during Fuchs's postconversion period focuses on a person's transcendental, athematic relationship with God that determines a person's goodness or badness: no longer does it matter soteriologically what a person does, in other words, whether a person's actions conform to natural law, but the moral quality of her fundamental option. Fuchs also displays a decided preference for a "dynamic" interpretation of the human person, which views her as a malleable, continually evolving being capable of self-development and self-creation. Whereas before his conversion Fuchs frequently presented the constants of human nature as sufficient conditions for deriving practical directives for action, in his postconversion writings these constants are very few and are capable of supporting only the most general statements about right behavior. Finally, Fuchs's emergent personalism, which emphasizes the necessity of considering the good of the whole human person in the totality of her concrete circumstances, eschews the abstraction that characterized his preconversion anthropology.

Reconstructing Natural Law: Karl Rahner's Transcendental Thomism and the Emergence of the Acting Subject

In one of his earliest postconversion articles, Fuchs poses a startling question: [W]hat is the morality of my personal ego, over and above the morality of my various actions?"[3] For the preconversion Fuchs, this question was unintelligible; for within Fuchs's traditional act analysis, a person's moral standing was virtually coextensive with the morality of her acts. Of course, mitigating circumstances such as erroneous knowledge, fear, or coercion sometimes limited the degree to which a wrong action affected a person's moral standing, but this limited qualification in no way undermines the direct link Fuchs maintained between the rightness or wrongness of actions and personal morality.

Fuchs's ability to distinguish the person from her acts stems directly from his appropriation of Karl Rahner's theological anthropology. Rahner, like other notable transcendental Thomists, developed his theological anthropology by isolating, analyzing, and articulating the implications of the necessary conditions of human subjectivity, or the necessary, a priori modes of being constitutive of the human person.[4] What emerged from Rahner's "turn to the subject" was a conception of the human person that radically challenged the theological anthropology underlying traditional Roman Catholic natural law theory, particularly its notions of human freedom, human acts, and salvation.

The thrust of Fuchs's postconversion theological anthropology is to reconstruct the meaning of salvation—and by extension the soteriological import of natural law—by uncovering and articulating the implications of a dimension of freedom, "basic freedom"[5] as Fuchs calls it, previously overlooked in Roman Catholic moral theology. Fuchs maintains that there are two types of human freedom: freedom of choice and basic freedom.[6] Roman Catholic moral theology's preoccupation with acts and the subjective responsibility for acts has led to an almost exclusive focus on freedom of choice, which concerns the moral agent's ability to choose freely between two or more courses of action and the presence of certain internal or external impediments, such as fear, ignorance, or coercion, which limit or perhaps even preclude free choice. There is, however, another sphere of human freedom, basic freedom, which is concerned not with discrete acts, but with the human person as a whole.[7] Whereas the object of freedom of choice is some specific act, the object of basic freedom is the human person herself. As Karl Rahner writes, "freedom is first of all the subject's being responsible for himself, so that freedom in its fundamental nature has to do with the subject as such and as a whole. In [basic] freedom the subject always intends himself, understands and posits himself. Ultimately he does not do *something*, but does *himself*."[8]

As Rahner mentions, basic freedom pertains not only to the human person as subject, but to the subject "as a whole." What does this mean? All persons experience varying degrees of freedom in their lives and our capacity to act freely is contingent upon a multitude of factors, both internal and external, including self-knowledge, psychological stability, genetic inheritance, upbringing, cultural values, and the quality of moral imagination. Although these factors impinge directly, and sometimes decisively, on the practical ability to act freely, they do not directly affect basic freedom. In Fuchs's and Rahner's view, these instances of internal and external conditioning of freedom affect isolated and partial aspects of the human person. The human person, however, is never coextensive with the sum total of her various parts.[9] As a subject, the human person is always capable of reflecting on the various ways she is conditioned; she can identify and analyze her psychological processes, her degree of self-control, and the conceptions of the good life offered by family, friends, and society that she has accepted and internalized. Simply by reflecting on these conditioned aspects of her being, however, the human person reveals herself as a unified, self-conscious subject capable of encompassing and transcending the various components of her being. Stated in the first person, when I reflect on myself, explain aspects of myself, and analyze myself, the "I" performing these operations necessarily affirms itself as something more than, and prior to, any components being investigated. In this sense, the human person as a subject is present to and aware of

herself in her totality as a creature that cannot be reduced to, or identified with, isolated, regional elements of her being, or the sum total of
these elements.[10]

From Fuchs's understanding of the human person as a subject, an
important corollary follows. Because I am always necessarily more
than the sum total of my analyzable elements, basic freedom, which
refers to the person as a whole, remains unaffected by conditioning
occurring on other levels of my being. Psychology, sociology, genetics,
biology, physics, medicine, and all the other sciences might establish
various cause-effect relationships that determine in varying degrees
the way I think, act, and understand myself, but these partial explanations say nothing about my existence as a whole, unified subject.[11] In her
"original experience"[12] of basic freedom the human person experiences
herself as a whole as open, undetermined, being given-over to herself,
and responsible for the manner in which she actualizes herself.[13]

Through the exercise of basic freedom the human person disposes
of herself as a whole and establishes her fundamental option, which
Fuchs characterizes as an abiding disposition arising from the human
person's acceptance or rejection of God that determines her moral
standing before God. There are two important preliminary points to
note about Fuchs's conception of fundamental option. First, the theological import of fundamental option is derived not simply from its capacity to actualize the person as a whole, but from its capacity to actualize
the person as a whole before God.[14] In Fuchs's Rahnerian theological
anthropology, one of the existentials of human existence—one of the
necessary a priori modes of being constitutive of the human person—
is transcendence. As spiritual beings, all of our intentional activities
have an inherent dynamism toward God.[15] Human knowing reaches
beyond all limited objects and horizons in a perpetual search to grasp
the ultimate horizon of human knowing, God. The drive impelling our
willing and loving likewise is not satisfied by finite objects but strives
to embrace the infinite object, God.[16] From the most mundane, commonplace acts to one's fundamental option that disposes of the person as
a whole, there is an intentionality underlying all human activity that
seeks God, and through this intentionality the human person's attempts
at self-realization and self-commitment are always made before God
and in reference to God as the ultimate horizon of human existence.[17]

Second, every person, regardless of her explicit religious convictions, is aware of this transcendental intentionality toward God, in
other words, every person implicitly acknowledges God as the remote
term of all her actions and her attempts at self-realization even when
this is not admitted explicitly.[18] In Rahner's metaphysical epistemology, the condition of the possibility for human transcendence is "the

pre-apprehension (*Vorgriff*)[19] of infinite reality" through which every person—Christian, Muslim, atheist, or agnostic—knows God as Father, Son, and Holy Spirit.[20] For our purposes, the only aspect of Rahner's controversial *Vorgriff* we wish to highlight is the level of consciousness on which it occurs. According to Rahner and Fuchs, this awareness of God as the ultimate horizon of all reality does not occur on the level of conceptual or thematic consciousness, but on the level of nonconceptual, unthematic consciousness where the subject is present to herself as a whole. On this level of human consciousness, the human person knows the Triune God as both source and term of her striving and loving and the presence before which self-realization occurs.[21]

This distinction between thematic and unthematic levels of human consciousness also pertains to self-knowledge. According to Fuchs, unthematic knowledge is the only port of entry to the human person as a whole. It is possible, of course, to objectify, conceptualize, and reflect on various components—dispositions, motives, intentions, values, and attitudes—of the human person. Reflection on these components, however, fails to grasp the subject as a whole, who cannot be objectified fully through thematic knowledge. As Fuchs writes,

> objective reflection on the self can never take in the whole self as subject; the subjective "I" which reflects and acts in this reflection remains, precisely as such, outside the "I" that is the object of reflection. . . . This consciousness is not objective, or even reflexive, but transcendental and unreflexive. [On this level of consciousness] [t]he person acting . . . is totally present to himself, not as object but as subject, not perceived but self-aware, not seen from outside but experienced in himself.[22]

As an act that disposes of the whole person, a fundamental option must be made and known by the person as a subject on that level of consciousness where the human person is aware of herself, and capable of actualizing herself, as a whole. Because, according to Fuchs, subjective self-awareness can never be objectified entirely or captured totally by conceptual reflection, the status of one's fundamental option always remains obscure to thematic awareness:[23] "The self-realization of the person as person before the Absolute . . . tends to escape thematic reflection; indeed, it cannot properly be accessible in the center of the 'I' to full thematic reflection."[24] In consequence, one might openly profess love for God, perform right actions, and show kindness toward friends and strangers alike, yet these thematically conscious activities do not necessarily indicate a fundamental option for God.[25] Nor is it licit in Fuchs's view to infer a negative fundamental option from wrong actions or beliefs.[26]

Thus, for Fuchs the human person as a subject is unthematically conscious of herself as a whole as an essentially free and undetermined being. She is also unthematically aware of God as the ultimate horizon of her knowing, willing, and loving, and of her transcendence as a spiritual being that implicitly tends toward God in every act. Conscious of this awareness of God and of herself as a whole, the human person cannot avoid engaging her basic freedom and disposing of herself as a whole either by accepting God in love as the source and term of her existence, or by refusing to love God in an "utterly destructive affirmation of self."[27] This self-commitment and self-disposal of the human person as a whole, through which God either is rejected, or accepted in love, is for Fuchs a fundamental option.

As a disposal and realization of the whole self, changing one's fundamental option is an infrequent occurrence: "This fundamental option brings about an abiding fundamental intention. The whole person is committed in this direction. Consequently, I believe that it is not so easy—not as easy as our moral textbooks seem to indicate—to change ourselves, to change what we are."[28] Although a reversal of one's fundamental option is always possible, the constancy and stability produced throughout the human person as the multiple layers of her being are integrated and aligned with her basic stance toward (or away from) God make a gradual intensification or diminution of one's fundamental option a more likely phenomenon.[29] Indeed, as Fuchs emphasizes, the self-disposal of the human person before God is always *totus sed non totaliter* (as a whole person, but not totally).[30] A fundamental option is not a definitive or final moment of self-realization, but a basic stance at a particular time that is always "immature and imperfect" and that can be solidified or weakened through subsequent acts of self-commitment.[31]

Most importantly, Fuchs's notion of fundamental option bears directly and decisively on his understanding of personal salvation. The preconversion Fuchs maintained that accepting the gift of salvation and acquiring merit depended on two conditions: the performance of right actions and the presence of charity through which acts are referred to God, our final end. Fuchs's appropriation of Karl Rahner's notion of fundamental option, however, undermines the soteriological import of categorial actions. The crucial issue for Fuchs is whether a person has committed herself as a whole in love for God, which is conceptually distinct from the ability to perform actions conforming to natural law. Can a rightly ordered person—in other words, one who has consistently acted according to natural law and cultivated habits conducive to acting rightly—still not be acting out of love for God? Conversely, is it possible to have made a fundamental option for God in love while also acting wrongly on occasion and possessing qualities that inhibit one's ability to act according to natural law? For Fuchs, the answer to both questions is yes. A fundamental option for God in love does not preclude the possibility of acting wrongly; nor does a negative fundamental option prohibit one from acting rightly. Good persons (i.e., those who have made a fundamental option for God in love) sometimes act wrongly because of misinformation, insufficient information, fear, inadequate self-control, anger, or lack of moral imagination. Similarly, bad persons sometimes act rightly although they are motivated by self-aggrandizement, selfishness, or the desire to avoid social reprobation, and sometimes bad persons act rightly by mistake.[32] For these reasons, the rightness or wrongness of a person's actions is not necessarily an accurate reflection of her fundamental option for God.[33]

Moreover, Fuchs argues, freely chosen acts are manifestations and expressions of an underlying reality; they arise from a person's character, disposition, attitudes, and values, all of which are conditioned by one's fundamental option. In this sense, the most basic and proper object of moral evaluation is the quality of one's fundamental option before God, which permeates and affects the entirety of one's being. As Fuchs writes, a fundamental option

> rises from the depths of the human heart, where man (in his freedom) makes his choices not for this or that particular good (or evil) but where he decides to commit his entire personal being for good or for evil—that is, where he makes a choice for faith, for love, and for following Christ, or where he chooses not to accept Christ's call. This fundamental choice in freedom is the basic and genuine decision, and is certainly more central than all the external and internal confessions of faith, love, and the following of Christ for, in the last analysis, such confessions are only expressions of the decisive commitment to faith, love, and the following of Christ. A fortiori, the fundamentally decisive commitment we have defined will be much more central and all-encompassing than one's free choices for individual tasks or right works because, in themselves, these latter are but the fruit and categorical expression of that same fundamental and profound decision of commitment.[34]

Thus, for Fuchs salvation concerns one's transcendental relationship with God, in other words, the manner in which one's basic freedom has been actualized before God. If I actualize myself as a subject in love for God, I have accepted the gift of salvation and am saved; if, on the other hand, I exercise my basic freedom in opposition to God and refuse my love, I am a sinner and outside the realm of salvation.[35] As such, salvation has no intrinsic, necessary relation to categorial actions; they might express the status of one's fundamental option, but unlike Fuchs's preconversion position, categorial actions are no longer directly linked to one's soteriological standing.[36] Fuchs writes, "inner-worldly actions [are] not directly concerned with salvation. Thus he who realizes all that is 'right' in this world and avoids what is 'wrong' is not yet, therefore, necessarily 'good' and within the realm of 'salvation.' "[37]

For the first time, Fuchs has clearly established the possibility—and legitimacy—of an antecedent moral evaluation of the person as distinct from her categorical acts through his appropriation of Karl Rahner's theological anthropology.[38] Based on this distinction between the person and her acts, Fuchs partitions the category of "morality" into two spheres: the transcendental, which concerns the moral quality of a person's self-realization through her fundamental option for or against God; and the categorial, which concerns the way in which concrete goods are realized through particular acts.[39] For Fuchs, as we have seen, the locus of salvation is the transcendental sphere, in other words, one's athematic relationship to God. The pivotal question for our study is, What is the soteriological import of the categorial dimension of morality?

The pertinence of this question appears when the broad structural features of Fuchs's postconversion natural law theory are outlined. As discussed in the previous chapter, Fuchs's intellectual conversion during the pontifical birth control commission precipitated many notable conceptual shifts in his natural law theory. But these conceptual shifts in his notions of moral competency, moral epistemology, the normativity of "nature," and the role of the individual moral agent, among others, all of which affected the substantive content of his postconversion natural law theory, did not alter the proper subject of natural law: categorial behavior. Natural law, both before and after Fuchs's conversion, is concerned with the right realization of the world, with actualizing certain concrete human goods, with regulating the manner in which goods are pursued, and with systematizing and articulating appropriate modes of behavior in moral norms, all of which are directly or indirectly concerned with categorial behavior. Even given this broad understanding of natural law, Fuchs's appropriation of Karl Rahner's theological anthropology raises pressing questions: If a person's transcendental relationship to God is the "decisive factor"[40] in determining her soteriological standing, has natural law, or more precisely, actions in accordance with natural law, become irrelevant to the issue of personal salvation?[41] Does Fuchs's turn to the subject unwittingly promote an antinomianism that cares only that an action is motivated by love for God, not whether it is right or wrong?

Although Fuchs distinguishes between the transcendental and categorial dimensions of morality and maintains that the former is the locus for determining personal salvation, he weaves a subtle connection between the two spheres that precludes any wholesale disjunction. A morally good person—in other words, someone who has accepted the gift of salvation by making a fundamental option for God in love—is not indifferent to the manner in which the world is realized. If one is morally good, Fuchs writes, "one tends toward the good";[42] one strives to cultivate qualities and habits that are conducive to acting rightly; one seeks to know natural law's requirements both generally and in concrete situations; and one attempts to act according to natural law:[43]

> In the area of categorial life, the moral goodness of the person as a whole expresses itself as an inclination of mind, intention, good-will, etc. The lack of such an intention would be a sign that the person is not "good" and does not live within the realm of "salvation." Personal moral goodness . . . is therefore also the will for the "right" realization of the world of man, that is, a realization which is good precisely for man: of the individual, of interpersonal relationships, of society, and of the material world. More exactly, it is the intention to try to find this rightness and, inasmuch as it is found, to realize it.[44]

Thus, Fuchs's insistence on internal moral goodness as the locus of salvation does not obviate the need for natural law; for the morally good person's disposition toward the good impels her to seek to discover natural law and to act in accordance with it. The critical link between one's fundamental option (goodness or badness) and categorial actions (rightness or wrongness), for Fuchs, therefore, is striving, or the effort one expends, to act rightly.[45] No longer does the rightness or wrongness of an act immediately and directly transfer to the moral agent's goodness or badness;[46] for as Fuchs demonstrates convincingly, in many instances actions are ambiguous and unreliable indicators of a person's moral standing. What matters soteriologically for Fuchs is the degree of striving to discover and adhere to natural law's demands.

What Is the Human Being? Human Nature and Personhood

Fuchs's Rahnerian turn to the subject represents only the initial movement in his effort to reconceive the anthropological foundations of natural law. Fuchs's appropriation of Karl Rahner's transcendental Thomism and his notion of the human person as a unified, whole subject treats the human person's transcendental relationship to God and the process of self-realization before God that determines her soteriological standing. Yet as both Fuchs and Rahner note, the human person is not exclusively a spiritual being, but a spirit-in-the-world, a being conditioned not only by her inherent spiritual, transcendental dynamism but by her constitution as a worldly creature whose givenness and facticity distinguish her from other beings, direct her to particular goods, and determine natural law's contents for her as a human being.[47]

As noted in earlier chapters, Fuchs's principal category for describing and analyzing the human *esse* was human nature, which served as the intelligible link between eternal law, or God's mind directing all things to their due ends, and natural law. By reflecting on human nature, Fuchs claimed it possible to discern a hierarchy of goods to which humans are directed and the appropriate manner of pursuing these goods. The hallmark of Fuchs's preconversion notion of human nature was its highly determinate character. On the level of absolute natural law, human nature grounded a series of concrete (and usually negative) moral norms that provided universal and immutable directives for action. In the sphere of relative natural law, once relevant information concerning the concrete situation was known, reflection on human nature was capable of yielding specific prescriptions or proscriptions. At the very least, therefore, Fuchs's notion of human nature functioned as a virtually sufficient condition for determining natural law's contents in any specific situation, and in many instances knowledge of human nature was the only condition necessary for determining natural law concretely.[48]

In his postconversion writings, however, Fuchs denies the ability to discern natural law's specific, concrete contents from human nature. Fuchs is not denying that human nature functions heuristically by determining a general conception of the human good and setting the broad parameters for acceptable conduct, only that it cannot support detailed, proximate moral conclusions by itself. Although such an unmistakable shift in human nature's function in natural law deliberation suggests that Fuchs had adopted another conception of human nature, such a conclusion cannot be verified; for Fuchs never produced a sustained, detailed analysis of human nature and its contents either before or after his intellectual conversion, thus rendering the possibility of comparison highly speculative. The most likely explanation that has substantial textual support is that the postconversion Fuchs realized that the moral norms and the judgments he had rendered on particular issues and actions were not conclusions derived directly and invariably from human nature, but the dictates of reason interpreting the inclinations given through human nature and determining the human good in concrete, particular contexts.[49] For the preconversion Fuchs, there was no substantial gap between human nature and concrete situations; for embedded in human nature were a series of moral norms that could be applied immediately, unambiguously, and directly in concrete situations. The postconversion Fuchs, in contrast, is aware that the movement from human nature to practical decisions is a process involving interpretation, evaluation, distinguishing relevant from irrelevant data, judging the correctness of beliefs and factual information, comparing the practical effects of various courses of action, drawing analogies and comparing one's situation to paradigm cases, and assessing the likely outcomes of one's action, all of which are the work of reason. For the postconversion Fuchs, reason is the critical link between the givens of human nature and practical moral decisions that concretize natural law's contents.[50] Human nature indicates general human goods and sets the outer parameters of acceptable behavior, but specific knowledge of natural law requires reason to interpret and assess the concrete situation, to evaluate potential courses of action, and to judge natural law's demands.[51]

Another reason for the sharp limitations Fuchs places on human nature's role in natural law deliberation is the conceptual distinction between factual data and moral judgments. Both nature and human nature convey physiological, biological, psychological, and sociological information about how humans function, cause-effect relationships at various levels of the human being, statistical probabilities between certain stimuli and responses, and conditions that either retard or enhance human functioning. Drawing on the is/ought distinction common in analytic philosophy,[52] Fuchs, however, insists that such factual information cannot determine which action is required by natural law in a particular situation; for "[m]oral categories cannot be deduced from ontological categories":[53]

> In fact, the only thing that we can grasp from the givenness of nature . . . is what it is, how it functions, and what its natural goal is (perhaps a goal reached in a variety of ways). By itself, therefore, nature discloses only its being to us, not an ethical obligation. Thus, the question of how we "should" make use of what is given in nature in a human and rational way is exclusively an ethical question that must be solved by human reason; it is a question of interpreting and evaluating the relevance of nature for human reality as a whole. . . . The study of what is given in natures does

not, as such, permit us to recognize any moral obligation, and the attempt to deduce a moral obligation from this source alone is revealed as a naturalistic fallacy.[54]

Fuchs is not implying that natural law has become exclusively an exercise of reason, or that natural law reasoning can generate conclusions without guidance from the givenness of human nature. Fuchs's distinction between factual information and moral obligations intends a much more limited claim: the "givenness" of human nature and the various facts derived from an observation of human functioning are not determinative of natural law; or stated differently, descriptive statements concerning human nature should not be equated with normative moral conclusions. Natural law analysis must consider the finalities of various levels of human nature and the goods they indicate, but this knowledge of human nature, however determinate, cannot indicate practical moral obligations without the intervention of reason assessing the relevant factors in a concrete situation and determining which goods should be actualized and in what manner. Human nature, then, functions for Fuchs as an indispensable, but insufficient, source for natural law analysis.[55] Regardless of the specificity of its contents, knowledge of it cannot provide practical directives in concrete situations.

Finally, the postconversion Fuchs is decidedly more cautious about the possibility of knowing human nature's contents. Very few aspects of human nature are known a priori—"body-soul unity, personality, accountability, interpersonality"[56]—and the remainder of human nature, if there is indeed a remainder, must be discovered a posteriori.[57] Moreover, contrary to Fuchs's preconversion confidence in the ability of "concrete human experience" to illuminate those components of human nature not given through revelation,[58] the postconversion Fuchs maintains that concrete experience in no way guarantees or automatically generates correct knowledge of human nature. The ability to grasp human nature's contents, for Fuchs, depends on the quality of one's insights, which in turn are conditioned by the presence or absence of a variety of factors, such as personal and cultural biases; insufficient or inaccurate factual information; underdeveloped hermeneutical skills to interpret factual information; a society's interest in promoting knowledge and academic study; and the decadence or vitality of prior philosophies, theologies, and anthropologies. Given the uncertainty and contingency of a posteriori knowledge, grasping the entirety of human nature will probably never occur, and the process of identifying various discrete components of human nature will most likely proceed incrementally as more empirical data is accumulated,[59] presuming, of course, that the contingencies listed above are favorable for the acquisition of knowledge.[60]

Circumscribing human nature's function in natural law deliberation was only a prelude to a more thorough reconstruction of the anthropological foundations of Fuchs's natural law theory. In his postconversion writings, the principal thrust of Fuchs's theological anthropology is to understand the human being as a concrete aggregate developing over time for whom natural law is determined not by the universal dictates of nature or human nature, but by whatever constitutes concrete, integral human flourishing. In contemporary terminology, Fuchs has shifted from human nature to the human "person"[61] as the locus of natural law deliberation.[62]

During the pontifical birth control commission these rival conceptions of the human being as the locus of moral normativity were at the heart of Fuchs's intellectual conflict. In the sphere of sexuality, Fuchs's preconversion natural law theory grounded moral objectivity in the natural end of intercourse: procreation. Within this framework, the particular circumstances of married couples were irrelevant to the morality of contraception. Yet Fuchs became aware during the course of the pontifical commission that the only permissible methods of birth control—total abstinence and the rhythm method—frequently undermined marital health and stability by causing tension, frustration, and emotional distance between spouses. The pivotal question for Fuchs was, Does natural law seek to protect the integrity of the natural end of intercourse or the well-being of concrete persons, in other words, of spouses and their families? By the close of the commission Fuchs had emphatically affirmed the latter, claiming that natural law can be determined only in reference to "the good of the whole person."[63]

Fuchs's conception of personhood signals four substantive alterations in the anthropological foundations of his natural law theory. First, to consider the human being as a person means to acknowledge that she "is a being of becoming, not a being created in [her] full development."[64] Fuchs increasingly portrays the human person as a dynamic, evolving entity whose *esse* undergoes continual modification through the values she embraces, the acts she performs, and through interaction with her environment.[65] The ideal of human perfection consistent with this notion of personhood is not the conservation and protection of natural givens, but the intentional and continual renovation of one's *esse* that renders a person capable of acting according to natural law. It is the duty of man constantly to make himself more a man, that is, always to develop himself further, and to bring into action the inner possibilities of the being that is called man. . . . It would certainly be false to say—because God has created man as he finds himself to be in actuality, therefore this is the best manner of existence for men. For God has created man *complete with the possibility of his development*, and indeed of *self-development.*[66]

Consistent with his methodological presupposition *agere sequitur esse,* Fuchs maintains that alterations of the human person's *esse* might warrant corresponding adjustments in the behavior considered to be required by natural law.[67] For Fuchs, however, not all changes in the human person require concomitant changes in natural law, nor is his emphasis on the human person's mutability an implicit or explicit rejection of stability in natural law's contents. The only conclusion following from his conception of the human person as a developing being is that changes in natural law "are not to be ruled out from the beginning."[68] Whether alterations of the human person's *esse* cause natural law to change is a matter to be determined concretely by considering whether the specific change actually requires different behavior in order to promote human well-being.

Second, Fuchs claims that to regard human beings as persons means that natural law must seek to enhance and promote the integral fulfillment of concrete, individual human beings. No longer are moral prescriptions or prohibitions derived from universally shared characteristics given through human nature, or discrete, isolated aspects of human beings, or the natural ends of certain types of actions, but from the totality of the human person in all her dimensions.[69]

In order to discover the moral in the use of physical reality and physical laws an understanding is necessary of the meaning, the significance and the importance of the given physical nature in the totality of the human person as such. The norm of correct moral behavior cannot simply be found in the fact of its conformity with physical nature as such, but rather in its conformity with the human person taken in his totality—not, therefore, without regard for the peculiarity of purely physical nature. . . . Thus it is not the physical law that has to be considered as a moral law and invoked to regulate the free actions of mankind, but the *"recta ratio"* which understands the *person* in the *totality* of his reality.[70]

This shift to concrete, integral human flourishing[71] as the locus of moral normativity is important in two respects. Because the human good comprises various levels of the human person—including the physiological, biological, psychological, social, and cultural—the process of uncovering natural law has become more interdisciplinary and empirical and requires input from the natural and social sciences. Thus, knowledge of natural law will be gained incrementally[72] as the sciences provide more accurate data on the human person and outline the ways in which her well-being is hindered or promoted at all levels.[73]

Furthermore, Fuchs's methodological shift away from metaphysics to empirical data to determine concrete, integral human flourishing renders all anthropologies inherently revisable. Until the total reality of the human person has been discovered completely, the possibility exists that further knowledge will reveal existing anthropologies as incomplete or erroneous. In turn, the dependence of natural law on the empirical sciences requires that judgments concerning natural law's contents should be regarded as provisional and potentially subject to revision as anthropological data is accumulated and our knowledge of the human person is expanded.

> When we construct ethical proposals for the person, we must always bear in mind that our knowledge of the total reality of the person is always extremely defective. This situation is precisely the one in which we find ourselves today. As knowledge increases or as plausible hypotheses are formed, one may possibly be required to revise earlier interpretations and ethical insights, judgments, and convictions. The new knowledge that one gains about the possibility of intervention in reality, whether in the technological world, in bioethics and human reproduction, in recent medical, psychological, and sociological knowledge about marriage and sexuality, or in the realm of interpersonal, national and international relationships, has the possibility of determining a new reflection on what hitherto counted as ethically insightful and defensible.[74]

Third, Fuchs's notion of personhood is intended to convey a new understanding of historicity. Prior to his intellectual conversion, historicity pertained to the sphere of relative natural law and became a relevant factor in moral deliberation when formal moral norms derived from absolute natural law were applied in concrete circumstances. As Fuchs liked to say, different historical circumstances sometimes require variable applications of the same formal moral norm in order to attain the human good: "The same immutable and eternal truth is being conditioned . . . to act in one way in this situation and in another way in that situation. It requires different measures in different situations: *diversa diversis mensuris mensurantur.*[75] The historical reality of original sin, for example, conditions the correct application of the formal moral norm "The state must be allowed to care for the common good." For *prelapsum* humans, this norm would disallow the state from exercising any force to achieve the common good because *prelapsum* humans would willingly cooperate with the state's directives. The selfishness, ill-will, avarice, and opportunism characteristic of *postlapsum* humans, on the other hand, would require the state to exercise some amount of force in order to achieve its objective, given by absolute natural law, to care for the common good because humans in this period of salvation history would cooperate with the state begrudgingly, or not at all.[76]

The purpose of Fuchs's preconversion notion of historical consciousness is to render Roman Catholic natural law theory more attentive to particular circumstances that vary among different societies and cultures and evolve, sometimes dramatically, over time. Yet in Fuchs's postconversion writings, historicity's influence on natural law has been expanded considerably and substantively. History still conditions natural law deliberation in the sense that evolving social, political, economic, and cultural circumstances sometimes warrant diverse moral judgments to realize human well-being. But Fuchs, unlike before his conversion, now regards historicity as an inherent subjective condition affecting the manner in which we understand ourselves and our world.[77] More precisely, history has become both an epistemological precondition for the acquisition of knowledge and a potential epistemological limitation of our ability to interpret data correctly.[78]

For the postconversion Fuchs, the meaning attributed to all reality, including the human person, is conditioned by one's *Weltanschauung,*[79] or general worldview, which comprises literally anything that seeks to render human beings intelligible: physics, physiology, biology, psychology, sociology, anthropology, philosophy, religion, theology, popular narratives, culture. In any historical period, the dominant *Weltanschauung* provides the concepts and categories employed to analyze and understand the human person, establishes acceptable methods of investigation and the type of information actively sought or ignored, and supplies various images, symbols, and paradigms intended to impart meaning to the human person and her place in the cosmos. This process of interpreting and understanding the human person, however, cannot escape historical embeddedness; it reflects both the concerns and pre-understandings of a particular historical community:[80] "The steady groping attempts of reason never take place outside history, never, as it were, in an air-free space or from a neutral standpoint."[81]

As human history has demonstrated frequently, the worldviews upon which our self-understandings are based have shifted and caused corresponding modifications in our conception of the human person. In the area of theology alone, our evaluations of religious freedom, the significance of marital love,[82] the inherent dignity of the human person, and the role of women have changed substantially in response to developments in our worldview.[83]

For Fuchs, the practical upshot of our historical embeddedness is that our conception of the human person must be regarded as provisional and partially incomplete. As new knowledge could lead us to revise, perhaps even repudiate, prior anthropologies or find them to be superior to existing anthropologies, as each generation's ability correctly to interpret and evaluate the human person could vary, and as the influence of certain sciences and disciplines could differ in particular historical periods, our understanding of the human person could change, along with our standards of what constitutes human flourishing: "As human beings are partially different in their self-perception, interpretations, and evaluations, it appears certain that new generations will partially change their way of proceeding in these matters with the passing of time."[84]

Fourth, Fuchs's term "person" is intended to highlight the autonomy that characterizes human participation in eternal law.[85] Both before and after his conversion, God's nature and will—eternal law—remained the ultimate source of morality according to Fuchs. The manner in which humans participate in eternal law, however, differs markedly. The preconversion Fuchs maintained that eternal law could be known indirectly, but accurately, by grasping human nature's contents, which revealed a hierarchy of human goods and the appropriate manner of pursuing them. For the postconversion Fuchs, participation in eternal law does not consist in obeying the moral order arising from nature or human nature; for neither gives "us information about moral problems or solutions"[86] or conveys God's will.[87] Instead, Fuchs claims, God has entrusted humans with the responsibility of discovering the human good for ourselves:[88]

> [The human person's] autonomy is understood not only as a fundamental possibility given to humanity by the God who has created and redeemed the world, but also as a task which has been entrusted to humanity. Man is commissioned to seek and to find a way of behaving which corresponds, in every one of his acts and deeds without exception, to his "being-as-spirit-in-a-body". . . . Man is to seek his being-as-God's-image not through letting himself

be told about it but through his own fashioning of right behavior, as well as through bringing himself to fulfillment.[89]

Although the language of autonomy suggests Kantian influences, Fuchs never claims that natural law is created by the human person. Natural law, for Fuchs, is a given, preexistent moral order that is valid whether recognized by humans or not. Fuchs's language is abundantly clear on this point: grasping natural law involves seeking and discovering the moral order corresponding to the good of the concrete human person.[90]

The human person's autonomy, according to Fuchs, necessitates that although recourse to certain authoritative moral sources—such as Scripture, official church teaching, or socially accepted moral norms—should always be a necessary part of natural law deliberation, they do not offer a comprehensive blueprint of acceptable moral behavior and thus are not adequate substitutes for rationally determining how integral human flourishing is best attained.[91]

In summary, for the postconversion Fuchs the human being is both "person and nature in one."[92] As beings with a nature, humans possess invariant and universally shared characteristics and inclinations that direct us to certain goods and provide a general orientation to the human good. As we have seen, however, Fuchs claims that knowledge of human nature is insufficient to determine practical courses of action.[93] Personhood, for Fuchs, remains the anthropological key to unlocking natural law concretely. In contrast to human nature, personhood signifies individuality, particularity, historicity, development, and concreteness. To consider human beings as persons, Fuchs maintains, requires that moral deliberation attend to humans as they actually exist in determinate places and times, as beings who change throughout their lives in response to various environmental, social, political, economic, and cultural circumstances, and who must use their reasoning ability to probe the findings of the physical and social sciences in order to discover the necessary components of integral human flourishing and how these components can best be attained amidst diverse peoples, circumstances, and situations.

An Assessment of Fuchs's Theological Anthropology: Contributions and Criticisms

From a historical perspective, the originality and creativity of Fuchs's attempt to reconstruct the anthropological bases of Roman Catholic natural law theory by wedding a traditional notion of human nature with contemporary personalism is undeniable. He was one of the first moral theologians to incorporate the insights of transcendental Thomism—human transcendence, fundamental option, subjectivity, athematic knowledge—into his natural law theory, which allowed him to reconceive the human person's relationship to God and to overcome the act analysis that dominated Roman Catholic moral theology since the collapse of high scholasticism. He was one of a handful of moral theologians who in the 1960s began attempting to reconcile a traditional Thomistic notion of universal human nature with emerging versions of personalism emphasizing the importance of individuality, particularity, and concrete human flourishing. He also has appropriated a contemporary notion of historical consciousness and on many occasions has continued to refine and clarify his understanding of historicity and its implications for Roman Catholic natural law theory. Fuchs stands as one of the significant moralists in this century offering a clear alternative to the theological anthropology of the neo-Thomist manualists, and his writings have been instrumental in the quest for a refurbished theological anthropology capable of grounding a credible and cogent natural law theory.

Nevertheless, Fuchs's theological anthropology, as it stands, is incomplete and suffers from certain flaws that militate against the possibility of formulating a natural law theory capable of identifying or ordering concrete human goods constitutive of human flourishing or of generating precise, normative conclusions about acceptable human conduct. I am not claiming, however, that the contents of Fuchs's theological anthropology misrepresent the human person or that they fail to provide the structural beginnings of an anthropology that, after some supplementation, could be serviceable for use in contemporary Roman Catholic natural law theory. My principal criticism is that even if the entirety of Fuchs's theological anthropology were true, it is questionable whether it provides sufficient content to begin resolving pressing practical moral issues.

Perhaps the most serious limitation of Fuchs's anthropology is its formal character.[94] As discussed above, human nature and personhood are the two principal descriptive categories of Fuchs's anthropology. Human nature represents the invariable and universal characteristics shared by all humans, whereas personhood seeks to capture concrete human beings as particular individuals conditioned by diverse environments and circumstances. When the specific contents of human nature and personhood are examined with a view toward identifying the salient components of each directing humans to certain goods, however, a recurrent pattern emerges: the generality of Fuchs's presentation precludes any determinate notion of the human good.

Fuchs's treatment of both human nature (both its a priori and a posteriori components) and personhood list the following characteristics of human beings: body-soul unity, personality,[95] responsibility, sociality,[96] orientation toward the Absolute, subjectivity, basic freedom, athematic knowledge of God,[97] mutability,[98] historicity,[99] moral autonomy,[100] the capacity for self-realization,[101] and an awareness that good should be pursued and evil avoided.[102] Although this account of the human being might provide a potent and fruitful basis for constructing a fundamental moral theology, its contribution toward identifying goods, even a general catalogue of goods, constitutive of human flourishing is marginal. With the exception of the social nature of humans, Fuchs's presentation of the human being resembles more a descriptive phenomenology of the necessary preconditions for being human than a normative account of the conditions and goods conducive of human well-being.

This could be remedied by a concrete anthropology; but Fuchs does not provide one, and his theoretical premises act formidably against an outside observer mastering sufficient information to develop one adequately. In order to generate a concrete anthropology, one would need to know how particular circumstances—regional and local, environmental, social, political, economic, and cultural—condition human well-being and what type of attributes or qualities best enable persons to actualize concrete goods in these circumstances. In itself, this is no small feat; for as Fuchs emphasizes, the aforementioned realities are susceptible to change, sometimes slowly and ponderously, but sometimes rapidly and tumultuously.[103] Moreover, the mutability of human beings raises the possibility that as particular groups, cultures, and societies have evolved over time and reinforced different sets of characteristics in response to diverse living conditions, we not only have to consider that prior anthropologies, legitimate in their day, might no longer capture the human being existing today,[104] but also that it might be necessary to develop plural anthropologies in order to account for the various ways in which humans have evolved differently.[105]

One undesirable consequence of the formality of Fuchs's theological anthropology is the apparent vacuity of Fuchs's criterion of integral human flourishing. For example, historicity entails changes in the human person, the natural environment, social and political structures, social roles, and the meanings attached to various aspects of human life (such as work, family, and relationships), yet Fuchs's analysis of historicity offers no guidelines to distinguish which changes in the human person or her world enhance or impede human well-being. Similarly, human autonomy requires that we search for norms and patterns of behavior constitutive of integral human flourishing, but Fuchs fails to specify how our autonomy should be exercised.

The practical upshot is that without further specifying the contents of human well-being, Fuchs's theological anthropology faces difficulties in identifying, ordering, and prioritizing the goods, commitments, and institutional arrangements that humans should pursue, and it offers few substantive criteria to determine legitimate from morally impermissible actions. As Cristina Traina rightly notes, the lack of specific content of Fuchs's theological anthropology means that it "could easily end up merely replacing the theological foundations of existing moral theological positions, or, on the other hand, justifying any moral conclusions at all."[106] Although it is extremely doubtful that, if pressed, Fuchs would claim that all moral conclusions are equally valid embodiments of moral truth, Traina is correct that nothing in Fuchs's theological anthropology, as it stands, immediately rules any moral judgment out of court.

A similar problem arises with Fuchs's claim that natural law can be determined only by considering "the human person taken in his totality."[107] One of Fuchs's principal complaints about traditional Roman Catholic natural law theory is that its philosophy of nature tended to locate moral normativity in certain isolated, discrete components of human beings in opposition to the good of the whole person.[108] The principle of totality, as employed by Fuchs, is intended to supplant the neo-Thomists's philosophy of nature and to extend natural law analysis to include anything impinging on concrete human well-being. Although the goal of rendering Roman Catholic natural law theory more cognizant of and receptive to the broad array of circumstances affecting humans concretely is laudable and fundamentally sound,[109] in order to make the criterion of "the good of the self, understood in its totality"[110] a meaningful and intelligible principle of natural law analysis there must be some standards to distinguish relevant from irrelevant data or circumstances, which in turn presupposes at least a general conception of what it means to be human, how humans function, what conditions contribute to human well-being, and what goods are worthy of being protected and actualized.

Yet once again, the lack of specific content in Fuchs's theological anthropology offers little substance to distinguish which parts of the total concrete reality are germane to making a correct moral judgment. This is not to suggest that there is not a fuller theological anthropology implicitly operative in Fuchs's natural law theory. As Fuchs's discussion of procured abortion strongly indicates, not all circumstantial data are relevant to the abortion decision, and there are concrete goods worthy of protection.[111] But by not considering these anthropological considerations explicitly, the criteria Fuchs employs to differentiate morally relevant from morally irrelevant circumstances and goods lack unity and appear somewhat arbitrary.[112]

On the positive side, Fuchs's Rahnerian turn to the subject, which provided Fuchs with the intellectual framework to begin differentiating between a person's moral standing and the moral quality of her actions and which culminated in Fuchs's distinction between personal moral goodness and categorial rightness, has successfully overturned the longstanding erroneous tendency in Roman Catholic moral theology (and in Fuchs's preconversion writing) to link salvation with the performance of actions conforming to natural law, which I criticized at length in chapter 2.[113] This is perhaps the most valuable contribution of Fuchs's postconversion theological anthropology, which will continue to offer fertile ground for understanding the human person and for situating natural law's soteriological significance.

The problem with Fuchs's preconversion understanding of the relation between acts conforming to natural law and personal salvation is that lacking any antecedent evaluation of the person, the sole criterion determining whether one's soteriological standing is improved is the actual performance of a right action (assuming the act is animated by charity).[114] By linking salvation with the performance of right actions, Fuchs's synthesis unwittingly leads to several implausible and erroneous conclusions: innocent mistakes negate the possibility of acquiring merit; those possessing more intellectual acumen are more likely to improve their soteriological standing because they are better able to discover natural law's contents than those less intellectually endowed; and factors largely, if not entirely, beyond a person's control—genetic inheritance, the quality of one's family life, upbringing, and moral education, and the decadence or vitality of one's society or culture—can affect the capacity to gain salvation insofar as they influence one's ability to act rightly.[115]

By distinguishing between the person and her acts and generating separate evaluative criteria for each, the postconversion Fuchs avoids all these errors. Because personal moral goodness depends on striving to order oneself properly, to discover natural law, and to act rightly, innocent mistakes no longer affect one's personal goodness. Indeed, wrong actions resulting from innocent mistakes might actually increase one's personal goodness if a sincere and reasonable effort has been made to gather relevant information and to act rightly.

Fuchs's goodness/rightness distinction also overcomes the latent intellectual moral elitism characteristic of his earlier preconversion position that was inherently biased against the unintelligent. Superior adeptness at gathering and interpreting factual information, knowing which moral principle applies to the situation at hand, assessing the moral relevance of circumstances, and judging the likely consequences of various actions still offer a distinct advantage in being able to determine natural law's contents in a particular situation, in other words, to know what is right. But superior intellectual acumen offering a particular moral agent greater insight into natural law no longer proves intrinsically advantageous in increasing moral goodness; for moral goodness is not necessarily enhanced by knowing natural law or performing right actions.

Finally, Fuchs's goodness/rightness distinction offers an intelligible and coherent basis for addressing the many unequal and largely accidental factors—including quality of family life and moral education, heredity, the decadence or vitality of one's culture, exposure to moral exemplars, or the presence or absence of psychological impairments—that directly or indirectly make one more or less well-ordered and capable of acting rightly. James Keenan frames the issue well:

> [C]onsider a woman who was abandoned during her youth and who notwithstanding the lack of being loved still attempts to love even in a restricted way. This person may conduct herself wrongly, yet, given her personal history, her striving to love is an indication of the personal moral goodness in her life. Similarly, a person suffering from neurosis may find his actual conduct sorely wanting, but in his attempts to become a more integrated person in order to serve the church, he too is good. Finally, consider the person born with a better-ordered personality than most people and whose family's financial and emotional support has fortified this personality. Is that better-ordered personality an indication of goodness or rightness? Is it simply a rightly ordered personality? And is not goodness, on the other hand, a question whether that person or any person strives to become even better so as to serve others?[116]

Fuchs, like Keenan, recognizes that differing native endowments and personal circumstances render persons more or less able to act rightly. Within Fuchs's preconversion framework, which measured moral goodness by the attainment of right actions, those disadvantaged by the vicissitudes of heredity, family, and other factors were significantly hampered in their ability to accept God's offer of salvation, even though they might be in no way responsible for the impediments or disorders that render them less able to act rightly. By adopting the goodness/rightness distinction and basing personal salvation on moral goodness—not on the performance of right actions—Fuchs has effectively severed the unwitting link he had forged between salvation and the innumerable random circumstances affecting every person's life. No longer does it matter soteriologically whether one is blessed or cursed by nature, whether one is talented or inept, or whether one is stifled or nurtured by friends, family, society, or culture. The sole criterion for assessing one's soteriological standing is now the effort a person makes to act rightly, given her internal and external circumstances, which makes the possibility of accepting God's offer of salvation in principle equally accessible to everyone.

In the final analysis, although Fuchs's postconversion theological anthropology succeeds convincingly on several levels, it remains questionable whether his reconstructed theological anthropology provides sufficient content to begin identifying concretely how natural law orders and guides our lives. One can read and analyze Fuchs's anthropology and marvel at the insightfulness of his appropriation of Karl Rahner's conception of transcendental Thomism. One can agree that natural law deliberation should begin to understand human beings as "persons" who evolve and develop throughout their lives. One can concur that humans are historical beings whose respective worldviews and self-understandings are conditioned by time and place. One can agree that natural law deliberation must be focused on the integral, concrete flourishing of individual human beings. Yet one can also fail to detect how these conceptual shifts in Fuchs's theological anthropology provide concrete direction for persons seeking to clarify and prioritize their commitments and to conform their actions to natural law.

In fairness to Fuchs, it should be mentioned that Fuchs never attempted to delineate a concrete anthropology that identifies specific human goods. Fuchs's proclivity as a German was to engage fundamental matters in moral theology, not to address more practical matters such as articulating and ordering concrete human goods or resolving particular cases. Unlike many American and English casuists, who often delve into precise—even excruciating—detail in their case analyses and exhibit no reluctance in articulating and ordering human goods, Fuchs preferred to address topics not immediately germane to the sphere of practical ethics.

Although Fuchs's inattention to more practical matters can be partially attributed to a simple lack of interest, I suspect that Fuchs's positions on certain foundational issues precluded, or at least strongly inhibited, the possibility of formulating a concrete anthropology or of resolving particular moral issues. First, as I mentioned earlier in this chapter, Fuchs does not regard the human person as an unchanging being; through our decisions, actions, and interaction with our environments we shape ourselves and become, for better or worse, different persons. The implication Fuchs draws from the human person's malleability and capacity for (at least partial) self-creation is that the concrete human good might change as humans change. Thus, we should be cautious about naming goods when, in fact, the determinant of human goods—concrete human beings as they are constituted—might be evolving and developing.

Second, Fuchs, I think, would consider even a concrete anthropology to have limited applicability in concrete situations. One of the main thrusts of Fuchs's natural law theory is to move practical moral deliberation away from abstractions and generalizations, whether these be moral norms or human goods, to a consideration of the concrete, and in many cases unique, circumstantial data impinging on the decision to act in a certain way: the specific moral agents involved and those affected by the action; the particular values and disvalues realized in the act; and the commitments and responsibilities of those in the situation, among others. In this sense, what is vitally important for Fuchs is not a thick, clearly ordered, and detailed anthropology, because even the most concrete anthropology, to the degree that it abstracts from specific individual moral agents and the circumstances in which they act, cannot capture the full reality of the situation and thus cannot indicate what constitutes *recta ratio*.

Thus, although I have criticized Fuchs's anthropology as being too formal to provide practical direction and advice, it is plausible, maybe even likely, that Fuchs would regard my criticism as a misguided attempt to expect a degree of specificity and clarity that no anthropology can possibly provide. Whatever the case, fairness to Fuchs requires that I acknowledge the reasons for Fuchs's reluctance to develop a fuller anthropology and at least entertain the possibility that his reasons were well-founded.

Although I applaud Fuchs's recognition that any anthropology, to the extent that it prescinds from individual moral agents and their circumstances, cannot indicate what constitutes concrete human flourishing, I still think that a thicker, more robust anthropology than Fuchs's is needed if natural law analysis is to begin ordering and prioritizing human goods and offering a coherent basis for adjudicating between conflicting values and courses of action. Lacking a more substantive anthropological basis, natural law analysis will be incapable of offering anything more determinate than general moral guidance and formal human values, which have very restricted applicability in the everyday lives of moral agents.

It is possible that with significant supplementation Fuchs's postconversion theological anthropology might provide an adequate basis for a natural law theory serviceable for use within Roman Catholic moral theology. From a historical perspective, the anthropological changes Fuchs and other moralists—Alfons Auer, Bruno Schüller, Franz Böckle, Louis Janssens, Bernard Häring, Fritz Tillmann, Gerard Gilleman— have proposed are relatively new. Perhaps given enough time and attention, the germinal insights of Fuchs's postconversion theological anthropology will bear enduring fruit. But at this point, I think it is limited in its ability to ground a natural law theory capable of generating substantive, concrete moral advice.

Notes

1. Josef Fuchs, *Personal Responsibility and Christian Morality*, trans. William Cleves et al. (Washington, D.C.: Georgetown University Press, 1983), 213–15. The section to which this citation refers is a summary of Josef Fuchs, "Sittliche Normen—Universalien und Generalisierungen" 52 (1974): 18–33.

2. Josef Fuchs, "Sin and Conversion," *Theology Digest* 14 (1966): 292–301; Josef Fuchs, *Human Values and Christian Morality*, trans. M. H. Heelan et al. (Dublin: Gill and Macmillan, 1970): 1–55, 92–111, 112–47; Fuchs, *Personal Responsibility*, 19–32, 53–68; and Josef Fuchs, *Theologia Moralis Generalis*, pars altera (Rome: Pontificia Universitatis Gregoriana, 1966), 204–22.

3. Fuchs, *Human Values*, 95.

4. See George Vass, *A Theologian in Search of a Philosophy*, 2 vols. (Westminster, Md.: Christian Classics, 1985), 1: 47–92 for a discussion of human subjectivity in Rahner's theological anthropology.

5. Karl Rahner's seminal article on basic freedom is found in Karl Rahner, "Theology of Freedom," in vol. VI of *Theological Investigations*, trans. Karl-H. Kruger and Boniface Kruger (New York: Seabury Press, 1969), 178–96.

6. Fuchs, *Human Values*, 93.

7. Fuchs, "Sin and Conversion," 292.

8. Karl Rahner, *Foundations of Christian Faith*, trans. William V. Dych (New York: Crossroad, 1989), 94.

9. Timothy P. Muldoon, "German Grisez on Karl Rahner's Theory of Fundamental Option," *Philosophy and Theology* 10, no. 1 (1997): 243.

10. Fuchs, *Human Values*, 95; and Rahner, *Foundations of Christian Faith*, 26–31.

11. Anne Carr, "Starting with the Human," in *A World of Grace*, ed. Leo O'Donovan (New York: Crossroad, 1986), 26.

12. Rahner, *Foundations of Christian Faith*, 26.

13. Fuchs, *Human Values*, 96; and Rahner, *Foundations of Christian Faith*, 96–97.

14. Fuchs, *Human Values*, 96; and Fuchs, "Sin and Conversion," 296.

15. Mark Lloyd Taylor, *God Is Love: A Study in the Theology of Karl Rahner* (Atlanta: Scholars Press, 1986), 51–60.

16. David Coffey, "Rahner's Theology of Fundamental Option," *Philosophy and Theology* 10 (1997): 257.

17. Fuchs, *Human Values*, 103. See also Jean Porter, "Salvific Love and Charity: A Comparison of the Thought of Karl Rahner and Thomas Aquinas," in *The Love Commandments*, ed. Edmund Santurri and William Werpehowski (Washington, D.C.: Georgetown University Press, 1992), 242–45.

18. Fuchs, *Human Values*, 124; and Fuchs, *Personal Responsibility*, 56–57.

19. For a perceptive discussion of the epistemological problems associated with Rahner's notion of *vorgriff*, see Patrick J. Burke, "Conceptual Thought in Karl Rahner," *Gregorianum* 75 (1994): 65–93.

20. Rahner, *Foundations of Christian Faith*, 33–35.

21. Fuchs, *Human Values*, 106.

22. Ibid., 105.

23. For discussions on the possibility of raising the status of one's fundamental option to explicit, thematic consciousness, see George Lobo, *Guide to Christian Living* (Westminster, Md.: Christian Classics, 1984), 344–49; Enda McDonagh, *Gift and Call* (Dublin: Gill and Macmillan, 1975), 64; and Timothy E. O'Connell, *Principles for a Catholic Morality* (San Francisco: Harper and Row, 1990), 57–66.

24. Fuchs, *Personal Responsibility*, 56.

25. Germain Grisez criticizes Fuchs on this point, claiming that it denies the soteriological import of free, self-determining, fully conscious choices. See German Grisez, *Christian Moral Principles*, vol. 1 of *The Way of the Lord Jesus* (Chicago: Franciscan Herald Press, 1983), 387–88.

26. Fuchs, *Personal Responsibility*, 98–99; and Fuchs, "Sin and Conversion," 294.

27. Fuchs, "Sin and Conversion," 296.

28. Ibid., 297.

29. Josef Fuchs, "Good Acts and Good Persons," in *Considering Veritatis Splendor*, ed. John Wilkins (Cleveland, Ohio: Pilgrim Press, 1994), 23.

30. Fuchs, *Theologia Moralis Generalis, pars altera* 147.

31. Fuchs, *Human Values*, 96.

32. Josef Fuchs, *Christian Ethics in a Secular Arena*, trans. Bernard Hoose and Brian McNeil (Washington, D.C.: Georgetown University Press, 1984), 53.

33. For criticism of fundamental option theory, insofar as it fails to indicate actions congruent with one's fundamental option, see Jean Porter, "Moral Language and the Language of Grace: The Fundamental Option and the Virtue of Charity," *Philosophy and Theology* 10 (1997): 171–81.

34. Fuchs, *Personal Responsibility*, 36.

35. Fuchs, "Sin and Conversion," 296.

36. Josef Fuchs, *Christian Morality: The Word Becomes Flesh*, trans. Brian McNeil (Washington, D.C.: Georgetown University Press, 1987), 97.

37. Fuchs, *Christian Ethics*, 53. See also Fuchs, *Personal Responsibility*, 36.

38. For others distinguishing between the moral quality of the person and her actions, see Klaus Demmer, *Deuten und Handeln* (Freiburg, Germany: Universitätsverlag, 1985); Klaus Demmer, "Erwängungen zum 'inrinsece malum,' " *Gregorianum* 68 (1987); James F. Keenan, "Can a Wrong Action Be Good? The Development of Theological Opinion on Erroneous Conscience," *Eglise et Théologie* 24 (1993); James F. Keenan, "Distinguishing Charity as Goodness and Prudence as Rightness: A Key to Thomas's Secunda Pars," *Thomist* 56 (1992); Bernard Hoose, *Proportionalism: The American Debate and Its European Roots* (Washington, D.C.: Georgetown University Press, 1987), 41–67; and Bruno Schüller, *Die Begründung sittlicher Urteile* (Düsseldorf, Germany: Patmos, 1980).

39. Fuchs, *Christian Ethics*, 51; and Fuchs, *Personal Responsibility*, 55.

40. Fuchs, *Human Values*, 106.

41. Most of the controversy surrounding the notion of fundamental option has centered on this issue. See John Finnis, *Fundamentals of Ethics* (Washington, D.C.: Georgetown University Press, 1983), 142–44; Joseph Boyle, "Freedom, the Human Person, and Human Action," in *Principles of Catholic Moral Life*, ed. William E. May (Chicago: Franciscan Herald Press, 1980); and Theodore Hall, "The Mysterious Fundamental Option," *Homiletic and Pastoral Review* 78 (1978): 12–20.

42. Fuchs, *Christian Morality*, 111.

43. Ibid., 23, 29, 107–9, 140; Josef Fuchs, *Moral Demands and Personal Obligations*, trans. Brian McNeil (Washington, D.C.: Georgetown University Press, 1993), 97.

44. Fuchs, *Christian Ethics*, 51.

45. Fuchs, *Christian Morality*, 61.

46. Cf. Josef Fuchs, *General Moral Theology*, pt. 1 (Rome: Pontificia Universitatis Gregoriana, 1963), 188.

47. Ronald Modras, "Implications of Rahner's Anthropology for Fundamental Moral Theology," *Horizons* 12 (1985): 73–79.

48. The distinction between human nature as a necessary or sufficient condition for knowing natural law is taken from Alan Gewirth, "Natural Law, Human Action, and Morality," in *The Georgetown Symposium on Ethics*, ed. Rocco Porreco (Lanham, Md.: University Press of America, 1984), 67–90. Gewirth distinguishes between human nature exhaustively defining or constituting the good (sufficient condition) and human nature setting "the outer limits on what can count as the good of man" and thus proving insufficient by itself "to define or provide the content of man's good" (necessary condition) (71).

49. Fuchs, *Christian Morality*, 45.

50. For a host of different reasons, the growing tendency in contemporary natural law theory is to minimize reliance on teleological conceptions of human nature, especially on what have come to be known as "thick" descriptions of human nature, in favor of equating natural law with practical reason, or *recta ratio* in Fuchs's case. See, for example, Lloyd Weinreb, *Natural Law and Justice* (Cambridge, Mass.: Harvard University Press, 1987); Grisez, *Christian Moral*

Principles, 173–204; John Finnis, *Natural Law and Natural Rights* (Oxford: Clarendon Press, 1980); Martin Rhonheimer, *Natural Law and Practical Reason: A Thomist View of Moral Autonomy,* trans. Gerald Malsburg (New York: Fordham University Press, 2000); Martha C. Nussbaum, "Aristotelian Social Democracy," in *Liberalism and the Good,* ed. R. Bruce Douglass, Gerald M. Mara, and Henry S. Richardson (New York: Routledge, Chapman, and Hall, 1990); Martha C. Nussbaum, "Nature, Function, and Capability: Aristotle on Political Distribution," in *Oxford Studies in Ancient Philosophy,* supplementary volume (New York: Oxford University Press, 1988); and Martha C. Nussbaum, "Aristotle on Human Nature and the Foundation of Ethics," in *World, Mind, and Ethics,* ed. J. E. J. Altham and Ross Harrison (Cambridge: Cambridge University Press, 1995). For perceptive criticisms of this tendency, see Russell Hittinger, "Varieties of Minimalist Natural Law Theory," *American Journal of Jurisprudence* 34 (1989); and Louise Antony, "Natures and Norms," *Ethics* 111 (2000).

51. Fuchs, *Personal Responsibility,* 66. See also Franz Böckle, *Fundamental Moral Theology* (Dublin: Gill and Macmillan, 1980), 183–98; and Martin Rhonheimer, *Natural Law and Practical Reason: A Thomist View of Moral Autonomy,* 307–36.

52. Fuchs, *Moral Demands,* 33.

53. Fuchs, *Human Values,* 145.

54. Fuchs, *Moral Demands,* 33. In a similar vein, Fuchs writes, "what man can read directly in physical nature as such is nothing more than *facts*—to which the *physical* laws of nature pertain. . . . In order to discover the moral in the use of physical reality and physical laws an understanding is necessary of the meaning, the significance and the importance of the given physical nature in the totality of the human person as such. . . . Thus it is not the physical law that has to be considered as a moral law and invoked to regulate the free actions of mankind, but the 'recta ratio' which understands the *person* in the *totality* of his reality" (Fuchs, *Human Values,* 143).

55. Wilhelm Korff, "Nature or Reason as the Criterion for the Universality of Moral Judgments," *Concilium* 150 (1981), 82–88 offers a similar assessment.

56. Fuchs, *Personal Responsibility,* 126. See also Fuchs, *Human Values,* 145, where he identifies dependence on an absolute, a social orientation to others, personality, freedom, and responsibility as the components of human nature known a priori.

57. Fuchs, *Human Values,* 145.

58. Josef Fuchs, *Natural Law: A Theological Investigation,* trans. Helmut Recker and John Dowling (New York: Sheed and Ward, 1965), 54.

59. Pamela Hall, *Narrative and Natural Law: An Interpretation of Thomistic Ethics* (Notre Dame, Ind.: University of Notre Dame Press, 1994), 99–101.

60. Fuchs, *Personal Responsibility,* 213.

61. For an assessment of the concept "person" in Christian ethics, see Hans Rotter, *Person und Ethik: Zur Grundlegung der Moral theologie* (Innsbruck, Austria: Tyrolia, 1993); Stanley Rudman, *Concepts of Person and Christian Ethics* (New York: Cambridge University Press, 1997); and Louis Jannsens, "Personalism

in Moral Theology," in *Moral Theology: Challenges for the Future*, ed. Charles E. Curran (Mahwah, N.J.: Paulist Press, 1990).

62. Fuchs, *Personal Responsibility*, 127; Fuchs, *Christian Ethics*, 93; and Fuchs, *Human Values*, 143, 182–83.

63. Josef Fuchs et al., "Final Report of the Pontifical Commission on Population, Family, and Birth," in *The Encyclical that Never Was*, Robert Blair Kaiser (London: Sheed and Ward, 1967), 8.

64. Fuchs, *Christian Ethics*, 119.

65. This developmental aspect in Fuchs's anthropology stems largely from Karl Rahner, who maintained that the human person's capacity for self-determination and self-creation is never complete until the moment of death. See Karl Rahner, "The Experiment with Man," in *Theological Investigations*, vol. 9, trans. Graham Harrison (New York: Herder and Herder, 1972), 213, where he writes, "In contradistinction to 'things' which are always complete and which are moved from one mode of completion to another, and thus are at the same time always in a final state and yet never determined, man begins his existence as the being who is radically open and incomplete. When his essence *is* complete, it is as he himself has freely created it" (emphasis in original).

66. Fuchs, *Human Values*, 117.

67. Fuchs, *Personal Responsibility*, 126–27.

68. Fuchs, *Human Values*, 43.

69. Fuchs, *Moral Demands*, 48.

70. Fuchs, *Human Values*, 143. See also Fuchs, *Personal Responsibility*, 212–13; and Fuchs, *Moral Demands*, 48, 58.

71. For a discussion of the criterion of integral human flourishing as it functions in natural law deliberation, see Cristina L. H. Traina, *Feminist Ethics and Natural Law* (Washington, D.C.: Georgetown University Press, 1999). Cf. Stephen Pope, "Scientific and Natural Law Analyses of Homosexuality," *Journal of Religious Ethics* 25 (1997): 110–21 who maintains that among revisionist moral theologians the criterion of integral human flourishing is problematic because of its imprecision and lack of substantive content.

72. Thomas R. Kopfensteiner, "Historical Epistemology and Moral Progress," *Heythrop Journal* 33 (1992): 48–50.

73. Fuchs, *Human Values*, 71. See also Hall, *Narrative and Natural Law*, 99–101.

74. Fuchs, *Moral Demands*, 22.

75. Fuchs, *Natural Law*, 95 quoting Thomas Aquinas's *Summa Theologiae*, I–II.104.3 ad 1.

76. Fuchs, *Natural Law*, 96.

77. See also Hans Rotter, "Zwölf Thesen zur heilgeschichtlichen Begründung der Moral," in *Heilgeschichte und ethische Normen*, ed. Hans Rotter (Freiburg, Germany: Herder, 1993).

78. See also Klaus Demmer, "Sittlicher Anspruch und Geschichtlichkeit des Verstehens," in *Heilgeschichte und ethische Normen*, ed. Hans Rotter (Freiburg, Germany: Herder, 1984).

79. Fuchs, *Moral Demands*, 97.

80. Thomas R. Kopfensteiner, "Globalization and the Autonomy of Moral Reasoning: An Essay in Fundamental Moral Theology," *Theological Studies* 54 (1993): 486–90.

81. Fuchs, *Christian Morality*, 15. For examples of scientific investigation mirroring and attempting to validate prevailing historical worldviews, see Stephen Jay Gould, *The Mismeasure of Man* (New York: W.W. Norton, 1981).

82. Fuchs, *Christian Morality*, 113.

83. Fuchs, *Personal Responsibility*, 16.

84. Fuchs, *Moral Demands*, 93.

85. Alfons Auer's *Autonome Moral und christlicher Glaube* (Düsseldorf, Germany: Patmos, 1971) was one of the earliest and most influential works on moral autonomy in Roman Catholic moral theology. For subsequent developments of the concepts of autonomy, see Böckle, *Fundamental Moral Theology*, 30–63; Tadeusz Styczen, "Autonome Ethik mit einen christlichen 'Proprium' als methodologisches Problems," in *Ethik im Kontext des Glaubens: Probleme—Grundsätze—Methode*, ed. Francesco Compagnoni and Dietma Mieth (Freiburg, Germany: Universitätsverlag, 1978); Klaus Demmer, "Die autonome Moral: Eine Anfrage an die Denkform," in *Fundamente der theologischen Ethik: Bilanz und Neuansätze*, ed. Adrian Holderegger (Freiburg, Germany: Universitätsverlag, 1996); and Martin Rhonheimer, "Sittliche Autonomie and Theonomie gemäß der Enzyklika 'Veritatis Splendor,' " *Forum Katholische Theologie* 10 (1994); and Rhonheimer, *Natural Law*, 181–251.

86. Fuchs, *Christian Ethics*, 96.

87. Ibid., 78. See also Fuchs, *Christian Morality*, 137.

88. For criticism of Fuchs's understanding of moral autonomy, see Russell Hittinger, "Natural Law and Catholic Moral Theology," in *A Preserving Grace*, ed. Michael Cromartie (Grand Rapids, Mich.: William B. Eerdmans, 1997), 16–19.

89. Fuchs, *Personal Responsibility*, 99.

90. Ibid., 59, 78; Fuchs, *Christian Morality*, 7, 57, 148; and Fuchs, *Moral Demands*, 41.

91. Fuchs, *Personal Responsibility*, 99.

92. Ibid., 127.

93. Ibid., 34–44.

94. Traina, *Feminist Ethics*, 191–92.

95. Fuchs, *Personal Responsibility*, 127.

96. Fuchs, *Human Values*, 187.

97. Ibid., 92–111.

98. Fuchs, *Personal Responsibility*, 42–43.

99. Fuchs, *Moral Demands*, 91–96.

100. Fuchs, *Christian Ethics*, 118; and Fuchs, *Personal Responsibility*, 98–99.

101. Fuchs, *Christian Morality*, 143–53.

102. Fuchs, *Moral Demands*, 111.

103. Ibid., 97.

104. Ibid., 95.

105. Fuchs, *Christian Morality*, 136–38.

106. Traina, *Feminist Ethics*, 193.

107. Fuchs, *Human Values*, 72, 143; and Fuchs, *Christian Ethics*, 10; Fuchs, *Christian Morality*, 147; Fuchs, *Moral Demands*, 58.

108. Fuchs, *Human Values*, 141–43.

109. For a discussion of the practical implications of the shift from "nature" to integral human flourishing as the locus of moral normativity, see Pope, "Scientific and Natural Law," 110–21.

110. Fuchs, *Christian Morality*, 147.

111. Fuchs, *Moral Demands*, 10–11.

112. Cristina Traina raises the same criticism of Fuchs's discussion of procured abortion: "The nurture of potentially social, conscious human life seems to be Fuchs's central criterion. Yet without further specification even this value produces arbitrary results. For instance, he hints that abortion is appropriate when there is no chance that a child will be born alive or develop into a conscious, marginally functional person, or when a mother's life is endangered. But usually we have more than two human lives to consider, and their needs often conflict. If context is everything, why does Fuchs arbitrarily exclude from consideration the mother's economic situation, other children she may have, the medical care available to her, and her own wishes and feelings?" (Traina, *Feminist Ethics*, 187).

113. See chapter 2.

114. Fuchs, *General Moral Theology*, pt. 1, 188.

115. See chapter 2.

116. James F. Keenan, "What Is Good and What Is Right," *Church* 5 (1989): 24.

5

The Core of Fuchs's Mature Natural Law Theory: *Recta Ratio* as the Proximate Norm of Morality

In the previous chapter the analysis focused on the latter portion of the traditional natural law methodological principle *agere sequitur esse*. I discussed the implications of Fuchs's attempt to revamp the anthropological underpinnings of his postconversion natural law theory by wedding a notion of universal human nature with contemporary personalism emphasizing historicity, mutability, personal development, and concrete, integral human flourishing. The focus of this chapter is to outline and critique several components of Fuchs's later natural law theory, focusing especially on the role of human reason in uncovering natural law. We begin with Fuchs's postconversion shift from nature to *recta ratio*, or right reason, as the proximate norm of morality.

Natural Law and *Recta Ratio*

One of the objectives of Fuchs's postconversion theological anthropology was to deconstruct the role and function of nature predominant in Roman Catholic moral theology during the twentieth century, which regarded nature as the visible manifestation of God's essence and will and the intelligible link between the eternal law and natural law. The preconversion Fuchs typified this position: "[T]he reality which we call 'nature' . . . comes directly from the hands of God. God speaks through it and reveals himself in it. It bears his features and it is his image."[1] Given this conception of nature as a revelation of God's will for humankind, Fuchs understood natural law as the moral demands arising from nature, and the focus of his natural law theory was to articulate the finalities and demands inherent in the order of nature.

The postconversion Fuchs, in sharp contrast, repudiates his earlier philosophy of nature and now claims that nature, although morally significant, is not determinative of natural law, nor is it a conduit between humankind and God mediating God's intentions for us.[2] Nature might indicate certain goods constitutive of human flourishing and might set the outer boundaries of acceptable behavior, but Fuchs denies that it can ground natural law concretely.[3] If nature is no longer the critical link between eternal law and natural law, what is? If God's essence and will cannot be discerned through the natural order, how can they be known?

As I hinted at briefly in the previous chapter, for the postconversion Fuchs *recta ratio* has displaced nature as the proximate norm of morality.[4] Consistent with his preconversion position, Fuchs still claims that natural law is a *"lex interna,"* a preexistent moral order grounded in the divine nature that is valid whether recognized by humans or not.[5] The crucial question for Fuchs is, How is this internal law recognized or discovered? Retrieving what he believes to be Thomas Aquinas's understanding of natural law,[6] Fuchs now claims that natural law is made manifest through the power of human reason, or more precisely, *recta ratio*, through which humans participate in eternal law.[7]

I will begin the analysis by discussing five features related to Fuchs's notion of *recta ratio* as the proximate norm of morality: (1) discovering natural law is a rational process dependent on human reason at every step in assessing the rightness or wrongness of actions; (2) grasping natural law through reason requires experience, and it occurs over time; (3) the magisterium has no special competency in determining *recta ratio*; (4) *recta ratio* admits a degree of legitimate moral pluralism; and (5) there is a general method to determine *recta ratio*.

Human Reason as the Port of Entry to Natural Law

In any specific situation in which a moral question is raised, whether that of a parent deciding how and where her child should be educated, a moral theologian attempting to determine the liceity of capital punishment, welfare reform laws, or current national environmental policy, or a mayor trying to assess how limited monies can be spent best in her local community, the goal of moral deliberation is to understand natural law and the specific course of action it indicates.

The element common to the parent, the moral theologian, and the mayor is that each one, throughout the entire process from initially raising the question, What should be done? to finally making a judgment as to the right course of action, relies on her reasoning ability. How does the parent assess the unique needs of her child, the strengths and weaknesses of various schools, the quality of faculty members and students? How does the moral theologian assess the cogency of moral norms dealing with capital punishment, detect possible racial biases operative in states allowing capital punishment, or comprehend the historical, cultural, or religious influences behind capital punishment? How does a mayor determine a community's most pressing needs, compare projected costs in relation to perceived benefits, or determine the legitimacy of requests from special interest groups promoting certain expenditures in exclusion to others?

For Fuchs, the answer to each question is "Through the use of human reason." Reason is the active, creative, and constructive dynamism behind the human person's multifaceted abilities to question, to interpret, to sort relevant from irrelevant information, to evaluate different courses of action, to detect rationalizations and deceptions, to nuance and draw distinctions, to develop and critique ideas, to offer justifying reasons for behavior or beliefs, to accept or reject actions or policies as right, to comprehend historical and cultural contexts, to draw inferences and conclusions, to establish cause and effect relationships, and to judge what should be done in the here-and-now.[8] Human reason, for Fuchs, is the sine qua non for knowing ourselves and our world and is the necessary condition for grasping natural law's contents and thereby determining right conduct.[9]

Absent the power of reason, there would be no way to determine how to prioritize and select human goods worthy of pursuit, what constitutes the good in particular situations, or what are the acceptable ways of actualizing human goods. Take, for example, the natural inclination given through human nature to be sociable, to seek the company of other human beings.[10] Although this natural inclination indicates a general human good—interaction with others—there are other human goods that are constitutive of human well-being as well, such as food, shelter, life, play, and physical and mental health.[11] Given these multifarious human goods, the question immediately arises, Which good should be pursued and actualized? for not all human goods can be realized simultaneously. The answer and the process of generating criteria to answer the question depend on human reason interpreting the needs of a particular community or individual, assessing the probability of actualizing certain goods, evaluating the relative importance of particular goods, and making a final judgment as to which good should be realized.

Let us assume for a moment that an individual has chosen to pursue the good of social intercourse with others. Here the person must choose from among a variety of possibilities, including joining a voluntary association, spending time with a casual acquaintance, renewing old or neglected friendships, seeking an intimate and long-term relationship, frequenting a popular local establishment such as a bar and grill, or seeking employment that requires frequent social contact. Once again, human reason is the operative dynamism that allows the individual to assess the attractiveness and viability of various options and to determine which course of action is best.[12]

Descending into further detail on any one of these potential options for satisfying the human good of social interaction and describing the necessity of human reason on this highly practical level only reiterates the main point of the preceding paragraphs: from beginning to end, from identifying and interpreting the contents of the human good, to selecting among various potential goods to be realized, to assessing alternative options, to finally grasping the practical option that best serves human well-being, human reason is the indispensable component for uncovering and understanding the human good.[13] Quoting Thomas Aquinas, Fuchs writes,

> The criterion [of self-realization and right conduct] is the insight of evaluating reason: "Bonum hominis est secundum rationem esse," "the good of the human person consists in his being in accord with reason," says Thomas Aquinas. Because reason has the possibility of arriving at self-understanding, and also at an understanding of individual realities, it can attempt to evaluate and discover which of the manifold possibilities of action best corresponds to the true good of the human person and to his development.[14]

At first glance, it might appear that Fuchs's postconversion natural law theory has shifted toward the Enlightenment rationalistic ideal of a detached, pure reason constructing a notion of the human good and corresponding normative guidelines solely through human reason without recourse to any personal or communal experience. The role of "experience" in grasping natural law will be discussed below.[15] For now, I want to point out that Fuchs's understanding of human reason's function in moral deliberation is not disconnected from the given reality of the human being. For Fuchs, it is simply impossible to grasp natural law independently of knowledge about human functioning, human needs, and the conditions necessary for human flourishing. Although the postconversion Fuchs regards anthropological data as facts from which no concrete normative moral conclusions can be immediately and directly derived, this does not imply that these facts concerning human beings are irrelevant to moral analysis or that they exercise no influence on human reason's deliberations.[16] It is morally significant that we are human beings whose natural drives, desires, and needs direct us to particular goods and impose limits on the possible patterns of behavior deemed to be consistent with human well-being. As Fuchs writes, "Reason . . . speak[s] a word which becomes for us a moral standard of measure, but in order to do this it absolutely must listen to the word of nature."[17]

The fundamental rationality of the process of discovering natural law and determining moral rightness means that the principal source of moral obligation for humans is human reason itself.[18] Because only reason can understand the human person and her world and render intelligible behavior conforming to natural law,[19] the locus of moral normativity, for Fuchs, is human reason.[20] To be sure, there are numerous potential fonts of moral wisdom available to the human person when confronting a particular decision, such as feedback from peers, colleagues, parents, and family members; scholarly insights; religious figures; Scripture; religious and philosophical ethical traditions; persons who have experienced similar situations; and respected community leaders. But the moral wisdom conveyed by any or all of these sources is neither self-validating nor authoritative unless affirmed by reason as cogent and intelligible embodiments of moral truth. For Fuchs, the "law of rationality"[21] operative in ethical experience necessitates that moral obligations be understandable, credible, and persuasive; there is no room in Fuchs's natural law theory either for a fideism that disregards the reasonableness of moral obligations or for a divine positivism that considers God's commands or laws as morally binding even if they appear "whimsical and meaningless" to human reason:[22] "The binding force of morality would be nonsense if it did not enjoy a fundamental ability to be perceived and understood. . . . If the information which is given to us in revelation is to be ethically meaningful . . . then the attainment of insight into the relationship between the information and moral behavior must be possible."[23]

Fuchs maintains that the reasoning process employed to determine natural law's contents is not deductive, resembling a syllogistic demonstration by generating normative moral conclusions from premises derived from the human *esse*.[24] Discovering natural law, for Fuchs, involves "not a metaphysical or logical thought pattern, but a form of reasoning which experiences and evaluates."[25] What this means, in practical terms, for Fuchs is that correct natural law reasoning should seek to accumulate sufficient information or evidence—not to provide "proofs"[26]—about the human person, the contexts in which she acts, and human well-being in order to make a considered judgment about the reasonable course of action. Because the human person and her world are historical realities susceptible to change, and because our human knowledge always falls short of understanding these realities in their totality, the most that can be expected of natural law reasoning is "moral certitude," or the probability that one's knowledge of natural law is correct, not "absolute" or "metaphysical" certainty, as Fuchs calls it.[27]

Although Fuchs insists that the process of uncovering natural law occurs through the use of human reason, he is receptive to the idea that reason might operate in different ways to attain moral knowledge. A moral theologian's deliberations on natural law might tend to be propositional and discursive, and in her quest for critical evaluation she might bring to explicit consciousness the many concepts, ideas, hermeneutical tools, notions of the human person, presuppositions, methods of argumentation, and criteria for ethical evaluation operative in her search for moral knowledge. For Fuchs, however, it is important not to dismiss the "common sense" insights[28] of those whose moral deliberations are not explicitly conscious and who might be less adept than the professional ethicist at articulating the thought processes employed to reach ethical conclusions, but who nonetheless display a notable ability to discern right behavior. Simply because someone's moral insights might be prior to explicit reflection, perhaps even "intuitive,"[29] does not imply, for Fuchs, that they are less than reasonable or that they cannot be "made the object of reflection."[30]

Grasping Natural Law through Human Reason Requires Experience, and It Occurs over Time

The language Fuchs consistently employs to describe the process of attaining rational insight into natural law—searching,[31] seeking,[32] finding,[33] discovering[34]—indicates that knowledge of natural law is neither innate nor immediately evident.[35] Unlike the preconversion Fuchs, who claimed that concrete moral obligations could sometimes be "read" immediately and indubitably from the natural order prior to experience,[36] the postconversion Fuchs insists that knowledge of natural law depends on lived experience[37] that makes manifest how human persons function, the conditions necessary for human fulfillment, and how actions either hinder or promote human well-being.[38]

As scholars have noted, the appeal to "experience" common in contemporary moral theology is often employed as a justification for a particular moral position not because of the reasonableness or persuasiveness of the position, but "because of the genesis and possession of the opinion by a particular person or group."[39] In other words, appeals to experience are sometimes used to circumvent discussion and evaluation of the contents of a particular moral belief by presenting experience as an authoritative, normative, and self-validating conclusion to an argument. But as these scholars have noted, appeals to experience might sometimes "function as a channel for bias, delusion, self-protection, rationalization, and self-deception,"[40] which necessitates that they all be subjected to critical assessment to determine whether or not they embody moral truth.

Fuchs's appeal to experience in order to know natural law does not have an implicit or explicit justificatory function. *Recta ratio*, or right reason, for Fuchs, is the measure of right conduct and as such assesses the validity of any appeal to experience. Fuchs's appeal to "experience [as] the starting point of personal morality"[41] is intended to highlight only the fact that insights into natural law—especially concrete knowledge of natural law—are gained incrementally as we become more familiar with human beings and learn more precisely and comprehensively the contents of human well-being.

To illustrate the role of experience, consider briefly the general pattern of moral development from childhood to adulthood.[42] Children receive their initial moral instruction through parents, relatives, social and educational institutions, caretakers, and other significant adults who through their own examples and pithy verbal instructions (Stop that or you will be punished! Be nice to your brother! Share your toys!) convey general guidelines for proper behavior. Children also, through imitation and playacting, assume various roles and begin to explore how people in these roles think, feel, and respond to normal situations and unusual predicaments. In addition, characters in story books, other children, and various symbols often convey—rightly or wrongly— certain standards of behavior. Throughout this socialization process, these multifarious experiences allow children to gain a broad range of insights about moral ideals, claims and expectations placed on them, social roles, harms and benefits, and acceptable forms of conduct.

As children mature into adults, their experiences lead them (one hopes) to a better understanding of right conduct and prompt the cultivation of skills and qualities—analogical reasoning, empathy, concern for oneself and others, critical thinking, courage—necessary for leading exemplary lives. The validity of earlier moral insights are tested for their correctness as young adults emerge as active assessors of moral truth embodied in, or absent from, certain ideals and behavioral norms. New experiences and knowledge provide a more comprehensive and accurate basis for judging the truthfulness of particular moral claims. Novel or unprecedented situations are no longer the occasion of panic or moral paralysis, but are rendered intelligible through comparison with analogous situations or by imaginatively envisioning entirely new solutions. Better ways of structuring relationships, social roles, institutions, and recurrent patterns of behavior are entertained.

The point I wish to make by this cursory treatment of moral development is that right behavior is a learned and socially mediated phenomenon, knowledge of which accumulates gradually as we experience and learn more about ourselves and the world.[43] We begin our lives unaware of right and wrong; in childhood we are initiated into the rudiments of proper conduct through a variety of sources; and as we progress into adulthood and accumulate more moral insights we gain a more critical and precise understanding of humans, human well-being, and the particular actions conducive to this end. As Pamela Hall writes, "[Natural] law must be learned in order to be efficacious as practical guidance, and such learning requires experience over time. We must discover what our good is and what is conducive to that good. In this way, we both understand and enact the natural law."[44]

For Fuchs, however, the value of experience lies not only in gaining general knowledge of human well-being or right patterns of behavior, or in recognizing the necessity of descending into history, as it were, to gain moral insights, but in being able to familiarize oneself with concrete particularities, with certain persons, groups, regions, issues, cultures, political and economic systems, and other contexts.[45] Unlike the preconversion Fuchs, who claimed that natural law's contents could be determined in many instances without knowledge of concrete circumstantial data beyond that necessary to determine which moral norm should be applied, the postconversion Fuchs repeatedly insists that natural law cannot be known in particular situations without detailed and accurate knowledge of the totality of circumstances.[46] Fuchs is not implying that all circumstantial data will be relevant to determining natural law's contents in a particular situation. He is simply noting that abstract or general knowledge does not suffice to make correct moral judgments in concrete situations.[47] For example, in order to raise a child well, knowledge of child psychology and development will probably be very helpful in providing certain benchmarks or criteria for assessing a child's progress and in offering certain methods for fostering proper overall development. The well-being of a particular child, however, requires attention to a number of circumstances unique to each child, including the need for structure or freedom; the desire for social contact or time spent alone; the amount of parental supervision necessary; the quality of social skills; or the amount and type of correction needed to counteract wrong actions or bad habits. Knowledge of parenting skills and methods that generally work well might be extremely valuable, but they cannot replace the indispensable role of intimate, detailed knowledge of a specific child's unique constitution and the ways in which her individual talents and well-being are best nurtured and her weaknesses overcome.

What emerges from Fuchs's use of human reason reflecting on experience is an essentially open-ended and ongoing method of uncovering and learning natural law that is, in principle, capable of revision through subsequent moral insights clarifying, correcting, repudiating, or developing earlier insights. This represents a significant departure from Fuchs's preconversion methodology, which grounded moral obligation not in the considered judgments of human reason, but in "nature." On the issue of artificial contraception, for instance, the preconversion Fuchs located moral normativity in the "natural" end of intercourse, procreation. By directly impeding the natural finality of the marital act, artificial contraceptives contravened the natural order and were deemed contrary to natural law by Fuchs. Within this framework does experiential data, understood very broadly, contribute to the determination of artificial contraception's liceity? Does it matter morally that artificial methods of contraception might be more effective than the rhythm method in regulating births? Does it matter that married couples using artificial contraception might be more satisfied with their sex lives, or that their marriages might be more stable and healthy? Does it matter that serious medical problems might arise for some women if they become pregnant? Does it matter if more babies afflicted by Down's Syndrome are born to couples using the rhythm method than those using artificial contraception? For the preconversion Fuchs, the answer is "no" because the process of uncovering natural law on this particular issue depends on knowing the natural finality of conjugal intercourse, not on the cumulative knowledge gained through the insights or empirical data of medical doctors, married couples, or anyone else.

The postconversion Fuchs, in contrast, claims not only that natural law analysis must consider the insights of married couples, population experts, medical doctors, social scientists, philosophers, and theologians to determine the liceity of artificial contraception, but maintains that recent advances in various disciplines have culminated in an entirely new understanding of conjugal intercourse and artificial contraception:

> The reasons in favour of this affirmation [of the use of artificial contraceptives] are of several kinds: social changes in matrimony and the family, especially in the role of the woman; lowering of the infant mortality rate; new bodies of knowledge in biology, psychology, sexuality and demography; a changed estimation of

the value and meaning of human sexuality and of conjugal relations; most of all, a better grasp of the duty of man to humanize
and to bring to greater perfection for the life of man what is given
in nature.[48]

This passage typifies the essential openness of natural law deliberation to new insights, new evidence, and advances in the physical and
social sciences that have altered our conception of the human person
and of appropriate interventions into human fertility. It is possible, of
course, to dispute the relevance of such data and the conclusion Fuchs
draws from them. What is incontestable, however, is that this passage
clearly indicates a new methodology operative in Fuchs's natural law
theory, which resembles what Bernard Lonergan calls a "moving viewpoint":[49] reason actively probing and seeking new information about
human beings and our world; new insights arising and being tested for
their cogency and validity; these insights, in turn, affirming, correcting,
complementing, or developing earlier insights; a more critical viewpoint emerging from the dynamic and constructive process of reason
accumulating and verifying insights; and the process repeating itself
indefinitely as more data is generated and further questions are raised
and answered.[50]

This adoption of a natural law methodology receptive to new insights and open to potential revision does not imply that all moral
judgments or moral norms are indeed provisional. Fuchs grants that
the cumulative knowledge generated by human reason reflecting on
experience and gaining more comprehensive and accurate insights into
the human person and patterns of behavior conducive to human well-
being might confirm the validity and correctness of earlier insights
which were codified in specific moral norms.[51] To this extent, there
might be a body of stable, enduring, and unvarying moral norms that
through centuries or millennia are continually affirmed as legitimate
embodiments of moral truth.[52] But their perennial validity as genuine
guidelines for human behavior is not a given;[53] they still must be
confirmed in each age by the proximate norm of morality—*recta ratio*—
as promoting human well-being.[54]

In Fuchs's mind, this methodological openness to new data and
insights is the only basis for a credible natural law theory capable not
only of further clarifying, refining, and specifying the moral wisdom
of the past, but of rendering intelligible the many emerging and unprecedented questions confronting the contemporary world. This latter
task, for Fuchs, represents perhaps the most pressing issue for natural
law analysis, which in the contemporary period has been confronted
by a daunting array of issues unknown before the twentieth century,

such as advances in medical technology, including genetic manipulation, cloning, and developments in reproductive technology; nuclear weaponry and the problems of disposing of radioactive waste; environmental issues, such as depletion of the ozone layer, accumulation of greenhouse gases, massive destruction of rain forests, and decreasing fresh water supplies worldwide; and agricultural problems, including the increasing use of hazardous chemicals, bioengineered crops, and soil compaction and erosion.[55] Solutions to these issues, in Fuchs's opinion, requires a natural law theory sufficiently flexible to respond to new data as they emerge and to devise innovative and ongoing responses to these issues as human reason continually assesses their affect on human flourishing.[56]

The Magisterium and Recta Ratio

The preconversion Fuchs was extremely pessimistic about the ability of the vast majority of humankind—more precisely, the nonmembers of the magisterium—of grasping natural law concretely. Like captives in Plato's cave, they possess nondescript, obscure images of natural law's full reality, an understanding of natural law's first—and most general—principles that offer only indeterminate advice when confronted by the practical question, What should I do?[57] The descent into particulars, according to Fuchs, proved to be bedeviling and was fraught with uncertainty and unintelligibility; for the massive subjective epistemological barriers induced by original sin prevent the consistent (or even infrequent) acquisition of detailed knowledge of natural law.[58]

The magisterium, however, does not suffer similar difficulties in grasping natural law concretely. Citing official documents from Vatican I's *Dei Filius* to Pius XI's *Casti Connubii* to Pius XII's *Humani Generis*, Fuchs affirms the magisterium's unique competency as the authentic interpreter of natural law, which allows it to know natural law from the most formal principles to the most detailed, proximate conclusions:[59] "The Church [i.e., the magisterium], as our guide on this way, has the obligation of proclaiming and protecting the entire moral law, including the natural law, even in as far as it has not been formally revealed and even down to its concrete applications."[60]

It should be noted that Fuchs's preconversion confidence in the magisterium's ability to comprehend and propose natural law correctly is not based on some functionalism or on the magisterium's own claims to competency in moral matters, but because Fuchs believed that God's grace bestowed on the magisterium superior insight into natural law, which virtually guaranteed that its moral teachings were free from error. This grace was initially given through episcopal ordination, which not only instilled in the bishop a persistent desire to grasp natural law more completely, but also made it easier for him to comprehend natural law, both revealed and unrevealed.[61] In consequence, a bishop, in Fuchs's opinion, represents a "teacher of truth," an "instrument of God," whose superior insight into natural law legitimizes the deference given to him by the faithful.[62] In addition, Fuchs cites the classic *assistentia Spiritus*, which though not guaranteeing infallibility to all the magisterium's interpretations of natural law, creates such a strong presumption in favor of the magisterium's teaching that no "personal conviction," however sincere, is capable of overriding it.[63] For both these reasons—grace given through episcopal ordination, and the ongoing *assistentia Spiritus*—Fuchs regarded the magisterium as a font of moral truth whose superior insight into natural law justifies its position as authentic interpreter of natural law.[64]

The marked enthusiasm characteristic of Fuchs's preconversion confidence in the magisterium's ability to grasp natural law correctly is conspicuously absent in Fuchs's postconversion writings. Whereas the preconversion Fuchs was unabashedly apologetic in his defense of the magisterium's competency in moral matters, the postconversion Fuchs is equally forthright about the magisterium's limits in interpreting and proposing natural law.

Fuchs's analysis of the magisterium's competency in moral matters focuses on four issues, the first of which is the magisterium's role in interpreting revelation. Fuchs notes that in the Second Vatican Council's *Dei Verbum*, which defined the magisterium's role in interpreting divine revelation, the council fathers state that the purpose of revelation is to transmit those truths necessary for the salvation of humankind.[65] Now, as discussed in chapter 4, Fuchs's distinction between goodness and rightness pertains directly to the question of salvation. Goodness, for Fuchs, consists in making a fundamental option for God in love, which manifests itself as a persistent striving to act rightly in the world. By making a fundamental option for God and disposing of ourselves as a whole in love for God, we accept God's gift of salvation and are saved.[66]

Given Fuchs's understanding of salvation, the magisterium's mandate, defined by the Second Vatican Council, to interpret and safeguard revelation for the purpose of leading all persons to salvation is not principally concerned with specific teachings on categorial behavior; for salvation, according to Fuchs, depends on moral goodness (i.e., the quality of one's fundamental option) rather than on acting rightly.[67] If the magisterium is to remain faithful to its task of preaching and teaching salvation, its focus must be on proclaiming "the salvific action of God" which, through grace, transforms the person interiorly from an "egotism that is closed in upon itself" to a state of love, generosity, and readiness to labor for "the right shaping of the world of man."[68]

Second, when the magisterium interprets natural law and teaches on the rightness or wrongness of certain behavior, it is important to recognize that few of its teachings, if any at all, are infallible.[69] The Second Vatican Council explicitly states that the magisterium's "infallibility is coextensive with the 'treasure of Divine Revelation,' " which, Fuchs writes, "logically excludes from the charism of infallibility . . . those moral questions which belong to the 'natural moral law' without being at the same time revealed."[70] Fuchs rejects the common argument that there are concrete moral truths so intimately connected with the *depositum fidei* that the charism of infallibility extends to a wide array of practical moral issues:[71]

> Ecclesiology normally states that to the questions of *depositum fidei* also belong matters not explicitly revealed but which have such an inner relationship to explicitly revealed truths that the latter cannot be defended without the acceptance of these other (not explicitly revealed) truths. However, it does not seem conceivable that the unlimited number of concrete questions regarding the moral rightness of "horizontal" acting have such a relationship and therefore belong to the competence of the magisterium in the same full sense as revealed truths do; again we could think of such questions as those belonging, for instance, to the biological, aerospatial, and political arenas.[72]

The practical upshot, for Fuchs, is that most official teaching deals with nonrevealed moral truths, and such teaching of the ordinary magisterium rarely enjoys infallibility and therefore is susceptible to error.

Third, contrary to his preconversion position,[73] Fuchs maintains that the *assistentia Spiritus* promised to the church is not limited to the magisterium. Although the Holy Spirit undoubtedly guides and assists the magisterium as it teaches natural law, Fuchs emphasizes that the Holy Spirit's assistance "is guaranteed to the Church *as a whole*," including "the individual missions" that pertain to persons outside the magisterium.[74] Beyond theologians who have "received an official commission" from the magisterium,[75] Fuchs does not specify to whom the individual missions refer, or the prerequisites for such a mission (a canonical mandate? formal training in moral theology? expertise on a particular moral issue? profession of Catholic faith?), but at the very least Fuchs does not consider the Holy Spirit's aid to be confined exclusively to the magisterium.

Moreover, Fuchs contends that it is impossible to determine when the Holy Spirit will intervene in the magisterium's teaching on a particular issue. As Fuchs writes, "there is no theological criterion which allows us to determine the period of time within which the Holy Spirit 'should intervene.' "[76] The magisterium's teachings on slavery, religious freedom, and taking interest on a loan, for instance, which were upheld for centuries, were eventually repudiated.[77] The lesson learned from these changes in official church doctrine, according to Fuchs, is that "erroneous moral teaching [can] persist within the Church for long periods of time,"[78] which makes it difficult, if not impossible, to determine when the Holy Spirit will intervene and guide the church to correct knowledge of natural law.[79]

Fourth, Fuchs argues that on moral matters unconnected to the "deposit of faith," in other words, those questions dealing with nonrevealed, noninfallible moral teaching, the magisterium, as such, enjoys no privileged competency to interpret natural law. Fuchs, it should be noted, is not denying in any way the magisterium's teaching authority. Fuchs accepts the magisterium as the legitimate authoritative body responsible for defining the Catholic Church's official moral doctrine. What Fuchs disputes is that the magisterium possesses any special competency to determine right or wrong behavior.

To clarify Fuchs's distinction between authority and competency, let me draw an analogy. The president of the United States possesses the authority, given by the U.S. Constitution, to send troops into battle, to veto legislation, and to nominate candidates for the Supreme Court. Yet even though the president's authority allows him or her to perform such tasks, it does not grant or somehow bestow on the president any special competency or ability to determine whether sending U.S. troops into battle is morally justified, or whether a respective piece of legislation should be vetoed, or who is best qualified to occupy a seat on the Supreme Court.

Similarly, although the magisterium possesses the institutional authority to interpret natural law and to propose norms of behavior for the church, its teaching authority is separate and distinct from its competency in moral matters, and its teaching authority does not necessarily entail that its moral judgments are correct or inherently superior to anyone else's.[80]

Moral competency, for Fuchs, rests on the ability to grasp natural law concretely, which in turn depends on several factors. Foremost among these is the personal goodness of the individual moral agent, which impels her to strive to discover what is right, to cultivate the qualities and characteristics necessary to become a well-ordered human being capable of acting rightly consistently, and to muster the will-power to perform right actions once they are known. Lacking personal moral goodness, a person might still occasionally act rightly, but she will not exhibit the enduring drive and desire to discover and to do what is right on a consistent basis.[81]

Another component of moral competency is knowledge of the subject matter in question.[82] To assess the environmental impact of contemporary North American farming practices, for example, one would need to become familiar with issues such as soil erosion; water contamination through pesticide, herbicide, and fertilizer use; the amount of fossil fuels (and thus air pollution) needed to produce different types of crops; the long-term effects (salinization and aquifer depletion) of irrigation; the costs and benefits associated with planting annual crops instead of perennials; and the potential environmental hazards of homogeneous monocultures of one or two crops compared to diversification and genetic variation of species.

Regardless of the issue at hand, whether it be Third World debt, the morality of warfare, or reproductive technology, the ability to assess its moral implications and to present thorough, detailed, accurate, and convincing analyses that identify problems and propose viable, persuasive solutions depends on knowledge of one's subject matter.

The third component of moral competency Fuchs identifies is knowledge of concrete particulars. One of the most consistent themes in Fuchs's postconversion natural law theory is the necessity of practical knowledge to determine natural law's contents in a concrete situation.[83] General knowledge of soil erosion causes and rates in North America, for instance, is vital for constructing national and state governmental policy designed to ensure the long-term sustainability of our topsoil. But for a particular farmer convinced of the moral rightness of preserving the quantity and quality of her topsoil for future generations, general knowledge does not suffice to provide practical directives for action. Integral to the farmer's attempt to limit topsoil erosion is concrete knowledge of her farmland, including its composition (percentage of humus, clay, rock, organic matter, or other components that are more or less susceptible to erosion), its structure (steep hills, moderate inclines, or flat expanses), average rainfall per year and frequency of rainfall, knowledge of possible preventive measures (trees, terracing, underground tiling, interspersing different crops in strips, crop rotation), and where these erosion protection measures should be placed to maximize topsoil retention.

Fuchs's critique of the magisterium's competency to interpret natural law focuses on the last two criteria, knowledge of a particular issue or subject, and practical knowledge of concrete situations. The magisterium's principal limitation, according to Fuchs, is that its members often are no more familiar with contemporary moral issues than the average lay person. Some bishops might be practicing moral theologians actively teaching or researching, some might have an interest in moral issues pertaining to their pastoral ministry, and some might not have thought seriously about moral issues since their seminary training. As a group, then, the magisterium is comprised of individuals with widely varying degrees of knowledge on certain topics, and who might or might not have any expertise on certain moral issues.

To this extent, Fuchs claims, it is erroneous to attribute to the magisterium any privileged ability to grasp natural law. The magisterium, in fact, might have extraordinary insight into some moral matters but have little familiarity with others. What is impermissible, however, is to grant the magisterium a privileged position in moral deliberation before knowing whether such privilege is warranted:

> Anyone who wishes to teach right behavior in international politics, change in tribal marriages, the correct realization of human sexuality in different phases, situations and cultures, etc., must be very competent in all these matters of human reality. It is clear that Christians as such, and the people involved in the church's magisterium as such, have no privileged competency with regard to such questions . . . If one wishes to give moral instructions and teachings concerning such human realities, inasmuch as they are human, one must acquire sufficient competence, receiving information from others who are more competent.[84]

The bishops, like all other human beings, are "in the same boat"[85] concerning the process of discovering natural law. They neither have direct access to God's will,[86] nor do they receive binding revelations from God,[87] nor does God somehow circumvent the limitations associated with human knowing,[88] thereby guaranteeing the magisterium indubitable knowledge of natural law. The magisterium discovers natural law by reflecting on human nature and concrete human beings, identifying goods necessary for human fulfillment, articulating appropriate ways of pursuing these goods, and continually reevaluating the considered judgments of one's culture or society as new anthropological data is uncovered, better ways of structuring relationships or institutions are proposed, or changing circumstances require a rethinking of acceptable human conduct. This process of discovering right behavior is incremental, ongoing, and requires insight and sustained attention and effort to be successful.

Just as physicians, teachers, or chemists spend considerable time studying their respective disciplines, sometimes over many years and in great detail, in order to become competent practitioners of their craft, the ability to understand moral issues or particular fields in sufficient depth, breadth, and nuance is a sine qua non for moral competency. For the magisterium to be considered competent to interpret natural law in a specific area of human life, according to Fuchs, its members must master the knowledge necessary to understand an issue thoroughly and to present convincing reasons for their position.[89]

The second component of Fuchs's critique of the magisterium's competency in moral matters represents a wholesale departure from his preconversion position. For the early Fuchs, the movement from general principles known by all without difficulty to more specific principles capable of offering directives for action in concrete situations was fraught with difficulties for those outside the magisterium. Subjective impediments engendered by original sin, the sometimes overwhelming complexity of details, and usually inadequate "scientific" instruction in moral matters bedeviled lay persons faced with practical decisions and rendered them largely incapable of correctly grasping natural law in concrete situations. The only way to rectify this deficiency was to turn to the magisterium, which alone could virtually guarantee that its teaching on natural law, even its most concrete, determinate, and detailed teaching, was correct.[90]

For the postconversion Fuchs, in contrast, the members of the magisterium are not exempt from the subjective impediments arising from original sin, nor are they inherently more able to render intelligible the complexity often encountered in concrete situations. The magisterium and the laity alike share essentially the same conditions, either positive or negative, affecting their ability to grasp natural law.[91] But for Fuchs, the pivotal issue is whether the magisterium is capable of considering the totality of circumstantial data surrounding a concrete situation, without which attaining *recta ratio* is impossible.[92] *Recta ratio*, the proximate norm of human conduct, cannot be attained by ascertaining what is right in a majority of cases, or in nearly all situations; *recta ratio* corresponds exclusively to the objectively right manner of acting in the here-and-now, considering all the morally salient elements of the situation.[93]

Given the degree of practical knowledge necessary to attain *recta ratio*, the one theoretically in the best position to know and assess the moral import of the totality of circumstantial data in a concrete situation is the person in that situation, who possesses knowledge about himself, the likely practical consequences of her action, the values and disvalues at stake in the various options available to her, and her responsibilities and commitments to others, all of which might be relevant to the decision at hand and thus applicable to the determination of *recta ratio*.

This does not imply the magisterium's teachings are irrelevant to the individual moral agent in the concrete situation. The magisterium's teachings on a wide variety of issues might prove to be highly reliable indicators of right behavior in specific situations. But it must not be forgotten that the magisterium's teachings are abstract, prefabricated, and fashioned by fallible human beings[94] whose ability to envision various contingencies potentially arising in concrete situations is questionable.[95] Stated differently, there is a conceptual gap between received teaching and *recta ratio*, and for received teaching to be morally binding, it must be judged to be consistent with *recta ratio* by someone familiar with the morally relevant elements of the concrete situation.

In the end, Fuchs's presentation of the magisterium's competency to interpret nonrevealed truths of natural law significantly circumscribes the magisterium's role in moral deliberation. Gone is Fuchs's earlier theology of the Holy Spirit, which identified the magisterium as the principal, perhaps even singular, object of the *assistentia Spiritus*. Gone is Fuchs's preconversion belief that the Holy Spirit's intervention in the process of discovering moral truth is limited to a specific time period, typically before the magisterium officially promulgates a particular moral teaching, which virtually guarantees the magisterium freedom from error. Gone is the belief that the magisterium's competency to teach natural law is unaffected by knowledge—or lack of knowledge—of its subject matter. Gone, too, is the notion that moral competency can be divorced from concrete, circumstantial knowledge.

For the postconversion Fuchs, there is in principle no inherent difference between the members of the magisterium and the rest of humankind in terms of discovering the concrete expression of natural law: all must reflect on the human person and the conditions necessary for human fulfillment in order to grasp natural law; all are subject to personal biases, limitations, and weaknesses arising from original sin; all must be familiar with a particular moral issue to be considered competent to offer credible, persuasive moral advice on it; and all are the recipients of God's grace in the search to discover right behavior.

The competency to teach nonrevealed natural law, then, cannot be attributed univocally to the magisterium. Its moral competency is contingent on the extent to which its teachings are the product of thorough investigation; an accurate, current, and relatively comprehensive understanding of the issue at stake; a willingness to strive to uncover what is right; and familiarity with circumstantial data relevant to the issue in question. At its best, the magisterium's teaching can display insightfulness, thoroughness, clarity, rigor, and persuasiveness that undeniably establish the competency to give moral advice on certain issues. At its worst, the magisterium's teaching can be based on inaccurate or partial information, poorly argued, unclear, too general, and perhaps erroneous in its conclusions.

Recta Ratio and Moral Pluralism

One of the most interesting tenets of Fuchs's postconversion natural law theory is the possibility of legitimate moral pluralism. In a very restricted way, the preconversion Fuchs recognized that natural law permitted different types of behavior in certain situations. This moral pluralism was limited typically to the various ways in which formal moral norms could be applied in concrete situations. For instance, the moral norm, "A worker must be paid a just wage" could be fulfilled in a number of ways depending on the cost of living in a particular region, the education and skill level of particular workers, and potential work hazards justifying higher compensation for greater personal risk, among others.[96] But other than these very limited instances of formal moral norms admitting a plurality of applications in concrete situations, moral pluralism was untenable in Fuchs's preconversion natural law theory.

In the domain of received teaching expressed propositionally through moral norms, the preconversion Fuchs regarded moral pluralism as an unacceptable mistake occasioned by ignorance, insufficient knowledge, or erroneous beliefs arising from subjective impediments due to original sin. On abortion, lying, artificial contraception, premarital sex, and a host of other moral issues the objective moral order articulated by the magisterium identified the proper manner of human behavior that allowed no deviation. In other words, received teaching on these issues was valid for all persons at all times, without exceptions or variations.[97]

The postconversion Fuchs, in contrast, contends that moral pluralism on the level of normative moral conclusions is not only acceptable in some cases, but actually desirable in order to attain true objectivity in concrete situations.[98] Fuchs, of course, is aware that an unrestrained moral pluralism could degenerate into a vulgar moral relativism, which denies any standards of acceptable behavior beyond an individual's own personal code of conduct, or that of one's particular culture or society. It should be noted that Fuchs is not endorsing a "radical pluralism"[99] that would most likely lead to a moral relativism precluding any cross-cultural or -societal standards of behavior. He is convinced, instead, that a more restricted pluralism is consistent with the proximate norm of morality, *recta ratio.*

Four potential causes of moral pluralism,[100] which Fuchs discusses to illustrate the phenomenon of legitimate moral pluralism, concern divergent interpretations of data, cultural constructs of the human person, potentially morally relevant local and regional differences, and developmental differences among nations or countries. The first cause of legitimate moral pluralism, according to Fuchs, stems from opposing interpretations of data concerning the human person and the necessary conditions for human well-being that support differing normative conclusions about human behavior. Unlike the preconversion Fuchs, whose philosophy of nature yielded unambiguous and univocal conclusions about the ends given through human nature, the postconversion Fuchs claims that "human reality cannot compel the practical reason . . . to arrive at one single and completely identical interpretation and evaluation of human reality,"[101] even in cases where there is no factual dispute about the data themselves.[102]

This inability of identical data to command a univocal interpretation is perhaps nowhere more apparent than in the longstanding debate on the moral status of the human embryo. Roman Catholic commentators usually agree that the infusion of a soul is a necessary prerequisite for individuality, at which point the embryo should be considered a human person enjoying the rights and privileges of all other human persons. But as different commentators interpret embryological data and the various processes the embryo undergoes in the first few weeks of development, there is considerable disparity about when these processes culminate in an individual embryo capable of receiving a soul. The problem for these commentators is not radically divergent worldviews, antinomic anthropologies, or disputes about factual data, but the significance and meaning that should be attached to the data.[103]

In these cases of differing interpretations of the same data, Fuchs claims that if a person has obtained the most comprehensive and accurate set of facts available, has striven to comprehend the data to the best of one's ability, and has arrived at an understanding of the data that is plausible and persuasive, she has attained *recta ratio* and it is legitimate to follow the course of action she considers correct.[104]

Another potential cause of legitimate moral pluralism arises from diverse cultural understandings of the human person, which generate different conceptions of acceptable human conduct and human well-being.[105] Fuchs writes,

It is conceivable, not only in particular cultures different from "ours" but also in "subcultures" within our more general culture, that there are convictions and visions of the world that—to the extent that they exist—are consequently the foundation of certain "objective" moral norms. That is, behavior in response to these convictions corresponds objectively to the reality of the world for these cultures, and therefore must be respected as such, although at the same time they are not acceptable for the rest of us.[106]

In his discussion of divergent types of behavior considered accept-able in different cultural contexts, Fuchs clearly wants to avoid a cul-tural imperialism that imposes behavioral homogeneity on people from diverse cultures. Indeed, in the preceding quotation Fuchs displays a notable degree of tolerance for behavior that coheres and is consistent with more basic beliefs about human beings and permissible conduct in a certain culture, even though such behavior might deviate from more widely held standards of behavior.

In Fuchs's discussion of different forms of marriage in African tribes (Fuchs does not specify whether polyandry, polygyny, or polyg-amy is the type of marriage in question), for example, he considers it possible that nonmonogamous marital arrangements might be right, given the conception of marriage and family life dominant in the respec-tive tribe:

> But might it not be assumed also that on the basis of dissimilar experiences, a heterogeneous self-concept and varying options and evaluations on the part of man (humanity) projecting himself into his future in human fashion—*secundum rectam rationem*—are en-tirely possible, and that these options and evaluations [concerning marriage] within the chosen system postulate varied forms of behavior?[107]

The consistent theme of Fuchs's analysis of certain types of behavior specific to particular cultures and normally at odds with commonly accepted standards of conduct is a willingness to entertain the possibil-ity that given the culture's belief system, their actions might correspond to *recta ratio*.

The interesting issue Fuchs's discussion of culture and moral plu-ralism raises is the justification of behavior. The preceding two quota-tions seem to indicate that actions can be justified by reference to a culture's dominant *Weltanschauung* and the consistency of actions with its worldview. The problem this position raises is that the experiences, concepts, and self-image comprising any particular culture's world-view and providing the background beliefs from which behavior arises might be misinterpreted or inaccurate. Thus, a justification of behavior based on consistency with a particular worldview is inadequate without attending to the truth or falsity of the larger network of beliefs grounding and justifying particular actions.

Oddly enough, although Fuchs seems very accepting of different cultures's beliefs and nowhere, to my knowledge, does he engage in any extensive critique of a particular culture's *Weltanschauung*, throughout his postconversion writings he consistently criticizes the concepts and anthropology underlying contemporary Roman Catholic moral theology and promotes distinct notions of God[108] and the human person[109] as correct. At least in his own Roman Catholic culture, Fuchs clearly does not regard all beliefs as equally plausible, nor does he exhibit any reluctance to propose a specific *Weltanschauung* or to argue at length against those in opposition.

Although Fuchs exhibits a considerable degree of receptivity toward the possibility of legitimate, diverse patterns of behavior in different cultural contexts, it is difficult to systematize or formulate any concrete criteria by which legitimate or illegitimate actions prompted by specific cultural understandings can be distinguished. Fuchs clearly wants to preserve those practices of different cultures that promote a positive sense of identity, purpose, solidarity, and meaning, but in the end he leaves many of the more pertinent questions unanswered.

Another component of moral pluralism arises from local and regional differences that might require diverse patterns of behavior to attain human well-being in a particular locale. In a small, tightly knit community characterized by a strong sense of obligation toward those less fortunate, Fuchs writes, meeting the basic needs of its members might best be accomplished through individual works of charity whereby those possessing the wherewithal to attend to the needs of others assume responsibility for ensuring a minimal standard of living for the disadvantaged. In larger urban areas where the poor tend to be geographically concentrated and neighborhoods lack the necessary social and economic structures to meet the basic needs of their inhabitants, ensuring a minimal standard of living might require more organized, institutional support capable of generating large amounts of external resources to counteract the impoverished conditions.[110]

Finally, legitimate moral pluralism might arise because developmental differences among countries create varying degrees of access to the resources necessary to enhance human well-being.[111] Proper medical treatment, for example, in less-developed countries might be considered primitive by U.S. standards, but given the limited medical resources available to physicians in these countries, their use of technology and medical techniques considered inferior to us might offer the best possibility of improving or restoring health, and therefore would correspond to *recta ratio* in those circumstances. The identical medical treatment, on the other hand, might be considered grossly inadequate and tantamount to malpractice in more developed countries where access to better technology and medical techniques is available.

Although Fuchs never attempts a systematic and thorough appraisal of the causes and limits of moral pluralism, the mere fact that he considers moral pluralism a legitimate response in certain situations represents a significant departure from his preconversion natural law theory. The principal thrusts of the preconversion Fuchs were universality and behavioral homogeneity. Other than the relatively limited number of formal moral norms admitting diverse concrete applications, natural law, for the preconversion Fuchs, consisted in a series of moral norms valid without regard to culture, nation, or social or economic situation. For the preconversion Fuchs, natural law typically allowed one, and only one, reasonable system of behavior, which was essentially the same for all human beings at all times.

The postconversion Fuchs, in contrast, does not consider a certain degree of moral pluralism an unacceptable deviation from objective morality that prevents human beings from grasping natural law correctly, nor does he believe that moral pluralism results from ignorance or character flaws. For the reasons mentioned above, moral pluralism is a legitimate response in certain situations. Indeed, as Fuchs writes, complete behavioral homogeneity would raise the suspicion that certain elements integral to attaining moral objectivity in concrete situations—historical and cultural contexts, varying access to resources to attain human well-being, and developmental differences among nations and regions—were either being overlooked or intentionally—and illicitly—omitted from consideration: "A certain plurality of solutions for situations which are only apparently equivalent is the price natural moral law ought to pay for the predicate of honor, *recta ratio*. A total lack of diversity in normative affirmations would nourish the doubt that these affirmations, if they truly take into account historical and cultural differences which are very important, lack a certain objectivity, without which there is no *recta ratio*."[112]

For Fuchs, then, moral pluralism is neither a lamentable state of affairs occasioned by inept human reasoning, nor is it a phenomenon that should be viewed with suspicion and hostility. Moral pluralism is sometimes warranted and should be welcomed as the correct manifestation of moral objectivity in concrete situations characterized by different morally relevant contexts that impinge on human well-being.[113] Although Fuchs offers no criteria which might clarify when or under what conditions moral pluralism is acceptable or desirable, at the very least the postconversion Fuchs makes clear that concretizing natural law's contents need not culminate in one exclusive behavioral response to moral issues, and that the quest to attain human flourishing in diverse cultural, historical, and social contexts might legitimately take different forms as humans discover the manifold ways in which human well-being can be attained.

Ascertaining *Recta Ratio:* The Emergence of a General Method to Determine Natural Law's Contents

The transition from nature or human nature to *recta ratio* as the proximate norm of morality created a vacuum in Fuchs's natural law theory immediately after his intellectual conversion. Unlike Fuchs's preconversion philosophy of nature, which yielded highly determinate and unambiguous conclusions about normative human conduct from an analysis of the finalities and order embedded in human nature, Fuchs's postconversion standard of right behavior, *recta ratio*, by itself offers little substantive indication of what natural law permits or forbids in concrete situations. Like the virtue of charity, *recta ratio* functions formally in moral deliberation, in other words, it contains no specific material content and cannot be reduced to, or identified exclusively with, any particular act or class of acts.

But the vacuum apparent in Fuchs's natural law theory immediately after his intellectual conversion stemmed not only from the formality of the proximate norm of morality, *recta ratio*. For approximately five years after Fuchs had repudiated his philosophy of nature and identified *recta ratio* as the standard by which actions are judged to be in accordance with, or contrary to, natural law, Fuchs never articulated any substantive criteria or a general method to determine whether human reason's moral evaluations and judgments had attained *recta ratio*, even though Fuchs's writings during this period are replete with references to *recta ratio*.[114] To be sure, Fuchs identified several necessary preconditions for human reason to be able to attain *recta ratio* in specific situations—a consideration of the concrete human person;[115] an assessment of the entire spectrum of circumstances present in a situation;[116] an evaluation of potentially relevant moral norms[117]—but these essential components of moral analysis indicate more that natural law reflection has been carried out in the right spirit, rather than identifying criteria that would give concrete direction to the moral agent's deliberations and allow her to assess whether her moral judgments correspond to *recta ratio*.

The first inkling of a method to determine *recta ratio* emerged in Fuchs's seminal article, "The Absoluteness of Behavioral Moral

Norms."[118] There Fuchs began to outline the criteria employed to assess whether an action conforms to *recta ratio*. Fuchs poses the question, "Do criteria for evaluating *recta ratio* exist? and then proceeds to list three standards. First, Fuchs writes, "A prime criterion is obviously correspondence of behavior ... to the meaning, in general, of being man and to the significance of particular givens—i.e., sexuality and marriage as *human* givens."[119] Fuchs goes on to say that the determination of the meaning of particular givens occurs not through an abstract metaphysical analysis of the human being, but through an assessment relying on experience and knowledge accumulated through reason continually reflecting on human beings and forging some understanding, however provisional, of human well-being.

Second, Fuchs claims that not only "the 'meaning' itself of experienced realities," but also "practical knowledge of the outcomes and consequences which determined modes of conduct can have" constitutes another criterion to assess the conformity of a moral judgment to *recta ratio*.[120] Although commentators have taken Fuchs's inclusion of consequences as one determinant of *recta ratio* to constitute "a giant step in the direction of a consequentialist methodology,"[121] with one moral theologian claiming Fuchs has proposed that "what one ought or ought not to do depends *entirely* on the consequences of an act,"[122] such far-reaching claims are unfounded. Fuchs, at this point, has not claimed that outcomes and consequences of acts are always morally relevant to determine an act's rightness or wrongness, nor has he articulated how they might affect the meaning of an act, nor has he indicated the relative importance of outcomes and consequences in comparison with the other determinants of *recta ratio*. Fuchs's inclusion of outcomes and consequences is not a misbegotten statement, but neither does the textual evidence support anything beyond the general statement that outcomes and consequences might be relevant to ascertain an act's conformity to *recta ratio*.

Third, another criterion Fuchs mentions is an act's "interpersonal significance and implications": "A basic criterion for true penetration of human reality, as well as for a just appraisal of experience, is found in the interpersonality of the human person. The conduct of individual persons in different areas of life has to be scrutinized in terms of its interpersonal significance and implications."[123] The intent of this criterion is to link actions to wider social contexts, in other words, to assess whether actions enhance social relations and strengthen community life or deleteriously affect a community's health and vitality.[124]

Having outlined three criteria to determine whether an act conforms to *recta ratio*, Fuchs takes up the practical issues of premarital intercourse and birth control and offers an assessment of how the determination of *recta ratio* proceeds in these situations:

> What must be determined is the significance of the action as a value or non-value for the individual, for interpersonal relations and for human society, in connection, of course, with the total reality of man and his society and in view of his whole culture. Furthermore, the priority and urgency of the different values implied must be weighed. By this procedure, man as assessor (the evaluating human society) arrives at a judgment, tentatively or with some measure of certitude, as to which mode of behavior might further man's self-realization and self-development.[125]

The principal thrust of this passage is to enlarge the scope of moral analysis to include a comprehensive account of the multiple values and disvalues in each act. As Fuchs writes, "Only the all-embracing view and total appraisal which, as such, determine the mode of action that is good for men, lead to a moral statement."[126] Far from limiting the determination of *recta ratio* to three criteria, Fuchs's practical illustration uncovers a drive toward a complete, panoramic understanding of an act and the potentially manifold human goods at stake in moral decisions.

Although the quest to attain an "all-embracing view and total appraisal" of an act is fundamentally sound and correct, absent some way to give content to *recta ratio* as the proximate norm of morality, Fuchs's notion of *recta ratio* could easily become a vacuous hodgepodge of general evaluative criteria that is practically meaningless and theoretically incapable of justifying any moral conclusion.[127]

Fuchs, however, offers an incipient account in "The Absoluteness of Behavioral Moral Norms" that begins to address *recta ratio*'s contents by appropriating significant portions of Peter Knauer's method of moral analysis. A few years prior to the publication of Fuchs's "The Absoluteness of Behavioral Moral Norms," Peter Knauer had published two influential studies on the principle of double effect[128] in which he claimed that the principle of double effect, properly understood, is "the fundamental principle of all morality,"[129] and offers a method to determine the rightness or wrongness of every human act. According to Knauer, the traditional function of the principle of double effect was to indicate when the causing of physical evils such as mutilation during surgery, killing innocent noncombatants during war, or killing an embryo during an operation for an ectopic pregnancy, was justified. The pivotal issue, in Knauer's opinion, is whether physical evil is intended directly or indirectly. If the former, the physical evil "becomes constitutive of the moral content of the act," which causes the act as a whole to be morally evil. If the latter, causing physical evil is justified and the act is considered morally right.

Knauer, however, departs substantially from the traditional understanding of the principle of double effect by claiming that the directness or indirectness of physical evil is not determined psychologically by the intention present in the moral agent's mind during an act—in other words, by what the moral agent was thinking about or desiring while performing an act—but by the presence of a "commensurate reason" for causing the physical evil.[130] A commensurate reason, in turn, exists only if physical evils caused during the pursuit of a particular value do not, in the long run, undermine the value being sought. For example, although the removal of a diseased organ causes a certain degree of physical evil (mutilation), it does not undermine the value being pursued (health) and thus constitutes a commensurate reason for causing the mutilation. If a surgeon were to remove more tissue than necessary to restore a person's health—regardless of whether the surgeon psychologically intended to remove additional tissue—this mutilation would not qualify as a commensurate reason because it would undermine the value being sought—health—and should be classified as a morally wrong action.[131]

In Knauer's opinion, the applicability of this method of determining moral rightness or wrongness goes far beyond the limited number of cases traditionally thought to be covered by the principle of double effect. Indeed, Knauer claims that the morality of all human actions ultimately rests on whether they are justified by a commensurate reason. The reason is that all human actions, without exception, cause some degree of physical evil, or "premoral physical evil" as Knauer calls it: "Every human act brings evil effects with it. The choice of a value always means concretely that there is denial of another value which must be given as a price in exchange."[132]

Knauer's conception of premoral physical evil is obviously more expansive than the traditional notion of *mala physica* and includes literally any disvalue or negative effect arising from the pursuit of human values, even when the only recognizable disvalue of a particular action is the fact that other values cannot be actualized at the same time. By studying for an examination, for instance, a student not only frequently suffers from lack of sleep, but also forecloses the possibility of actualizing other values at the same time, such as recreating, socializing, tutoring other students, or writing term papers. Thus, for Knauer, because every action, however laudable, involves creating some degree of premoral physical evil, all human actions—whether explicitly acknowledged or not—must be justified by a commensurate reason.

This brief outline of Knauer's interpretation of the principle of double effect is not intended to explicate or clarify the subtleties of Knauer's presentation, nor to indicate the problems that subsequent commentators raised with Knauer's interpretation.[133] My purpose is to provide the general background for the emerging natural law methodology apparent in Fuchs's "The Absoluteness of Behavioral Moral Norms," which relied heavily on Knauer's insights. In particular, Fuchs accepted Knauer's distinction between moral and premoral physical evil (Fuchs's premoral evil = Knauer's premoral physical evil) and claimed that the presence of premoral evil in an action, by itself, does not indicate whether an action is right or wrong. Killing, for example, is a grave premoral evil; but killing can be justified under certain circumstances. It is interesting to note that although Fuchs accepts Knauer's moral/premoral evil distinction, he does not indicate precisely the meaning of his phrase "premoral evil" or whether it is to be understood as synonymous with Knauer's expansive notion of any disvalue arising from the performance of an act, including the disvalue of being unable to actualize other values simultaneously, or whether premoral evil should be restricted to the traditional notion of *mala physica*—which refers only to bodily harms. Because Fuchs's practical illustrations of premoral evils treat only bodily harms and he does not offer any definition of premoral evil, it is difficult to establish his meaning precisely.

The second substantial component of Knauer's thought that Fuchs appropriated into his emerging natural law methodology was the necessity of a proportionate reason (= Knauer's commensurate reason) to justify the actualization of premoral evil. In his clearest statement on the justificatory role of proportionate reason—and his natural law methodology in general—Fuchs writes,

> [W]hen is human action, or when is man in his action (morally) good? Must not the answer be: when he intends and effects a human good (value), in the premoral sense—for example, life, health, joy, culture, etc. (for only this is *recta ratio*); but not when he has in view and effects a human nongood, and evil (nonvalue) in the premoral sense—for example, death, wounding, wrong, etc. What if he intends and effects good, but this necessarily involves effecting evil also? We answer: if the realization of the evil through the intended realization of good is justified as a proportionally related cause, then in this case only good was intended.[134]

Fuchs's structural analysis of the process of justifying the presence of premoral evil is comparable to Knauer's. The crucial issue for Fuchs, as for Knauer, is intentionality, in other words, How is the moral agent's intention evaluated when an action creates a certain amount of premoral evil? Or stated more explicitly in Knauer's terms, How is it determined whether a moral agent directly or indirectly intends premoral evil? For Fuchs, the moral quality of one's intention is determined by the presence or absence of a proportionate reason for causing premoral evil.

What Fuchs fails to specify is the meaning of proportionate reason. Although he cites Knauer's "The Hermeneutic Function of the Principle of Double Effect" immediately after stating that causing premoral evils is justified by a "proportionally related cause," Fuchs nonetheless omits an explanation that would allow his readers a precise understanding of his working notion of proportionate reason.

Thus, Fuchs's "The Absoluteness of Behavioral Moral Norms" signals a pronounced shift in his method of determining moral rightness and wrongness, but the ambiguity surrounding his conceptions of premoral evils and proportionate reason disallows any definite conclusions from being drawn about the validity of Fuchs's emerging natural law methodology, and it certainly is not sufficiently clear to provide moral agents with concrete directives which specify *recta ratio*'s contents and offer guidelines for ordering their lives and prioritizing their values.

In an article published ten years later,[135] Fuchs provided much-needed clarifications of the issues raised above and offered a clearer understanding of his natural law methodology. First, Fuchs's notion of premoral evils is now identical to Knauer's: anything of disvalue to human beings—even the nonrealization of certain human values resulting from the pursuit of other values—constitutes a premoral evil:

> Premoral evil [concerns] the well-being of human beings in the different areas of human reality. Such evils are, for example, illness, death, underdevelopment, depression, cultural deprivation, etc.— in short, anything in the earthly, human areas that in one way or another is opposed to the well-being and development of the human being. . . . [M]an is very limited in his actions in this world: he cannot realize premoral human goods or values without realizing premoral human evils at the same time and in the same act. Cultural values require the nonrealization of certain other human goods or values, accumulation of riches can cause poverty to others, the potentially high values of celibate life condition the nonrealization of the high values of married life (and vice versa), etc. The nonrealization of human goods and values is a premoral evil for human beings.[136]

Second, Fuchs offers a notion of what constitutes a proportionate reason justifying the creation of premoral evils. Fuchs writes,

> [B]ecause of the coexistence of premoral goods and premoral evils in every human act, we must determine the moral rightness or wrongness of every act by considering all goods and evils in an act and evaluating whether the evil or the good for human beings is prevalent in the act, considering in this evaluation the hierarchy of values involved and the pressing character of certain values in the concrete.[137]

For Fuchs, then, human actions are always attendant by premoral disvalues. Even in situations where a legitimate human value is sought and no perceptible negative effects are caused by the action, premoral disvalue is still realized insofar as other human values could not be actualized simultaneously. To determine whether the premoral disvalues of an act are morally justified, the moral agent must undertake a "comparative evaluation"[138] of the entire array of premoral values and disvalues and ascertain whether the former are more prevalent than the latter. If so, the action conforms to *recta ratio* and is morally right. If not, the action is contrary to natural law and is therefore morally wrong.

One of the major criticisms leveled against Fuchs's method for determining *recta ratio* is the difficulty—some say the impossibility—of undertaking any comparative evaluation of qualitatively different values, or what is call the "incommensurability problem."[139] In order to assess the prevalence of values over disvalues in any given action, Fuchs's critics claim, there must be some homogeneous measure or common denominator which serves as an intelligible basis for comparison. For example, the values and disvalues of eating certain foods such as apples, breakfast cereal, steak, or fish can be assessed from a variety of homogeneous measures, such as calories, fat content, cholesterol level, or amount and type of vitamins present, protein, or calcium. Because of the existence of common denominators to assess the values and disvalues of each type of food (e.g., calories, fat content), it is possible to render a comparative evaluation of the merits of each food. The incommensurability problem arises when no common denominator exists to compare the values and disvalues present in an action. A comparison of the values of eating a meal (nourishment), going for a walk (exercise), or taking a nap (rest) cannot be made, according to Fuchs's critics, because there is no univocal standard by which the benefits and disvalues of each can be measured.[140] As Germain Grisez asks rhetorically, "[H]ow many appetizing meals in a French restaurant give enjoyment comparable to that of a happy marriage? How many satisfactions of desires for particular objectives are comparable to the satisfaction of one's desire to be a good father, an excellent philosopher, or a faithful follower of Jesus?"[141]

Fuchs concedes that a "*quantitative* mathematical calculation of . . . *qualitatively* different elements involved in [an] action" is impossible.[142] But he also claims that this does not foreclose the possibility of determining the prevalence of premoral values and disvalues in an act. Fuchs presents two solutions to the incommensurability problem, which in the final analysis might be the same substantively. First, Fuchs claims that even though a comparative evaluation might not be made consciously, so that a person, if asked, could not provide explicit criteria by which premoral values and disvalues are compared, it does not follow that a valid comparative assessment has not been made. As Fuchs writes, "Causing an 'evil for man' is not morally wrong in every case. All that seems necessary is that it be justified by a comparative evaluation of all the elements of the total actual situation, without such evaluation having necessarily to take place on the plane of conscious reflection."[143] Although in this quote Fuchs makes no reference to Karl Rahner's epistemology, which posits the existence of an extensive realm of unthematic knowledge that always remains beyond the grasp of conceptualization and thematization, a Rahnerian influence could be operative here. If this is so, the comparative evaluation necessary to assess the premoral values and disvalues realized in any action would take place in that realm of consciousness inaccessible to thematic awareness.

The difficulty with this interpretation is that it contradicts the thrust of Fuchs's natural law theory—making the determination of moral rightness and wrongness as explicit as possible by knowing one's subject matter and concrete circumstances—by offering persuasive and credible reasons for a particular position, and by identifying the spectrum of premoral values and disvalues at stake in potentially divergent patterns of action. Unthematic knowledge, to be sure, plays a pivotal role in Fuchs's understanding of human subjectivity and the realization of oneself before God, but in the sphere of ascertaining moral rightness and wrongness, there seems to be little room in Fuchs's writings for basing moral evaluations or judgments on unthematic knowledge, which would have the tendency to privatize natural law deliberation.

A more plausible interpretation, in my opinion, is that Fuchs is referring to "intuitions"[144] that are not unthematic in his or Rahner's sense of the term, but also do not properly belong to analytic, discursive modes of thought. An experienced bicyclist, for example, requires no conscious advertence to the mechanics of pedaling, balancing, and accelerating and decelerating, yet the bike rider is aware, on some level, of her coordinated, purposeful activities. Long-married, loving spouses are often aware of each other's mental and emotional conditions without explicitly focusing attention on each other. Walking from point A to point B often requires numerous insights that help one avoid objects and other impediments, even though one might be mentally preoccupied with work, family, or some other important concern. In short, humans have the capacity to understand even though such acts of understanding elude explicit consciousness and occupy that gray and perhaps opaque area between unthematic knowledge and fully conscious awareness of one's mental operations and insights. As Fuchs writes, "The terms *ratio, recta ratio,* derive from the Scholastic tradition [and] signify . . . rather than specifically discursive thinking, an evaluative observing-understanding-judging, which can also occur 'intuitively.' "[145]

The difficulty inherent in this solution to the incommensurability problem is that unless the intuitions determining the proportion of premoral values to disvalues can be brought to explicit consciousness, so that there can be some degree of public discussion and examination of the moral decision-making process, Fuchs's method of determining moral rightness and wrongness must necessarily remain inaccessible to outside observers. In addition, absent any way to bring one's analysis of premoral values and disvalues to explicit, thematic consciousness, there seems to be little hope of fruitful moral dialogue and analysis in the face of disagreements. If, for example, I have a strong intuition that suicide is wrong but cannot publicly articulate the reasons for my moral judgment or for why I find premoral disvalues prevalent in the act of suicide, there is little chance of rendering the moral status of suicide intelligible to my interlocutors or readers, and perhaps even less chance of convincing anyone that suicide is morally wrong based solely on my conviction, however sincere and strongly held, that suicide is contrary to natural law.

Fuchs's other rejoinder to his critics is that the "common sense" moral judgments of people have consistently proven to be capable of determining moral rightness and wrongness accurately: "There is . . . an act of understanding and evaluating by *the person as a whole*—an act that is often not the product of reflection but of common sense— that humanity has always believed and shown itself to be capable of."[146] Assuming that the "common sense" to which Fuchs refers could be raised to explicit consciousness and discussed publicly, this solution to the incommensurability problem enjoys initial plausibility.[147] Take, for example, the case of a man sitting on a beach reading a book who notices a child beginning to drown. Suppose this man is a strong, capable swimmer experienced in water rescue techniques. Should he continue reading his book and let the child drown, or should he interrupt his reading and save the child? The "common sense" response, which I imagine would garner near unanimous approval, would be that the value of human life is far greater than the value of continuing reading a book, and that it would be morally wrong for the man not to attempt a rescue.[148]

Although it might be true that many people lead laudable lives based on their common sense convictions, and there are probably many good persons who act rightly consistently without any elaborate theoretical constructs consciously guiding their decisions, in the end Fuchs's appeal to common sense once again fails to clarify an intelligible way of determining the prevalence of values over disvalues in an act. To be sure, Fuchs's attention to the differing levels of awareness in our moral experiences honors the fundamental insight that many, if not most, of the right decisions made by people are not attendant by extensive, explicit, discursive moral reasoning. To this extent, Fuchs has succeeded in identifying a valid component of moral reasoning that deserves closer attention from moralists. But by not sufficiently explaining what he has identified, Fuchs lacks tangible criteria to distinguish common sense from common nonsense, which leaves little hope that Fuchs's appeal to common sense will be able to provide sufficient moral content to order people's lives and prioritize their commitments, and even less hope that it will be able to adjudicate the merits of competing moral claims. Like Fuchs's contention that determining the prevalence of values over disvalues occurs intuitively, his appeal to common sense creates more obscurity than it solves and ultimately renders the process of assessing values and determining moral rightness and wrongness ambiguous events that evade public inspection or explicitly conscious rational critique.

These criticisms do not imply, however, that Fuchs's method of determining moral rightness or wrongness by considering the prevalence of values or disvalues in an act is, as Fuchs's critics claim, "absurd," literally incoherent,"[149] "senseless," or "unintelligible."[150] The common conviction among Fuchs and like-minded moral theologians is that in concrete situations human beings can discern a hierarchy of values and can determine the proportion of values and disvalues likely to be actualized in different courses of action. Of course, assessing the potentially manifold consequences of an action is always fraught with a certain degree of uncertainty and is limited by the incapacity of human reason accurately to predict all contingencies. But this does not negate Fuchs's contention that values differ in their contribution to human well-being and that humans can assess the relative importance of particular values when confronted with different behavioral options.[151] As Edward Vacek writes, the human mind "function[s] more complexly than a computer" and is able rationally to choose between goods such as "apples and oranges" or between "a Julia Child meal and a van Gogh painting"[152] even in the absence of a common denominator by which to evaluate supposedly incommensurable human goods. Vacek continues, "Anyone who could not make such a comparison of these 'incomparables' would have to be value-blind, bereft of value judgment."[153]

The indisputable appeal of Fuchs's method of determining moral rightness and wrongness is that it recognizes gradations of values (human goods) and honors the widespread belief that not all goods are equally integral to human flourishing. We can and do make judgments that saving a boy from drowning is more important than reading a book; we can and do assess the relative worth of becoming a scientist, teacher, carpenter, or a beach bum; we can and do determine whether a life of voluntary poverty and simplicity is more morally laudable than life of consumerism and the pursuit of material goods; we can and do make moral judgments about the merits of allocating tax monies for welfare, space exploration, wilderness preservation, road construction, or law enforcement. In every sphere of human life, humans make moral judgments that explicitly or implicitly acknowledge certain human goods as more constitutive of human fulfillment and more worthy of pursuit.

This being said, the major lacuna in Fuchs's method of determining moral rightness or wrongness—which is also acknowledged by influential moral theologians as perhaps the greatest structural weakness of the whole "proportionalist" school of thought[154]—is an inadequate explanation of how humans assess competing values and disvalues and compare apparently qualitatively different values.[155] To rely, as Fuchs does, on intuition or common sense to justify a comparative evaluation of values and disvalues does appeal to the widespread experience of being able to discern and differentiate higher and lower values in concrete situations, but to the extent that Fuchs cannot make more explicit exactly how this comparative evaluation takes place, the ambiguity of his reliance on these types of moral awareness plays into Grisez's and Finnis's charge that moral decisions based on Fuchs's natural law method tend to be arbitrary and are all too often determined by personal preference, or a desire to conform to social pressures or expectations.

With Lisa Sowle Cahill, I suspect that at the root of Fuchs's inability to articulate a convincing, explicit way to assess the value of diverse human goods is an underdeveloped anthropology,[156] which I criticized at length in the preceding chapter. Although Fuchs adeptly

appropriates Karl Rahner's strand of transcendental Thomism and successfully reconstructs the acting subject according to the building codes
issued by mid–to late–twentieth-century transcendental Thomism,
Fuchs's postconversion theological anthropology resembles more a
phenomenological analysis of the necessary preconditions for being
human—transcendence, historicity, unthematic awareness of God, subjectivity—rather than an analysis of the goods constitutive of human
well-being from which a normative account of a hierarchy of values
could be constructed. If Fuchs's anthropology contained a thicker, more
detailed assessment of human well-being and identified the location
and relative importance of particular goods within an overarching
hierarchy of goods, he could overcome his critics's contention that any
comparative evaluation of values and disvalues is ultimately arbitrary
by showing how the particular values and disvalues at issue in a
concrete situation affect human well-being and at what level.

In the end, then, the question of whether Fuchs has succeeded in
offering an intelligible method to determine *recta ratio* remains unanswered. Fuchs, like Vacek, Cahill, McCormick, and a host of other
reputable moral theologians, refuses to accept that values—even alleg-
edly incommensurable values—cannot be legitimately compared, and
that our choices based on these comparative analyses are nothing more
than arbitrary decisions lacking any foundation in reality. Yet to date
Fuchs has not offered, in my opinion, sufficiently cogent evidence
explaining how an assessment of the values and disvalues in an act
are compared.

Contributions and Criticisms

In my estimation, one of Fuchs's greatest contributions to contemporary
natural law theory is the recognition that knowledge of natural law is
learned incrementally as we reflect on human well-being and discover
more precisely how human flourishing is best attained.[157] Prior to his
intellectual conversion, Fuchs's natural law theory was bereft of any
notion that natural law was uncovered gradually by reason reflecting
on experience in an ongoing and inherently open-ended process conditioned positively by competent, well-informed analysis and undermined and obscured by social and cultural biases, ideological
entrenchment, and inaccurate information about human beings and
their world; for natural law, according to the preconversion Fuchs, was
rendered intelligible through the *ordo naturae* that was not only readily
manifest and perceptible (at least to the members of the magisterium),
but also provided an invariant basis for universal and timeless moral
judgments valid for all people at all times.

For the postconversion Fuchs, in contrast, the supposition that knowledge of natural law can be gained completely through an unfettered and comprehensive view of the *ordo naturae* is patently false. Part of the reason for this shift is that the postconversion Fuchs no longer thinks nature is the locus of moral normativity, although it is morally significant.[158] Another reason is that the *esse* from which action follows is no longer invariable human nature, but the evolving and developing human person who continually modifies her existence as she progresses through history, which necessitates a more incremental approach in grasping changes in the human person as they occur over time in order to account for the fundamental natural methodological principle *agere sequitur esse*.[159] But prescinding from these reasons for Fuchs's postconversion contention that natural law is learned gradually, the principal reason for Fuchs's shift is a more realistic epistemology that is based not on the special assistance from the Holy Spirit to secure knowledge of natural law, or sanctifying grace given through episcopal ordination that unclouds a bishops mind and allows him to grasp natural law clearly and unambiguously,[160] but on the quality of one's moral insights.[161]

Moral insights, according to Fuchs, are gained by understanding the human person, our world, and the necessary conditions for human well-being. As one would expect, these insights are partial and fragmentary, never completely comprehending the totality of reality. As Fuchs writes, humans are "always in the stage of learning";[162] we seek to extend our knowledge of human functioning and human well-being by isolating identifiable components of the human person, developing different disciplines to study human existence in its manifold aspects (e.g., physiology, biology, psychology, sociology, philosophy, or theology). By continually uncovering new information about human beings we come to a greater and more detailed and precise understanding of ourselves. This process, however, is for Fuchs radically open-ended and indeterminate. We continually attempt to refine, improve, clarify, and extend our prior insights with further insights that offer a more comprehensive and accurate conception of human beings. Over and over this (one hopes) self-correcting process continues, never quite providing the much sought after omniscient God's-eye view of humankind, but gradually accumulating more information that further reveals the human person.

Thus, for Fuchs, knowledge of natural law, which is inseparable from knowledge of the human person and her world, does not come all at once in a momentous flash of insight that conveys our *esse* and the contents of the numerous disciplines that accumulate extensive information on discrete components of human beings; it comes through the hard-won fruits of consistently and patiently asking questions, seeking answers, sorting through information, testing hypotheses, judging the evidence, examining the validity of ideas (both present and past), and reflecting on decisions, actions, policies, programs, moral principles, and ideals. In this way, we gradually come to learn what actions truly promote human flourishing and are further able to implement and codify our accumulated moral wisdom.

Fuchs's presentation of the incremental process of gaining knowledge of natural law is strongly corroborated by recent historical studies documenting moral doctrine as an evolving, fluid phenomenon.[163] There are periods of stasis and certain plateaus in the history of any particular moral doctrine, but the defining characteristic of moral thought is the progressive attempt either to purify and solidify existing doctrine by adducing better reasons, making more cogent arguments, extending principles and concepts, or refuting opposing ideas, or to change doctrine by appealing to new information, exposing structural or substantive flaws, exposing contradictions or inconsistencies, or— perhaps—even inaugurating a paradigm shift that challenges the theoretical foundations on which a moral doctrine is based. Either way, moral reflection does not arrive at some bedrock set of truths impervious to further insights that need no further substantiation or verification to retain their persuasiveness. Bedrock moral truths there might be, but their legitimacy must be continually reassessed and reaffirmed as humans confront new issues, examine their moral beliefs, and gradually come to some understanding of how human well-being can be achieved in potentially unprecedented situations.

The practical advantages of Fuchs's idea that knowledge of natural law is gained incrementally are twofold. First, although it cannot explain the process of development of moral doctrine, it would certainly help alleviate the fear and trepidation many in the Roman Catholic community experience when confronted by changes in the Catholic Church's official moral doctrine. If Fuchs is correct that our knowledge of natural law always remains incomplete and partial, a change in moral doctrine could be conceived as a valuable moment in the ongoing process of purifying, supplementing, and possibly correcting our moral beliefs, rather than as a direct affront to the magisterium's credibility to teach on moral matters.[164]

Another advantage of conceiving natural law as learned incrementally over time is the methodological openness to further supplementation and revision as more anthropological data is accumulated, as the implications of patterns of behavior and social and economic policies are understood more clearly and in greater detail, and as potentially unprecedented moral issues arise. This methodological openness is essential if Roman Catholic natural law theory is to continue appropriating relevant insights gained from the social and physical sciences in an attempt to understand and specify further natural law's contents and how they bear upon contemporary moral questions.

Another valuable contribution Fuchs's notion of *recta ratio* makes to contemporary natural law theory is its recognition of the importance of knowledge of concrete circumstances.[165] Prior to his conversion, Fuchs's understanding of natural law, especially the sphere of absolute natural law, was dominated by a universalism that disregarded circumstantial data as irrelevant ontological accidents that bore no meaning for an assessment of right and wrong. Moral objectivity resided in abstract (though not indeterminate) moral principles generated through an equally abstract analysis of human nature, which were then applied in concrete situations without regard to any circumstance, whether personal, familial, cultural, economic, or social.[166]

The postconversion Fuchs, however, reiterates time and again that concrete knowledge is necessary to determine *recta ratio*.[167] *Recta ratio* cannot be ascertained by knowing what is right generally, what was right in the past, or what is right in the vast majority of cases. *Recta ratio* corresponds exclusively to what is objectively right in *this* situation, in the here-and-now constituted by the totality of circumstances.

This insistence on concrete knowledge to determine *recta ratio* must be understood properly. Fuchs is not embracing some form of situationism that claims every concrete situation is new and unique and thus calls for an original solution, nor is he asserting that time-honored moral wisdom expressed propositionally in moral norms cannot adequately capture the morally salient elements of a particular situation, nor is he implying that all circumstantial data are relevant to a moral decision. Fuchs is only maintaining that in order to determine *recta ratio*, knowledge of concrete particulars and how they impinge on human well-being are essential. As Fuchs writes, the determination of right and wrong concretely requires consideration of "the mode and 'color' of the nuanced particularity of the individual or societal situation, and in the contextualized givenness of the person."[168]

The force of Fuchs's contention that concrete knowledge is necessary to ascertain *recta ratio* is apparent when a wide variety of decisions pregnant with moral meaning and directly related to human well-being are considered: whether to get married, to take religious vows, or to remain single; when to have children and how many children to have; where and how children are to be educated; the selection of a particular career path or occupation; how to contribute to the life of the community; how to nurture healthy relationships; whether and how to support charitable organizations; and where to spend disposable income, among others. To make these choices in a manner that contributes to human well-being, and thus to attain *recta ratio*, requires intimate knowledge of a variety of circumstances such as personality, commitments, resources, talents, interests, personal limitations and constraints, amount of disposable income, and a community's needs, to mention a few. To attain integral, concrete human flourishing, it seems to me, there is no adequate substitute for well-informed moral agents who possess detailed, accurate knowledge of concrete particulars and who can use this information constructively to determine which course of action is beneficial to human welfare.

It is interesting to note that despite Fuchs's repeated admonitions that *recta ratio* is impossible to attain without knowledge of concrete circumstances, and despite his contention that it is the moral theologian's task to delve into practical matters,[169] Fuchs rarely ventures into the practical domain by considering moral issues or particular cases. When he does, his analyses resemble general, sometimes vague, ruminations on potentially relevant values that should be taken into consideration, and his principal strategy centers around posing questions that remind moral agents of the wide array of human goods at stake.[170] Part of Fuchs's refusal to engage practical matters undoubtedly stems from his German proclivity for more fundamental matters, which is relatively foreign to his American counterparts who generally show much greater interest in providing detailed, and sometimes painstakingly elaborate, answers to concrete moral issues or cases. Another reason is that Fuchs is simply honoring his methodological premise that attaining *recta ratio* requires knowledge of concrete circumstances, and as a moral theologian not privy to the circumstantial data surrounding a particular case or situation, Fuchs is not competent to judge whether a certain choice accords with *recta ratio* or not.

Thus, although Fuchs correctly—and unrelentingly—drives home the indispensable need for concrete knowledge to determine *recta ratio*, he leaves me wondering how practical moral reasoning should proceed in concrete matters. Lacking any substantive illustration that incarnates in greater detail the evaluative task of comparing values and disvalues, Fuchs's readers are left in the dark concerning how to adjudicate between conflicting values, how to sort relevant from irrelevant information, how analogies are to be drawn and paradigms utilized, and how to prioritize values. A good lesson in practical moral reasoning, of course, cannot begin to solve the numerous situations that could possibly arise. But lacking a better notion of how practical moral reasoning operates in concrete situations, Fuchs natural law theory and its predicate of honor—*recta ratio*—cease to clarify and illuminate the moral life in precisely the most interesting and vital moment.

Furthermore, Fuchs's conspicuous lack of attention to practical matters not only leaves individual moral agents with little sense of how to reason in concrete situations, but it also poses a more fundamental question as to whether Fuchs has produced a natural law theory serviceable for use within Roman Catholic moral theology. One of the criteria employed to assess the validity of any moral theory is the specific conclusions it reaches on concrete moral issues. Structural soundness, methodology, consistency, anthropological, philosophical, and theological presuppositions, and correctness of principles and maxims are potential bones of contention that might vitiate, in whole or in part, a moral theory's legitimacy. Yet equally important and open to dispute are the concrete, normative moral conclusions drawn by employing a particular moral theory. To this extent, a substantive evaluation of Fuchs's notion of *recta ratio* as it pertains to practical matters cannot be undertaken for lack of information. Perhaps Fuchs could demonstrate the soundness of his conception of *recta ratio* on a practical level by analyzing and explicating in further detail the operations of reason in a concrete situation and the various conceptual devices used to determine moral rightness or wrongness. But this pedestrian, yet vitally important, task has not yet been undertaken by Fuchs, which leaves a formidable, nagging question mark surrounding a significant component of his natural law theory.

Yet I believe Fuchs's natural law theory offers a much better basis for analyzing long-term moral issues raised not by individual, discrete actions but by the cumulative effects of certain patterns of behavior, even though each discrete action comprising these patterns is relatively benign by traditional standards. Let me illustrate by an example currently receiving much attention among agronomists: soil erosion on farmland in the United States.

From the beginning of this century to approximately the late 1970s soil erosion each year on American farms averaged nine tons per acre per year. Subsequent to the late 1970s, soil erosion was reduced to approximately five tons per acre per year due to the introduction of better farming techniques, and has remained at this level. At these rates, it takes about sixteen to thirty years for one inch of topsoil to erode. Under natural conditions, topsoil is created at a rate of one inch every 300 to 1,000 years,[171] which is equivalent to the formation of approximately 1½ tons of topsoil per acre per year.[172] The cumulative results are staggering: since the beginning of this century, the United States has suffered a net loss of approximately two billion tons of topsoil every year due to agricultural use![173] In Iowa alone, which supplies 12 percent of the world's supply of corn and a slightly less percentage of its soybeans, scientists estimate that from one-third to one-half of the topsoil has eroded since the beginning of this century.

The principal cause of the erosion problem is keeping the topsoil in a continually disturbed state. Unlike perennial crops which, after the initial planting, return year after year, do not require any subsequent soil disturbance, and develop intricate and widespread root systems that hold topsoil tightly in place during rainstorms or severe winds, modern agriculture, which is dependent almost exclusively on high-yield, annual hybrid crops that must be replanted every year, cultivated several times during the course of the growing season, and do not develop extensive root systems to hold topsoil in place, are continually disturbing the topsoil and thereby leaving it openly exposed to the elements.

Traditional Roman Catholic natural law analysis does not possess the moral vocabulary or conceptual tools to make sense of the topsoil erosion problem in the United States. The hallmark of Roman Catholic natural law deliberation from the twentieth-century neo-Thomist manualists to Finnis and Grisez is not only its exclusive focus on the human act as the sole locus of moral evaluation, but its reliance on the direct/indirect distinction to assess which effects or consequences enter into the moral evaluation of an act. Within this framework, any effect or consequence of an act outside the moral agent's intention is classified as indirect and does not affect the liceity of the act. Effects or consequences intended by the moral agent, however, are relevant to a moral assessment of an act.

This type of natural law analysis becomes unintelligible when applied to the topsoil erosion problem. First of all, no human act causes soil erosion—wind and rain do. Farmers simply create the condition—disturbed topsoil—whereby naturally occurring events can, when and if they occur, wreak far more havoc than they normally would under natural conditions. Second, the acts most proximately responsible for topsoil erosion—plowing and cultivating—are not directly intended to cause topsoil erosion, and thus the long-term effects of these practices would be excluded from the traditional moral evaluation of these respective acts. In the acts of cultivating and plowing topsoil, a farmer is simply intending to prepare the topsoil for eventual planting, or intending to eradicate weeds that compete with his crops for valuable minerals and nutrients. Neither intention could be considered morally wrong in any sense.

The disconcerting upshot of this strain of natural law analysis is that although enormous environmental degradation occurs unabatedly year after year, not only is no one held morally accountable because nobody directly intends to cause topsoil erosion, but it fails morally to assess the many influential forces, policies, and structures that either make it difficult for farmers to adopt another form of agriculture more conducive to topsoil retention or that make it so financially attractive to pursue short-term economic gain at the expense of long-term environmental consequences that only those farmers with enormous moral fiber willing to endure perhaps years of comparatively below average earnings are able to resist. For natural law analysis adequately to confront the issue of topsoil erosion in the United States, it must move beyond its traditional concepts and methods of analysis and somehow bring into moral consideration all those factors—government policies, agribusiness, consumer demand and preference, modern technology—that determine in differing degrees the trajectory of U.S. agriculture and actively resist and discourage any change in the status quo.

Fuchs's natural law theory, in my opinion, provides a more solid basis for confronting this issue in its root causes. The extremely attractive quality of Fuchs's method of natural law analysis is that by bringing the totality of premoral values and disvalues of an act into consideration, it connects individual, discrete acts to larger structures and schemes of recurrence that either hinder or promote human flourishing. Fuchs places no restrictions on whether premoral values and disvalues must be proximately or remotely connected to an act, directly or indirectly intended, long-term or short-term, probable or improbable, or great or insignificant, to be included in the assessment of moral rightness or wrongness. Moral analysis of an action, according to Fuchs, must take into consideration literally "anything in the earthly, human areas that in one way or another is opposed [or conducive] to the well-being and development of human beings"[174] that is associated in any way with the action.

If my interpretation of Fuchs is correct, this means that we must begin connecting our moral assessment of actions with the larger institutions, structures, long-term effects, and patterns of production and consumption that our actions support and legitimize, albeit in widely varying degrees. Similar to a rock thrown into a calm pond, causing waves to ripple across the entire pond's surface, the meaning, import, and effects of certain actions—and the premoral values and disvalues they support or create—reverberate throughout various spheres of human life.

When applied to the practical issue of topsoil erosion in the United States, Fuchs's method of analysis provides much needed clarity that begins to expose the root causes of topsoil erosion and sheds new light on the moral import of individual actions. Although many factors contribute to topsoil erosion in the United States, the principal contributory factor is Americans' insatiable appetite for beef. Although the

United States population constitutes approximately 4 percent of the world's population, it consumes 23 percent of all the beef produced in the world.[175] Over 70 percent of all the grain grown in the United States is used to feed livestock, the overwhelming majority of which is fed to cows.[176] Although American agriculture's astounding levels of production have consistently and vocally been praised for "providing food for the world,"[177] the indisputable fact is that the single most influential force in U.S. agriculture today is our lucrative beef market, which virtually dictates the types of crops grown and the amount of acres in production, and is supported heavily by federal government subsidies designed to ensure a steady stream of cheap grain in order to provide Americans with a relatively inexpensive and ample supply of beef.

Compared to other grain fed animals, cattle are the most inefficient converters of energy into meat, needing sixteen pounds of grain to produce one pound of meat (16:1). The grain-to-meat ratios of other animals are significantly lower: hogs 6:1, turkeys 4:1, chickens 3:1, and catfish 1:1.[178] This conversion inefficiency alone, which is the cause of an enormous amount of grain being wasted every year because of our refusal to substitute other meat sources for beef, is cause for grave concern. But the principal problem with beef production in the United States is that the grains most frequently fed to cattle—corn and soybeans—are responsible for the overwhelming majority of topsoil erosion in America. Americans' proclivity not only for beef, but for fatty beef,[179] necessitates that cattle spend at least three months before slaughter feeding almost exclusively on a diet of corn and soybeans, which represents the most cost-effective way for cattle farmers to produce the requisite fat content American consumers prefer.[180] Cost effectiveness, however, is directly opposed to long-term topsoil retention; for corn and soybeans are the principal culprits of the massive amount of topsoil erosion in the United States this past century. Their relatively sparse root systems offer scant protection during rainstorms or high winds; they need to be replanted each year, which leaves the topsoil in a perpetually disturbed—and highly erodable—state; and they require frequent cultivation to be protected from competing weeds in order to attain their maximum grain output, which also requires more topsoil disturbance.

The links between topsoil erosion and beef production in the United States are undeniable, although rarely, if ever, direct. Principally because of Americans' demand for beef, a major component of our agricultural system is rapidly depleting our topsoil at historically unprecedented levels which will take thousands of years to replenish at natural rates. Moreover, the gradual institutionalization of American agriculture has culminated in a powerful array of social and economic forces resistant to change that might reverse the decline of our topsoil: multinational corporations responsible for producing agricultural chemicals have a vested interest in the continued production of corn and soybeans; universities and faculty members benefiting financially from research into different genetic strains of corn and soybeans have much to lose if production levels decline; farm machinery and implement companies making tractors, combines, plows, and cultivators depend for their livelihood on the continued demand for corn and soybean production related machinery; and cattle farmers, both large and small, stand to lose millions of dollars if their cheap supply of grain became more scarce or expensive.[181]

Within Fuchs's method of natural law analysis, the moral import of discrete, individual acts such as buying and consuming beef, tilling and cultivating topsoil, growing corn and soybeans, or promoting government subsidies for farmers producing corn and soybeans can be assessed only by taking into account all the reasonably foreseeable premoral values and disvalues associated with the respective act,[182] including the disvalue that such act fosters patterns of behavior or supports institutions, practices, or policies that create the necessary conditions for an extraordinary amount of topsoil erosion to occur. Perhaps the singularly most important contribution of Fuchs's natural law methodology is its ability to account for the interconnectedness of individual acts and larger schemes of recurrence (such as topsoil erosion) affecting human well-being. Even though premoral values and disvalues might be far removed in time and place from individual acts, and even though no direct causal relationship exists between acts and the many values and disvalues they reinforce and perpetuate, Fuchs's methodology not only allows for, but requires, that natural law analysis consider the manifold links, sometimes remote and subtle, between individual acts and their consequences.

On a practical level, this means that the act of buying and consuming a hamburger, for instance, to the extent that it creates demand for a food production system and practices that are highly deleterious to topsoil quantity and supports and perpetuates an agricultural system unsustainable in the long-term, is connected to these disvalues and can be assessed morally only by including these disvalues in the overall determination of the act's rightness or wrongness. This does not imply, of course, a blanket condemnation of beef consumption, nor that consumers are solely accountable or most proximately responsible for topsoil loss related to beef production. The lengthy causal trail between topsoil erosion and consumers includes a host of intermediaries, all of which are more directly involved in the farming practices and policies that inevitably lead to excessive topsoil erosion. But the absence of a direct causal link between beef consumers and topsoil erosion does not mean that a moral assessment of beef consumption can ignore its long-term environmental effects or simply classify these effects as unintended consequences beyond the scope of a particular action's rightness or wrongness.

Many of the long-term problems confronting us today—global warming, depletion of the ozone layer, dwindling fisheries worldwide, species extinctions, underdevelopment of and massive poverty in Third World countries, and rapid deforestation of tropical rain forests—are comparable to the issue of topsoil erosion: most are caused indirectly and unintentionally by individuals or institutions; none are caused by individual acts per se, but by the cumulative negative effects of individual acts over long periods of time; many of those contributing to these problems are separated geographically and causally from the problems themselves, and might never experience personally the hardships inflicted upon those most immediately affected by these conditions; and most cannot be associated exclusively with one readily identifiable cause, but with a multitude of partial causes that have roots in lifestyle choices, business practices, governmental and corporate policies, and other forces conditioning and reinforcing patterns of behavior inimical to human well-being in the long run.

Fuchs's natural law methodology, which requires that all foreseeable premoral values and disvalues of an action be included in its moral evaluation, rightly recognizes that the implications of actions, especially consistent patterns of actions, often extend far and wide and affect human well-being in a multitude of ways. If my interpretation of Fuchs's natural law methodology is correct, however, it offers a plausible and sorely needed conceptual basis for confronting many of these problems by making moral agents consider the moral import of their discrete, individual actions more panoramically and comprehensively. It forces us to look beyond the immediate effects of our actions to the potential structures, institutions, and practices they support or legitimize. It makes individual moral agents consider the cumulative long-term effects of their actions and the probable outcomes of their behavior.[183] It draws attention to the long, potentially complicated, yet undeniable trail of causality that links actions to larger schemes of recurrence, and raises our awareness of the interconnectedness of human life and behavior. And finally, it counteracts the myopia that all too easily and self-servingly discounts the full moral import of our actions and often blithely refuses to acknowledge participation in and responsibility for, albeit in varying degrees, conditions impeding human flourishing. Not a bad beginning for Roman Catholic natural law theory as it begins to tackle the many pressing, systemic moral problems confronting us in the early twenty-first century.

Notes

1. Josef Fuchs, *Natural Law: A Theological Investigation*, trans. Helmut Recker and John Dowling (New York: Sheed and Ward, 1965), 60.

2. Josef Fuchs, *Christian Morality: The Word Becomes Flesh*, trans. Brian McNeil (Washington, D.C.: Georgetown University Press, 1987), 137.

3. Josef Fuchs, *Human Values and Christian Morality*, trans. M.H. Heelan et al. (Dublin: Gill and Macmillan, 1970), 112; Josef Fuchs, *Moral Demands and Personal Obligations* (Washington, D.C.: Georgetown University Press, 1993), 94–96; Josef Fuchs, *Personal Responsibility and Christian Morality*, trans. William Cleves et al. (Washington, D.C.: Georgetown University Press, 1983), 129; and Josef Fuchs, *Christian Ethics in a Secular Arena*, trans. Bernard Hoose and Brian McNeil (Washington, D.C.: Georgetown University Press, 1984), 120, 145.

4. James F. Keenan, "Josef Fuchs at Eighty, Defending the Conscience while Writing from Rome," *Irish Theological Quarterly* 59 (1993): 206–7.

5. Fuchs, *Personal Responsibility*, 127; and Fuchs, *Christian Ethics*, 120.

6. Fuchs, *Christian Morality*, 52, 147–48; and Fuchs, *Personal Responsibility*, 73. For discussions of reason in Thomas Aquinas's natural law theory, see Vernon J. Bourke, "Is Thomas Aquinas a Natural Law Ethicist?" *Monist* 58 (1974); Frank J. Yartz, "Order and Right Reason in Aquinas' Ethics," *Mediaeval Studies* 37 (1975); and Laurent Sentis, "La Lumière Dont Nous Faisons Usage," *Revue des Sciences Philosophiques et Théologiques* 79 (1995).

7. Fuchs, *Personal Responsibility*, 208–10; and Fuchs, *Moral Demands*, 40.

8. Franz Böckle, *Fundamental Moral Theology* (Dublin: Gill and Macmillan, 1980), 215–22. See also Jean Porter, *Natural and Divine Law: Reclaiming the Tradition for Christian Ethics* (Grand Rapids, Mich.: William B. Eerdmans, 1999), 85–98, for an analysis of reason in Medieval natural law theory.

9. Fuchs, *Christian Morality*, 15, 52–53.

10. Fuchs, *Human Values*, 145.

11. This illustrative list is mine, not Fuchs's.

12. Fuchs, *Moral Demands*, 54–55.

13. Fuchs, *Personal Responsibility*, 130.

14. Fuchs, *Christian Morality*, 147–48. See also Fuchs, *Moral Demands*, 113, where he discusses three levels of inclinations in human beings as presented by Thomas Aquinas (*Summa Theologiae*, 5 vols., trans. Fathers of the English Dominican Province [1911; reprint, Westminster, Md.: Christian Classics, 1981], I–II.94.2)—those shared with all beings, those shared with all animals, and those unique to humans—and identifies human reason as the principal human good.

15. See Böckle, *Fundamental Moral Theology*, 222–28.

16. For the relationship between reason and nature, see also ibid., 199–222; Franz Böckle, "Nature as the Basis of Morality," in *Personality Morals*, ed. Joseph A. Selling (Leuven, Belgium: Leuven University Press, 1988); and Wilhelm Korff, "Nature or Reason as the Criterion for the Universality of Moral Judgments," *Concilium* 150 (1981).

17. Fuchs, *Christian Ethics*, 95.

18. Fuchs, *Personal Responsibility*, 95–96. For a different perspective, see William C. Spohn, *Go and Do Likewise* (New York: Continuum, 1999).

19. See also Martin Rhonheimer, *Natural Law and Practical Reason: A Thomist View of Moral Autonomy*, trans. Gerald Malsbary (New York: Fordham University Press, 2000), 318–20.

20. Fuchs, *Personal Responsibility*, 129–30.

21. Ibid., 98.

22. Ibid., 97. Cf. Pope John Paul II, *Veritatis Splendor* (Boston: St. Paul Books and Media, 1993), #36.

23. Fuchs, *Personal Responsibility*, 97.

24. Fuchs, *Human Values*, 145.

25. Fuchs, *Personal Responsibility*, 93.

26. Fuchs writes, "[M]oral questions are not resolved through logical and clear deductions from the concrete being-human. Rather, moral 'solutions' are an evaluative insight and understanding capable of corresponding to the concrete conduct of being human in each specific situation. Therefore it is not possible to 'prove' such 'solutions' in the strict sense of the word; we can only explain and describe them, make them intelligible" (ibid., 67).

27. Ibid., 179, 182; and Fuchs, *Christian Ethics*, 122.

28. Fuchs, *Moral Demands*, 42.

29. Fuchs, *Personal Responsibility*, 128.

30. Josef Fuchs, "The Absolute in Morality and the Christian Conscience," *Gregorianum* 71 (1990): 701; Fuchs, *Personal Responsibility*, 128; Fuchs, *Christian Ethics*, 10. See also Mercier's attempt to explore the implications of symbolism in Fuchs's natural law theory (Ronald Amos Mercier, "What Is Nature? The Development of Josef Fuchs' Thought on Moral Normativity" [Ph.D. diss., Regis College, 1993], 174–93).

31. Fuchs, *Christian Morality*, 7.

32. Fuchs, *Personal Responsibility*, 99.

33. Ibid., 125.

34. Fuchs, *Human Values*, 142.

35. Ibid., 144.

36. Fuchs, *Natural Law*, 7.

37. For constructive proposals on the role of experience in moral theology, see Margaret A. Farley, "The Role of Experience in Moral Discernment," in *Christian Ethics: Problems and Prospects,* ed. Lisa Sowle Cahill and James F. Childress (Cleveland, Ohio: Pilgrim Press, 1996); and Susan L. Secker, "Human Experience and Women's Experience," in *The Annual of the Society of Christian*

Ethics, ed. D. M. Yeager (Washington, D.C.: Georgetown University Press, 1991).

38. Fuchs, *Personal Responsibility,* 130.

39. George P. Schner, "The Appeal to Experience," *Theological Studies* 53 (1992): 44.

40. Stephen Pope, "Scientific and Natural Law Analyses of Homosexuality," *Journal of Religious Ethics* 25 (1997): 116.

41. Fuchs, *Personal Responsibility,* 93.

42. The following description of moral development is heavily dependent on Jean Porter, *Moral Action and Christian Ethics* (Cambridge: Cambridge University Press, 1995), 174–77.

43. Fuchs, *Moral Demands,* 40–41.

44. Pamela M. Hall, *Narrative and Natural Law: An Interpretation of Thomistic Ethics* (Notre Dame, Ind.: University of Notre Dame Press, 1994), 99. See also Fuchs, *Moral Demands,* 55.

45. Fuchs, *Moral Demands,* 114, 117.

46. Fuchs, *Personal Responsibility,* 100, 130, 183, 197; Fuchs, *Christian Ethics,* 6, 40; and Fuchs, *Human Values,* 145, 187–88.

47. See Bernard Hoose, "Proportionalists, Deontologists, and the Human Good," *Heythrop Journal* 33 (1992) for an insightful critique of the limits of abstraction in moral theology.

48. Josef Fuchs et al., "Final Report of the Pontifical Commission on Population, Family, and Birth," in *The Encyclical That Never Was* by Robert Blair Kaiser, (1967; reprint, London: Sheed and Ward, 1987), 10.

49. Bernard J. F. Lonergan, *Insight: A Study of Human Understanding* (New York: Longmans, Green, 1958), xxiii–xxx.

50. Fuchs, *Moral Demands,* 98–99.

51. Ibid., 22.

52. Fuchs, *Personal Responsibility,* 209–12.

53. James Keenan makes this point concerning the principle of double effect (James F. Keenan, "The Function of the Principle of Double Effect," *Theological Studies* 54 [1993]: 294–95).

54. Fuchs, *Personal Responsibility,* 129–30.

55. Fuchs, *Moral Demands,* 97.

56. Ibid., 114–15.

57. Fuchs, *Natural Law,* 151.

58. Ibid., 145–46.

59. Josef Fuchs, *General Moral Theology,* pt. 1 (Rome: Pontificia Universitatis Gregoriana, 1963), 55.

60. Fuchs, *Natural Law,* 158.

61. Josef Fuchs, "Weihsakramentale Grundlegung kirchlicher Rechtsgewalt," *Scholastik* 16 (1941): 515.

62. Ibid., 516.

63. Fuchs, *Natural Law,* 159.

64. Ibid., 158–60.

65. Fuchs, *Christian Ethics*, 50. See Austin Flannery, ed., *The Conciliar and Post Conciliar Documents: Vatican Council II*, vol. 1, rev. ed. (Northport, N.Y.: Costello Publishing, 1988), 750–53.

66. Fuchs, *Christian Morality*, 14–17, 21–26; Fuchs, *Christian Ethics*, 50–54; Fuchs, *Moral Demands*, 96–97; and Josef Fuchs, "Good Acts and Good Persons," in *Considering Veritatis Splendor*, ed. John Wilkins (Cleveland, Ohio: Pilgrim Press, 1994), 22–23.

67. Fuchs, *Moral Demands*, 142. Cf. Gustave Ermecke, "Die Bedeutung von 'Humanwissenschaften' für Moraltheologie," *Theologische Zeitschrift* 26 (1975): 126–40.

68. Fuchs, *Christian Morality*, 20–21.

69. For a more extended discussion of the magisterium's infallibility, see Francis A. Sullivan, *Magisterium: Teaching Authority in the Catholic Church* (Mahwah: N.J.: Paulist Press, 1983), 79–152.

70. Fuchs, *Christian Ethics*, 60.

71. Richard A. McCormick, *The Critical Calling: Reflections on Moral Dilemmas since Vatican II* (Washington, D.C.: Georgetown University Press, 1989), 96–100. For a synopsis of the different levels of official moral teaching, see Avery Dulles, "The Hierarchy of Truths in the Catechism," *Thomist* 58 (1994).

72. Fuchs, *Christian Ethics*, 60.

73. Fuchs, *Natural Law*, 158–59.

74. Fuchs, *Christian Ethics*, 148 (emphasis added).

75. Ibid.

76. Ibid., 62.

77. Fuchs, *Personal Responsibility*, 179.

78. Fuchs, *Christian Ethics*, 62. See also Bruno Schüller, "Remarks on the Authentic Teaching of the Magisterium of the Church," in *The Magisterium and Morality*, Readings in Moral Theology, no. 3, ed. Charles E. Curran and Richard A. McCormick, (Ramsey, N.J.: Paulist Press, 1982), 26–31 for specific instances of error in the magisterium's teaching.

79. Fuchs, *Moral Demands*, 194.

80. Fuchs, *Christian Ethics*, 61. See also Joseph A. Komonchak, "Authority and Its Exercise," in *Church Authority in American Culture*, ed. Philip J. Murnion (New York: Crossroad, 1999), 29–46 who bases teaching authority on the trust engendered among the faithful by the magisterium.

81. Fuchs, *Christian Morality*, 140; and Fuchs, *Christian Ethics*, 51.

82. Fuchs, *Christian Ethics*, 57–58, 148; Fuchs, *Christian Morality*, 115; and Fuchs, *Personal Responsibility*, 184.

83. Fuchs, *Human Values*, 145–46, 187–88; Fuchs, *Personal Responsibility*, 100, 130; Fuchs, *Christian Ethics*, 6, 40; Fuchs, *Christian Morality*, 147; and Fuchs, *Moral Demands*, 42, 48, 105, 114, 117.

84. Fuchs, *Christian Morality*, 115.

85. Fuchs, *Moral Demands*, 142.

86. Fuchs, *Christian Morality*, 54.

87. Fuchs, *Moral Demands*, 142.

88. Ibid., 194. See also John P. Boyle, "The Natural Law and the Magisterium," in *The Magisterium and Morality*, Readings in Moral Theology, no. 3, ed. Charles E. Curran and Richard A. McCormick, (Ramsey, N.J.: Paulist Press, 1982), 446–52.

89. Fuchs, *Christian Ethics*, 148.

90. Fuchs, *Natural Law*, 145–62.

91. Fuchs, *Moral Demands*, 142.

92. Fuchs, *Human Values*, 72.

93. Fuchs, *Personal Responsibility*, 128–29.

94. Schüller, "Remarks on the Authentic Teaching of the Magisterium," 16–17.

95. Fuchs, *Human Values*, 72.

96. Josef Fuchs, "Naturrecht und positives Recht," *Stimmen der Zeit* 163 (1958–59): 133.

97. The aforementioned issues pertain both to absolute natural law, which comprises that body of timeless and universally valid moral norms, and relative natural law, which comprises those moral norms applicable for all *postlapsum* humans. Technically speaking, moral norms derived from relative natural law would not be valid for persons before the Fall. But for the purposes of our analysis, the distinction between *pre-* and *postlapsum* humans is inconsequential.

98. For contemporary discussions of moral pluralism, see Benedict Ashley, "The Loss of Theological Unity," in *Being Right*, ed. Mary Jo Weaver and R. Scott Appleby (Bloomington: Indiana University Press, 1995); Lawrence C. Becker, "Places for Pluralism," *Ethics* 102 (1992); John Kekes, *The Morality of Pluralism* (Princeton: Princeton University Press, 1993); C. Ben Mitchell, "Is That All There Is? Moral Ambiguity in a Postmodern Culture," in *Challenge of Postmodernism*, ed. David S. Dockery (Wheaton, Ill.: Bridgepoint/Victor, 1995); Karl Wilhelm Merks, "Das Recht Anders zu sein: Eine Chance für die Moral: Pluralismus zwischen Freiheit und Verantwortlichkeit," *Bijdragen* 55 (1994); and David B. Wong, "Coping with Moral Conflict and Moral Ambiguity," *Ethics* 102 (1992).

99. Fuchs, *Moral Demands*, 113.

100. These examples are not intended as a comprehensive catalogue of the causes of moral pluralism, only as means to illustrate the various ways *recta ratio* might yield different normative moral conclusions in concrete situations. Fuchs was not interested in developing a theory of moral pluralism, only in explaining how it related to natural law deliberation.

101. Fuchs, *Moral Demands*, 26.

102. Ibid., 22.

103. For a debate that illustrates well the problem of interpreting empirical data, see Mark Johnson, "Delayed Hominization," *Theological Studies* 56 (1995); Mark Johnson, "A Rejoinder to Thomas Shannon," *Theological Studies* 58 (1997); Jean Porter, "Individuality, Personal Identity, and the Moral Status of the Preembryo: A Response to Mark Johnson," *Theological Studies* 56 (1995); Thomas

A. Shannon, "Delayed Hominization: A Response to Mark Johnson," *Theological Studies* 57 (1996); and Thomas A. Shannon, "A Further Postscript to Mark Johnson," *Theological Studies* 58 (1997).

104. Fuchs, *Christian Morality*, 136.

105. See also Gerard J. Hughes, "Is Ethics One or Many?" in *Catholic Perspectives on Medical Morals*, ed. Edmund D. Pellegrino, John P. Langan, and John Collins Harvey (Dordrecht, The Netherlands: Kluwer Academic Publishers, 1989), 184–91.

106. Fuchs, *Moral Demands*, 106.

107. Fuchs, *Personal Responsibility*, 132.

108. See Fuchs, *Christian Morality*, 28–49, 50–61.

109. See Fuchs, *Human Values*, 92–111.

110. Fuchs, *Personal Responsibility*, 60–61.

111. Ibid., 132, 214; and Fuchs, *Christian Morality*, 137.

112. Fuchs, *Personal Responsibility*, 70–71.

113. Ibid., 214; Fuchs, *Christian Morality*, 137; and Fuchs, *Moral Demands*, 111.

114. See, for example, Fuchs, *Human Values*, 112–47.

115. Ibid., 145.

116. Ibid., 72.

117. Ibid., 28–29.

118. Josef Fuchs, *Personal Responsibility and Christian Morality*, trans. William Cleve et al. (Washington, D.C.: Georgetown University Press, 1983), 115–52. This article was first published as "The Absoluteness of Moral Terms," *Gregorianum* 52 (1971): 415–57. Unless noted otherwise, all citations refer to the version in *Personal Responsibility and Christian Morality*.

119. Fuchs, *Personal Responsibility*, 130.

120. Ibid.

121. Richard A. McCormick, "Reflections on the Literature," in *Moral Norms and Catholic Tradition*, no. 1 of *Readings in Moral Theology*, ed. Charles E. Curran and Richard A. McCormick (Ramsey, N.J.: Paulist Press, 1979), 294.

122. John R. Connery, "Morality of Consequences: A Critical Appraisal," in *Moral Norms and Catholic Tradition*, no. 1 *Readings in Moral Theology*, ed. Charles E. Curran and Richard A. McCormick (Ramsey, N.J.: Paulist Press, 1979), 245 (emphasis added).

123. Fuchs, *Personal Responsibility*, 130.

124. For this criterion, Fuchs cites William van der Marck, who writes, "The real (formal) difference between acts which are externally (materially) completely alike arises from the essentially inter-subjective character of all human acts . . . The most fundamental and ultimate thing that can be said about a human act is that it is community-forming or community-breaking— it makes for a communal relationship, or rejects it" (William van der Marck, *Love and Fertility* (London: Sheed and Ward, 1965), 33–34.

125. Fuchs, *Personal Responsibility*, 131.

126. Ibid., 131.

127. See Cristina L. H. Traina, *Feminist Ethics and Natural Law* (Washington, D.C.: Georgetown University Press, 1999), 193.

128. Peter Knauer, "La détermination du bien et du mal moral par le principe du double effet," *Nouvelle Revue Théologique* 87 (1965): 356–76; Peter Knauer, "The Hermeneutic Function of the Principle of Double Effect," in *Moral Norms and Catholic Tradition*, no. 1 of *Readings in Moral Theology*, ed. Charles E. Curran and Richard A. McCormick (Ramsey, N.J.: Paulist Press, 1979). For a shortened English version of the first article, see Peter Knauer, "The Principle of the Double Effect," *Theology Digest* 15 (1967).

129. Knauer, "Hermeneutic Function," 1.

130. Ibid., 27.

131. Ibid., 30–31.

132. Ibid., 16.

133. For early commentary on Knauer's articles, see Connery, "Morality of Consequences;" Paul Quay, "Morality by Calculation of Values," in *Moral Norms and Catholic Tradition*, no. 1 of *Readings in Moral Theology*, ed. Charles E. Curran and Richard A. McCormick (Ramsey, N.J.: Paulist Press, 1979); and Albert Di Ianni, "The Direct/Indirect Distinction in Morals," in *Moral Norms and Catholic Tradition*, no. 1 of *Readings in Moral Theology*, ed. Charles E. Curran and Richard A. McCormick (Ramsey, N.J.: Paulist Press, 1979).

134. Fuchs, *Personal Responsibility,* 136.

135. Fuchs, *Christian Ethics*, 71–90.

136. Ibid., 81–22.

137. Ibid., 82.

138. Ibid., 84.

139. Germain Grisez, "Against Consequentialism," *American Journal of Jurisprudence* 23 (1978): 29–41; Fuchs, *Personal Responsibility*, 156–61; William E. May, *An Introduction to Moral Theology* (Huntington, Ind.: Our Sunday Visitor, 1994), 119–23; John Finnis, *Fundamentals of Ethics* (Washington, D.C.: Georgetown University Press, 1983), 86–94; John Finnis, *Natural Law and Natural Rights* (Oxford: Clarendon Press, 1980), 118–25; and John Finnis, *Moral Absolutes: Tradition, Revision, and Truth* (Washington, D.C.: Catholic University of America Press, 1991), 18–24. Peter Knauer also claimed that there is no common measure to assess qualitatively different values (Knauer, "Hermeneutic Function," 11–12).

140. For an overview of the incommensurability problem, see Bernard Hoose, *Proportionalism: The American Debate and Its European Roots* (Washington, D.C.: Georgetown University Press, 1987), 81–91.

141. Grisez, "Against Consequentialism," 35.

142. Fuchs, *Moral Demands*, 42. Garth Hallett, in contrast, claims that it is legitimate to compare qualitatively different values and that Grisez's incommensurability thesis is actually a pseudo-problem. See Garth Hallett, "The 'Incommensurability' of Values," *Heythrop Journal* 28 (1987): 373–87; and Garth

Hallett, *Greater Good: The Case for Proportionalism* (Washington, D.C.: Georgetown University Press, 1995), 23–29.

143. Fuchs, *Personal Responsibility,* 164–65.

144. Fuchs, *Human Values,* 145; Fuchs, *Personal Responsibility,* 128; and Fuchs, *Christian Ethics,* 10.

145. Fuchs, *Personal Responsibility,* 128.

146. Fuchs, *Moral Demands,* 42.

147. Lisa Sowle Cahill offers a similar assessment of common sense, stating that "good moral common sense never has been and is not now to be replaced in *practice* by conceptual analysis . . ." (Lisa Sowle Cahill, "Teleology, Utilitarianism, and Christian Ethics," *Theological Studies* 42 [1981]: 618).

148. Interestingly, as I understand Grisez's and Finnis's positions, both of which maintain that life and knowledge are equally basic and incommensurable goods that cannot be lexically ordered, it would be morally permissible for the man on the beach either to continue reading his book and let the child drown or to attempt to save the child. Because neither action directly attacks a basic good, either action is equally morally permissible.

149. Germain Grisez, *Christian Moral Principles,* vol. 1 of *The Way of the Lord Jesus* (Chicago: Franciscan Herald Press, 1983), 153.

150. Finnis, *Fundamentals of Ethics,* 87, 89.

151. Fuchs, *Moral Demands,* 42, 51 n. 23.

152. Edward Collins Vacek, "Proportionalism: One View of the Debate," *Theological Studies* 46 (1985): 304.

153. Ibid.

154. See Cahill, "Teleology," 617; Pope, "Scientific and Natural Law," 116–21; and Vacek, "Proportionalism," 304. It should be noted that Fuchs disavowed any connection to proportionalism until very late in his academic career, and then only in a very restricted sense. See Fuchs, *Moral Demands,* 44–45.

155. Hoose, "Proportionalists, Deontologists, and the Human Good," 187.

156. Commenting on the same problem in Richard McCormick's presentation of proportionality, Lisa Sowle Cahill writes, "One pertinent and undeniable shortcoming in McCormick's sort of innovative teleology is that, in the absence of a classical or medieval metaphysics and anthropology, it is no mean task to discern and agree upon the precise relations of values in the hierarchy upon which the theory depends. . . . It is possible to enjoin or to prohibit absolutely certain resolutions of value conflicts only in the light of knowledge of the ways in which such resolutions impinge on human nature. This is why the achievement of some consensus on the hierarchical relations of potentially conflicting values (e.g., premoral values), while so elusive, is so vital" (Cahill, "Teleology," 617). See also James J. Walter, "The Foundation and Formulation of Norms," in *Moral Theology: Challenges for the Future,* ed. Charles E. Curran (Mahwah, N.J.: Paulist Press, 1990), 146.

157. For a similar assessment of the incremental nature of knowledge of natural law see Hall, *Narrative and Natural Law,* 99; and Kenneth R. Melchin, "Moral Knowledge and the Structure of Cooperative Living," *Theological Studies* 52 (1991).

158. Fuchs, *Moral Demands*, 59.

159. Fuchs, *Personal Responsibility*, 126.

160. Fuchs is not denying that the Holy Spirit is operative in leading us to knowledge of natural law, or that sanctifying grace given through episcopal ordination is unhelpful in determining natural law's contents. His only point is that the Holy Spirit's assistance and God's grace do not circumvent the normal processes of human knowing.

161. Fuchs, *Personal Responsibility*, 93; and Fuchs, *Christian Morality*, 148.

162. Fuchs, *Moral Demands*, 22.

163. John T. Noonan, *The Scholastic Analysis of Usury* (Cambridge, Mass.: Harvard University Press, 1956); John T. Noonan, *Contraception: A History of Its Treatment by the Catholic Theologians and Canonists* (Cambridge, Mass.: Harvard University Press, 1965); John T. Noonan, "Development in Moral Doctrine," *Theological Studies* 54 (1993): 662–77; and John Maxwell, *Slavery and the Catholic Church* (London: Barry Rose Publishers, 1975).

164. John Ford, one of the moral theologians on the papal birth control commission, framed the issue in precisely these terms: If the magisterium were to change its teaching on artificial contraception it would not only raise doubts about its position as authentic interpreter of natural law, but would cast an ominous shadow of doubt over the entire corpus of received teaching. See John C. Ford et al., "The Birth Control Report: II: The Conservative Case," *Tablet* (29 April 1967): 485.

165. Traina, *Feminist Ethics*, 185–86. For an excellent article on the importance of concrete, circumstantial knowledge, see Hoose, "Proportionalists, Deontologists, and the Human Good," 181–87.

166. James F. Keenan, "Josef Fuchs and the Question of Moral Objectivity in Roman Catholic Moral Reasoning," *Religious Studies Review* 24 (1998): 253.

167. Fuchs, *Human Values*, 187–88; Fuchs, *Personal Responsibility*, 100, 136–37; Fuchs, *Christian Ethics*, 6, 40, 107; and Fuchs, *Moral Demands*, 3, 41–42, 105.

168. Fuchs, *Moral Demands*, 114. As Cristina Traina accurately characterizes Fuchs's position, "Concrete, local wisdom is the key to objectivity [for Fuchs]" (Traina, *Feminist Ethics*, 185).

169. Fuchs writes, "And the moral theologian suffers no slight to his dignity by venturing into the more practical domain of casuistry; it is part of his task to do so" (Fuchs, *Human Values*, 41).

170. See Fuchs, *Moral Demands*, 74–87.

171. Wes Jackson, *New Roots for Agriculture* (Lincoln: University of Nebraska Press, 1980), 17.

172. R. Neil Sampson, *Farmland or Wasteland: A Time to Choose* (Emmaus, Penn.: Rodale Press, 1981), 124.

173. Ibid., 116–17.

174. Fuchs, *Christian Ethics*, 83.

175. Jeremy Rifkin, *Beyond Beef* (New York: Penguin, 1993), 154.

176. Ibid., 160.

177. This deceptive bit of political propaganda, which in many instances is explicitly or implicitly intended to evoke nationalistic pride and satisfaction in the fact that American agriculture can export grain to feed the starving masses in Third World countries, obscures the fact that 66 percent of America's grain exports are fed to livestock, not people, which in many instances are then imported to America for us to consume. See ibid., 162.

178. Francis Moore Lappé, *Diet for a Small Planet* (New York: Ballantine, 1982), 70.

179. Most Americans have probably never eaten beef produced exclusively by grass fed cattle, which compared to grain fed beef tends to be dry, tough, and generally less palatable. For an account of the historical and cultural forces operative in Americans's preference for grain fed beef, see Rifkin, *Beyond Beef*, 40–64.

180. The United States Department of Agriculture's beef grading system (choice, prime, select, standard) is based on fat content. The higher the fat content of a cut of beef, the higher the grade it receives from USDA inspectors. See ibid., 96–98.

181. Marty Strange, *Family Farming: A New Economic Vision* (Lincoln: University of Nebraska Press, 1988), 31–42

182. Fuchs, *Christian Ethics*, 80–82.

183. See Cynthia S. W. Crysdale, "Revisioning Natural Law: From the Classicist Paradigm to Emergent Probability," *Theological Studies* 56 (1995): 478.

6

Natural Law, Christian Faith, and Moral Norms

Introduction

Although natural law analysis has been a mainstay of Roman Catholic moral theology throughout the twentieth century, employed to address peoples of all nations on a wide variety of moral issues, significant voices of discontent began to emerge in the mid-twentieth century claiming there existed considerable antinomy between the dominant natural law tradition and the fullness of the Christian moral life. By deriving normative moral conclusions from the perceived natural order and virtually ignoring the import of Christian sources of moral wisdom (except as proof texts intended to justify positions already held), whether these be specific teachings of Jesus or prominent themes in Scripture such as discipleship, Christian love, the kingdom of God, forgiveness, or compassion, critics asserted, albeit on varying grounds, that natural law is not synonymous with Christian morality and that any ethic based on natural law must inevitably culminate in a desiccated and partial version of the total Christian moral life.

Fritz Tillmann (1874–1953), a former scripture scholar, was one of the first Roman Catholic moral theologians to criticize the dominant neo-Thomist natural law tradition and represents perhaps the most decisive break from the neo-Thomist manualists. In Tillmann's works on Christian ethics[1] there is no intention of revamping or dialoguing with the existing natural law tradition. Tillmann's singular purpose was to reestablish the link between Scripture and Christian ethics, which had been effectively severed by the neo-Thomist manualists through their fusion of morality with canon law. Both in methodology and theological presuppositions, Tillmann rejected the presentation of Christian morality portrayed by the neo-Thomist manualists and proposed an entirely different basis for the Christian moral life: following Christ.[2]

For Tillmann, Christian morality finds its source in the visible image of God, Jesus, who represents the norm of morality for humankind. Through Christ, God's intentions for humans have been clearly revealed, and we must conform our lives to Jesus by following the example he set.[3] Tillmann's notion of following Christ does not imply a literal imitation of Jesus: following Christ involves considerably more plasticity and originality, and means a devotion to Christ and a willingness to assume the conscious role of Christ's disciple who shares and understands Christ's mission, religious vision, and relationship to the Father. In this sense, following Christ does not entail carbon copies of Jesus intent on performing exactly the same actions as Jesus, but the appropriation of Christ's religious and moral consciousness, which is then translated into action.[4]

Gérard Gilleman (b. 1910), another influential moral theologian critical of the dominant natural law tradition, particularly that of twentieth-century neo-Thomist manualists, chides the manualists for having "systematized into a science the pulsing vitality of concrete Christian life."[5] The language of commandments, law, obligation, and principles dominating the neo-Thomist manualists' presentation of morality ignores the "soul of the Christian tradition," God's love, which has been graciously offered to all through Christ and which draws us into intimate communion with God: "The core of the 'good news' was this: God is charity; and we no longer are merely His creatures or participations, but we are really His sons, invited *in Filio* to communion with the Father. With this the whole world was renewed; man could no longer live as before."[6]

Gilleman does not jettison the role of natural law in moral deliberation; the formal function of charity, according to Gilleman, necessitates that proximate ends be set by reason grasping the natural order, which in turn are referred to our ultimate end, God, through charity.[7] Gilleman's principal complaint is that natural law theorists have misrepresented the moral life as a quest to obey and fulfill a series of (usually minimal) moral obligations instead of a concrete response to the spiritual dynamism present in every person that seeks nothing less than direct union with God in mutual love. Our being and actions receive their principal meaning from the fact that we are ordered toward God and all of our actions should be manifestations of creatures expressing our response to God's love. To the extent that natural law prescinds from the finality and intentionality present in our being and actions, it must be considered "a section artificially cut out from the real, complete [Christian] morality" that distorts and differs radically from the reciprocal love that constitutes the basis of the Christian moral life.[8]

Bernard Häring (1912–98), the noted Redemptorist at the Roman Alfonsianum, was another critic of the neo-Thomist natural law tradition who was perhaps most responsible for the demise of the neo-Thomist manuals of moral theology. Häring eschewed the abstraction and theological sterility of Roman Catholic natural law theory that seemed to him a moral philosophy detachable and separate from Christian faith. His popular three volume work, *The Law of Christ*,[9] greatly influenced by Tillmann, also attempted to ground Christian morality in Scripture, not in philosophical notions of nature or human nature. As Häring writes, "Moral theology in all its considerations must flow from the word of God."[10]

According to Häring, the moral and religious lives can be distinguished, but not separated. Scripture portrays the moral life as an invitation to a life of discipleship in Christ by responding to God's salvific work and by accepting the grace continually and individually prompting us to conversion. This grace-filled *metanoia* is always prior to any moral law: before any sense of obligation or duty, the Christian must understand morality as a summons by God to follow the exemplar of the moral life, Jesus, and to respond to God's initiative and self-communication by modeling her life on Jesus' example. Only then is it possible properly to understand the theological import of the moral law as a concrete expression of one's adherence to Christ.[11]

Häring's insistence on the priority of Scripture in moral theology leads to a presentation of Christian morality markedly at odds with the dominant neo-Thomist manuals. In the *Law of Christ*, for example, Häring introduces nearly every section with a relevant biblical passage and then proceeds to discuss particular topics related to the respective biblical verse(s). Häring's intent in using scripture as the prelude to a subsequent substantive analysis of a moral issue was not to confirm preestablished positions, but as a normative source to give trajectory and content to his discussion. Although Häring's undifferentiated appeal to Scripture raises numerous questions about his methodological consistency and the precise role the Bible plays in moral deliberation, there is little doubt that his goal to "expound the most central truths in the light of the inspired word of the Bible"[12] represented a new emerging genre of moral theology that contrasted starkly in numerous ways with traditional Roman Catholic natural law theory.

These early attempts to bring the Christian faith to bear on the moral life were extremely successful in raising questions about the adequacy of Roman Catholic natural law theory and in forcing moral theologians of all stripes to clarify the relationship between the Christian faith and natural law.[13] Buoyed especially by the Second Vatican

Council's instruction that moral theology "should draw more fully on the teaching of holy Scripture and should throw light upon the exalted vocation of the faithful in Christ,"[14] the movement begun by Gilleman, Tillmann, and Häring gained momentum and subsequently led to a lively and protracted debate that has continued to the present day.[15]

Throughout this ongoing discussion after the Second Vatican Council, Fuchs has been one of the pivotal figures clarifying issues and proposing constructive solutions to a host of challenges. In both his commentaries on the Second Vatican Council's documents[16] and in his articles dealing with the relationship between Christian faith and natural law,[17] Fuchs has consistently defended the validity of natural law while also attempting to honor the realities of the Christian faith. The purpose of this section is to develop Fuchs's unique contribution to the question of the relationship between Christian faith and natural law and to critique his understanding of natural law's function within the wider context of the Christian moral life.

Christian Morality and Natural Law

Although natural law comprises an indispensable component of Christian morality, Christian morality is not reducible to or coextensive with natural law. Similar to Fuchs's preconversion synthesis of the natural and supernatural orders, which partitioned the moral life into two distinct, but related, spheres, with natural law serving as a receptacle for the supernatural order and remaining intrinsically open to fulfillment on a higher level,[18] the postconversion Fuchs also regards natural law as one component within the more comprehensive sphere of Christian morality. The distinction Fuchs draws between natural law and Christian morality, which is functionally equivalent to his preconversion natural/supernatural distinction, occurs between the categorial and transcendental dimensions of Christian morality.[19]

The categorial component of Christian morality concerns material conduct, the rightness or wrongness of which is determined solely by its conformity to natural law.[20] *Recta ratio*, which is attained by human reason reflecting on experience and grasping the course of action consistent with concrete, integral human flourishing, is the measure of right and wrong conduct in the categorial sphere. On this plane of morality, the objective of all persons—Christian or non-Christian—is the same: to employ our reasoning capacity in order to understand the human person and to determine how our actions and the various human goods affected by our actions—such as relationships, social, political, and economic structures, family life, personal commitments, or the common good—should be ordered and actualized. Accordingly, the evaluative criteria, methodology, and types of analyses "by which we must determine which kind of human conduct is truly human, that is, in accordance with right reason, are in themselves the same for all men"[21] on the plane of categorical morality.[22]

The transcendental[23] dimension of Christian morality, on the other hand, refers to a person's relationship with God, which is conceptually distinct from the particular manner of expressing this relationship through action in the categorial sphere. According to Fuchs, there are two aspects of one's transcendental relationship with God, one unthematic and the other thematic. First, there is a specific Christian intentionality that tends toward God as the remote term of our existence. This Christian intentionality should not be confused with the concept of intent used to assess the liceity of an action in traditional Roman Catholic moral theology (i.e., object, intent, and circumstances). Fuchs's notion of Christian intentionality is borrowed from Karl Rahner and presupposes the basic tenets of Rahner's theological anthropology.[24] As a transcendent, spiritual being, the human person's activities have an inherent dynamism toward God. Human knowing reaches beyond all limited objects and horizons in a perpetual search to grasp the ultimate horizon of human knowing, God. The drive impelling our willing and loving likewise is not satisfied by finite objects but strives to embrace the infinite object, God. From the most mundane to the most momentous actions, there is an intentionality underlying all human activity that seeks God, and through this intentionality all human actions are made before God and in reference to God as the ultimate horizon of human existence.[25]

This intentionality, according to Fuchs, is both Christian and unthematic. Fuchs, like Rahner, claims that our transcendental intentionality tends toward God as Father, Son, and Holy Spirit because of our unthematic knowledge of God. Although Fuchs is more ambiguous than Rahner about the total contents of the realm of unthematic knowledge,[26] Fuchs clearly maintains that the term of human transcendence, God, is known not as an undifferentiated entity grounding our existence and the rest of creation, but in the full reality of God as the Trinity.[27] Thus every person—Christian, Muslim, Buddhist, atheist, or agnostic—is unthematically aware in every human action of the Christian God as the source and term of her striving.

The second aspect of the human person's transcendental relationship to God concerns the thematic recognition of God who is revealed in Scripture and tradition and has become manifest in the person of Jesus. In other words, this component of one's transcendental relationship to God is the sphere in which Christian faith, understood broadly as the constellation of explicitly conscious beliefs (incarnation, resurrection, salvation) values (poverty, hospitality, forgiveness), stories (the Good Samaritan, creation), concepts (divinity, omnipotence), attitudes (reverence, awe, joyfulness), and practices (worship, prayer, contemplation), gives rise to the religious life characterized by various rituals, sacraments, and participation in a faith community.[28] Through this explicit awareness of God and God's saving action in history, we forge our self-understanding as Christians, reflect on the meaning of the world, our position in the cosmos, and the import of the mysteries of faith, and in conscious recognition of this ongoing divine-human relationship seek to respond to God in love.

Although Fuchs claims that the influence of explicit Christian faith on morality is principally motivational,[29] the Christian faith also provides a realm of meaning that impinges on the content of the moral life.[30] On perhaps the most fundamental level, the Christian faith motivates the Christian to strive for rightness and to be a moral person.[31] It also motivates Christians to embrace and incarnate certain broad values or general "moral stances"[32] such as simplicity, neighbor love, concern for the poor, and compassion.[33] The Christian faith might provide reasons for particular types of behavior, such as St. Paul exhorting the Corinthians to avoid prostitution because their bodies are temples of the Holy Spirit and should not be degraded through illicit sex.[34] Finally, it might provide an intelligible religious context that lends legitimacy to certain choices for Christians, such as voluntary virginity or celibacy.[35] On all these levels, the Christian faith, Fuchs claims, "animates" the moral life, and gives "a deeper and richer meaning" to our behavior.[36]

For Fuchs, then, Christian morality comprises three distinct components: (1) categorial behavior, the rightness of wrongness of which is determined by natural law; (2) an unthematically conscious Christian intentionality, through which every person, regardless of her particular religious faith (or lack thereof), recognizes the Christian God as the remote term of her striving, willing, and acting; and (3) explicit, thematic Christian faith that is manifested through one's religious life and affects the moral life by its motivational power and the meaningful context it provides for the Christian.[37]

Most of the controversy surrounding the relationship between natural law and Christian morality during the latter half of the twentieth century has focused on (1) and (3), more specifically, on the issues whether and how the Christian faith affects the material content of behavior.[38] Fuchs's critics contend that by separating the thematically religious component of Christian morality from the realm of categorial behavior, not only has Fuchs failed to grasp that the content of categorial behavior is sometimes determined by religious faith, in other words, "faith involves fundamental decisions (with definite content) in moral matters,"[39] but he has erroneously constructed a notion of Christian morality in which the determination of the moral rightness or wrongness of concrete actions is "untouched and detachable from faith,"[40] thereby effectively eviscerating the Christian faith's ability to exercise a normative influence on categorial behavior.

Before addressing the central issue in this debate—the normativity of Christian faith for material conduct—I want to examine in more detail the precise ways in which Fuchs claims that natural law analysis, which concerns the determination of right and wrong categorial behavior, is dependent on Christian faith. Although Fuchs maintains that explicit, thematic Christian faith "influences," "penetrates," and "enriches"[41] categorial behavior, Fuchs sets clear limits on the possible ways the relationship between Christian faith and natural law analysis can be construed.

First, perhaps the most pronounced dependency of natural law deliberation on Christian faith is anthropological.[42] Both the pre- and postconversion Fuchs subscribes to the fundamental methodological principle *agere sequitur esse*,[43] which requires that before any normative statements about human conduct can be made, there must be sufficient knowledge about the human person, the goods to which we are ordered, and the conditions necessary for human flourishing. Although the Christian faith might not offer a systematic, comprehensive anthropological account of the human person, it does convey vital elements that serve as indispensable aids for understanding the human *esse*. The anthropological claim that the human person is created in the image and likeness of God, for example, which bestows on the human person inalienable dignity and value, at the very least creates a strong bias against any action, policy, or structure that views or treats humans instrumentally, and might serve as a guiding principle for more specific moral claims such as particular human rights.[44] The doctrine of original sin, which explains the persistent tendency present in every human being to act destructively, also might be useful in formulating social policies that effectively limit the possibility of individual biases leading to harmful consequences, and on an individual level it might create a healthy sense of self-criticism that counteracts our proclivities to rationalize and deceive ourselves.[45] From the theological doctrines of creation, redemption, and salvation to the Christian understandings of suffering, discipleship, and eschatology, the anthropological implications of the Christian faith confer a "deepened insight"[46] into human beings and offer "a specific vision of the person and the world that makes it easier to attempt to discern valid norms of rightness."[47]

Another dependency of natural law on Christian faith is axiological. In the quest to identify values conducive to human well-being, the Christian faith offers the moral agent a certain "ethos"[48] in which particular values are enshrined and promoted as constitutive of a genuinely human moral life.[49] Peacefulness, compassion, concern for the poor and vulnerable, forgiveness, and the equitable distribution of the earth's resources are a few of the many enduring values that have been widely accepted by the Christian community as integral components of the moral life.

A third type of dependency between natural law and Christian faith is epistemological. Because of the anthropological vision supplied by Christian faith that makes manifest particular aspects of the human person, and because of the Christian ethos that conveys and promotes certain values constitutive of human well-being, the Christian, according to Fuchs, enjoys an epistemological advantage over non-Christians to the extent that the truths of the Christian faith make it easier to discover right behavior in some concrete situations.[50] As Fuchs writes, the Christian faith, which "gives to believers a vision and evaluation of man that are impossible at least in the same way and to the same degree, for nonbelievers,"[51] helps Christians "discover norms and judgments [consistent with natural law] more easily and securely."[52]

It should be noted that the epistemologically privileged position of Christians asserted by Fuchs is limited. Fuchs is not claiming that Christians act (or have acted) more morally than non-Christians, or that the truths of the Christian faith are sufficient to solve every contemporary moral issue, or that Christian faith somehow renders superfluous the findings of the sciences and philosophy, or that Christians are able to circumvent the normal, fallible processes of human knowing in arriving at moral truth. The epistemological advantage of Christians over non-Christians must be understood as a difference in degree, not in kind. To the extent that the Christian faith conveys truths about the human person and particular values conducive to human well-being, this body of knowledge theoretically increases the probability that the Christian will find it easier to discern right and wrong behavior in some instances.

Despite these three types of dependency of natural law on Christian faith, Fuchs denies any normative dependency between the material content of morality and Christian faith. The question that has continually been debated by theologians the past thirty years[53] is, Does Christian morality depend on the Christian faith for its material content? Stated differently, Does the Christian faith provide normative material content for contemporary Christians, so that moral norms and concrete judgments can be legitimately inferred, deduced, or derived from the

Christian faith?[54] Typically those answering these questions affirmatively hold that some source such as God's action in history, Jesus' words, St. Paul's moral instructions, or the "clear and constant" teaching of the church[55] constitutes a binding moral imperative indicating what Christians ought to do both then and now.[56]

In one of his early postconversion articles, Fuchs seems to endorse this position, stating that the Christian faith "not only motivates human conduct more deeply and inspires it, but it will also determine the *content* of our conduct."[57] In subsequent articles, however, Fuchs repudiates this statement and offers two reasons why the Christian faith cannot determine the material content of behavior in the manner described above. First, the exclusive source of moral obligation, according to Fuchs, is the judgment of human reason that a particular action promotes human well-being. The "law of rationality"[58] operative in ethical experience requires that every potential font of moral wisdom be intelligible, credible, and persuasive; to gain the consent of the moral agent there must be an insight into the information (e.g., Scripture, church teaching) that grasps cogent reasons for accepting the information as correct and applicable in the concrete situation and that understands that the implementation of the information in question is conducive to human flourishing. As Fuchs writes of revelation, which can be generalized to include all potential sources of moral information generated by the Christian faith, "The binding force of morality would be nonsense if it did not enjoy the fundamental ability to be perceived and understood. . . . If the information which is given to us in revelation is to be ethically meaningful . . . then the attainment of insight into the relationship between the information and moral behavior must be possible."[59]

For Fuchs, then, neither a fideism that disregards the reasonableness of moral obligations, nor a divine positivism that considers God's commands or laws as morally binding even when they appear erroneous to human reason, nor the attempt directly and immediately to derive normative material content from some authoritative Christian source of moral wisdom, is legitimate; for they all overlook, or overtly disregard, that moral obligations arise only through human reason determining that a particular action, norm, or policy conforms to *recta ratio,* which for Fuchs is the sine qua non for determining normative material content in concrete situations.[60]

Fuchs's argument against inferring, deducing, or deriving normative moral conclusions from the Christian faith, it should be noted, is applicable even to those time-tested Christian sources of moral wisdom that throughout human history have been recognized as perennial embodiments of moral truth. The moral injunctions of the Ten Commandments and the Sermon on the Mount, for example, although conveying moral knowledge that has been consistently affirmed by Christians in every age, do not in themselves dictate how Christians must act or not act. As Fuchs writes, the reason these and other components of the Christian moral tradition have attained such longstanding and notable prominence is because Christians, by reflecting on the human situation and determining what types of actions promote human well-being, have time and again concluded that the moral wisdom contained in them is reasonable, persuasive, and promotes the objective of human well-being, in other words, that it corresponds to *recta ratio*.[61] In Fuchs's mind, this corroborates his principal contention that it is not the Christian faith that determines the material content of behavior, but the discerning, evaluative work of human reason assessing concrete situations, the values at stake, and the validity of the Christian moral tradition and judging which particular action serves human welfare in the given circumstances.[62]

The second reason why the material content of behavior cannot be inferred, deduced, or derived from the Christian faith lies in the process of justifying moral beliefs. Any appeal to some aspect of the Christian faith as an authoritative source for a particular norm or action, which commonly takes the form of "God (or the Bible or the Church's teaching authority) forbids X . . . therefore we must not do X," implicitly relies on the belief that a moral position can be justified by reference to the respective Christian source.[63] This belief, however, fails to acknowledge that such sources are not self-justifying, and that any appeal to them must be further justified by "the fundamental moral experience of the human person,"[64] or the judgment of *recta ratio*.

Take, for example, an appeal to the Bible to condemn homosexual behavior (Leviticus 18:22, 20:13; 1 Corinthians 6:9; Romans 1:26–7). Presupposing that these texts do offer an unequivocal condemnation of homosexual behavior in all circumstances,[65] is a Christian's position that homosexual behavior is morally wrong justified by appealing to these texts? For Fuchs, the answer is "no." If the further question is asked, How is the material content of these biblical passages morally justified? an immediate problem arises. Is the moral content of the Book of Leviticus justified by appealing to the Book of Leviticus? Is St. Paul's condemnation of homosexual behavior justified by citing St. Paul's other letters? Is any appeal to the Bible justified by appealing to the Bible itself? The circularity apparent in this manner of justifying moral belief reveals that the appeal to the Bible as an authoritative source from which moral positions can be immediately derived is flawed; for in order to justify the Bible's moral contents as valid imperatives for Christians, one must appeal to an extrabiblical source, which

Fuchs claims is, and has always been, the considered judgments of Christians employing their reasoning power to discern what is morally right.[66]

For Fuchs, then, Christian ethics cannot dispense with natural law analysis. The Christian faith might be a treasure trove of moral wisdom, conveying moral insights gained, tested, and purified throughout Christian history and offering moral knowledge applicable to a wide variety of contemporary moral issues. But, Fuchs claims, the Christian faith cannot supplant the creative, constructive role of human reason, which alone is capable of determining right and wrong concretely. Christians should reflect upon and try to bring the moral wisdom embedded in our faith tradition to bear on concrete choices; we should use the anthropological knowledge generated by various Christian sources to understand the human person better and more comprehensively;[67] we should strive to cultivate attitudes and dispositions—for example, love of neighbor, concern for the poor and vulnerable, and kindness—that Christians have consistently endorsed as integral to the moral life;[68] and we should meditate on the life and works of Christ and try to understand the values he promoted.[69] With only one proviso—that the material content of behavior not be determined directly by the Christian faith—moral deliberation for Christians, in Fuchs estimation, should be permeated by our faith tradition.

Although most of Fuchs's postconversion writings on the relationship between Christian faith and natural law have usually focused on the role of isolated, pithy, propositional forms of explicit moral instruction such as the Ten Commandments or Jesus' words or St. Paul's exhortations and whether the substance of these instructions determine the material content of behavior for contemporary Christians,[70] it is important not to overlook Fuchs's larger contribution to the debate on constructing a Christian ethic that honors both the realities of the Christian faith and the normative function of human reason in ascertaining right conduct. In my opinion, Fuchs's insights provide a solid foundation for situating natural law deliberation in the larger content of Christian morality.

As we discussed in the preceding chapter,[71] the process of discovering and learning right behavior is an incremental, ongoing, and open-ended process in which humans, by continually reflecting on their experience, forge their basic beliefs (moral and nonmoral), come to some understanding of the human person, and grasp the capacity of certain actions to promote or impede human well-being. Throughout this process, humans are continually presented with potentially morally relevant data from a number of sources, including popular culture, parents and peers, the media, religious figures, community leaders, narratives, the social and physical sciences, and dominant social roles and ideals. The Christian, just like the non-Christian, must employ her reasoning power to sort through this information, to construct a plausible and coherent conception of one's purpose and meaning in life, and to identify values and particular goals and types of behavior congruent with one's respective *Weltanschauung*.

Thus, the process of learning correct behavior is essentially the same for Christians and non-Christians.[72] Both use the creative and constructive power of reason during every stage of this process, from understanding factual information, to interpreting data, to evaluating the moral import of the data, to testing the adequacy of moral beliefs, to making concrete moral judgments. Although the general contours of this process of learning right behavior is the same for all people, the Christian differs from the non-Christian in that her faith tradition occupies a privileged position in her personal and moral formation. This does not imply that the Christian faith is the exclusive source of moral information for the Christian; for moral insights, as Fuchs clearly demonstrates, arise from manifold sources.[73] It does entail, however, that the Christian's faith tradition is not simply one font of moral wisdom among other equally relevant sources of moral information, but one that makes a pressing claim upon the Christian for sustained attention and consideration.

As the Christian reflects on her religious tradition and assesses the many beliefs, values, and ideals presented to her, the substance of the Christian tradition begins to give shape and content to her notions of human well-being and the particular types of actions conducive to this end.[74] Let me be clear: our notion of the human good and the specific content attached to it, although constructed by human reason, is formed in part for the Christian by her religious tradition. For example, as a Christian begins formulating some conception of human well-being, she will most likely encounter a variety of Christian sources indicating that poverty and oppression are incompatible with concrete, integral human flourishing: the caustic remonstrations of the biblical prophets denouncing corruption and greed, which directly or indirectly deprive the neediest of the basic necessities of life; Jesus' parables and preaching on poverty and caring for the poor; the practice of early Christian churches of sharing goods in common and distributing food to the neediest; or saints such as Mother Teresa, whose explicit mission was to care for the poorest of the poor, or Peter Claver, who attended to the needs of slaves forced to live in wretched conditions.

This consideration of the moral wisdom conveyed by the Christian tradition might not provide solutions to concrete, contemporary moral issues. A Christian might in the end disagree with specific teachings or general values promoted by her religious tradition, or she might not find the received moral wisdom sufficiently critical or nuanced. But these reservations do not negate the contention that as the Christian surveys the moral knowledge embedded in her religious tradition and continually reassesses its legitimacy and truthfulness, certain components of the Christian moral tradition will exercise a formative influence on her moral consciousness and self-understanding, which in turn affect the content of her notion of human well-being.[75]

Thus, the Christian faith and human reason are, for Fuchs, mutually conditioning aspects in the process of learning right behavior.[76] The *Weltanschaaung* of the Christian faith provides stories, certain values, moral exemplars, and types of behavior which exert influence on the Christian's moral beliefs and give content to her understanding of the reasonableness of actions and their impact on human flourishing. Reason, for its part, provides the dynamic, constructive component of the search for right behavior by interpreting the moral knowledge contained in the Christian tradition, assessing its validity, testing its insights, developing certain themes or concepts, and continually extending, and perhaps correcting, the moral wisdom of the Christian tradition in an ongoing attempt to construct an ethic capable of honoring both the substance of Christianity and the demand confronting Christians in every age to propose coherent, plausible answers to the pressing moral issues of the day.[77]

Fuchs's synthesis of Christian faith and natural law deliberation, in my opinion, succeeds on two important points. First, it adequately addresses the problems raised by critics of the Roman Catholic natural law tradition, especially the earlier critics who initially raised these issues, that beyond a few theological presuppositions necessary to link human reason or the natural order to the divine mind ordering creation and drawing all things to their due ends, natural law deliberation resembled a self-sufficient moral philosophy divorced from any discernible, substantive connection to the Christian faith. In outlining the anthropological and epistemological dependencies of natural law analysis on the Christian faith, as well as developing the reciprocally conditioning relationship between the moral wisdom of the Christian tradition and human reason, Fuchs has aptly demonstrated the formative influence of the Christian faith on the Christian's self-understanding, which in turn gives meaning and content both to foundational moral concepts—the human good, right, and wrong—and also to particular values and types of behavior affecting human well-being. Although the preconversion Fuchs typified the position that natural law deliberation is a practical exercise in moral philosophy legitimized by a few presuppositions drawn from natural theology, the postconversion

Fuchs shows effectively how Christian sources of moral wisdom—for example, Jesus, the Bible, or Christian saints—enhance natural law deliberation and contribute to our understanding of right behavior and human flourishing.[78]

Second, Fuchs's synthesis rightly upholds the longstanding natural law axiom that knowledge of right behavior is in principle accessible to non-Christians,[79] even though in some instances the Christian faith enables Christians to discern right conduct "more easily and securely."[80] The pivotal issue for Fuchs is the ability to attain insight into the human person and the contents of human well-being, which lead to determinate moral judgments about specific types of behavior. As Fuchs claims, by virtue of the power of reason shared by all human beings, the ability to understand human well-being and the actions consistent with this overarching end belongs to every person, which renders the possibility of grasping natural law, in whole or in part, in principle available to everyone.

This assertion, of course, does not imply that everyone is equally capable of grasping natural law. Individual strengths and weaknesses, the quality of moral instruction, the decadence or vitality of one's culture, and a host of other factors either limit or enhance one's practical ability to comprehend right behavior. The point of Fuchs's contention that knowledge of natural law is in principle accessible to all persons, however, is not intended to address the empirical issue of the knowledge of right behavior possessed by any individuals or groups, but to solidify the autonomy of the ethical sphere and to avoid the untenable conclusion that, lacking Christian faith, humans would be bereft of moral insights and incapable of understanding themselves and discovering behavior that promotes their well-being.

The practical upshot of Fuchs's claim that natural law's contents are accessible to those outside the Christian faith is that Christians can—and should attempt to—learn about right behavior from non-Christians. Although the anthropological implications of the Christian faith might prove advantageous in some instances in the quest to discover natural law,[81] this assertion is a far cry from contending that the Christian faith is a sufficient source for determining right conduct in all concrete situations, or that the moral insights of non-Christians cannot frequently complement, extend, or perhaps even correct the moral insights gained by Christians reflecting on moral issues in the "light of the Gospel."[82] To this extent, natural law deliberation must at least be receptive to non-Christian currents of thought, and ideally should actively seek insights from non-Christians that contribute to our understanding of human beings and the behavior conducive to human well-being.[83]

Natural Law and the Validity of Moral Norms

Fuchs's shift from nature or human nature to *recta ratio* as the proximate norm of morality produced a corresponding shift in his understanding of the origin, function, and limitations of moral norms. Prior to his intellectual conversion, Fuchs considered the natural order and the finalities embedded in nature to ground a series of moral norms, regulating the entirety of human behavior, that could be applied directly by moral agents in concrete situations to determine what ought to be done. Although the moral norms derived from relative natural law[84] were context dependent[85] and in some limited cases could be modified to account for different historical, cultural, political, and social contexts, the overriding thrust of Fuchs's preconversion natural law theory, especially in the realm of absolute natural law, was to construct a series of hierarchically ordered, immutable, universally applicable moral norms arising necessarily from the natural order.[86]

The transition to *recta ratio* as the proximate norm of morality undermined most of the theoretical superstructure upon which Fuchs's understanding of moral norms had been erected. Moral norms went from an expression of the demands inherent in an invariant, epistemologically accessible human nature to the manifestation of human reason reflecting on experience, recognizing the impact of particular actions on human well-being, formulating guidelines to protect and promote human goods, and further specifying and revising these guidelines over time as subsequent moral insights offered a better understanding of proper conduct. The emergence of *recta ratio* as the port of entry to natural law also meant that moral objectivity could no longer be attained simply by applying prefabricated moral norms in concrete situations, but by considering all potentially relevant aspects of the particular situation and using one's reasoning ability to determine right and wrong behavior. In this sense, moral norms might indicate certain premoral values to be pursued or premoral disvalues to be avoided, but their principal function is pedagogical, not normative, in other words, to guide and clarify human reason's deliberations in particular situations without dictating concretely what ought to be done. In what follows, I develop and critique Fuchs's postconversion understanding of the origin, function, and limitations of moral norms, addressing in the latter portion of this section the highly disputed issue in contemporary Roman Catholic moral theology of the validity of exceptionless moral norms.

Moral norms, according to Fuchs, are the product of a lengthy deliberative process in which a particular community, by reflecting on the meaning of the human person, human well-being, and the role of actions in promoting or hindering this end, synthesizes and makes manifest its moral judgments in propositional form.[87] This ongoing process involves both an active appropriation of received communal wisdom and the further revision and refinement of moral norms as communities generate additional moral insights and attempt to determine what types of behavior are congruent with human well-being in their circumstances.

This process of formulating, solidifying, and revising moral norms is highly experiential. Moral norms are not "read" from the natural order, nor are they self-evident or a priori truths.[88] Similar to the process involved in determining right and wrong behavior in concrete situations—separating relevant from irrelevant information, interpreting and understanding data, evaluating the values at stake, and judging which action is consistent with human well-being[89]—the process of formulating and specifying moral norms involves an active appropriation of a community's received moral wisdom, the testing and validation of its contents, and the ongoing clarification and possible revision of moral norms, all of which depend on practical experience that makes it possible for human reason to understand the moral import of structures, institutions, and particular patterns of behavior.[90]

The genesis of moral norms in reason reflecting on experience in an ongoing, open-ended search to discover right, or perhaps better, conduct means that moral norms might exhibit a certain degree of plasticity to account not only for the variable social, cultural, economic, and political contexts in which humans live and act,[91] but also because the concrete realities of human life—including the human person herself[92]—and our general worldview that provides the meaningful context through which reality is evaluated, are capable of change and development.[93] In the area of theology alone, our evaluations of religious freedom, the significance of marital love,[94] the inherent dignity of the human person, and the role of women have changed substantially in response to insights modifying our *Weltanschauung*, which have entailed a corresponding modification of the moral norms applicable to these respective issues.[95]

Moreover, there is a certain degree of malleability to many of the institutions and practical circumstances that condition human behavior: political and economic institutions erected to benefit humans are sometimes restructured and the scope of their activities curtailed or expanded; new technologies affecting human well-being raise unprecedented questions and possibilities; and changes affecting family life, the workplace, the physical environment, and economic security and stability occur frequently throughout the world, all of which entail variable responses and moral norms sufficiently adaptable to concrete, local conditions to safeguard human well-being in these potentially changing circumstances.

Thus, the process of reducing natural law to a series of ordered moral norms will not culminate entirely in a body of immutable, universally valid moral norms.[96] To be sure, there might be a substantial collection of moral norms that throughout human history has correctly been affirmed as reliable indicators of right or wrong behavior regardless of historical, cultural, social, economic, or political circumstances. But according to Fuchs this does not obviate the legitimacy—even the necessity—of context dependent moral norms fashioned with specific conditions in mind that can be modified and revised to meet the exigencies of a potentially changing world.[97] As Fuchs writes, "The fact of the (active) changing of man and his world, along with a more dynamic and evolutionary understanding of the order of earthly reality, can lead to new types of behavior and behavioral norms."[98]

Given the fact that moral norms represent the cumulative moral wisdom of a community and the innumerable insights that have contributed over time to their specific contents, their importance for discerning right behavior in the here-and-now is considerable. Fuchs would agree with Jean Porter, who writes, the "ability to follow rules [norms] is one of the most fundamental capacities that a (potentially) rational creature can possess. Without this capacity, persons can neither emerge as fully rational social beings, nor can they act or sustain a course of activity."[99] As embodiments of a community's values and moral judgments, moral norms offer invaluable advice to moral agents attempting to attain *recta ratio* in concrete situations. Norms help people separate relevant from irrelevant information; they indicate premoral values and disvalues; they convey social roles and ideals that give meaning and purpose; they offer specific paradigms and criteria for practical moral reasoning; and on a more personal level they can counteract—or at least impede—the destructive tendencies of rationalization, self-deception, or lack of self-control which sometimes obfuscate and warp moral deliberation for self-serving ends.[100]

This being said, Fuchs emphasizes that despite their indispensable role in natural law analysis, moral norms have limitations that must be clearly acknowledge to avoid the mistaken assumption that attaining *recta ratio* consists simply in obeying moral norms (i.e., applying them directly in concrete situations) or that the entirety of natural law can be codified into moral norms. The purpose of moral norms, Fuchs asserts, is to help people discern right behavior in concrete situations. In the process of attempting to determine *recta ratio,* however, there exists a conceptual gap between a particular moral norm formulated to regulate behavior in the situation at hand and the judgment of reason; for in every concrete situation a moral agent must determine whether the norm correctly indicates a solution and should be accepted as valid or whether the norm is deficient in some way and should be rejected, both of which reveal that the judgment of human reason in a concrete situation is prior to and ultimately more authoritative than the respective norm. This "innovative activity," as Fuchs describes it, in which human reason goes beyond the norm and judges its applicability in the given circumstances, occurs in every moral decision:

> [A moral system] must have its own innovative element; something that is not already contained in what exists but derives from the person making the ethical decision even if it is only the judgment that an ethical answer that already exists is the *correct* answer, in concreto, to the person's problem. . . . Thus, the already existing answer that is appropriated receives—innovatively—a final nuance and meaningfulness that it did not have in the abstract, already existing formulation that was appropriated. In other words, the human person who decides or acts takes, in every instance, an innovative step beyond the statement of the already existing and appropriated norm. One's ethical decision and ethical conduct are never only the execution of a norm.[101]

This quotation illustrates well why *recta ratio* and received moral norms, even widely accepted ones, are not necessarily synonymous. Moral norms might create a strong, *prima facie* case for or against a certain action, but to the extent that human reason determines the validity of a norm in a concrete situation, moral normativity is shown to reside in the considered judgments of human reason, not the moral norm itself. Thus, only insofar as moral norms embody *recta ratio* in the concrete do they possess the capacity to be morally obligatory.[102]

Another potential limitation of moral norms stems from their human genesis. Because moral norms originate in a particular community and are products of human interpretation, evaluation, and judgment, the validity of moral norms is dependent on the quality of a community's moral deliberation and insights. In general, this means that moral norms might embody both the best and worst qualities of a community, from pernicious biases, erroneous values, and intellectual obtuseness to extraordinary insightfulness, self-consciously critical inquiry, and a correct ordering of priorities. Most importantly, however, Fuchs claims that the epistemological limitations associated with human knowing should interject a healthy sense of realism into our reliance on moral norms in concrete situations. Our knowledge of the human person and human flourishing, which for Fuchs is an indispensable prerequisite for constructing valid moral norms, is always incomplete: "When we construct ethical proposals for the person, we must always bear in mind that our knowledge of the total reality of the person is always extremely defective."[103]

In addition, the process of formulating moral norms might be affected by the inability of human reason to grasp morally relevant contexts and circumstances, which could render a respective norm deficient in two different ways. First, it is possible that the construction of a norm was faulty or incomplete, either through the unintentional omission of important contextual information, or by disregarding relevant factual data that would have restricted the scope and applicability of the norm, or by failing to specify in sufficient detail the precise circumstances for which the norm was intended,[104] all of which might culminate in a moral norm being either too broad and unclear or insufficiently attentive to morally relevant information in certain contexts to be able to capture *recta ratio* in a concrete situation.

Moral norms might also be rendered inapplicable in certain cases not because of any substantive flaw in the formulation process, but because of the limited human ability to predict future contingencies. An integral component of the process of formulating and revising moral norms is the imaginative act of posing hypothetical questions ("What if . . . ?) to see if some possible future scenario could perhaps reveal deficiencies in either the scope or content of a respective moral norm.[105] This imaginative, mental exploration of various possible, even highly implausible, exigencies is an integral moment in the ongoing attempt to test and verify the accuracy and persuasiveness of particular moral norms.[106] But Fuchs warns that despite the fundamental value of such activity, we must realize that the power of human reason to envision all future contingencies or developments potentially affecting the validity of moral norms is restricted. Humans do not possess indubitable knowledge of the future; we make informed predictions, based on past experiences and the current state of knowledge, of what the future is likely to bring. Sometimes these prove to be highly accurate, in other cases they fail miserably. Whatever the case, the potential future scenarios and circumstances we envision, whether well- or ill-informed, remain in the end fallible predictions that cannot attain certainty.[107]

On a practical level, the inability of human reason to predict the future and thus to capture fully the contexts and circumstances in which humans must act means that preformulated moral norms might suffer several deficiencies which render them inapplicable. They might have been formulated for specific political, economic, cultural, or social conditions that no longer exist, or that might have changed significantly enough to call into question the validity of a formerly widely accepted moral norm.[108] New technologies or developments—such as in vitro fertilization, nuclear weaponry, cloning, worldwide deforestation, or global warming—might call for entirely unprecedented moral norms, or possibly the substantive revision of existing moral norms to attain human well-being.[109] Insights gained from discoveries in biology, physiology, psychology, sociology, anthropology, or philosophy might improve our understanding of the human person and the conditions necessary for human flourishing, which would necessitate a corresponding alteration in the moral norms erected to protect and promote certain human goods.[110]

Fuchs's intent in outlining the potential deficiencies of prefabricated moral norms is not to engender an aura of skepticism or doubt about the possibility of employing norms to determine right and wrong behavior. As Fuchs writes, moral norms are "indispensably important" in conveying a community's collective moral wisdom and in forming and guiding persons as they develop their moral sensibilities and are confronted by concrete choices.[111] The reason for Fuchs's emphasis on the potentially manifold limitations of moral norms is to highlight the fact that attaining *recta ratio*, which should be the moral agent's sole concern in every situation, is not necessarily enhanced by following or simply applying moral norms. As human creations, moral norms reflect their source, fallible human beings whose moral insights vary in quality, precision, comprehensiveness, and foresight. Thus, the appropriation of moral norms must always be attendant by a healthy realism that acknowledges both that norms are usually valuable aids in the search for right behavior and should be given the benefit of the doubt, and that norms, for the reasons mentioned above, should not always be unquestionably accepted as valid embodiments of *recta ratio* in concrete situations.[112] As Fuchs writes frequently, quoting Thomas Aquinas, moral norms are valid *ut in pluribus* (in the majority of cases),[113] but this prima facie validity can be overridden if, for whatever reason, there is a disjunction between a norm's specific directive and the type of behavior deemed to be consistent with human well-being in a concrete situation.

Thus, for Fuchs, the value of norms in the quest to uncover natural law is principally their pedagogical service in guiding and instructing moral agents: "[T]he function of norms is then 'only' pedagogical. They are guides to right actualization—that is, they are not intended, being abstract, to be an easy solution, nor can they even, at least normally, designate with precision their own range of validity. Yet, practically speaking, they are indispensably important, because no one who is incorporated in a community is without norms."[114] From early childhood to adolescence and continuing throughout the rest of our lives, moral norms direct us to the human good, indicate premoral values and disvalues that should be considered in concrete decisions, provide relatively stable bases for analogical reasoning to resolve new, and potentially unprecedented, issues and cases, and promote behavioral patterns that are gradually internalized and appropriated, which help create individual moral agents habituated to act rightly. Moral norms, for Fuchs, initiate human beings into the moral community and continually guide and aid moral agents in the search for right behavior by providing proven benchmarks that form our characters over time and offer usually reliable behavioral standards protecting and promoting human well-being.

Exceptionless Moral Norms?

One of the most hotly disputed issues in Roman Catholic moral theology in the latter half of the twentieth century is the existence of exceptionless moral norms. Although the situation ethics controversy in the 1940s and 1950s focused on the validity of exceptionless moral norms and raised many of the issues that would later be resurrected and reexamined, this lively and sometimes rancorous debate on situation ethics was conceived largely as a Catholic versus Protestant affair clearly divided along denominational lines, with Catholics, including Fuchs, defending the validity of exceptionless moral norms and Protestants—Karl Barth, Emil Brunner, and Helmut Thielicke—denying them.[115] Especially after the interventions of the Holy Office and Pope Pius XII in the 1950s,[116] there was virtually no public questioning by any reputable Catholic moral theologian of the validity of exceptionless moral norms.

The contemporary debate on exceptionless moral norms, in contrast, has witnessed a growing number of influential Catholic moral theologians, especially American and European moralists, raising substantive doubts about, and sometimes denying, the existence of exceptionless moral norms.[117] Although none of these moralists question the legitimacy and function of moral norms in natural law deliberation, they do doubt the ability to formulate norms valid at all times and in all circumstances without any exceptions. This has engendered strong criticism from several philosophers and theologians,[118] including Pope John Paul II,[119] who for various reasons contend that although many norms might be valid only in particular contexts, there is a body of universal and immutable moral norms that transcend historicity and cultural and social circumstances and properly deserve the designation "exceptionless."

Fuchs has been one of the most influential—and criticized—participants in this ongoing debate. During his postconversion writings Fuchs has consistently objected to the idea of exceptionless moral norms, although as we shall see his reservations are limited and should be understood precisely to avoid the erroneous impression, which is sometimes conveyed by Fuchs's critics, that Fuchs's position undermines some of the most widely revered moral norms in the Christian tradition.[120] In what follows, I focus on Fuchs's unique contribution to the debate on exceptionless moral norms and offer an assessment of the adequacy of his position.

Before considering substantive matters, it is vitally important to recognize two points. First, the controversy surrounding exceptionless moral norms has focused on one specific class of norms.[121] Nobody denies that formal moral norms such as "Be just," "Be fair," and "Always show respect for others," which forbid injustice, unfairness, and disrespect, are always valid. These formal norms, however, fail to specify what particular types of acts are forbidden and by themselves do not offer any substantive, material solutions to concrete questions dealing with justice, fairness, and respect: Is it just to execute a prisoner convicted of murder? Is it fair to discipline children differently for comparable misdeeds? Does welfare reform requiring welfare recipients to work a specified number of hours per week disrespect them as persons?

Nor does anyone dispute that analytic moral norms such as "Do not commit murder" or "Do not be cruel"[122] are exceptionless. This class of norms contains an evaluative component that renders any act contrary to them to be immoral.[123] For example, because "murder" is functionally equivalent to "unjustified homicide," any act determined to be murderous is, by definition, morally unjustified and therefore wrong. Likewise, a cruel act, which involves inflicting unjustified suffering on someone or something, is always wrong. Although analytic moral norms presuppose certain general circumstances to determine whether an act is regulated by a respective norm (e.g., the prohibition of murder requires that a homicide not be an instance of self-defense, or killing during war, or an unintentional accident), these circumstances are not enumerated in the norm itself.

A third class of valid, exceptionless norms, which articulates specific circumstances for an act to be considered wrong, also is not disputed by anyone. "Do not kill your spouse out of anger or jealousy," "Do not kick a dog for pleasure," and "Do not take someone else's property without her permission merely to make her mad" are instances in which the moral quality of an act, neither right nor wrong in itself, is determined by the specific circumstances surrounding it.

Kicking a dog to prevent it from mauling your leg, or to remove it quickly from the path of an oncoming car, for example, is morally permissible, whereas kicking it simply because you dislike dogs or because you enjoy seeing animals in pain is always wrong.

The only class of norms at issue in the contemporary controversy over exceptionless moral norms is that prohibiting concrete, specifiable actions in which the object chosen by the moral agent and described in factual, nonevaluative,[124] "morally neutral language"[125] is always wrong, regardless of any attendant circumstances.[126] Furthermore, these exceptionless moral norms remain valid in any context or circumstances, past, present, or future. Nothing that might arise, whether foreseeable or not, could render these norms inapplicable or make the concrete actions forbidden by them morally right.[127]

The second crucial point to remember before addressing Fuchs's position on exceptionless moral norms is that Fuchs draws a sharp distinction between theoretical and practical considerations. A theoretical assessment of the validity of exceptionless moral norms is an abstract, speculative, and hypothetical enterprise intended to test the possible grounds for accepting or rejecting the central claim that there exist exceptionless moral norms which proscribe certain acts as wrong ex objecto, regardless of context or circumstance. The theoretical nature of this endeavor, which by design tests limits and considers imaginative questions, means that the conclusions reached might or might not have any direct, immediate relation to the applicability or worth of supposedly exceptionless moral norms in everyday life. It is possible to conclude that it is theoretically untenable to subscribe to the view that any moral norm can be considered exceptionless in the manner described above while simultaneously affirming that this has no impact on the moral norms currently operative and regarded as correct.[128] For example, although one might be able to imagine circumstances in which the norm "Do not intentionally engage in sexual intercourse with someone other than your spouse" would be inapplicable, the current absence of these circumstances and the inability to foresee the emergence of these circumstances in the near or distant future means that the norm, on a practical level, should be considered exceptionless.

Fuchs's writings on exceptionless moral norms, it should be noted at the beginning, address principally their theoretical—not practical—adequacy. Fuchs neither examines any concrete, specific behavioral moral norms, nor does he imply, suggest, or conclude that his theoretical position has any immediate relevance to the adequacy of currently operative moral norms. As Fuchs writes, regardless of whether exceptionless moral norms are affirmed or denied on a theoretical level, this has no direct bearing on the substantial body of moral norms to which humans conform their everyday behavior, and it certainly does not undermine their practical worth and efficacy.[129]

In perhaps the most succinct exposition of his position on the validity of exceptionless moral norms, Fuchs writes,

> [C]an behavioral moral norms be universal at all, in the sense of being applicable always, everywhere and without exception, so that the action encompassed by them could never be objectively justified? Traditionally we are accustomed to speak of an *intrinsece malum.*
>
> Viewed theoretically, there seems to be no possibility of behavioral norms of this kind for human action in the inner-worldly realm. The reason is that an action cannot be judged morally at all considered purely in itself, but only together with all the circumstances and intention. Consequently, a behavioral norm, universally valid in the full sense, would presuppose that those who arrive at it could know or foresee adequately all the possible combinations of the action concerned with circumstances and intentions, with (premoral) values and nonvalues (*bona* and *mala 'physica'*). A priori, such knowledge is not easily attainable. . . . [130] Add to this that the conception opposed to this does not take into consideration the significance for an objective understanding of morality attached to, first, practical experience and induction, second, civilization and cultural differences, third, man's historicity and 'creative' perceptions. . . .
>
> Theoretically, no other answer seems possible: one cannot easily formulate universal norms of behavior in the strict sense of *intrinsece malum.*[131]

Although the language of this paragraph does not constitute an unequivocal denial of the theoretical possibility of formulating exceptionless moral norms ("there *seems* to be no possibility of moral norms of this kind"; "one cannot *easily* formulate universal norms of behavior"),[132] Fuchs clearly believes it is highly difficult, if not virtually impossible, to construct exceptionless moral norms that preclude certain types of behavior as morally wrong *ex objecto*.

Two of the four reasons Fuchs offers to justify his doubt about the possibility of formulating exceptionless moral norms were discussed above in the section on moral norms in general. First, the essentially open-ended character of natural law analysis, in which reason continually reflects on human experience in an ongoing attempt to determine *recta ratio* in the given social, cultural, economic, and political circumstances, means that there is an inherent provisionality in our moral norms.[133] As humans gain greater insight into human well-being and the particular types of actions conductive to this end in specific contexts, there might need to be a corresponding adjustment in the content of certain moral norms. This does not imply, of course, that moral norms are constantly in flux or that new moral insights continually call for a revision or reformulation of longstanding moral norms. But as products of the ongoing process of human reason reflecting on experience and synthesizing the judgments of *recta ratio* in propositional form, moral norms are always susceptible to change and should be regarded as provisional embodiments of a community's moral wisdom that can, and sometimes should, be further specified or revised as we learn more about proper behavior.[134]

Second, Fuchs also notes that moral norms, as human creations originating in a determinate historical community conditioned by a particular *Weltanschauung* and cultural and social values, might present a particular action as always and everywhere morally wrong which in reality is only a reflection of the respective community's moral beliefs and does not warrant the designation "exceptionless" outside its community of origin.[135] As Fuchs writes, because our moral judgments and norms can never escape historical embeddedness entirely,[136] we must be extremely wary of importing our cultural and social standards into our moral norms, which limits their range of applicability and renders them exceptionless only in a certain contexts:

> [M]ust it not be supposed that the behavioral norms encountered in a particular civilization or cultural area were formulated partly in consideration of just this civilization and culture, hence for them alone? And this despite the fact that definitive or generally valid norms of conduct were actually intended, simply because the possibility of other civilizations and cultures was not taken into consideration.[137]

The third component of Fuchs's critique of exceptionless moral norms, which was not discussed in the prior section, is anthropological.[138] For Fuchs, the human person is historical in the sense that her being is malleable and changeable; she is a dynamic, evolving entity who is modified by the values she embraces, the acts she performs, her interaction with the environment, and her cultural and social upbringing. As "a being of becoming, not a being created in [her] full development,"[139] the human person and the particular trajectory the gradual unfolding of her *esse* takes is somewhat unpredictable.

Consistent with the natural law methodological principle *agere sequitur esse*, Fuchs claims that the human person's historicity and her capacity for development and change, which when actualized could substantially modify her being and the conditions necessary for her well-being, raises the possibility that concomitant adjustments in the body of moral norms designed to protect and enhance human well-being might have to be undertaken. Applied specifically to exceptionless moral norms, the human person's mutability entails that norms correctly considered exceptionless for certain persons or societies in particular stages of development might suffer exceptions as humans evolve and require different types of structures, institutions, and behavior to attain concrete, integral human flourishing. Whether alterations of the human person's *esse* are in fact sufficient grounds for revising or rejecting previously exceptionless moral norms, however, can only be determined concretely by considering whether the specific change actually requires different moral norms to attain human well-being.[140]

Although these first three considerations correctly indicate potential obstacles to formulating exceptionless moral norms, their conditional natures do not pose any inherent limitations or impediments on the possibility of constructing valid exceptionless moral norms. The ongoing, open-ended process of human reason reflecting on experience *might* eventually lead to the conclusion that some exceptionless moral norms are not actually exceptionless. A critical awareness of cultural and social embeddedness *might* reveal that supposedly exceptionless moral norms are reflections of a particular people's moral beliefs and are valid only in their communal context. The development of and change in the human person's *esse might* indicate that exceptionless moral norms need to be revised to promote human well-being. These considerations cumulatively engender a healthy sense of humility about the potentially manifold difficulties involved in asserting that exceptionless moral norms are valid everywhere and always, regardless of circumstances and contexts. But they do not present any insurmountable objections to the theoretical notion of exceptionless moral norms.

Fuchs, however, in the quotation above from "The Absoluteness of Behavioral Moral Norms" presents another critique that is, I believe, a decisive blow to the theoretical possibility of constructing exceptionless moral norms. The force of this epistemological critique is not dependent on the realization of certain future conditions, only on the fact that humans are not omniscient beings capable of predicting the future in precise detail. The gravamen of Fuchs's objection is that in order to claim that some norm is exceptionless and the action it prohibits can never be morally justified, one would have to foresee all possible combinations of circumstances that might arise in the future to claim with surety that the norm will admit no exceptions at any time. As Fuchs writes, "a behavioral norm, universally valid [i.e., exceptionless] in the full sense, would presuppose that those who arrive at it could know or foresee adequately all the possible combinations of the action concerned with circumstances and intentions."[141]

One could try to rebut Fuchs's objection by pointing out that a respective moral norm has been consistently valid throughout human history and has been repeatedly affirmed throughout all cultures and peoples, and that there is no remotely imaginable combination of circumstances which might someday vitiate the norm's legitimacy. This rebuttal, however, fails to address the substance of Fuchs's objection. This critique of exceptionless moral norms does not dispute the fact that some norms have been tested over long periods of time and have proven exceptionless in all prior situations, nor does it dispute that humans might never be able to conceive of circumstances in which a particular exceptionless moral norm would not apply. Proponents of exceptionless moral norms claim that certain actions are immoral *ex objecto* and can never, under any circumstances, be justified. To substantiate this claim, proponents of exceptionless moral norms must be able to foresee all possible combinations of circumstantial data that will arise in the future in order to know that a respective exceptionless moral norm will not be defective in any concrete situation. If they cannot, there is no way of knowing that exceptionless moral norms actually will obtain in future circumstances, which directly undermines their argument for the validity of exceptionless moral norms.

One need not delve deeply into epistemological theory to grasp the force of Fuchs's critique of exceptionless moral norms. Although humans are capable of a broad array of insights and in many instances are remarkably adept at predicting the occurrence of certain events and contingencies, this ability to foresee future circumstances and the ways in which individual lives, societies, cultures, and political and economic systems actually unfold is limited. We can collect information, consult experts, read the latest literature, study historical precedents, and based on this knowledge make intelligent, educated, well-informed predictions about the future, but in the end these entirely reasonable predictions are, to a certain extent, guesses that might or might not be correct.

As Fuchs writes, our knowledge of human beings and our world is always incomplete; we possess neither comprehensive knowledge of the human person or of the various disciplines which render humans and our world intelligible—for example, biology, physics, medicine, sociology, politics, economics, psychology, philosophy, and theology—nor indubitable knowledge about the practical effects of these disciplines and the various ways in which they might alter human life and the pursuit of the human good.[142] Just as the contemporary world of computers, air travel, intercontinental communication, automobiles, nuclear power and weapons, and industrial mechanization was unforeseeable for a Paleolithic hunter-gatherer or a medieval monk, the circumstances of our future are similarly unforeseeable in their precise lineaments.

Thus, the claim that certain moral norms are exceptionless always and everywhere on a theoretical level cannot be sustained. To the extent that humans cannot foresee future circumstances and thus cannot know that exceptionless moral norms will be valid in concrete situations, the notion of intrinsically evil acts morally wrong *ex objecto* needs to be rejected. Again, this does not imply that on a practical level we should doubt the validity of longstanding, widely accepted, exceptionless moral norms. As Fuchs writes, "Despite misgivings on the level of theory, we get along very well with norms of this kind."[143] Contrary to Fuchs's critics, rejecting the theoretical possibility of exceptionless moral norms does not, on a practical level, entail that moral agents must constantly anticipate exceptions to moral norms and stand ready to contravene the collective moral wisdom conveyed through moral norms.[144] In our daily lives we should regard the accumulated moral judgments synthesized in moral norms and tested over long periods of time as correct and indicative of *recta ratio*.[145] There might arise instances in the near or distant future that will reveal defects in certain widely accepted moral norms and render them inapplicable in specific concrete situations, but this possibility should not influence one's practical, everyday readiness and willingness to accept received ethical wisdom as valid.

Fuchs's presentation of moral norms, both moral norms in general and exceptionless moral norms, represents a significant, fruitful contribution to Roman Catholic natural law theory that succeeds on several levels. First, Fuchs correctly identifies the function of moral norms as guides or aids to the determination of right conduct, which can never substitute adequately for the necessary task of reason considering the premoral values and disvalues present in the totality of a respective situation and judging what is morally right in the given circumstances. *Recta ratio*, as Fuchs repeatedly insists, cannot be equated with what is generally the case, or what obtains in the vast majority of situations; it can be determined only through an analysis of the concrete particularities of a situation in the here-and-now.

In practice this means that moral norms exercise an auxiliary or pedagogical function in moral deliberation:[146] they initiate us into the community and convey behavioral guidelines reflecting a community's considered moral judgments; they help moral agents distinguish between relevant and irrelevant data; they indicate premoral values and disvalues that impinge on human well-being; and they provide valuable advice in determining moral rightness and wrongness in concrete situations. But Fuchs correctly cautions that acting rightly does not consist simply in applying moral norms to particular cases, nor should the moral life be considered a quest to fulfill and obey moral norms; for moral norms "basically offer nothing more than assistance"[147] that cannot decisively indicate what should be done in a concrete situation: "it is impossible to receive the complete ethical answer to ethical questions from already existing norms and answers. What is ethically right and correct for an individual or a particular society can never be determined completely by already existing and general ethical statements."[148]

Second, Fuchs's analysis of human reason as the genesis of moral norms offers a persuasive basis for explaining the emergence and validity—perhaps even necessity—of the ongoing revision and specification of moral norms. As products of human insight, moral norms originate in determinate communities in response to particular needs to promote or prevent certain patterns of behavior affecting human well-being. In any community moral deliberation represents an ongoing attempt to render intelligible, or at least more intelligible, the types of relationships, structures, institutions, and actions befitting human beings. As communities experience various types of change—environmental, technological, intellectual, political, economic, social, or cultural[149]—and seek to understand how human well-being can best be attained under these conditions, it should not be surprising that moral norms might need to be supplemented, partially corrected, or perhaps even repudiated.[150] As Mark Johnson writes, these changes, whether momentous or barely perceptible, call for an innovative response:

> Human beings develop in an evolving environment where their physical setting, sociopolitical institutions, and communal relations are typically in a process of very gradual change, though one that is infrequently punctuated with moments of more radical and rapid transformation. To adapt to such a changing complex of physical, interpersonal, and cultural interactions requires imagination, the ability to transform and adjust our categories, social relations, and institutional commitments. We really must be innovators, if we hope to meet in an intelligent way the demands of these various sorts of change that confront us daily in all aspects of our lives. We must decide which attitudes, traits of character, human goods, and actions serve our purposes and aims within communities that represent continuing and developing moral traditions. This will involve critically scrutinizing our own purposes and values, as

well as imaginatively envisioning alternative perspectives and possibilities for human flourishing.[151]

But Fuchs's argument for the ongoing revision and specification of moral norms is not simply that our moral norms must be adjusted to meet the demands of an evolving world. Because moral norms are not self-justifying or self-validating, their legitimacy must continually be reassessed to determine whether they accurately embody *recta ratio*.[152] The prior insights and judgments that constitute the authoritative bases of moral norms need to be tested to see if they correctly indicate right and wrong behavior. The scope and content of our moral norms must be reexamined to determine whether they are too broad and unspecified, or fail to account for morally relevant information, or perhaps are based on untenable presuppositions. Thus, moral norms do not represent a static body of precepts that can be assumed to be valid in every age;[153] as products of human reason reflecting on experience in an ongoing, open-ended process of determining *recta ratio* in concrete, historical situations, moral norms are intrinsically susceptible to revision and mirror the dynamism of human reason assessing the validity of prior judgments, revising and further specifying received wisdom, and perhaps generating new moral norms that indicate better ways of structuring our lives and ordering our priorities.[154]

Finally, Fuchs's analysis of the limitations of moral norms in natural law deliberation has important implications for our understanding of moral agency. If, as Fuchs claims, moral norms originate in human reason and their validity depends on the quality of human insights,[155] the paramount concern of Roman Catholic moral theology should be to equip moral agents with the resources necessary to attain moral insights that are accurate, persuasive, credible, and well-informed; for without a community of moral agents capable of attaining *recta ratio* consistently and making good moral judgments, the possibility of accomplishing the secondary, derivative task of formulating correct moral norms based on a community's moral insights appears negligible.

Furthermore, as I argued earlier,[156] moral norms are not capable of providing definitive, concrete answers to many of the issues arising in human life. Even if it were possible to master the entire corpus of received teaching, it is inconceivable that this knowledge could indicate to an individual moral agent what should or should not be done in every concrete situation.[157] In addition, it is doubtful that many of the moral questions affecting concrete, integral human flourishing can be resolved by referring to moral norms: whether to get married, to take religious vows, or to remain single; the selection of a career path or particular occupation; how to contribute to the life of one's community;

or how to spend disposable income. These and many other moral questions cannot be answered by hauling out prefabricated moral norms; for they depend intimately on detailed knowledge of concrete particulars—commitments, resources, talents, limitations, personality traits, and other external circumstances—that can be obtained only by individual moral agents in the situation.

Fuchs, I am certain, would agree wholeheartedly with this assessment. Moral agency is not simply a matter of identifying the correct moral norm and applying it in a situation, but of being able to judge the validity of a moral norm, and if necessary to move innovatively beyond preestablished moral norms if *recta ratio* so indicates.[158] This suggests that the church's traditional role in natural law deliberation of proposing and promulgating moral norms needs to be supplemented by the equally important task of enhancing moral agency by attempting to create capable and competent individual moral agents whose skills allow them to negotiate uncharted territory, to understand the values protected and promoted in moral norms, to assess critically the self-understandings, social roles and ideals, and structures and institutions prevalent in a particular age, and to cultivate the personal qualities that will serve them well in all stages of life. These objectives, it seems to me, should be the focus of the church's energy in the moral arena if the laudable goal of concrete, integral human flourishing is to become a reality.

Notes

1. Fritz Tillmann, ed., *Handbuch der katholischen Sittenlehre,* 4 vols. (Düsseldorf, Germany: Druck und Verlag L. Schwann, 1934).

2. Fritz Tillmann, *Die Idee der Nachfolge Christi,* vol. 2 of *Handbuch der katholischen Sittenlehre* (Düsseldorf, Germany: Druck und Verlag L. Schwann, 1934), 5.

3. Ibid., 2: 6.

4. Vincent MacNamara, *Faith and Ethics: Recent Roman Catholicism* (Washington, D.C.: Georgetown University Press, 1985), 29.

5. Gérard Gilleman, *The Primacy of Charity in Moral Theology,* rev. Rene Carpentier, trans. William F. Ryan and André Vachon (Lanham, Md.: University Press of America, 1959), xxix.

6. Ibid., xxii.

7. Ibid., 29–48.

8. Ibid., 220–21.

9. Bernard Häring, *The Law of Christ,* 3 vols., trans. Edwin G. Kasper (Westminster, Md.: Newman Press, 1961–66).

10. Ibid., 2: xxi.

11. Ibid., 1: 72.

12. Ibid., 1: viii.

13. For a historical treatment of a related question, the moral theologian's self-understanding, see Peter Black and James F. Keenan, "The Evolving Self-Understanding of the Moral Theologian," *Studia Moralia* 39 (2001): 291–327.

14. Austin Flannery, ed., *The Conciliar and Post Conciliar Documents: Vatican Council II*, vol. 1, rev. ed. (Northport, N.Y.: Costello Publishing, 1988), 720.

15. For a discussion of the major figures and disputed issues in the debate between proponents of a *Glaubensethik* and natural law theorists, see MacNamara, *Faith and Ethics*, 9–55.

16. Josef Fuchs, *Human Values and Christian Morality*, trans. M. H. Heelan et al. (Dublin: Gill and Macmillan, 1970), 1–55, 56–75; and Josef Fuchs, *Christian Morality: The Word Becomes Flesh*, trans. Brian McNeil (Washington, D.C.: 1987), 19–27.

17. Fuchs, *Human Values*, 112–47; Josef Fuchs, *Personal Responsibility and Christian Morality*, trans. William Cleves et al. (Washington, D.C.: Georgetown University Press, 1983), 19–31, 32–50, 53–68, 69–83, 84–111; Fuchs, *Christian Morality*, 3–18; and Josef Fuchs, *Christian Ethics in a Secular Arena*, trans. Bernard Hoose and Brian McNeil (Washington, D.C.: Georgetown University Press, 1984), 3–14, 15–28, 110–27.

18. Josef Fuchs, *Natural Law: A Theological Investigation*, trans. Helmut Recker and John Dowling (New York: Sheed and Ward, 1965), 163–80.

19. Fuchs, *Personal Responsibility*, 55, 65.

20. Ibid., 88.

21. Fuchs, *Human Values*, 131.

22. Ibid., 121. Cf. Norbert J. Rigali, "The Uniqueness and Distinctiveness of Christian Morality and Ethics," in *Moral Theology: Challenges for the Future*, ed. Charles E. Curran (Mahwah, N.J.: Paulist Press, 1990), 74–93.

23. See Anne Carr, "Starting with the Human, in *A World of Grace*, ed. Leo O'Donovan, 1986), 17–22; and Ronald Modras, "Implications of Rahner's Anthropology for Fundamental Moral Theology," *Horizons* 12 (1985): 70–72 for explanations of Rahner's transcendental/categorial distinction and his understanding of intentionality.

24. For an extended discussion of Fuchs's Rahnerian theological anthropology, see chapter 4.

25. Fuchs, *Human Values*, 103. See also Karl Rahner, *Foundations of Christian Faith*, trans. William V. Dych (New York: Crossroad, 1989), 31–35.

26. Rahner claims that unthematic knowledge encompasses "the infinity of reality" (Rahner, *Foundations of Christian Faith*, 33). Beyond knowledge of the triune God, Fuchs never elaborates on the total content of unthematic knowledge, although his extensive appropriation of Rahner's theological anthropology suggests that Fuchs probably considers unthematic knowledge to include more than simply knowledge of the Trinity.

27. Fuchs, *Human Values*, 123–24.

28. Fuchs, *Personal Responsibility*, 203.

29. Fuchs, *Human Values,* 125; and Fuchs, *Personal Responsibility,* 27, 37, 63–64, 75, 102.

30. The following examples illustrating the Christian faith's influence on the content of and motivations for certain actions pertain only to the realm of thematic knowledge in which the Christian, with explicit, fully thematic consciousness of her faith tradition, brings her faith to bear on the moral life.

31. Fuchs, *Personal Responsibility,* 75.

32. MacNamara, *Faith and Ethics,* 42.

33. Fuchs, *Personal Responsibility,* 64.

34. Ibid.; and Fuchs, *Human Values,* 125.

35. Fuchs, *Human Values,* 168.

36. Fuchs, *Personal Responsibility,* 64.

37. Fuchs *Human Values,* 129–30.

38. For discussions on the relationship between the Christian religion and categorial behavior, see Richard A. McCormick, "Does Religious Faith Add to Ethical Perception?" in *The Distinctiveness of Christian Ethics,* Readings in Moral Theology, no. 2, ed. Charles E. Curran and Richard A. McCormick (Ramsey, N.J., Paulist Press, 1980); Josef Blank, "Does the New Testament Provide Principles for Modern Moral Theology?" *Concilium* 25 (1967); William K. Frankena, "Is Morality Logically Dependent on Religion?" in *Religion and Morality,* ed. John P. Reeder, Jr. (Garden City, N.Y.: Anchor Press, 1973); James J. Walter, "The Dependence of Christian Morality on Faith," *Eglise et Théologie* 12 (1981): 237–77; Norbert J. Rigali, "On Christian Ethics," *Chicago Studies* 10 (1971); Rigali, "Uniqueness and Distinctiveness of Christian Morality;" Stanley Hauerwas, *The Peaceable Kingdom* (Notre Dame, Ind.: University of Notre Dame Press, 1983), 50–71; Bruno Schüller, "Autonomous Ethics Revisited," in *Personalist Morals,* ed. Joseph A. Selling (Leuven, Belgium: Leuven University Press, 1988); Gerard J. Hughes, "A Christian Basis for Ethics," *Heythrop Journal* 13 (1972); Gerard J. Hughes, *Authority in Morals* (Washington, D.C.: Georgetown University Press, 1978); Michael Simpson, "A Christian Basis for Ethics," *Heythrop Journal* 15 (1974); Dietmar Mieth, "Autonomy of Ethics—Neutrality of the Gospel?" *Concilium* 155 (1982); and Joseph Cardinal Ratzinger, "The Church's Teaching Authority—Faith—Morals," in *Principles of Christian Morality,* trans. Graham Harrison (San Francisco: Ignatius Press, 1986).

39. Ratzinger, "Church's Teaching Authority," 72.

40. MacNamara, *Faith and Ethics,* 43.

41. Fuchs, *Personal Responsibility,* 101.

42. See also Klaus Demmer, "Moralische Norm und theologische Anthropologie," *Gregorianum* 54 (1973).

43. Fuchs, *Personal Responsibility,* 213–15.

44. Ibid., 181.

45. Fuchs, *Christian Ethics,* 25.

46. Fuchs, *Christian Morality,* 13.

47. Josef Fuchs, *Moral Demands and Personal Obligations* (Washington, D.C.: Georgetown University Press, 1993), 102.

48. Fuchs, *Christian Morality*, 12.

49. Fuchs, *Christian Ethics*, 58.

50. Fuchs, *Personal Responsibility*, 180; Fuchs, *Christian Morality*, 13; and Fuchs, *Moral Demands*, 102.

51. Fuchs, *Christian Ethics*, 25.

52. Fuchs, *Christian Morality*, 61.

53. For recent articles addressing the salient points of this discussion, see James J. Walter, "The Question of the Uniqueness of Christian Morality: An Historical and Critical Analysis of the Debate in Roman Catholic Ethics," in *Method and Catholic Moral Theology: The Ongoing Reconstruction*, ed. Todd A. Salzman (Omaha, Nebraska: Creighton University Press, 1999); and Jean Porter, "The Natural Law and the Specificity of Christian Morality: A Survey of Recent Work and an Agenda for Future Research," in *Method and Catholic Moral Theology: The Ongoing Reconstruction*, ed. Todd A. Salzman (Omaha, Neb.: Creighton University Press, 1999).

54. Walter, "Dependence of Christian Morality," 254, 274; and MacNamara, *Faith and Ethics*, 69–70.

55. See Ratzinger, "Church's Teaching Authority," 66, n. 13.

56. Fuchs, *Christian Morality*, 71–72.

57. Fuchs, *Personal Responsibility*, 64. For commentary on Fuchs's article, see Philippe Delhaye, "Questioning the Specificity of Christian Morality," in *The Distinctiveness of Christian Ethics*, Readings in Moral Theology, no. 2, ed. Charles E. Curran and Richard A. McCormick, (Ramsey, N.J.: Paulist Press, 1980); and Rigali, "Uniqueness and Distinctiveness of Christian Morality," 74–86.

58. Fuchs, *Personal Responsibility*, 98.

59. Ibid., 97. See also Bruno Schüller, "A Contribution to the Theological Discussion of Natural Law," in *Natural Law and Theology*, Readings in Moral Theology, no. 7, ed. Charles E. Curran and Richard A. McCormick (Mahwah, N.J.: Paulist Press, 1991), 72–98.

60. Fuchs, *Personal Responsibility*, 79, 128; and Fuchs, *Christian Ethics*, 146.

61. Fuchs, *Christian Morality*, 5–7.

62. Ibid., 13–14.

63. For an extended analysis of this position, see Hughes, *Authority in Morals*, esp. chapter 1.

64. Fuchs, *Christian Morality*, 6.

65. This presupposition that homosexual behavior is condemned in these biblical texts is solely to illustrate the role of the bible in justifying moral positions, not to establish that a careful exegesis of these passages would in fact reveal a condemnation of homosexual behavior.

66. Fuchs, *Personal Responsibility*, 119–20; and Fuchs, *Christian Morality*, 203.

67. Fuchs, *Personal Responsibility*, 181.

68. Fuchs, *Christian Ethics*, 13.

69. Fuchs, *Christian Morality*, 109–10.

70. Fuchs, *Personal Responsibility*, 64, 73; and Fuchs, *Christian Morality*, 9–14, 66–74.

71. For a fuller discussion of the process of learning natural law's contents, see chapter 5.

72. Fuchs, *Personal Responsibility*, 95–98.

73. Fuchs, *Moral Demands*, 54–55.

74. Gerard Hughes, who claims that the moral beliefs embedded in the Christian tradition must always be confirmed by an independent source (human reason), fails to acknowledge the mutually reinforcing relationship between faith and reason in which what is considered reasonable and right is influenced by faith. See Hughes, *Authority in Morals*, chapter 1.

75. Fuchs, *Christian Morality*, 11. This point is also made by Simpson, "A Christian Basis for Ethics," 289.

76. This hermeneutical element in Fuchs's thought, which posits a reciprocally conditioning relationship between faith and reason, should not be overlooked. Some of the more influential proponents of an autonomous ethic, such as Bruno Schüller and Gerard Hughes, present an Enlightenment notion of reason in which reason operates independently from Christian faith in the process of forging moral beliefs and determining the content of the human good. Fuchs, in contrast, although distinguishing faith and reason for the purpose of analysis, wants to move away from Schüller's and Hughes's position by portraying faith and reason not as separate realities existing alongside each other in relative isolation, but as realities involved in an ongoing dialectical relationship. For an illuminating discussion of this understanding of faith and reason in the works of several notable European moral theologians attempting to construct an autonomous ethic in the context of Christian faith, see James F. Keenan and Thomas R. Kopfensteiner, "Moral Theology Out of Western Europe," *Theological Studies* 59 (1998): 115–19.

77. Fuchs, *Personal Responsibility*, 123–25; Fuchs, *Christian Morality*, 9–17; and Fuchs, *Moral Demands*, 102–3.

78. Cf. Kevin A. McMahon, "Josef Fuchs and the Question of a Distinctively Christian Morality," in *Faith Seeking Understanding: Learning and the Catholic Tradition*, ed. George C. Berthold (Manchester, N.H.: St. Anselm College Press, 1991), 240. For an analysis of how Christian sources of moral wisdom enhanced natural law deliberation in the writings of medieval theologians, see Jean Porter, *Natural and Divine Law: Reclaiming the Tradition for Christian Ethics* (Grand Rapids, Mich.: William B. Eerdmans, 1999), 121–77.

79. Fuchs, *Christian Morality*, 65, 138.

80. Fuchs *Human Values*, 131; Fuchs, *Christian Ethics*, 58; Fuchs, *Christian Morality*, 61, 139, 207; and Fuchs, *Moral Demands*, 102.

81. Fuchs, *Christian Ethics*, 58.

82. Fuchs, *Personal Responsibility*, 41.

83. Fuchs, *Human Values*, 139.

84. For an extended discussion of absolute and relative natural law in Fuchs's writings, see chapter 1.

85. The singularly most important factor conditioning relative natural law's contents, according to the preconversion Fuchs, is original sin. Practically, this means that most of the moral norms derived from relative natural law are universally applicable to all persons after the Fall. See Fuchs, *Natural Law*, 85–122.

86. Josef Fuchs, *General Moral Theology*, pt. 1 (Rome: Pontificia Universitatis Gregoriana, 1963), 42–43.

87. Fuchs, *Personal Responsibility*, 123–24, 178–79; Fuchs, *Christian Ethics*, 10; and Fuchs, *Moral Demands*, 105.

88. Fuchs, *Personal Responsibility*, 188.

89. Ibid., 128.

90. Fuchs, *Christian Ethics*, 10.

91. Fuchs, *Personal Responsibility*, 142.

92. Ibid., 42.

93. Fuchs, *Moral Demands*, 97.

94. Fuchs, *Christian Morality*, 113.

95. Fuchs, *Personal Responsibility*, 16.

96. Fuchs, *Christian Ethics*, 145. As Fuchs writes, "[I]f behavioral norms are to be operative, the entire pertinent reality (including the social factor) has to be taken into account and enter into the judgment. The a priori, hence universal, ahistorical social ethics that stands opposed to this, that provides norms in advance for every social reality, sacrifices the indispensable objectivity and therefore validity of duly concrete solutions to an a priori universalism. The critical question, then, is . . . [moral] objectivity, or the 'truth' of the action which must be in conformity with the whole concrete reality of man (of society)" (Fuchs, *Personal Responsibility*, 133).

97. Ibid., 179. In a similar vein, Mark Johnson argues that the genesis, meaning, and function of moral norms must be connected to the communal context in which they emerged: "The mistake is to peel off a specific [norm] from its embodiment in the historically developing moral experience of a people. Whatever moral [norms] there are have their meaning and usefulness only within the horizon of an evolving moral tradition. The mistake is thus to divorce the [norm] from its experiential origins within a particular historical, political, social, economic, and psychological context" (Mark Johnson, *Moral Imagination* [Chicago: University of Chicago Press, 1993], 104).

98. Fuchs, *Personal Responsibility*, 2.

99. Jean Porter, *Moral Action and Christian Ethics* (Cambridge: Cambridge University Press, 1995), 190.

100. Fuchs, *Personal Responsibility*, 47.

101. Fuchs, *Moral Demands*, 114.

102. Fuchs, *Personal Responsibility*, 128, 192.

103. Fuchs, *Moral Demands*, 22.

104. Fuchs, *Human Values*, 73.

105. For a signal example of this methodology of exploring implausible, yet possible, scenarios to test the validity of moral norms, see Derek Parfit,

Reasons and Persons (Oxford: Clarendon Press, 1987), especially 12–13, 21–22, and 38.

106. Fuchs, *Christian Ethics*, 10.

107. Fuchs, *Human Values*, 73; Fuchs, *Personal Responsibility*, 48; and Fuchs, *Christian Morality*, 141.

108. Fuchs, *Personal Responsibility*, 132, 142.

109. Fuchs, *Human Values*, 73.

110. Fuchs, *Personal Responsibility*, 179.

111. Ibid., 146.

112. Fuchs, *Christian Morality*, 130–32.

113. Fuchs, *Personal Responsibility*, 142, 193; Fuchs, *Christian Ethics*, 71; and Fuchs, *Moral Demands*, 106.

114. Fuchs, *Personal Responsibility*, 146.

115. For an examination of the issues and figures involved in the situation ethics debate and their respective positions on exceptionless moral norms, see chapter 1.

116. See Pope Pius XII, "The Christian Conscience as an Object of Education," *Catholic Documents* 8 (1952): 1–7; Pope Pius XII, "Address to the World Federation of Catholic Young Women," *Catholic Documents* 8 (1952): 15–20; and John C. Ford and Gerald Kelly, *Contemporary Moral Theology*, 2 vols. (Cork, Ireland: Mercier Press, 1958–63), 1: 123.

117. For some of the more important works on this topic, see Fuchs, *Personal Responsibility*, 115–52; Fuchs, *Christian Ethics*, 71–90; Lisa Sowle Cahill, "Contemporary Challenges to Exceptionless Moral Norms," in *Moral Theology Today: Certitudes and Doubts* (St. Louis, Mo.: Pope John XXIII Center, 1984); Charles E. Curran, "Absolute Norms in Moral Theology," in *Norm and Context in Christian Ethics*, ed. Gene H. Outka and Paul Ramsey (New York: Charles Scribner's Sons, 1968); John Giles Milhaven, *Toward a New Catholic Morality* (Garden City, N.Y.: Doubleday, 1970), 15–28; and Richard A. McCormick, *Ambiguity in Moral Choice* (Milwaukee, Wisc.: Marquette University Press, 1973).

118. John Finnis, *Moral Absolutes: Tradition, Revision, and Truth* (Washington, D.C.: Catholic University of America Press, 1991); William E. May, *Moral Absolutes: Catholic Tradition, Current Trends, and the Truth* (Milwaukee, Wisc.: Marquette University Press, 1989); William E. May, *An Introduction to Moral Theology* (Huntington, Ind.: Our Sunday Visitor, 1991), 107–38; Germain Grisez, "Moral Absolutes: A Critique of the View of Josef Fuchs, S.J.," *Anthropos* 2 (1985); and Josef Seifert, "Absolute Moral Obligations towards Finite Goods as Foundation of Intrinsically Right and Wrong Actions," *Anthropos* 1 (1985).

119. Pope John Paul II, *Veritatis Splendor* (Boston: St. Paul Books and Media, 1993), #79–83.

120. See, for example, Grisez, "Moral Absolutes."

121. For a clear, succinct survey of the various types of moral norms, see Cahill, "Contemporary Challenges to Exceptionless Moral Norms," 122–25 from which the following examples are drawn.

122. Fuchs, *Personal Responsibility*, 188

123. For a fuller analysis of analytic moral norms, see Jean Porter, *Moral Action and Christian Ethics* (Cambridge: Cambridge University Press, 1995), 18–23.

124. Finnis, *Moral Absolutes*, 2.

125. May, *Moral Absolutes*, 25.

126. Pope John Paul II summarizes the position well: " 'there exist acts which *per se* and in themselves, independently of circumstances, are always seriously wrong by reason of their object' " (John Paul II, *Veritatis Splendor*, #80, quoting his earlier *Reconciliatio et Paenitentia*, #17).

127. Fuchs, *Christian Ethics*, 73–74.

128. Fuchs, *Personal Responsibility*, 140–41.

129. Ibid., 141.

130. The wording of this sentence has been altered from the original, which reads, "A priori, such knowledge is not attainable" (Josef Fuchs, "Absoluteness of Moral Terms," *Gregorianum* 52 [1971]: 449).

131. Fuchs, *Personal Responsibility*, 140. This last sentence has also been altered from the original: "*Theoretically*, no other answer seems possible: Probably there can be no universal norms of *behavior* in the strict sense of '*intrinsece malum*' " (Fuchs, "Absoluteness of Moral Terms," 450).

132. The original version of this article reads substantially the same: "there *seems* to be no possibility of norms of this kind for human action"; "*Probably* there can be no universal norms" (Fuchs, "Absoluteness of Moral Terms," 449–50; emphasis added).

133. For a fuller discussion of this issue, see chapter 5.

134. Fuchs, *Personal Responsibility*, 209–12; Fuchs, *Christian Morality*, 139–40; and Fuchs, *Moral Demands*, 22, 98–99, 114–15.

135. Fuchs, *Moral Demands*, 106.

136. Fuchs, *Christian Morality*, 15.

137. Fuchs, *Personal Responsibility*, 132.

138. See also Klaus Demmer, "Erwängungen zum 'intrinsece malum,' " *Gregorianum* 68 (1987).

139. Fuchs, *Christian Ethics*, 20.

140. For criticisms of Fuchs's argument that alterations of the human person might undermine the validity of exceptionless moral norms, see Finnis, *Moral Absolutes*, 24–28; and May, *Moral Absolutes*, 43–46.

141. Fuchs, *Personal Responsibility*, 140.

142. Fuchs, *Moral Demands*, 22.

143. Fuchs, *Personal Responsibility*, 141–42.

144. See Finnis, *Moral Absolutes*, 20–24; and Seifert, "Absolute Moral Obligations," 82–84.

145. Fuchs, *Personal Responsibility*, 141–42.

146. Ibid., 129, 146.

147. Fuchs, *Christian Morality*, 130.

148. Fuchs, *Moral Demands*, 116.

149. Ibid., 97–99.

150. Ibid., 116–17.

151. Mark Johnson, *Moral Imagination* (Chicago: University of Chicago Press, 1993), 109.

152. Fuchs, *Personal Responsibility,* 129.

153. Ibid., 179.

154. Ibid., 131–32.

155. Fuchs, *Christian Ethics,* 7.

156. Ibid., 91–94.

157. For similar arguments, see Fuchs, *Human Values,* 42; Fuchs, *Personal Responsibility,* 47; Fuchs, *Christian Ethics,* 107; and Fuchs, *Moral Demands,* 116.

158. Fuchs, *Moral Demands,* 117.

Conclusion

Fuchs and the Future of Roman Catholic Natural Law Theory

As a historical figure, Josef Fuchs serves as a weather vane for twentieth-century Roman Catholic natural law theory. During his preconversion period (1941–66) Fuchs emerged as an astute defender of the received tradition whose natural law theory, although considerably more theologically sophisticated than his neo-Thomist counterparts, reflected many of their preoccupations and presuppositions: an understanding of natural law dominated by an exceedingly confident metaphysics of human nature that served as the invariable, intelligible, and epistemologically accessible link between eternal law and natural law; the conviction that human nature yields—or can yield with a modicum of reflection on historical circumstances—an ordered series of moral norms capable of determining what ought to be done in any conceivable situation; the belief that moral objectivity resides in moral norms, which can be applied immediately and directly in concrete situations to attain moral rightness; a strong role for the magisterium, which by virtue of its superior insight into natural law enjoys privileged access to knowledge of right and wrong behavior, in formulating moral norms; and finally, a negligible role for the individual moral agent, who is exclusively responsible for forming her conscience according to received teaching to ensure that she is able to select the correct moral norm to be applied in her respective situation.

The upheaval and foment besetting Roman Catholic natural law theory during the 1960s, arising initially during the papal birth control commission's deliberations and reaching its zenith during the maelstrom of controversy following the publication of Pope Paul VI's *Humanae Vitae*, signaled a new beginning for Roman Catholic natural law theory. Although contraception was the proverbial spark that ignited the fire, the ensuing debate quickly moved far beyond this restricted issue and the general consensus among moral theologians then was that the structural defects uncovered in traditional Roman Catholic natural law theory during the contraception debate were systemic and foundational and could not be rectified by subtle adjustments or better distinctions.

Fuchs has been one of the most productive thinkers in Roman Catholic natural law theory since the 1960s. His willingness and ability to address fundamental matters proved to be highly opportune and fruitful during a period in which basic, foundational issues needed to be addressed. Consistent with the nature of the task, Fuchs began the project of reconstructing Roman Catholic natural law theory from the bottom up, so to speak, by addressing perhaps the most basic question: What is the human being? Adeptly appropriating the insights of Karl Rahner's transcendental Thomism, Fuchs explored the implications of human subjectivity, personhood, transcendence, fundamental option, and historicity, which culminated in a theological anthropology sharply at odds with his former notion of the human being as a composite of human nature and ontological accidents.

After this initial Rahnerian turn to the subject, Fuchs turned his attention to methodological and substantive matters in Roman Catholic natural law theory, and for the next thirty-odd years returned time and again to issues such as the role of reason in natural law deliberation, the necessity of experience in discovering natural law, the function and validity of moral norms, the soteriological import of natural law, moral competency, moral epistemology, and the role of the individual moral agent. What emerged during this period of sustained, deliberate reconstruction of Roman Catholic natural law theory was an understanding of natural law that at the beginning of the twenty-first century has garnered the allegiance of many of the most influential contemporary Roman Catholic moralists: reason reflecting on experience—not metaphysics—as the port of entry to natural law; natural law as a socially and historically mediated phenomenon that must be learned incrementally over time in a process inherently open to revision and supplementation; the distinction between goodness and rightness, which identifies striving to know and to do what is right—not actually performing right actions—as the decisive soteriological issue; the potential disjunction between abstract, preformulated moral norms and concrete, integral human flourishing as grasped by *recta ratio;* detailed, concrete knowledge of one's subject matter as the sine qua non of moral competency; and the moral agent not as an applicator of received teaching, but as an active assessor of moral truth who might have to propose innovative, unprecedented solutions in some instances.

Fuchs and his like-minded colleagues have initiated a reconstruction of Roman Catholic natural law theory that, in my opinion, has the potential to reap enormous long-term benefits for Roman Catholic moral theology. In its broad outline, I believe Fuchs's natural law theory provides a solid, persuasive, and cogent platform for reenvisioning natural law and for tackling many of the pressing moral issues that are likely to require sustained attention in the near future. Of course, the success of this project of refurbishing natural law is not preordained; as with any relatively new movement, cracks in its foundation are likely to appear, its germinal insights will need to be developed and solidified, and any incompleteness will have to be rectified. As I indicated in the second half of this study, although I agree with the fundamental bases and trajectory of Fuchs's postconversion natural law theory, there are crucial issues that will require significant attention if the project Fuchs began will eventually culminate in a natural law theory serviceable for use within Roman Catholic moral theology. In the hope of contributing to this endeavor, let me briefly outline a few areas that need attention if Fuchs's project is to succeed.

Perhaps the most pressing—and potentially difficult—topic is theological anthropology. Although Fuchs's masterful appropriation of Karl Rahner's transcendental Thomism has provided pivotal ideas and concepts—basic freedom, fundamental option, transcendence, the subject as a whole—that have altered the moral vocabulary and landscape of Roman Catholic moral theology, Fuchs's Rahnerian analysis of human subjectivity has left unaddressed the issue more immediately germane to natural law theory: the goods to which humans are directed. Even if Fuchs's Rahnerian anthropology is accepted as correct in its entirety, we are still left with perplexing, unanswered questions: How should one's fundamental option be expressed through particular actions? How should the disposal of oneself as a whole before God be reflected or incarnated categorially? How should we actualize ourselves through concrete, determinate choices?

Even to begin to tackle these questions, there must be a fuller understanding of what it means to be human, whether humans are inherently ordered to particular goods, what these goods are, and whether an order exists among these goods. This issue is vitally important; for the practical moral assessment of particular structures, institutions, relationships, and actions cannot commence without some conception of the human goods they promote or protect and the relative importance of these respective goods for human well-being. A close reading of Fuchs will uncover a partial list of goods—reason, sociability, life, and a loving relationship with God—that begin to give more content to his anthropology, but the paucity of this catalogue of human goods does not begin to exhaust the multifarious goods constitutive of human flourishing.

Fuchs's theological anthropology, like that of other influential revisionist theologians, incorporates distinct strands of thought that seem to tug in opposite directions. On the one hand, although Fuchs never outlines in any detail the contents of human nature, he is entirely sympathetic to the idea of a human nature that is comprised of various natural inclinations directing humans to certain goods. In this sense, Fuchs posits a teleological order of nature that establishes certain ends as constitutive of human well-being, even though the natural order does not dictate how these ends should be actualized in concrete situations. On the other hand, Fuchs clearly wants to supplement his theological anthropology with an understanding of personhood, which connotes historicity, change, self-creation, cultural and social embeddedness, and perhaps most importantly, an individuality that refuses to identify human beings simply as members of the human race sharing common inclinations and attributes, but as distinct selves whose needs, personalities, plans, and concrete well-being differ from person to person.

This wedding of human nature and contemporary personalism might prove to be a highly potent anthropological basis for Roman Catholic natural law theory, but at this time many of the finer points of this synthesis remain unclear: How determinate are the goods to which human nature directs us? Can these goods be pursued in different ways by different individuals? How malleable or rigid are our natural inclinations? Are there limits to our capacity for self-creation? If so, what are they? Does human historicity allow for the possibility of cross-cultural critiques of behavior? Or does our historical embeddedness and conditioning limit our ability to make normative judgments about behavior in other cultures and societies? What individual characteristics are morally relevant to natural law analysis? Gender? Ethnicity? Social role? Nationality?

The second issue that requires further attention is moral epistemology. One of the most persistent criticisms of Fuchs's method of determining the rightness or wrongness of specific actions is the impossibility of comparing qualitatively different human goods, or the incommensurability problem. Lacking any common standard by which to assess the value of disparate goods, Fuchs's critics contend, the process of determining the prevalence of premoral values or disvalues of various actions is bound to be arbitrary.

The issue raised by the incommensurability problem is of considerable importance to Roman Catholic natural law theory. If qualitatively different goods cannot be rationally commensurated or compared, there is no possibility of establishing an objective hierarchy of goods or of measuring the value of different actions that actualize supposedly incommensurable goods. In Grisez and Finnis's natural law theory, the incommensurability thesis culminates in a "scorched-earth policy" that denies any objective basis for preferring or choosing any basic good over another, and leaves the pursuit of these goods "to the vagaries of subjective temperament or cultural conditioning"[1] as long as one's actions do not directly attack or undermine a basic good.

On a practical level, the incommensurability thesis leads to scenarios that jar our moral sensibilities: because there is no common denominator to compare the worth of the goods of life or play, for example, there can be no objective basis for valuing the act of attempting to save a man suffering a heart attack more than playing a round of golf. Nor is there any objective basis for valuing a life dedicated to community activism, or scholarship and teaching, or direct service to the poor over a life centered around surfing or playing sports.

The incommensurability thesis contradicts the widely held conviction that certain human goods are more valuable than others, and there are valid reasons for preferring some goods over others. Every day, each person is presented with manifold potential human goods that can be actualized. But rarely do we experience these goods as incommensurable and incapable of being ordered hierarchically. Some are judged to be essential to human well-being and worthy of sustained, deliberate pursuit and protection, others are regarded as instrumental goods, valuable as necessary conditions for the attainment of higher goods, and some are considered only marginally important to a life well-lived. Throughout this process, we reveal ourselves as beings capable of determining the relative worth of goods for human well-being, even in the absence of a common denominator to compare qualitatively different goods.[2]

If Fuchs's project of refurbishing Roman Catholic natural law theory is to succeed, a moral epistemology needs to be developed that better explains the process of comparing premoral values and disvalues and how determining the prevalence of the former over the latter is based not on arbitrary judgments but on objective reality. The implausibility of the incommensurability thesis suggests that Fuchs and his like-minded colleagues are on the right track in asserting that humans do not need some common denominator to assess the relative worth of supposedly incommensurable goods for human well-being. But at this point, the epistemological basis for Fuchs's notion of moral reasoning lacks clarity and needs attention.

This being said, Fuchs's postconversion natural law theory, as it stands, represents a significant accomplishment that has corrected many of the shortcomings of traditional Roman Catholic natural law theory. By distinguishing between goodness and rightness and correctly identifying the singular soteriological issue as striving to know and to do what is right—not actually performing right actions—Fuchs has not only effectively eliminated the disturbing intellectual moral elitism underlying the traditional synthesis between the natural and supernatural orders that was inherently biased against the unintelligent and their ability to cooperate with God in their salvation, but he has also interjected a much needed egalitarianism into his understanding of personal salvation that levels the soteriological playing field, so to speak, so that differences in native talents, familial, cultural, or social background, or any other accidental conditions that either hinder or enhance one's ability to uncover natural law concretely and to perform right actions do not affect one's ability to respond to God's gift of salvation, thereby making the possibility of accepting salvation in principle equally accessible to everyone, regardless of their lot in life.

Fuchs's analysis of moral competency, which identifies three integral facets of being able to discover natural law consistently—personal goodness, knowledge of one's subject matter, and knowledge of concrete circumstances—offers a much needed corrective to the tendency in the Roman Catholic Church to regard the magisterium as the guarantor of moral rightness, regardless of the magisterium's qualifications to decide particular moral issues. To be sure, Fuchs never challenges the magisterium's institutional competency to speak officially for the church on moral matters, but on the issue of moral competency, Fuchs has correctly asserted that it cannot rest only on invocations of the Holy Spirit's assistance or on the magisterium's own claim to be the authentic interpreter of natural law, but also on the aforementioned qualities that must be present for anyone to grasp natural law concretely and consistently.

Fuchs's natural law theory also offers an insightful and timely critique of the preceptive understanding of natural law dominant in twentieth century Roman Catholic moral theology. Even a brief perusal of the neo-Thomist manuals of moral theology that served as the principal texts in seminaries worldwide from the late 1800s to the mid-1900s cannot fail to detect a fervent enthusiasm for reducing natural law to a series of clear, unambiguous, and usually universal moral norms that yielded specific directives for the laity to follow. Eternal law, the natural inclinations, the function and power of human reason, the magisterium's statements on natural law's perceptibility, and the distorting effects of original sin all received obligatory, albeit cursory, treatment in the neo-Thomists's tracts on natural law, which effectively served as theological and philosophical window dressing for the more important matter to follow: moral norms, and the innumerable aspects of life they regulate.

Although Fuchs never discounts the validity of moral norms and their instrumental role in conveying a community's cumulative moral wisdom, Fuchs continually beckons his readers to a more realistic appraisal of moral norms in natural law deliberation. Moral norms are only as accurate as their sources, human reason and judgment. They express both our limited capacity of imagination and insight, as well as our concerns and preoccupations as historically embedded beings attempting to order our lives and prioritize our commitments. As such, moral norms should be approached with neither unbridled confidence nor persistent skepticism, but with a critical awareness that they represent the considered, reflective judgments of a fallible human community in an ongoing quest to discover how human well-being can best be attained in its particular circumstances.

Furthermore, Fuchs's repeated insistence on concreteness as the necessary condition for grasping natural law raises our awareness that moral decisions always occur in determinate, here-and-now situations and that the abstract, preformulated moral norms might not always be directly applicable in concrete situations. This attention to concreteness, to the range of circumstances that actually occur in a situation as well as to the influence of actions and patterns of behavior on concrete human well-being, represents one of the most pronounced—and valuable—facets of Fuchs's postconversion natural law theory.

For too long in Roman Catholic moral theology the attainment of moral objectivity has been equated with the direct application of received teaching in one's situation. Fuchs's analysis of the potential disjunction between a moral norm's directive and the right course of action in the given concrete circumstances, however, discredits this notion of moral objectivity and interjects a healthy dose of realism into our understanding of the role and function of moral norms in natural law deliberation. Moral norms might enjoy prima facie validity and serve as usually reliable indicators of right and wrong behavior, but their acceptance is based on the insight, tested over time and repeatedly confirmed in a variety of circumstances, that they enhance concrete human well-being. In this sense, moral objectivity does not reside in moral norms, however well-received; it emerges only through the insight of an individual moral agent whose knowledge of concrete circumstances and the various premoral values and disvalues at stake allow her to discern the right course of action in the immediate situation.

Finally, as Roman Catholic natural law theory enters the twenty-first century it will have to face an unprecedented constellation of moral issues that pose long-term hazards to the health and well-being of humans worldwide. The confident, almost arrogant, pursuit of material progress and development characteristic of industrialized countries these past two centuries, which has been marketed as a sure-fire panacea for many of the ills afflicting humankind and has become the dominant and largely unquestioned force behind most Western social, political, and economic systems, has recently fallen under sharp criticism for the many adverse side-effects and sometimes outrageous injustices it has caused, institutionalized, and continues to perpetuate.

The mobility and convenience offered by the automobile, perhaps the crowning glory of the industrial revolution, has been gained by expelling enormous amounts of carbon dioxide, the leading cause of global warming, into the atmosphere. Transnational corporations, which possess the capital, technological sophistication, information, and resources to provide Westerners with the best, least expensive products available anywhere in the world frequently treat Third World countries as playgrounds for their money-making ventures, extracting vast quantities of natural resources, displacing indigenous peoples indiscriminately, and typically benefiting only the wealthy and politically influential in these countries. Technological innovations responsible for being able to build bigger, more efficient fishing boats have lead to depleted fisheries worldwide, sometimes to the point where once bountiful fishing grounds have been closed to commercial fishing indefinitely. Industrialized farming and its implements of choice—heavy machinery, pesticides, fertilizers, herbicides, genetically modified crops, irrigation—have produced disastrous effects that unquestionably impact long-term human well-being: historically unprecedented levels of topsoil erosion; widespread contamination of underground aquifers and farm wells; salinization of millions of acres of farmland; chemical residues on foods, the long-term hazards of which are unknown; widespread destruction of native ecosystems and the flora and fauna they once supported; and the extinction of many locally adapted—and genetically superior—crops that for thousands of years supplied a highly reliable source of nutrition for subsistence farmers and their local communities.

In my opinion, issues such as these which are ultimately caused by a desire for better material standards of living for people in First World countries and which produce worldwide, long-term threats to human well-being will be the critical moral issues of the twenty-first century. The possibility of constructing a plausible critique of these practices, however, must come to grips with the lengthy and often confusing trail of causality that makes it difficult to isolate and identify those responsible for a respective problem. It is easy to condemn the excessive amount of topsoil erosion in the United States, for example, yet equally difficult to pinpoint the culprit(s) or cause(s). Are the farmers who keep topsoil in a perpetually disturbed state the principal malefactors? What about American consumers whose demand for relatively large amounts of fatty beef make it financially attractive to farmers to produce those types of crops—corn and soybeans—most conducive to topsoil erosion? What about government agricultural policies that increase the financial incentive to grow corn and soybeans? How about the role of American agribusinesses, from heavy machinery manufacturers, to local implement dealers, to seed distributors, all who support and promote the agricultural status quo that inevitably culminates in historically unprecedented amounts of topsoil erosion? What about professors and agricultural researchers in American universities whose single-minded dedication to engineering the highest yielding strains of corn and soybeans has consciously neglected perennial crops that are much better at preventing topsoil erosion?

Topsoil erosion, like many other problems posing a long-term threat to human well-being, is not the product of one readily identifiable act; it is the cumulative, unintended, gradual effect of many acts and practices that are benign in themselves. Moreover, its causes and the structures supporting the types of farming practices that lead to excessive topsoil erosion are partial and manifold and include a host of intermediaries, from the consumer who demands fatty beef from cows fed on corn and soybeans, to government programs rewarding corn and soybean farmers financially, to agronomists who convince farmers that there is no viable alternative to growing corn and soybeans, to university researchers who refuse to explore and develop alternatives to the current monoculture of corn and soybeans.

If Roman Catholic natural law theory is to have an impact on long-term problems such as topsoil erosion, dwindling fisheries worldwide, deforestation, global warming, and the appalling income disparity between First and Third World countries, among others, it must begin to assess the moral import of individual actions more comprehensively by identifying and critiquing not only the immediate, proximate effects they produce, but also the particular schemes of recurrence, structures, institutions, and long-term consequences they create, support, and legitimize.

Fuchs's natural law theory succeeds admirably at this. By insisting that all premoral values and disvalues of an action be considered to determine its rightness or wrongness, whether proximate or remote, or direct or indirect, or slight or readily apparent, Fuchs has effectively expanded our understanding of an action's moral import to include all the repercussions for and influences on human well-being. In a very practical sense, Fuchs's natural law analysis alters the way we should think about the morality of many everyday, commonplace actions. Fuchs natural law theory requires automobile owners, for example, to consider the full range of values and disvalues potentially associated with automobile production, ownership, and use: How and to what extent are automobiles contributing to global warming? What are the ecological effects of strip mining for iron ore? How many and what kinds of toxic wastes are generated by manufacturing automobiles? How do corporations treat citizens of Third World countries where they extract natural resources? Does their activity in Third World countries benefit the poor and less fortunate? Is automobile transportation more or less efficient than public transportation? Could money spent on purchasing and maintaining an automobile be spent in better ways? Does the need for fossil fuels to power our automobiles create a predisposition to use force to protect our oil interests in other countries?

Automobile production and use, like many other actions common in contemporary American life, create various benefits and costs, involve a host of institutions, networks, and intermediaries, and support and reinforce multiple patterns of behavior, all of which detract from or enhance human well-being. In my opinion, only if natural law analysis begins to acknowledge and account for the interconnectedness of actions and the larger schemes of recurrence they cause, support, or perpetuate, as Fuchs's natural law theory does, will it be able not only to offer an accurate assessment of the full moral import of discrete, individual actions, but also to raise awareness that human well-being is not confined to emotionally wrenching, once-in-a-lifetime, momentous decisions that are the warp and woof of dilemma ethics, but includes many of the ordinary, mundane actions that constitute daily life and shape the larger world in which we live for better or worse, from the types of foods we buy and consume, to the way we treat friends, colleagues, and co-workers, to the businesses we frequent, to the way in which we spend disposable income, to the types of energy we use, to the material standard of living we pursue.

Fuchs's natural law theory has left a rich legacy to Roman Catholic moral theology, and subsequent moralists will undoubtedly benefit from the many ideas that Fuchs has articulated, developed, and refined during his academic career. In both his willingness and ability to tackle fundamental questions in Roman Catholic natural law theory, Fuchs stands unparalleled in twentieth-century Roman Catholic moral theology. For over fifty years Fuchs has returned time and again to basic issues such as moral objectivity, moral epistemology, moral competency, the role of nature, reason, and experience in natural law deliberation, the relation between actions and personal salvation, the validity of moral norms, and the role of the individual moral agent. And for over thirty years Fuchs has offered the key ingredients and insights that have restored the credibility of natural law in Roman Catholic circles and have provided the substantive beginnings of a cogent, persuasive natural law theory that can be fruitfully developed by subsequent commentators. Although some of the finer points of Fuchs's synthesis still need to be addressed, the many fundamental matters he has masterfully explored and effectively settled have gone a long way toward constructing a natural law theory serviceable for use within Roman Catholic moral theology.

Notes

1. Russell Hittinger, *A Critique of the New Natural Law Theory* (Notre Dame, Ind.: University of Notre Dame Press, 1987), 78.

2. For critiques of the incommensurability problem, see Edward Collins Vacek, "Proportionalism: One View of the Debate," *Theological Studies* 46 (1985): 303–306; and Garth Hallett, "The 'Incommensurability' of Values," *Heythrop Journal* 23 (1987).

Bibliography

Works by Josef Fuchs

Fuchs, Josef. "The Absolute in Morality and the Christian Conscience." *Gregorianum* 71 (1990): 697–711.

——. "The Absoluteness of Moral Terms." *Gregorianum* 52 (1971): 415–58.

——. *Christian Ethics in a Secular Arena*. Translated by Bernard Hoose and Brian McNeil. Washington, D.C.: Georgetown University Press, 1984.

——. *Christian Morality: The Word Becomes Flesh*. Translated by Brian McNeil. Washington, D.C.: Georgetown University Press, 1987.

——. *De Castitate et Ordine Sexuali*. Rome: Pontificia Universitatis Gregoriana, 1959.

——. "De Valore Legis Naturalis in Ordine Redemptionis." *Periodica de Re Morali, Canonica, et Liturgica* 44 (1955): 45–64.

——. "Ehelehre der Kirche und Eheleben der Christen." *Die neue Ordnung* 5 (1952): 413–17.

——. "Elterliche Verantwortung für das kommende Geschlecht." *Scholastik* 26 (1951): 222–43.

——. "Die Ehezwecklehre des h. Thomas von Aquin." *Theologische Quartalschrift* 128 (1948): 398–426.

——. "Ethique objective et éthique de situation." *Nouvelle Revue Théologique* 78 (1956): 798–818.

——. *General Moral Theology*. Pt. 1. Rome: Pontificia Universitatis Gregoriana, 1963.

——. "Good Acts and Good Persons." In *Considering Veritatis Splendor*, edited by John Wilkins. Cleveland: Pilgrim Press, 1994.

——. *Human Values and Christian Morality*. Translated by M. H. Heelan, Maeve McRedmond, Erika Young, and Gerard Watson. Dublin: Gill and Macmillan, 1970.

——. *Lex Naturae. Zur Theologie des Naturrechts*. Düsseldorf, Germany: Patmos, 1955.

——. "Der Liebe als Aufbauprinzip der Moraltheologie." *Scholastik* 29 (1954): 79–87.

——. *Moral Demands and Personal Obligations*. Translated by Brian McNeil. Washington, D.C.: Georgetown University Press, 1993.

————. "Morale théologique et morale de situation." *Nouvelle Revue Théologique* 76 (1954): 1073–85.

————. *Natural Law. A Theological Investigation.* Translated by Helmut Recker and John Dowling. New York: Sheed and Ward, 1965.

————. "Naturrecht und positives Recht." *Stimmen der Zeit* 163 (1958–59): 130–41.

————. " 'Operatio' et 'Operatum' in Dictamine Conscientiae." In *Thomistica Morum Principia II*, 71–9. Communicationes et Acta V Congressus Thomistici Internationalis, Rome, 13–17 September 1960. Rome: Catholic Book Agency.

————. *Personal Responsibility and Christian Morality.* Translated by William Cleves et al. Washington, D.C.: Georgetown University Press, 1983.

————. "Positivistisches Naturrecht?" *Orientierung* 20 (1956): 113–15, 127–29.

————. *Die Sexualethik des Heiligen Thomas von Aquin.* Cologne: J. P. Bachem, 1949.

————. "Sin and Conversion." *Theology Digest* 14 (1966): 292–301.

————. "Sittliche Normen—Universalien und Generalisierungen." *Münchener Theologische Zeitschrift* 1 (1974): 18–33.

————. *Situation und Entscheidung. Grundfragen christlicher Situationsethik.* Frankfurt: Knecht, 1952.

————. "Situationsethik." *Seelsorgehilfe* 4 (1952): 245–55, 273–78.

————. "Situationsethik in theologischer Sicht." *Scholastik* 27 (1952): 161–82.

————. *Theologia Moralis Generalis.* Pars altera. Rome: Pontificia Universitatis Gregoriana, 1966.

Fuchs, Josef, Pierre de Locht, Michel Labourdette, Raymond Sigmond, Alfons Auer, and Paul Anciaux. "Final Report of the Pontifical Commission on Population, Family, and Birth." In *The Encyclical That Never Was* by Robert Blair Kaiser, 3–18. 1967; reprint, London: Sheed and Ward, 1987.

Fuchs, Josef, Philippe Delhaye, and Raymond Sigmond. "The Argument for Reform." *Tablet*, 6 May (1967): 510–13.

Secondary Sources

Antony, Louise. "Natures and Norms." *Ethics* 111 (2000): 8–36.

Aquinas, Thomas. *Summa Theologica.* 5 vols. Translated by the Fathers of the English Dominican Province. 1911; reprint, Westminster, Md.: Christian Classics, 1981.

Arendt, Hannah. *The Origins of Totalitarianism.* New York: Harcourt Brace, 1975.

Arnhart, Larry. *Darwinian Natural Right: The Biological Ethics of Human Nature.* Albany: State University of New York Press, 1998.

Ashley, Benedict. "The Loss of Theological Unity." In *Being Right*, edited by Mary Jo Weaver and R. Scott Appleby. Bloomington: Indiana University Press, 1995.

Auer, Alfons. *Autonome Moral und christlicher Glaube.* Düsseldorf, Germany: Patmos, 1971.

Augustine, Saint. *The Confessions of St. Augustine.* Translated by John K. Ryan. New York: Doubleday, 1960.

Barth, Karl. *The Doctrine of Creation,* Vol. 3, Bk. 4, *Church Dogmatics.* Edited by G. W. Bromiley and T. F. Torrance. Translated by A. T. Mackay, T. H. L. Parker, Harold Knight, Henry A. Kennedy, and John Marks. Edinburgh: T. & T. Clark, 1961.

————. *The Doctrine of God,* Vol. 2, Bk. 1, *Church Dogmatics.* Edited by G. W. Bromiley and T. F. Torrance. Translated by T. H. L. Parker, W. B. Johnston, Harold Knight, and J. L. M. Hairie. Edinburgh: T. & T. Clark, 1957.

————. *The Doctrine of God,* Vol. 2, Bk. 2, *Church Dogmatics.* Edited by G. W. Bromiley and T. F. Torrance. Translated by G. W. Bromiley, J. C. Campbell, Iain Wilson, J. Strathearn McNab, Harold Knight, and R. A. Stewart. Edinburgh: T. & T. Clark, 1957.

Becker, Lawrence C. "Places for Pluralism." *Ethics* 102 (1992): 707–18.

Besanceney, Paul H. " 'Situation Ethics' or the 'New Morality.' " *American Ecclesiastical Review* 137 (1957): 100–104.

Biggar, Nigel. *The Hastening that Awaits: Karl Barth's Ethics.* Oxford: Clarendon Press, 1993.

Black, Peter and James Keenan. "The Evolving Self-Understanding of the Moral Theologian." *Studia Moralia* 39 (2001): 291–327.

Blank, Josef. "Does the New Testament Provide Principles for Modern Moral Theology?" *Concilium* 25 (1967): 9–22.

Blum, Lawrence. *Moral Perception and Particularity.* New York: Cambridge University Press, 1994.

Böckle, Franz. *Fundamental Moral Theology.* Dublin: Gill and Macmillan, 1980.

————. "Nature as the Basis of Morality." In *Personalist Morals,* edited by Joseph A. Selling. Leuven, Belgium: Leuven University Press, 1988.

Böckle, Franz, ed. *Das Naturrecht im Disput.* Düsseldorf, Germany: Patmos, 1966.

Böckle, Franz and Ernst Wolfgang Böckenforde, eds. *Naturrecht in der Kritik.* Mainz, Germany: Matthias-Grunewald, 1973.

Bourke, Vernon J. "Is Thomas Aquinas a Natural Law Ethicist?" *Monist* 58 (1974): 52–66.

Boyer, C. "Morale et surnaturel." *Gregorianum* 29 (1948): 527–43.

Boyle, John P. "The Natural Law and the Magisterium." In *The Magisterium and Morality,* Readings in Moral Theology, no. 3., edited by Charles E. Curran and Richard A. McCormick. Ramsey, N.J.: Paulist Press, 1982.

Boyle, Joseph. "Freedom, the Human Person, and Human Action." In *Principles of Catholic Moral Life,* edited by William E. May. Chicago: Franciscan Herald Press, 1980.

Brennan, J. M. *The Open-Texture of Moral Concepts.* New York: Harper and Row, 1977.

Broglie, G. de. "De gratuitate ordinis supernaturalis ad quem homo elevantus est." *Gregorianum* 29 (1948): 435–63.

Brunner, Emil. *The Divine Imperative.* Translated by Olive Wyon. Philadelphia: Westminster Press, 1947.

Buckley, Joseph. *Man's Last End*. St. Louis, Mo.: B. Herder Book Co., 1949.

Burke, Patrick J. "Conceptual Thought in Karl Rahner." *Gregorianum* 75 (1994): 65–93.

Cahill, Lisa Sowle. "Contemporary Challenges to Exceptionless Moral Norms." In *Moral Theology Today: Certitudes and Doubts*. St. Louis, Mo.: Pope John XXIII Center, 1984.

——. "Teleology, Utilitarianism, and Christian Ethics." *Theological Studies* 42 (1981): 601–29.

Carr, Aidan M. "The Morality of Situation Ethics." *Catholic Lawyer* 5 (1959): 67–83.

Carr, Anne. "Starting with the Human." In *A World of Grace*, edited by Leo O'Donovan. New York: Crossroad, 1986.

Coffey, David. "Rahner's Theology of Fundamental Option." *Philosophy and Theology* 10 (1997): 255–84.

Connell, Francis. *Outlines of Moral Theology*. Milwaukee, Wisc.: Bruce Publishing, 1953.

Connery, John R. *Abortion: The Development of the Roman Catholic Perspective*. Chicago: Loyola University Press, 1977.

——. "Morality of Consequences: A Critical Appraisal." In *Moral Norms and Catholic Tradition*, Readings in Moral Theology, no. 2, edited by Charles E. Curran and Richard McCormick. Ramsey, N.J.: Paulist Press, 1979.

Crowe, Michael Bertram. Book review of Josef Fuchs's *Natural Law*. *Irish Theological Quarterly* 33 (1966): 275–77.

Crysdale, Cynthia S. W. "Revisioning Natural Law: From the Classicist Paradigm to Emergent Probability." *Theological Studies* 56 (1995): 464–84.

Cunningham, Robert L. Introduction to *Situationism and the New Morality*, edited by Robert L. Cunningham. New York: Appleton-Century-Crofts, 1970.

Curran, Charles E. "Absolute Norms in Moral Theology." In *Norm and Context in Christian Ethics*, edited by Gene H. Outka and Paul Ramsey. New York: Charles Scribner's Sons, 1968.

Davis, Henry. *Moral and Pastoral Theology*. 4 vols. 7th edition. London: Sheed and Ward, 1958.

Dawidowicz, Lucy S. *A Holocaust Reader*. West Orange, N.J.: Behrman House, 1976.

Delhaye, Philippe. "Questioning the Specificity of Christian Morality." In *The Distinctiveness of Christian Ethics*, Readings in Moral Theology, no. 2, edited by Charles E. Curran and Richard A. McCormick. Ramsey, N.J.: Paulist Press, 1980.

de Locht, Pierre. *Les Couples et l'Eglise*. Paris: Centurion, 1975.

de Lubac, Henri. *Surnatural*. Paris: Aubier, 1946.

Deman, T. "Sur l'organisation du savior morale." *Recherches des Sciences Philosophiques et Théologiques* 23 (1934): 258–80.

Demmer, Klaus. "Die autonome Moral—eine Anfrage an die Denkform." In *Fundamente der theologischen Ethik. Bilanz und Neuansätze*, edited by Adrian Holderegger. Freiburg, Germany: Universitätsverlag, 1966.

————. *Deuten und Handeln*. Freiburg, Germany: Universitätsverlag, 1985.

————. "Erwängungen zum 'intrinsece malum.' " *Gregorianum* 68 (1987): 613–37.

————. "Hermeneutische Probleme der Fundamentalmoral." In *Ethik im Kontext des Glaubens. Probleme—Grundsätz—Methoden*, edited by Francesco Campagnoni and Dietmar Mieth. Freiburg, Germany: Universitätsverlag, 1978.

————. *Leben in Menschenhand*. Freiburg, Germany: Universitätsverlag, 1987.

————. "Moralische Norm und theologische Anthropologie." *Gregorianum* 54 (1973): 263–305.

————. "Die Moraltheologische Diskussion um die Anwendung Sterilisierender Medikamente. Versuch einer Uebersicht." *Theologie und Glaube* 53 (1963): 415–35.

————. "Sittlicher Anspruch und Geschichtlichkeit des Verstehens." In *Heilgeschichte und ethische Normen*, edited by Hans Rotter. Freiburg, Germany: Herder, 1984.

————. *Sittlich handeln aus Verstehen. Strukturen hermeneutisch orientierter Fundamentalmoral*. Düsseldorf, Germany: Patmos, 1980.

Di Ianni, Albert. "The Direct/Indirect Distinction in Morals." In *Moral Norms and Catholic Tradition*, ed. Charles E. Curran and Richard A. McCormick. Ramsey, N.J.: Paulist Press, 1979.

Dirks, Walter. "How Can I Know What God Wants of Me?" *Cross Currents* 5 (1955): 76–92.

Donnelly, Philip J. "Discussions on the Supernatural Order." *Theological Studies* 9 (1948): 213–49.

Dulles, Avery. "The Hierarchy of Truths in the Catechism." *Thomist* 58 (1994): 369–88.

Dupré, Louis. "Situation Ethics and Objective Morality." In *Situationism and the New Morality*, edited by Robert L. Cunningham. New York: Appleton-Century-Crofts, 1970.

Egenter, Richard. "Kasuistik als christliche Situationsethik." *Münchener Theologische Zeitschrift* 1 (1950): 54–65.

————. *Von der Freiheit der Kinder Gottes*. Freiburg, Germany: Herder, 1949.

Ermecke, Gustave. "Die Bedeutung von 'Humanwissenshaften' für Moraltheologie." *Theologische Zeitschrift* 26 (1975): 126–40.

Farley, Margaret A. "The Role of Experience in Moral Discernment." In *Christian Ethics: Problems and Prospects*, edited by Lisa Sowle Cahill and James F. Childress. Cleveland, Ohio: Pilgrim Press, 1996.

Finnis, John. *Fundamentals of Ethics*. Washington, D.C.: Georgetown University Press, 1983.

————. *Moral Absolutes: Tradition, Revision, and Truth*. Washington, D.C.: Catholic University of America Press, 1991.

————. *Natural Law and Natural Rights*. Oxford: Clarendon Press, 1980.

Flanagan, Owen. *Varities of Moral Personality*. Cambridge, Mass.: Harvard University Press, 1991.

Flannery, Austin, ed. *The Conciliar and Post Conciliar Documents: Vatican Council II*, Vol. 1. Rev. edition. Northport, N.Y.: Costello Publishing, 1988.

Ford, John C., and Gerald Kelly. *Contemporary Moral Theology*. 2 vols. Cork, Ireland: Mercier Press, 1958–63.

Ford, John C., Jan Visser, Marcellinus Zalba, and Stanilas de Lestapis. "The Birth Control Report: II: The Conservative Case." *Tablet* April 29, 1967: 478–85.

Frankena, William K. "Is Morality Logically Dependent on Religion?" In *Religion and Morality*, edited by John P. Reeder, Jr. Garden City, N.Y.: Anchor Press, 1973.

Gallagher, John A. *Time Past, Time Future: An Historical Study of Catholic Moral Theology*. Mahwah, N.J.: Paulist Press, 1990.

Gewirth, Alan. "Natural Law, Human Action, and Morality." In *The Georgetown Symposium on Ethics*, edited by Rocco Porreco. Lanham, Md.: University Press of America, 1984.

Gilleman, Gérard. *The Primacy of Charity in Moral Theology*. Translated by William F. Ryan and André Vachon, rev. Rene Carpentier. London: Burns and Oates, 1959.

Gleason, Robert W. "Situational Morality." *Thought* 32 (1957–58): 533–58.

———. *Situational Morality*. Albany, N.Y.: Magi Books, 1968.

Gould, Stephen Jay. *The Mismeasure of Man*. New York: Norton, 1981.

Grisez, Germain. "Against Consequentialism." *The American Journal of Jurisprudence* 23 (1978): 21–72.

———. Book review of Josef Fuchs's *Natural Law*. *Month* 34 (1965): 330–31.

———. *Christian Moral Principles*, vol. 1, *The Way of the Lord Jesus*. Chicago: Franciscan Herald Press, 1983.

———. "Moral Absolutes. A Critique of the View of Josef Fuchs, S.J." *Anthropos* 2 (1985): 154–201.

Grootaers, Jan. "The Papal Commission." In *On Human Life*, edited by Peter Harris. London: Burns and Oates, 1968.

Gustafson, James. *Protestant and Roman Catholic Ethics*. Chicago: University of Chicago Press, 1978.

Hall, Pamela M. *Narrative and Natural Law: An Interpretation of Thomistic Ethics*. Notre Dame, Ind.: University of Notre Dame Press, 1994.

Hall, Theodore. "The Mysterious Fundamental Option." *Homiletic and Pastoral Review* 78 (1978): 12–20.

Hallett, Garth. *Greater Good: The Case for Proportionalism*. Washington, D.C.: Georgetown University Press, 1995.

———. "The 'Incommensurability' of Values." *Heythrop Journal* 28 (1987): 373–87.

Häring, Bernard. *The Law of Christ*. 3 vols. Translated by Edwin G. Kasper. Westminster, Md.: Newman Press, 1961–66.

———. *My Witness for the Church*. Translated by Leonard Swidler. Mahwah, N.J.: Paulist Press, 1992.

Hauerwas, Stanley. *The Peaceable Kingdom*. Notre Dame, Ind.: University of Notre Dame Press, 1983.

————. *With the Grain of the Universe: The Church Is Witness and Natural Theology.* Grand Rapids, Mich.: Brazos Press, 2001.

Helm, Paul, ed. *Divine Commands and Morality.* New York: Oxford University Press, 1981.

Hilsdale, Paul. "The Real Threat of Situation Ethics." *Homiletic and Pastoral Review* 58 (1957): 173–78.

Hildebrand, Dietrich von. *True Morality and Its Counterfeits.* New York: McKay, 1955.

Hirschmann, Hans. "Im Spiegel der Zeit." *Geist und Leben* 25 (1951): 300–304.

Hittinger, Russell. *A Critique of the New Natural Law Theory.* Notre Dame, Ind.: University of Notre Dame Press, 1987.

————. "Natural Law and Catholic Moral Theology." In *A Preserving Grace,* edited by Michael Cromartie. Grand Rapids, Mich.: William B. Eerdmans, 1997.

————. "Varieties of Minimalist Natural Law Theory." *American Journal of Jurisprudence* 34 (1989): 133–70.

Hoose, Bernard. *Proportionalism. The American Debate and Its European Roots.* Washington, D.C.: Georgetown University Press, 1987.

————. "Proportionalists, Deontologists and the Human Good." *Heythrop Journal* 33 (1992): 175–91.

Hughes, Gerard J. *Authority in Morals.* Washington: Georgetown University Press, 1978.

————. "A Christian Basis for Ethics." *Heythrop Journal* 13 (1972): 27–43.

————. "Is Ethics One or Many?" In *Catholic Perspectives on Medical Morals,* edited by Edmund D. Pellegrino, John P. Langan, and John Collins Harvey. Dordrecht, The Netherlands: Kluwer Academic, 1989.

Hürth, Francis. "Instructio Supremae Sacrae Congregationis S. Officii: De Ethica Situationis." *Periodica de Re Morali, Canonica, Liturgica* 45 (1956): 137–204.

Hürth, Francis, and P. M. Abellan. *De Principiis, De Virtutibus et Praeceptis.* Rome: Pontificia Universitatis Gregoriana, 1948.

Jackson, Wes. *New Roots for Agriculture.* Lincoln: University of Nebraska Press, 1980.

Janssens, Louis. "Morale conjugale et progestogènes." *Ephemerides Theologicae Lovanienses* 34 (1963): 787–826.

————. "Personalism in Moral Theology." In *Moral Theology: Challenges for the Future,* edited by Charles E. Curran. Mahwah, N.J.: Paulist Press, 1990.

John Paul II, Pope. *Veritatis Splendor.* Boston: St. Paul Books and Media, 1993.

Johnson, Mark. "Delayed Hominization." *Theological Studies* 56 (1995): 743–63.

————. *Moral Imagination.* Chicago: University of Chicago Press, 1993.

————. "A Rejoinder to Thomas Shannon." *Theological Studies* 58 (1997): 708–14.

Jone, Heribert, and Urban Adelman. *Moral Theology.* 2d edition. Westminster, Md.: Newman Bookshop, 1946.

Jonsen, Albert R., and Stephen Toulmin. *The Abuse of Casuistry.* Berkeley: University of California Press, 1988.

Kaiser, Robert Blair. *The Encyclical That Never Was: The Story of the Pontifical Commission on Population, Family, and Birth, 1964–66.* London: Sheed and Ward, 1987.

Kaufman, Philip S. *Why You Can Disagree and Remain a Faithful Catholic.* New York: Crossroad, 1995.

Keane, Philip. *Christian Ethics and Imagination.* Ramsey, N.J.: Paulist Press, 1984.

Keenan, James F. "Can a Wrong Action Be Good? The Development of Theological Opinion on Erroneous Conscience." *Eglise et Théologie* 24 (1993): 205–19.

———. "Distinguishing Charity as Goodness and Prudence as Rightness: A Key to Thomas's *Secunda Pars.*" *Thomist* 56 (1992): 407–26.

———. "The Function of the Principle of Double Effect." *Theological Studies* 54 (1993): 294–315.

———. "Josef Fuchs and the Question of Moral Objectivity in Roman Catholic Moral Reasoning." *Religious Studies Review* 24 (1998): 253–58.

———. "Josef Fuchs at Eighty, Defending the Conscience while Writing from Rome." *Irish Theological Quarterly* 59 (1993): 204–10.

———. "The Problem With Thomas Aquinas's Concept of Sin." *Heythrop Journal* 35 (1994): 401–20.

———. "Virtue Ethics: Making a Case as It Comes of Age." *Thought* 67 (1992): 115–27.

———. "What is Good and What is Right." *Church* 5 (1989): 22–28.

Keenan, James F., and Thomas R. Kopfensteiner. 1998. "Moral Theology Out of Western Europe." *Theological Studies* 59 (1998): 107–35.

Kekes, John. *The Examined Life.* University Park: Pennsylvania State University Press, 1988.

———. "Human Nature and Moral Theories." *Inquiry* 28 (1985): 231–45.

———. *The Morality of Pluralism.* Princeton, N.J.: Princeton University Press, 1993.

———. *Moral Tradition and Individuality.* Princeton, N.J.: Princeton University Press, 1989.

———. *Moral Wisdom and Good Lives.* Ithaca, N.Y.: Cornell University Press, 1995.

Kenny, J. P. "Reflections on Human Nature and the Supernatural." *Theological Studies* 14 (1953): 280–87.

Knauer, Peter. "La détermination du bien et du mal moral par le principe du double effet." *Nouvelle Revue Théologique* 87 (1965): 356–76.

———. "The Hermeneutic Function of the Prinicple of Double Effect." In *Moral Norms and Catholic Tradition,* Readings in Moral Theology, no. 1, edited by Charles E. Curran and Richard A. McCormick. Ramsey, N.J.: Paulist Press, 1979.

———. "The Principle of the Double Effect." *Theology Digest* 15 (1967): 100–104.

Koch, Antony, and Arthur Preuss. *A Handbook of Moral Theology.* 5 vols. 3d edition. St. Louis, Mo.: B. Herder Book, 1925.

Komonchak, Joseph A. "Authority and Its Exercise." In *Church Authority in American Culture,* edited by Philip J. Murnion. New York: Crossroad, 1999.

Kopfensteiner, Thomas R. "Globalization and the Autonomy of Moral Reasoning: An Essay in Fundamental Moral Theology." *Theological Studies* 54 (1993): 485–511.

———. "Historical Epistemology and Moral Progress." *Heythrop Journal* 33 (1992): 45–60.

Korff, Wilhelm. "Nature or Reason as the Criterion for the Universality of Moral Judgments." *Concilium* 150 (1981): 82–88.

Kunicic, J. " 'Ethicae situationis' multiplex error." *Divus Thomas* 60 (1957): 305–13.

Lappé, Francis Moore. *Diet for a Small Planet*. New York: Ballantine, 1982.

Leo XIII, Pope. *Rerum Novarum*. In *The Papal Encyclicals, 1878–1903*, edited by Claudia Carlen. 1891; reprint, Raleigh, N.C.: McGrath Publishing, 1981.

Lobo, George. *Guide to Christian Living*. Westminster, Md.: Christian Classicsm, 1984.

Lonergan, Bernard J. F. *Insight. A Study of Human Understanding*. New York: Longmans, Green, 1958.

———. *Method in Theology*. New York: Herder and Herder, 1972.

———. *A Second Collection*, edited by William F. J. Ryan and Bernard J. Tyrrell. London: Darton, Longman, and Todd, 1974.

———. *A Third Collection*, edited by Frederick E. Crowe. Mahwah, N.J.: Paulist Press, 1985.

Lovin, Robin W. *Christian Faith and Public Choices: The Social Ethics of Barth, Brunner, and Bonhoeffer*. Philadelphia: Fortress Press, 1984.

MacNamara, Vincent. *Faith and Ethics. Recent Roman Catholicism*. Washington, D.C.: Georgetown University Press, 1985.

Mahoney, John. *The Making of Moral Theology: A Study of the Roman Catholic Tradition*. Oxford: Clarendon Press, 1989.

Malevez, L. "L'espirit et désir de Dieu." *Nouvelle Revue Théologique* 69 (1947): 1–31.

Manser, Anthony. *Sartre: A Philosophic Study*. London: Althone Press, 1966.

Manser, Anthony, and Albert Kolnai. "Symposium on Existentialism." *Aristotelian Society Supplementary Volume* 37 (1963): 11–51.

Marshall, John. "The Council and the Commission." *Tablet* September 21, 1968: 933–34.

———. "The Door That Closed." *Tablet* July 23, 1988: 835, 837.

———. "Inside the Commission." *Tablet* July 24, 1993: 938–39.

Maxwell, John. *Slavery and the Catholic Church*. London: Barry Rose, 1975.

May, William E. *An Introduction to Moral Theology*. Huntington, Ind.: Our Sunday Visitor, 1991.

———. *Moral Absolutes: Catholic Tradition, Current Trends, and the Truth*. Milwaukee, Wisc.: Marquette University Press, 1989.

McClory, Robert. *Turning Point*. New York: Crossroad, 1995.

McCormick, Richard A. *Ambiguity in Moral Choice*. Milwaukee, Wisc.: Marquette University Press, 1973.

————. *The Critical Calling: Reflections on Moral Dilemmas Since Vatican II.* Washington, D.C.: Georgetown University Press, 1989.

————. "Does Religious Faith Add to Ethical Perception?" In *The Distinctiveness of Christian Ethics,* Readings in Moral Theology, no. 2, edited by Charles E. Curran and Richard A. McCormick. Ramsey, N.J.: Paulist Press, 1980.

————. "Reflections on the Literature." In *Moral Norms and Catholic Tradition,* edited by Charles E. Curran and Richard A. McCormick. Ramsey, N.J.: Paulist Press, 1979.

McDonagh, Enda. *Gift and Call.* Dublin: Gill and McMillan, 1975.

McGrath, Alister E. *Nature,* vol. 1, *A Scientific Theory.* Grand Rapids, Mich. William B. Eerdmans, 2001.

McHugh, John A., and Charles J. Callan. *Moral Theology: A Complete Course Based on St. Thomas and the Best Modern Authorities.* 2 vols. New York: Joseph F. Wagner, 1929.

McMahon, Kevin A. "Josef Fuchs and the Question of a Distinctively Christian Morality." In *Faith Seeking Understanding: Learning and the Catholic Tradition,* edited by George C. Berthold. Manchester, N.H.: St. Anselm College Press, 1991.

McShea, Robert J. *Morality and Human Nature: A New Route to Ethical Theory.* Philadelphia: Temple University Press, 1990.

Melchin, Kenneth R. "Moral Knowledge and the Structure of Cooperative Living." *Theological Studies* 52 (1991): 495–523.

Mercier, Ronald Amos. "What Is Nature? The Development of Josef Fuchs' Thought on Moral Normativity." Ph.D. diss., Regis College, 1993.

Merks, Karl Wilhelm. "Das Recht Anders zu sein: Eine Chance für die Moral: Pluralismus zwischen Freiheit und Verantwortlichkeit." *Bijdragen* 55 (1994): 2–23.

Michel, Ernst. *Der Partner Gottes. Weisungen zum christlichen Selbstverstandnis.* Heidelberg, Germany: Lambert Schneider, 1946.

Midgley, Mary. *Beast and Man: The Roots of Human Nature.* Ithaca, N.Y.: Cornell University Press, 1978.

Mieth, Dietmar. "Autonomy of Ethics—Neutrality of the Gospel?" *Concilium* 155 (1982): 32–39.

Milhaven, John Giles. *Toward a New Catholic Morality.* Garden City, N.Y.: Doubleday, 1970.

Mitchell, C. Ben. "Is That All There Is? Moral Ambiguity in a Postmodern Culture." In *Challenge of Postmodernism,* edited by David S. Dockery. Wheaton, Ill.: Bridgepoint/Victor, 1995.

Modras, Ronald. "Implications of Rahner's Anthropology for Fundamental Moral Theology." *Horizons* 12 (1985): 70–90.

Moore, Kenneth. "Situational Ethics." *American Ecclesiastical Review* 135 (1956): 29–38.

Muldoon, Timothy P. "Germain Grisez on Karl Rahner's Theory of Fundamental Option." *Philosophy and Theology* 10 no. 1 (1998): 227–54.

Newman, J. "The Ethics of Existentialism." *Irish Ecclesiastical Record* 77 (1952): 321–32, 421–31.

Niebuhr, Reinhold. "The Concept of 'Order of Creation' in Emil Brunner's Social Ethic." In *The Theology of Emil Brunner,* edited by Charles W. Kegley and Robert W. Brethall. New York: Macmillan, 1962.

Noldin, H., and A. Schmitt. *Summa Theologiae Moralis.* 3 vols. Innsbruck, Austria: Sumptis and Typic Feliciani Rauch, 1940.

Noonan, John T. *Contraception: A History of Its Treatment by the Catholic Theologians and Canonists.* Cambridge, Mass.: Harvard University Press, 1965.

———. "Development in Moral Doctrine." *Theological Studies* 54 (1993): 662–77.

———. *The Scholastic Analysis of Usury.* Cambridge, Mass.: Harvard University Press, 1956.

Nussbaum, Martha C. "Aristotle on Human Nature and the Foundations of Ethics." In *World, Mind, and Ethics,* edited by J. E. J. Altham and Ross Harrison. Cambridge: Cambridge University Press, 1995.

———. "Aristotelian Social Democracy." In *Liberalism and the Good,* edited by R. Bruce Douglass, Gerald M. Mara, and Henry S. Richardson. New York: Routledge, Chapman, and Hall, 1990.

———. *The Fragility of Goodness: Luck and Ethics in Greek Tragedy and Philosophy.* Cambridge: Cambridge University Press, 1986.

———. "Nature, Function, and Capability: Aristotle on Political Distribution." In *Oxford Studies in Ancient Philosophy,* supplementary vol. New York: Oxford University Press, 1988.

O'Connell, Timothy E. "Changing Roman Catholic Moral Theology: A Study in Josef Fuchs." Ph.D. diss., Fordham University, 1974.

———. *Principles for a Catholic Morality.* San Francisco: Harper and Row, 1990.

Oden, Thomas C. *The Promise of Barth.* Philadelphia: Lippincot, 1969.

Parekh, Bhikhu. "Is There a Human Nature?" In *Is There a Human Nature?,* edited by Leroy S. Rouner. Notre Dame, Ind.: University of Notre Dame Press, 1997.

Parfit, Derek. *Reasons and Persons.* Oxford: Clarendon Press, 1987.

Patrick, Anne E. *Liberating Conscience.* New York: Continuum, 1997.

Pius XI, Pope. *Casti Connubii.* In *The Papal Encyclicals 1903–39,* edited by Claudia Carlen. 1930; reprint, Raleigh, N.C.: McGrath, 1981.

———. *Quadragesimo Anno.* In *The Papal Encyclicals 1903–39,* edited by Claudia Carlen. 1931; reprint, Raleigh: McGrath, 1981.

Pius XII, Pope. "Address to the World Federation of Catholic Young Women." *Catholic Documents* 8 (1952): 15–20.

———. "The Christian Conscience as an Object of Education." *Catholic Documents* 8 (1952): 1–7.

———. *Humani Generis.* In *The Papal Encyclicals 1939–1958.* Edited by Claudia Carlen. 1950; reprint, Raleigh, N.C.: McGrath, 1981.

Plumwood, Val. *Feminism and the Mastery of Nature.* New York: Routledge, 1997.

Pope, Stephen. *The Evolution of Altruism and the Ordering of Love.* Washington, D.C.: Georgetown University Press, 1994.

———. "Scientific and Natural Law Analyses of Homosexuality." *Journal of Religious Ethics* 25 (1997): 89–126.

Porter, Jean. "Individuality, Personal Identity, and the Moral Status of the Preembryo: A Response to Mark Johnson." *Theological Studies* 56 (1995): 763–70.

———. *Moral Action and Christian Ethics.* Cambridge: Cambridge University Press, 1995.

———. "Moral Language and the Language of Grace: The Fundamental Option and the Virtue of Charity." *Philosophy and Theology* 10 (1997): 169–98.

———. *Natural and Divine Law: Reclaiming the Tradition for Christian Ethics.* Grand Rapids, Mich.: William B. Eerdmans, 1999.

———. "The Natural Law and the Specificity of Christian Morality: A Survey of Recent Work and an Agenda for Future Research." In *Method and Catholic Moral Theology: The Ongoing Reconstruction*, edited by Todd A. Salzman. Omaha, Neb.: Creighton University Press, 1999.

———. "Salvific Love and Charity: A Comparison of the Thought of Karl Rahner and Thomas Aquinas. In *The Love Commandments*, edited by Edmund Santurri and William Werpehowski. Washington, D.C.: Georgetown University Press, 1992.

Prümmer, Dominic. *Handbook of Moral Theology.* Translated by Gerald W. Shelton, edited by John Gavin Nolan. New York: P. J. Kennedy and Sons, 1957.

Quay, Paul. "Morality by Calculation of Values." In *Moral Norms and Catholic Tradition*, Readings in Moral Theology, no. 1, edited by Charles E. Curran and Richard A. McCormick. Ramsey, N.J.: Paulist Press, 1979.

Quelquejeu, Bernard. "Diversity in Historical Moral Systems and a Criterion for Universality in Moral Judgment." *Concilium* 150 (1981): 47–53.

Quirk, Michael J. "Why the Debate on Proportionalism is Misconceived." *Modern Theology* 13 (1997): 500–524.

Rahner, Karl. "The Experiment with Man." In *Theological Investigations,* vol. 9. Translated by Graham Harrison. New York: Herder and Herder, 1972.

———. *Foundations of Christian Faith.* Translated by William V. Dych. New York: Crossroad, 1989.

———. *Nature and Grace.* Translated by Dinah Wharton. New York: Sheed and Ward, 1964.

———. "On the Question of a Formal Existential Ethics." In *Theological Investigations*, vol. 2. Translated by Karl-H. Kruger. Baltimore, Md.: Helicon Press, 1963.

———. "Theology of Freedom." In *Theological Investigations,* vol. 6. Translated by Karl-H. and Boniface Kruger. New York: Seabury Press, 1969.

Ratzinger, Joseph Cardinal. 1986. "The Church's Teaching Authority—Faith—Morals." In *Principles of Christian Morality*. Translated by Graham Harrison, 47–73. San Francisco: Ignatius Press, 1986.

Rauch, W. *Abhandlungen aus Ethik und Moraltheologie.* Freiburg, Germany: Herder, 1956.

Reitlinger, Gerald. *The Final Solution: The Attempt to Exterminate the Jews of Europe, 1939–1945.* New York: A. S. Barnes, 1961.

Reuss, Josef M. "Eheliche Hingabe und Zeugung. Ein Diskussionsbeitrag zu Einem differenzierten Problem." *Theologische Quartalschrift* 143 (1963): 454–67.

Rhonheimer, Martin. *Natural Law and Practical Reason: A Thomist View of Moral Autonomy.* Translated by Gerald Malsbary. New York: Fordham University Press, 2000.

———. "Sittliche Autonomie und Theonomie gemäss der Enzyklika 'Veritatis Splendor.'" *Forum Katholische Theologie* 10 (1994): 241–68.

Rifkin, Jeremy. *Beyond Beef.* New York: Penguin, 1993.

Rigali, Norbert J. "On Christian Ethics." *Chicago Studies* 10 (1971): 227–47.

———. "The Uniqueness and Distinctiveness of Christian Morality and Ethics." In *Moral Theology: Challenges for the Future,* edited by Charles E. Curran, 74–93. Mahwah, N.J.: Paulist Press, 1990.

Rommen, Heinrich A. *The Natural Law: A Study in Legal and Social History and Philosophy.* 1947; reprint, Indianapolis, Ind.: Liberty Fund, 1998.

Rotter, Hans. *Person und Ethik: zur Grundlegung der Moraltheologie.* Innsbruck, Austria: Tyrolia, 1993.

———. "Zwölf Thesen zur heilsgeschichtlichen Begründung der Moral." In *Heilgeschichte und ethische Normen,* edited by Hans Rotter. Freiburg, Germany: Herder, 1984.

Rudman, Stanley. *Concepts of Person and Christian Ethics.* New York: Cambridge University Press, 1997.

Sabetti, Aloysius, and Timothy Barrett. *Compendium Theologiae Moralis.* Rome: Frederick Pustet, 1916.

St. John-Stevas, Norman. *The Agonizing Choice.* London: Eyre and Spottiswoode, 1971.

Sampson, R. Neil. *Farmland or Wasteland: A Time to Choose.* Emmaus, Pa.: Rodale Press, 1981.

Schner, George P. 1992. "The Appeal to Experience." *Theological Studies* 53 (1992): 40–59.

Schüller, Bruno. "Autonomous Ethics Revisited." In *Personalist Morals,* edited by Joseph A. Selling, 61–70. Leuven, Belgium: Leuven University Press, 1988.

———. *Die Begründung sittlicher Urteile.* Düsseldorf, Germany: Patmos, 1980.

———. "A Contribution to the Theological Discussion of Natural Law." In *Natural Law and Theology,* Readings in Moral Theology, no. 1, edited by Charles E. Curran and Richard A. McCormick. Mahwah, N.J.: Paulist Press, 1991.

———. "Remarks on the Authentic Teaching of the Magisterium of the Church. In *The Magisterium and Morality,* Readings in Moral Theology, no.

3, edited by Charles E. Curran and Richard A. McCormick. Ramsey, N.J.: Paulist Press, 1982.

Secker, Susan L. "Human Experience and Women's Experience." In *The Annual of the Society of Christian Ethics*, edited by D. M. Yeager. Washington, D.C.: Georgetown University Press, 1991.

Seifert, Josef. "Absolute Moral Obligations towards Finite Goods as Foundation of Intrinsically Right and Wrong Actions." *Anthropos* 1 (1985): 57–94.

Sentis, Laurent. "La Lumière Dont Nous Faisons Usage." *Revue des Sciences Philosophiques et Théologiques* 79 (1995): 49–69.

Shannon, Thomas A. "Delayed Hominization: A Response to Mark Johnson." *Theological Studies* 57 (1996): 731–34.

———. "A Further Postscript to Mark Johnson." *Theological Studies* 58 (1997): 715–17.

Simpson, Michael. "A Christian Basis for Ethics?" *Heythrop Journal* 15 (1974): 285–97.

Slater, Thomas. *A Manual of Moral Theology*. 2 vols. 3d edition. New York: Benzinger Brothers, 1908.

Smith, Gerard. "The Natural End of Man." *Proceedings of the American Catholic Philosophical Association* 23 (1949): 47–61.

Sohngen, G. "Die biblische Lehre von der Gottebenbildlichkeit des Menschen." *Münchener Theologische Zeitschrift* 2 (1951): 52–76.

Spohn, William C. *Go and Do Likewise*. New York: Continuum, 1999.

Strange, Marty. *Family Farming: A New Economic Vision*. Lincoln: University of Nebraska Press, 1988.

Styczen, Tadeusz. "Autonome Ethik mit einen christlichen 'Proprium' als methodologisches Problem." In *Ethik Im Kontext des Glaubens. Probleme—Grundsätze—Methode*, edited by Francesco Compagnoni and Dietmar Mieth. Freiburg, Germany: Universitätsverlag, 1978.

Sullivan, Francis A. *Magisterium: Teaching Authority in the Catholic Church*. Ramsey, N.J.: Paulist Press, 1983.

Tanner, Norman, ed. *Decrees of the Ecumenical Councils*. 2 vols. Washington, D.C.: Georgetown University Press, 1990.

Taylor, Charles. *The Ethics of Authenticity*. Cambridge, Mass.: Harvard University Press, 1991.

———. *Sources of the Self: The Making of the Modern Identity*. Cambridge, Mass.: Harvard University Press, 1989.

Taylor, Mark Lloyd. *God is Love: A Study in the Theology of Karl Rahner*. Atlanta, Ga.: Scholars Press, 1986.

Thiéffry, M. "Stérilization hormonale et morale chrétienne." *Nouvelle Revue Théologique* 83 (1961): 135–58.

Thielicke, Helmut. *Foundations*, vol. 1, *Theological Ethics*. Edited by William H. Lazareth. Translated by John W. Doberstein. Philadelphia: Fortress Press, 1966.

Tillmann, Fritz, ed. *Handbuch der katholischen Sittenlehre*. 4 vols. Düsseldorf, Germany: Druck und Verlag L. Schwann, 1934.

Traina, Cristina L. H. *Feminist Ethics and Natural Law*. Washington, D.C.: Georgetown University Press, 1999.

Ullmann-Margalit, Edna. "Revision of Norms." *Ethics* 10 (1990): 756–67.

Vacek, Edward Collins. "Proportionalism: One View of the Debate." *Theological Studies* 46 (1985): 287–314.

van der Marck, William. *Love and Fertility*. London: Sheed and Ward, 1965.

Vass, George. *A Theologian in Search of a Philosophy*. 2 vols. Westminster, Md.: Christian Classics, 1985.

Vermeersch, Arthur. *Theologiae Moralis*. 3d edition. 3 vols. Rome: Pontificia Universitas Gregoriana, 1933.

Wallace, W. A. "Existential Ethics In a Thomistic Appraisal." *Thomist* 27 (1963): 493–515.

Walter, James J. "Christian Ethics: Distinctive and Specific?" In *The Distinctiveness of Christian Ethics*, Readings in Moral Theology, no. 2., edited by Charles E. Curran and Richard A. McCormick. Ramsey, N.J.: Paulist Press, 1980.

———. "The Dependence of Christian Morality on Faith." *Eglise et Théologie* 12 (1981): 237–77.

———. "The Foundation and Formulation of Norms." In *Moral Theology: Challenges for the Future*, edited by Charles E. Curran. Mahwah, N.J.: Paulist Press, 1990.

———. "The Question of the Uniqueness of Christian Morality: An Historical and Critical Analysis of the Debate in Roman Catholic Ethics." In *Method and Catholic Moral Theology: The Ongoing Reconstruction*, edited by Todd A. Salzman. Omaha, Neb.: Creighton University Press, 1999.

Warnock, Mary. *The Philosophy of Sartre*. London: Hutchinson, 1965.

Wassamer, Thomas A. "A Re-Examination of Situation Ethics." *Catholic Educational Review* 57 (1959): 20–37.

Weinreb, Lloyd. *Natural Law and Justice*. Cambridge, Mass.: Harvard University Press, 1987.

Wong, David B. "Coping with Moral Conflict and Moral Ambiguity." *Ethics* 102 (1992): 763–84.

Wulf, Hans. "Gesetz und Liebe in der Ordnung des Heils." *Geist und Leben* 22 (1949): 356–67.

Yartz, Frank J. "Order and Right Reason in Aquinas' Ethics." *Mediaeval Studies* 37 (1975): 407–18.

Zalba, Marcellinus. "Casus de usu artificii contraceptivi." *Periodica de Re Canonica, Morali, et Liturgica* 51 (1962): 167–92.

———. *Theologiae Moralis Compendium: Juxta Constitutionem Deus Scientiarum.* 2 vols. Madrid, Spain: Editorial Catolica, 1958.

Index

LaVergne, TN USA
15 October 2009
160978LV00004B/9/A

9 780878 403820